Serving the People
of God's Presence

Serving the People of God's Presence

A Theology of Ministry

TERRY L. CROSS

Baker Academic

a division of Baker Publishing Group
Grand Rapids, Michigan

Published by Baker Academic
a division of Baker Publishing Group
PO Box 6287, Grand Rapids, MI 49516–6287
www.bakeracademic.com

Printed in the United States of America

Library of Congress Cataloging-in-Publication Data
Names: Cross, Terry L., author.
Title: Serving the people of God's presence : a theology of ministry / Terry L. Cross.
Description: Grand Rapids, Michigan : Baker Academic, a division of Baker Publishing Group, 2020. | Includes bibliographical references and index.
Identifiers: LCCN 2020012717 | ISBN 9781540960580 (paperback) | ISBN 9781540963512 (casebound)
Subjects: LCSH: Church work. | Christian leadership. | Pastoral theology.
Classification: LCC BV4400 .C69 2020 | DDC 253—dc23
LC record available at https://lccn.loc.gov/2020012717

Unless otherwise indicated, Scripture quotations are from THE HOLY BIBLE, NEW INTERNATIONAL VERSION®, NIV® Copyright © 1973, 1978, 1984, 2011 by Biblica, Inc.® Used by permission. All rights reserved worldwide.

Scripture quotations labeled ESV are from The Holy Bible, English Standard Version® (ESV®), copyright © 2001 by Crossway, a publishing ministry of Good News Publishers. Used by permission. All rights reserved. ESV Text Edition: 2016

Scripture quotations labeled KJV are from the King James Version of the Bible.

Scripture quotations labeled NASB are from the New American Standard Bible® (NASB), copyright © 1960, 1962, 1963, 1968, 1971, 1972, 1973, 1975, 1977, 1995 by The Lockman Foundation. Used by permission. www.Lockman.org

Scripture quotations labeled NCV are from the New Century Version®. Copyright © 2005 by Thomas Nelson. Used by permission. All rights reserved.

Scripture quotations labeled NKJV are from the New King James Version®. Copyright © 1982 by Thomas Nelson. Used by permission. All rights reserved.

Scripture quotations labeled NRSV are from the New Revised Standard Version of the Bible, copyright © 1989 National Council of the Churches of Christ in the United States of America. Used by permission. All rights reserved.

Scripture quotations labeled RSV are from the Revised Standard Version of the Bible, copyright 1946, 1952 [2nd edition, 1971] National Council of the Churches of Christ in the United States of America. Used by permission. All rights reserved worldwide.

Excerpts in chapter 5 from Terry L. Cross, "Romans 16: Women in Leadership?," The Doctrine & Polity Committee for the Church of God, http://churchofgod .org.s3.amazonaws.com/downloads/doctrine-and-polity-papers/Cross-Romans -16-English.pdf, are used with permission of the Church of God.

20   21   22   23   24   25   26   7   6   5   4   3   2   1

This book is dedicated to my
five-year-old grandson,

Luke Edward Snider,

my "best buddy."

Contents

Acknowledgments

The contents of this book propose some radical changes to the way Christians "do" church in the twenty-first century. Having established the need for a renewal of the theological foundation of the church in a previous volume, I turn now to provide the nuts and bolts of how to put such an ecclesiology into practice.

Given the rather radical nature of the proposal here, I have felt it necessary to extend my ideas to colleagues, students, pastors, and friends. They have offered immense help over the past decade or so. The associate dean of the School of Religion at Lee University, Dr. Rickie Moore, has read and engaged most of the material here, always probing me to think more deeply about the work of the Spirit in the church. A longtime friend, Dr. Larry Bergeron, has also read the manuscript and provided helpful direction, especially insight from his years in pastoral ministry.

Faculty in the School of Religion have responded to various aspects of my proposal, providing practical suggestions along the way. Much of what I have come to propose here is a result of many years of dialogue with these colleagues over the direction that theological education and ministerial training should take in this era of tectonic shifts in culture. Theological education across North America is experiencing challenges to enrollments for full-time ministry students—what does this mean for training future church leaders in the present? Further, what does this mean for the future of the church itself and for educational models for how to train ecclesial leaders? These questions have absorbed me in the past decade, and the faculty in our school have added immensely to my understanding of what we face. While none of them may recognize their own ideas in this proposal, each of the twenty-eight women and men has contributed to this theological dialogue. Two chairs work with me daily to make our school function effectively in training more than three hundred ministry students each semester. Dr. Mark Walker, chair of the Department of Christian Ministries (and the next president of Lee University), and Dr. Skip Jenkins, chair of the Department of Theology, have each brought into the dialogue their own expertise in leadership and historical theology respectively. Dr. Paul Conn, our current president at Lee University, is retiring after thirty-four years to become the chancellor. He has offered me unfailing support in so many ways throughout my years of teaching and administrating, for which I am very grateful.

Further, around one thousand students in my systematic theology classes over the past fifteen years have interacted with some version of various chapters. Their input has been immeasurable—especially in relation to the clarity of expressing the proposals here. Emma Posey and Grace Anne Cochrane, two of my student workers, have read versions of these chapters as well, offering very helpful suggestions for the sake of clarity from a student's perspective.

Working with the staff at Baker Academic has been sheer joy. From the beginning, Dr. Dave Nelson has nurtured this project, believing that it meets a need among God's people today. This encouragement has provided the impetus needed to complete these two companion volumes. The project editor, Jennifer Hale, has continued to bring sensitivity to the purpose of this book, as well as an extraordinary level of excellence to the editing process. Quite literally, this project would not be where it is without their enthusiasm and attention to detail.

The companion volume to this book (*The People of God's Presence: An Introduction to Ecclesiology* [Grand Rapids: Baker Academic, 2019]) was dedicated to the memory of my grandparents, who taught me so much about serving God's people and making room for the presence of God among us. This volume is dedicated to my five-year-old grandson, Luke, in the hope that the church of the future will help him understand what it means to make room for God's presence and other humans so that he, too, may discover the joy of being a priest unto God, ministering to others by bearing Christ to the world.

Abbreviations

General

alt.	altered		OT	Old Testament
ca.	circa		Q(Q)	question(s)
n.s.	new series		rev.	revised
NT	New Testament			

Bible Versions

Alter	Alter, Robert. *The Hebrew Bible: A Translation with Commentary.* 3 vols. New York: Norton, 2019.		NET	The NET Bible (New English Translation)
			NIV	New International Version
ESV	English Standard Version		NJB	The New Jerusalem Bible
GNT	Good News Translation		NKJV	New King James Version
HCSB	Holman Christian Standard Bible		NLT	New Living Translation
			NRSV	New Revised Standard Version
KJV	King James Version		Phillips	*The New Testament in Modern English*, J. B. Phillips
NASB	New American Standard Bible		REB	Revised English Bible
NCV	New Century Version		RSV	Revised Standard Version
NEB	New English Bible			

Old Testament

Gen.	Genesis		1 Kings	1 Kings
Exod.	Exodus		2 Kings	2 Kings
Lev.	Leviticus		1 Chron.	1 Chronicles
Num.	Numbers		2 Chron.	2 Chronicles
Deut.	Deuteronomy		Ezra	Ezra
Josh.	Joshua		Neh.	Nehemiah
Judg.	Judges		Esther	Esther
Ruth	Ruth		Job	Job
1 Sam.	1 Samuel		Ps(s).	Psalm(s)
2 Sam.	2 Samuel		Prov.	Proverbs

Eccles.	Ecclesiastes	Obad.	Obadiah
Song	Song of Songs	Jon.	Jonah
Isa.	Isaiah	Mic.	Micah
Jer.	Jeremiah	Nah.	Nahum
Lam.	Lamentations	Hab.	Habakkuk
Ezek.	Ezekiel	Zeph.	Zephaniah
Dan.	Daniel	Hag.	Haggai
Hosea	Hosea	Zech.	Zechariah
Joel	Joel	Mal.	Malachi
Amos	Amos		

New Testament

Matt.	Matthew	1 Tim.	1 Timothy
Mark	Mark	2 Tim.	2 Timothy
Luke	Luke	Titus	Titus
John	John	Philem.	Philemon
Acts	Acts	Heb.	Hebrews
Rom.	Romans	James	James
1 Cor.	1 Corinthians	1 Pet.	1 Peter
2 Cor.	2 Corinthians	2 Pet.	2 Peter
Gal.	Galatians	1 John	1 John
Eph.	Ephesians	2 John	2 John
Phil.	Philippians	3 John	3 John
Col.	Colossians	Jude	Jude
1 Thess.	1 Thessalonians	Rev.	Revelation
2 Thess.	2 Thessalonians		

Bibliographic Sources

AF   Holmes, Michael W., ed. and trans. *The Apostolic Fathers: Greek Texts and English Translations*. 3rd ed. Grand Rapids: Baker Academic, 2007.

ANF   *Ante-Nicene Fathers*

BDAG   Danker, Frederick W., Walter Bauer, William F. Arndt, and F. Wilbur Gingrich. *Greek-English Lexicon of the New Testament and Other Early Christian Literature*. 3rd ed. Chicago: University of Chicago Press, 2000.

CD   Barth, Karl. *Church Dogmatics*. Edited by T. F. Torrance and G. W. Bromiley. Translated by G. W. Bromiley et al. 13 vols. Edinburgh: T&T Clark, 1936–.

CSEL   Corpus Scriptorum Ecclesiasticorum Latinorum

Inst.   Calvin, John. *Institutes of the Christian Religion*. Edited by John T. McNeill. Translated by Ford Lewis Battles. 2 vols. Library of Christian Classics 20–21. Philadelphia: Westminster, 1975.

KD   Barth, Karl. *Die kirchliche Dogmatik*. 13 vols. Munich: Kaiser, 1932; Zurich: Evangelischer Verlag, 1938–.

NICNT   New International Commentary on the New Testament

NIGTC   New International Greek Testament Commentary

OS   Calvin, John. *Joannis Calvini Opera selecta*. Edited by Peter Barth, Wilhelm
        Niesel, and Dora Scheuner. 5 vols. Munich: Kaiser, 1926–52.
TDNT   *Theological Dictionary of the New Testament*. Edited by G. Kittel and
        G. Friedrich. Translated and edited by G. W. Bromiley. 10 vols. Grand Rapids:
        Eerdmans, 1974–2006.
TWOT   *Theological Wordbook of the Old Testament*. Edited by R. Laird Harris,
        Gleason L. Archer Jr., and Bruce K. Waltke. 2 vols. Chicago: Moody, 1980.
WA   Weimarer Ausgabe. *D. Martin Luthers Werke: Kritische Gesammtausgabe*.
        Weimar: Hermann Böhlau & successors, 1883–2009.
WBC   Word Biblical Commentary
WUNT   Wissenschaftliche Untersuchungen zum Neuen Testament

Introduction

Serving the People of God's Presence

The Christian church of the twenty-first century will need to change some of its long-held traditions and practices or face the prospect of becoming a footnote in the history of Western societies that are marked by post-Christian secularism. That was a governing motivation for my previous book on ecclesiology, where I addressed theological foundations of the church.[1] The church needs to return to a more biblically attuned and theologically astute basis for its nature and mission. While I have spent time reassessing a theology of the church with regard to its nature and mission previously, in this book I move forward on the basis of that previous theological inquiry to provide a reconsideration of the structures and practices of the church, particularly as these relate to leadership and ministry. Since the theological foundation offered in the previous book is essential for understanding the direction in which the present book moves, I shall rehearse briefly the key aspects of my ecclesiological proposal before engaging the question of structures and practices. I have proposed a rather radical agenda for the re-formation of the local church, both in its understanding of itself and in its structural setup. It is to that task of filling out the practical details of how the people of God's presence could operate as the church in contemporary society that we will turn in this work.[2]

---

1. Terry L. Cross, *The People of God's Presence: An Introduction to Ecclesiology* (Grand Rapids: Baker Academic, 2019).

2. While the manuscript for this book was completed before March 2020, I received the galleys in April, during the coronavirus pandemic and shelter-in-place requirements. Businesses and churches throughout the world have shuttered their doors in order to limit the spread of COVID-19. Life is not "normal" in the world today. Fear of the invisible virus is a stalwart contagion among us all. This is also true for the church, where challenges to providing ministry in quarantine settings have provoked new ways to share the gospel (livestreaming, devotional videos, drive-in church services, and a host of ingenious ways to connect with people who are shut-in). The radical nature of my proposal in this book was not written with this emergency situation

Essential Dimensions of the Church

The main thesis for which I previously argued regarding the church can be stated as follows: the church is the people of God's *direct* presence, who have been transformed by an encounter with God at a core level of their being—perhaps even a precognitive level. From this basic idea, I build an ecclesiology around the concept of the people of God as well as the power of God's presence among and in us. While for many ecclesiologies the church has been considered as a means of distributing God's grace, I argue that such a view diminishes the direct work of God in our lives, making us reliant on the all-too-human ecclesiastical institution for spiritual benefits from God's hand. This problem, I suggest, is not simply a Catholic, Orthodox, or Protestant one; it is prevalent regardless of one's church affiliation. Is the church a divinely established means by which God's grace is doled out to people? Such a sacramental view of the church's mission distorts the true nature of the church and places God at least one step removed from relating to humans. Is the church as institution the sole means of connecting with God? While I admit that God uses various media through which to encounter humans (including the church), I do not view such an instrumental use as a determinative factor in the transformation necessary for *being* God's people and for *doing* the work of God's people.

In contrast with such sacramental styles of ecclesiology, where the church is viewed as a channel of God's grace, I propose a view of the church as a people whom God has encountered *directly*. Even if various visible media (like a pillar of fire or a cloud) are used by God due to his invisible nature, I suggest that *within* the encounter with a medium still remains something of God's direct presence that connects immediately (i.e., without mediation) to our human spirits.

Among the various encounters we may have with God, I propose that the encounter with the risen Christ at a core level of our being demands a response on our part at some point. The Spirit of God re-presents the risen Christ to our spirits, giving us the opportunity to submit to the truth offered there or to deny it. If we respond positively to the re-presentation of Christ, we are immediately inserted by the Spirit into the body of Christ (1 Cor. 12:12–13).

---

in mind, but the recommendations are even more relevant given the state of things across the world. Christians have learned quite unexpectedly that the church is not the building but the people of God. We long for personal interaction with *people* in our congregations; the building simply provides the convenience for our gatherings. I remain steadfast in my proposal here that a radical re-formation of the church is needed for the twenty-first century. The proposal offered here outlines a possible way to consider such foundations so that we may restructure our notions of church for this century—whatever the world may look like after this coronavirus pandemic.

While I cannot rehearse the details supporting my argument here, it is the theological cornerstone of my proposal for a re-formation of the church in the twenty-first century.[3] Due to the central role that the presence of God the Spirit plays in connecting and communicating with God's people, as well as establishing and maintaining the church, I have called this a *pneumatic* ecclesiology.[4]

A difficulty arising from my proposal is one that has plagued free-church or believers' church models for several centuries. Most evangelical ecclesiologies have also inherited this problem. If humans choose to accept Christ on an individual basis, then what is the rationale for the church? In other words, if a personal relationship with Christ is individually determined, then what is the purpose for the local body of Christ? If a believer chooses Christ, then it seems that becoming part of a local church is a matter of choice as well (or voluntary association, as some have called it). If this is the case, then why do we need the church? A style of Enlightenment individualism threatens to rear its head quite prominently in many ecclesiological endeavors, including mine.

Here is where a crucial theological point has been missing in some reflections on the church. I argue that the nature of God comes to be reflected in the nature of the people of God. What does this mean? The God who encounters humans is the Triune God whose nature is *loving relationality*. Within the society that is triune, Father, Son, and Spirit operate in perfect communion and union, while maintaining their distinctions. Since the days of the early church, theologians have used a Greek term to describe the way Father, Son, and Spirit are distinct yet interpenetrate each other; the word is περιχώρησις | *perichōrēsis*. The idea inherent within this word group is "to dance around"; another possibility is "to make room for." The loving relationality within the life of the Trinity freely makes room for the Other, first *within* the trinitarian relations, and second *outside* of those inner relations. God's love "makes room for" creation. God's love "makes room for" human beings—even sinful human beings. In the rich fellowship that is the Trinity, God's life overflows

3. The theological basis for this proposal is worked out in chaps. 1–3 of *The People of God's Presence*.

4. The term "pneumatic" seems better suited to my emphasis on the Spirit's role than words like "charismatic" or even "Pentecostal," which are both fraught with difficulties in the current North American context. Words like "charismatic" and "Pentecostal" have a specific history in the twentieth century; their common use today tends to lay more stress on the *gifts* of the Spirit—especially the more demonstrable ones. This ecclesiology is not focused on manifestations of the gifts of the Spirit but on the motivator and mover of our lives of discipleship as we follow Christ together. Gifts are a part of this ecclesiology, but the Spirit as the Gift-giver is central. As such, "pneumatic" seems more precisely suited for connoting my intended meaning.

with bounty and grace so that even humans are called to share in the feast of the life of God. In this way, creation itself is an act of grace in that God did not *have* to create out of some need, but God wanted to share—in some sense—God's life with creatures that were not God. Hence, the nature of God is a rich, loving fellowship that overflows to those beings in creation who are not God. From eternity, God was "bent" toward humanity in the created world, not out of some external need but out of an inner, gracious, overflowing love. This loving nature of God toward the "Other" resulted in the mission of God (*missio Dei*) whereby the Son was sent to earth to become a human in order to reconcile humans to God. Thus, the *being* of God is reflected in the *doing* of God. The nature of God corresponds precisely with the mission of God.

I do not triumphantly expect that the people of God will reflect God's nature and mission accurately and consistently on this earth—after all, I have been around churches all of my life and realize that we do not always clearly represent the nature of the God we serve. Nonetheless, I do believe that the Spirit of God within believers transforms and empowers them to begin to offer to this world a reflection of the Trinity here and now as well as a "provisional representation" of the world to come.[5] This is a point often overlooked in ecclesiology—namely, that believers are partakers in God's nature so that transformation occurs in God's presence, thereby creating wholeness and integrity of our *being* and *doing*.

Further, intimately connected with this reasoning is a rather pressing question among Western societies today—namely, Why church? Only as we are continually encountering God's transforming presence within the gathered community of Jesus Christ where we *practice* the faith together can we begin to reflect the true image of our loving, relational God. In other words, we *need* the church in order to do the work that God has called us to do. It is here that a key insight concerning Paul's understanding of the function of the body of Christ comes to assist us in developing our own ecclesiology. It is from Christ, who is the head, that the whole body "grows and builds itself up in love, as each part does its work" (Eph. 4:16). Each believer is joined to other believers in the same way that supporting ligaments hold together the various parts of the human body. Only as each part of the body is "fitted and

---

5. This phrase, "provisional representation," comes from Karl Barth's discussion of the church as commissioned to be "a provisional representation to humanity as it is sanctified in Jesus Christ" (*CD* IV/2:698). By being a concrete reality of the future state of humanity, the community of faith exists as a witness to the eschatological reign of God. A similar phrase is found in a discussion of the believers' church by Wayne F. Groff, "A Believing People: Theological Interpretation," in *The Concept of the Believers' Church: Addresses from the 1968 Louisville Conference*, ed. James Leo Garrett Jr. (Scottdale, PA: Herald, 1969), 66. Groff says that the church is a "provisional representation and agency of God's kingdom purpose."

held together by what every joint supplies" and follows what it is supposed to do "according to the proper working of each individual part" will the whole body grow through building itself up in love (Eph. 4:16 NASB). Growing in Christ demands growing *together with* other people in a local community.

To what end is such corporate spiritual growth? The goal is that we become thoroughly equipped to do the work of ministry—to service (Eph. 4:12). This requires the transforming presence of God among us and in us. It is not within our own natures to love the way God loves; our natures must experience the transforming power of the Spirit in order to bring the presence of Christ to the world today. *We* cannot minister to the needs of people—only Christ can do that. Nevertheless, Christ has chosen to do that *through humans—through the people of God in the power of the Spirit.*

Therefore, gathering as the people of God allows us to experience God together in ways that transform us individually and corporately. We learn to "make room for God's presence" in gathered worship, in preaching and hearing the Word of God, in petitionary prayer for others, in celebrating various practices ordained by Christ, and in sharing other practices that mark our earthly existence together as fellow believers. By so doing, we learn "to make room for" the Other.

In my previous work, I also noted the specific tasks of the people of God when gathered in community. I made a distinction between those tasks occurring within the gathered congregation and those tasks outside of it in missional outreach.[6] Why? I argued that the primary tasks when gathered together were to "glorify God and enjoy God forever" (using the line from the Westminster Catechism of 1647). Primarily, this means that we glorify God through our worship together. The people of God's presence lift their minds and hearts upward toward God in worship so that God's presence encounters them directly in return, bringing with it the motivation and power to do the work of mission with the heart of Christ, not their own selfish concerns. We cannot truly worship God without considering the plight of fellow humans. God's presence propels us out into the world of hurt and devastation, empowering us to bring Christ to those in need.

Hence, gathered worship is primary in setting the proper tone and motivation for our work, sanctifying our natures so that we may become proper vessels for God's presence, transforming our lives into a reflection of the love of God in action. In this way, the perichoretic nature of our God—where Father, Son, and Spirit make room for each other *and* for the radically Other (humans)—becomes the nature of our own existence in the world whereby

6. Cross, *People of God's Presence*, chaps. 4 and 5 respectively.

we make room for God's presence among us and then make room for God's presence with us in the world. Believers cannot naturally "make room for" the Other; such radical consideration for "the Other" is simply not part of our human capacity in this world. Indeed, it is a gift of God's transforming presence that trains our lives to focus on God in worship and on others both within and without the gathered congregation.

These are the basic features of the previous ecclesial proposal.[7] It is the purpose of this present volume to build on these theological foundation points in order to ask practical questions so that we may determine how such a people could operate in the world today. Before moving on to the specific details of this practical aspect of the proposal, it is important to understand why this is necessary. My argument here is essentially that the theological focus on the people of God's presence and the encounter with God provides little value for the people of our century if it is not combined with an understanding of some of the problems that we have inherited from current models of the church and ministry.

Structural Flaws in the Contemporary Church

The Outward Form Disguises Its True Identity?

Were we to gather any group of churchgoers in an informal setting, it would not take much prying to get them to rehearse stories of ways they know churches have harmed someone they know or even themselves. The people of God's presence have often been "housed" within institutional structures that do not seem to fit the glory of the treasure within the vessel. Evangelical scholar James I. Packer notes something significant about this outward form of the church—its structural organization.

> But what is the church? The fact that we all first meet the church as an organized society must not mislead us into thinking that it is essentially, or even primarily, that. There is a sense in which *the outward form of the church disguises its true nature rather than reveals it*. Essentially, the church is not a human organization as such, but a divinely created fellowship of sinners who trust a common Savior, and are one with each other because they are all one with Him in a union realized by the Holy Spirit. Thus the church's real life, like that of its

7. I have decided to give a summary of these ideas from *The People of God's Presence* instead of quoting that volume or providing a host of references that were already given there. Obviously, readers will benefit most from engaging that book in more detail. What I have offered here is simply a minimal flow of the argument so that the reader may be able to fit the chapters here into the overall ecclesial framework I have proposed there.

individual members, is for the present "hid in Christ with God," and will not be manifested to the world until He appears.[8]

The emphasized words in Packer's statement illustrate the nature of the problem: "the outward form of the church disguises its true nature rather than reveals it." The human dimension of the church's organization and leadership has become a mask for whatever divine kernel of the true church remains underneath it. Thus, Packer encourages us to ignore the disguise—the visible costume of church structure—and focus instead on the invisible nature of the true church. While these words come from 1962, the sentiment they express still remains with us. The church often seems hidden under the trappings of contemporary ecclesial culture or disguised under the apparel of long-held tradition. But does it have to be this way? As Karl Barth has suggested, the order, life, and proclamation of the church should witness to the world a promise of the future kingdom—"there is already on earth a community whose order is based on that great alteration of the human situation and directed towards its manifestation" (CD IV/2:721).

Does the *structure* of the church really matter today? Are we to concede that since humans are involved in the functioning of a local church we need not expect things to be any different? What if the outward form of the church no longer disguised its true nature but *revealed it*? What if the visible church— even the one with a human face!—began to reflect more closely the heavenly paradigm of the life of the Triune God? Daniel Migliore speaks directly to this question: "The practices of the church and the way the church organizes its common life say at least as much to the world around it as does its verbal witness."[9]

The way we set up church structure for leadership and ministry reflects what we think about the church. In other words, what we *do* as a church gathered together in a local place reveals a great deal about who we think we *are* as a church. It also reveals how we think about our God, because something will always be reflected about how we envision God in our outward manifestation of being the church—for good or ill. To be sure, I am not suggesting that there is *one* biblically sanctioned model for church government and leadership. As we shall see, I remain unconvinced that any particular governmental model is mandated biblically. However, there are multiple cues from the New Testament that provide us with some rich material for how we may set up the structure

8. James I. Packer, "The Nature of the Church," in *Basic Christian Doctrines*, ed. Carl F. H. Henry (Grand Rapids: Baker, 1962), 242 (emphasis mine).
9. Daniel L. Migliore, *The Power of God and the gods of Power* (Louisville: Westminster John Knox, 2008), 68.

of the local congregation and how we are to relate with each other in our congregations in ways that allow God's presence in us to be manifested, not disguised, to others. We shall engage these in later chapters.

Given the fact that thus far I have proposed a view of the church that centers on the *invisible* presence of God, why should I be concerned about the *visible* structures of the church? Because humans are both spiritual and material beings, we cannot divorce ourselves from the material aspects of our lives, even when we speak of the spiritual dimensions of God's work in us. God has chosen to work *in* and *with* humans in order to accomplish his goals. We are coworkers with God (1 Cor. 3:9). Just as God understood the necessity of becoming flesh in Jesus the Christ in order to communicate with and rescue humans, so, too, God the Spirit "enfleshes" Godself in the work of his people in order to offer the presence and ministry of Christ to humans in the present.[10] It is the work of the Spirit to make the presence of Christ alive and real through the instrumentality of human lives that have been transformed by his presence. Such ministry may be appropriately designated "incarnational," as long as it is understood that the church *is not* Jesus Christ but through the power of the Spirit is able to bring along the presence of Christ with it into the world (*CD* IV/3.2:788, 720).

Therefore, as Karl Barth notes, Christ *is* the church in the sense that Christ is its "very root" (*CD* IV/3.2:788), but the reverse of that statement—namely, "the church *is* Christ"—cannot apply, since we are dealing here not with a continuation of the incarnation of Christ but with a continuation of the *ministry* of Christ. Such a reversal of the subject and predicate would be blasphemous (*CD* IV/3.2:720; *CD* IV/1:317–18). Hence, ministry of the church may be "incarnational" only in the sense that it follows the pattern of Philippians 2:5–8, whereby the Son of God "humbled himself" in order to become a human being and serve among us. It is *not* incarnational in the sense that *we are* Jesus Christ. No, indeed! We *reflect* the image of Christ into which we have been changed, but we are not *alter Christus*—another Christ (*CD* IV/3.2:786).

In his work devoted to the church, Emil Brunner proposes a rather stark idea of eliminating any institutional remnant of the church and focusing instead on the more mystical fellowship of the Spirit. He argues that this was

---

10. Throughout the book, I vary the reflexive pronoun for God from "Godself" to "himself." The former term is a recent neologism meant to overcome the difficulty in English of not having a genderless reflexive pronoun to refer to God. I acknowledge that God is neither male nor female but is above these designations, because God is Spirit. Whenever possible, I have used "Godself." But in those instances where the use of "Godself" leads to awkward syntax and cadence, I use "himself" as the reflexive pronoun for God.

the condition of the first-century church and one to which we need return. The *ekklēsia* of the New Testament was a *Christusgemeinde* (a community of Christ) not *eine Institution, ein Etwas* (an institution, a Something).[11] In other words, the first-century church was more invisible than visible, which Brunner lauds as something we should recoup.

At various points throughout the *Church Dogmatics* IV, Barth takes on Brunner's proposal found in the latter's *Misunderstanding of the Church*. In an extensive section dealing with the "order of the community" and what Barth calls "canon law," he argues that a church without law or institutional structure is not appropriate for the *communio sanctorum* (CD IV/2:676). While Brunner may long for a "pure fellowship of persons" (*eine Gemeinschaft von Personen*),[12] Barth argues that such a mystical community abandons "its life to chance and caprice and confusion" and will be a "contradiction to the Holy Spirit of Jesus Christ" as much as one that is enslaved to its laws (*CD* IV/2:681). Barth describes Brunner as declaring with exasperation, "What we need is the Holy Ghost!" To which Barth replies, "Of course we do. But . . ." (*CD* IV/2:681). Without the institutional aspects of the community, we cannot remain the church, because we will run into a disorder that will diminish and disguise the true church.[13] In other words, the visible church and its observable aspects of order help its continuance. To remove all aspects of institutional visibility would dissolve the church into an invisible phenomenon that probably would disappear entirely into a mystical mist of a nonphysical, nonhistorical entity.

Nevertheless, I feel strongly drawn toward Brunner's wistful idealism for the church. There are so many tentacles of humanity wrapped around the institutional church today that often I wish for a drastic surgery to remove

11. Emil Brunner, *Das Mißverständnis der Kirche* (Stuttgart: Evangelisches Verlagswerk, 1951), 12.

12. Brunner, *Das Mißverständnis der Kirche*, 12.

13. Such a strong plea for the visible structure of the church seems to go unheard by some theologians who accuse Barth of being too abstract and having no human agency. The extensive sections within *CD* IV/2 that relate to "canon law," as Barth calls it, clearly work against this. For one such charge, see Nicholas M. Healy, "The Logic of Karl Barth's Ecclesiology: Analysis, Assessment and Proposed Modifications," *Modern Theology* 10, no. 3 (July 1994): 253–70, here 258. Healy discusses Barth's idea of the difference between *die wirkliche Kirche* (the true church) and *die Scheinkirche* (mere semblance of a church) in *KD* IV/2:695–98; *CD* IV/2:614–17. See also Joseph L. Mangina, *Karl Barth: Theologian of Christian Witness* (Louisville: Westminster John Knox, 2004), 185, who notes that Barth has been "heavily criticized for being abstract" in his ecclesiology and possessing "insufficient human content." I attempt to argue against these charges in "Let the Church Be the Church: Barth and Pentecostals on Ecclesiology," in *Karl Barth and Pentecostal Theology: A Convergence of Word and Spirit*, ed. Frank Macchia, Andrew Gabriel, and Terry L. Cross, Systematic Pentecostal and Charismatic Theology Series, ed. Wolfgang Vondey and Daniela Augustine (New York: Bloomsbury, forthcoming).

all the human ganglia from God's house. Yet, with Barth, I understand that humans cannot operate as God's people without some human aspect of a society. Packer's sad conclusion noted above is that we simply have to wait for the *eschaton* to experience the pure form of the church. I cannot believe that God gathers his people into a local body to leave them deficient in reflecting together the true character of their God. Instead, I believe that the people of God's presence were meant to reflect—*through their very human existence as the church*—the nature of the God who called them together and sends them out into the world. Why give up on the Spirit's ability to transform our human institutions and endeavors called "church" and thereby surrender any attempt to bear Christ to the world in identifiable fashion? What if, as Barth describes, the paradigm of the heavenly community became proleptically present in some fashion here on earth? What if the church were a place whose order and organization offered a glimpse of the heavenly kingdom instead of a view of our earthly (carnal) striving for power? It is my contention that Pentecost marks a new era for God's people in this world—one that ushers a taste of the powers of the age to come into this present age. With this rushing in of the Spirit, the people of God's presence can and should expect some evidence of the future life here and now.

It is true that the church is a human institution—but it is also true that it is a miracle of God's own creation. It is by the Holy Spirit that we are drawn to Christ and then gathered together into the body of Christ. Cannot this same Spirit work with, in, and through the very human believers who are being transformed daily into the image of Christ so that the church will be more than its collective human sentiment for something better in this life or the next? Instead of the either/or of Spirit versus institutionalism, the pneumatic ecclesiology that I present here will offer a both/and approach.

Leading and Serving the People of God's Presence

Another significant structural flaw in the contemporary church is the level to which the gathered people of God have become "spectators" of Christianity instead of "participants." Nowhere is this more evident than in the realm of what we have come to call "ministry." Ministry has become the domain of professionals. The local congregation pays someone who has been trained (usually) to do the work of pastor so that the needs of the group can be attended to by one who knows what he or she is doing.[14] Over the centuries, the church has tended to divide the clergy from the laity, especially when it

---

14. In the next chapters I shall engage this issue more deeply.

comes to doing the work of ministry. It will be my contention in this book that such a view of ministry misunderstands the nature of leading the people of God's presence as well as the nature of ministry itself. The result of such a clergy/laity view is an inappropriate expectation on one or more clergy in a local congregation to do ministry while laypeople contribute to the upkeep of the system. The New Testament paradigm seems to view the entire people of God as doing the work of ministry. To be clear, however, I will not propose doing away with traditional ministry itself but will rather propose retooling how it could be done.

When reconsidering the structure of the church based on the theological claims that I have provided, one of the most important concerns relates to leadership of God's people. Why is this an important issue with respect to renewal of the structure of the church? It is because the way people lead frequently disguises the true identity of the church instead of demonstrating it. Perhaps the clearest example of this is found among leaders whose style is power driven. Autocrats among God's people leave a field of human debris, as if a spiritual tornado had hit God's house. While this may be most evident among churches that are called "independent" in terms of their lack of relation to a denomination or association that provides oversight, the problem of abuse of power does not land solely in such fertile spheres. There are plenty of examples in the church today of pastors who have welded together religious guilt and spiritual demands to such a degree that followers, intending to do the right thing, end up following something or someone other than Jesus Christ.

In an attempt to address this problem of spiritual abuse of power, I shall offer a theological critique of the concept of power that often lies at the center of such manipulative authoritarianism. The church of the twenty-first century must provide leaders who understand that Christ reversed the point of power from something that lorded over others to something that serves others with love.[15]

To be clear, I shall not propose a leaderless church! Such a utopian idealism cannot exist within this sphere of human existence. God desires to use humans and in so doing recognizes that we need leaders. However, future leaders will need to understand in more than intellectual ways that the power of God is found in the powerlessness of Christ's love in the face of the cross. Pagans and unbelievers may "lord it over" people, but Christ-followers must have none of that. Christian leaders operate with an authority based on love,

15. For the concepts derived from a "reversal of power," I am indebted to Migliore, *The Power of God and the gods of Power*, 68–71. We shall engage Migliore's fruitful discussion in greater detail in a later chapter.

not coercion. Whoever wants to be first must first learn to be a servant. How could leadership be any different for followers of Jesus Christ?

Given the basic reshaping of meaning for ministry in the church that I propose here, how are leaders supposed to lead? My proposal will certainly require a different set of skills for leaders of a local congregation from what was considered requisite in the past. In such a setting, ministerial training cannot prepare future leaders for merely duplicating the patterns of ecclesial leadership of the past where the minister is the "professional" who does the work of ministry and the people pay her or him for doing that work. This paradigm only serves to broaden and solidify the gap between "clergy" and "laity," thereby distancing God's people even further from their own calling to minister to others in the body of Christ and the world.

Leading will need to focus on training the people of God to do the work of *ministry* or *service*. This structural model is radically different from previous ones—especially as evidenced in Western societies. Instead of training one person to do work of ministry *for* the body of Christ, ministerial leadership training will need to focus on equipping the people of God to do the work of ministry. In this paradigm, leading will not be so much doing ministry oneself as *showing others how to do ministry* and then releasing them into doing it within the setting of the local congregation. In other words, leaders will need to "make room for" others among God's people to join in the work of ministry. In the chapters that follow, I shall propose details for how such a re-formation of the structure of the local church might look as well as how those who lead such churches might operate. However, before considering structure itself, we must examine more closely a theology of ministry.

A Biblical Background to Ministry

Introduction

A common paradigm for ministry today among many churches in Western societies is to relegate the majority of ministerial work to paid clergy whose professional training has (hopefully) provided them with the tools to do the various forms of work we call ministry. It is this widely accepted model for ministry that I believe needs to be reconstructed so that the church may rise to its calling in this century. It is my proposal that the structural framework of the local church and the paradigm for leadership must be radically reformed so that a more authentic form of ministry may flourish among God's people.

In this chapter, we begin an investigation for a different framework by engaging in a theological inquiry into ministry. To do so, we will return to scriptural examples of ministry as well as trace some historical trajectories from the early church in order to see how ministry functions developed over several centuries. Before proposing new paradigms for leadership and ministry among God's people, it is necessary that we excavate the early sources in order to discern any principles that may be found there for God's people today. While it will be clear that we cannot retrieve some pristine form of New Testament government or leadership per se, it will also be clear that we must retrieve something of the theology of ministry and leadership that is present there in order to function today as the people of God's presence.[1]

Some Biblical Foundations for Ministry

Diakon– *Words*

One place to begin a theology of ministry is with an understanding of the terms used for this activity in the New Testament. Perhaps the word that best characterizes the activity of the people of God's presence is found in the word "ministry." The people of God minister to the Lord, to one another, and to the world. Rooted in words that underscore the concept of serving others, the English verb "to minister" comes from the Latin word *ministrare*. In the New Testament, the concept is rooted in three different sets of Greek words. The first and most prominent set stems from the Greek noun διακονία | *diakonia*[2] ("service" or "ministry") or the verb διακονεῖν | *diakonein*[3] ("to serve" or "to minister"). Related to these words is διάκονος | *diakonos*, which is usually translated as "one who renders service to another" or "a minister." From these basic *diakon–* root words we get our English word "deacon." For over a century, scholars have understood the primary or basic meaning of this word to have arisen from a concept of service in which one "waits at table" for others.[4] Acts 6 has provided the paradigmatic example for this type of *diakonia*: Hellenistic Jews complained that their widows were overlooked in

---

see variation in usage of these titles and development. The New Testament does not have one understanding of any of these ministries. They are all in a state of flux." See Kevin Giles, *Patterns of Ministry among the First Christians*, 2nd ed. (Eugene, OR: Cascade Books, 2017), 8. The truth of this statement will become clearer as we work through the next two chapters. However, I do believe there are principles that can guide our ecclesiological endeavors, and it is these that we will highlight in the end.

2. Used thirty-four times in the NT, *diakonia* can mean "serving, service, waiting, or ministering." However, we will also see that its "semantic range" should include service that is done on behalf of a master or representing someone else; such serving would include the work of an emissary or ambassador. This latter expansion of the meaning of *diakon–* words has been proposed recently through extensive research by John Collins in the classical and Hellenistic Greek documents of the era that predate or are contemporaneous with the first-century Christian writings. I will engage Collins's work further below. See John N. Collins, *Diakonia: Reinterpreting the Ancient Sources* (New York: Oxford University Press, 1990).

3. Used thirty-seven times in the NT, *diakonein* can mean "to wait, attend on, serve, relieve, assist, or minister to." It may also refer to actions on behalf of someone else (as Collins has shown).

4. Hermann Beyer, "διακονέω," *TDNT* 2:84. The various uses in the NT of the verb and noun are provided in excellent detail by Beyer, but the extrabiblical uses of this verb in classical and Hellenistic Greek that have been discovered more recently have outlined much more than menial service. The entry for *diakonia* in BDAG (1979, 2nd ed.) follows Beyer's description precisely. It means service, aid, support, and serving as necessary for a meal's preparation. As John Collins notes, however, the entry for *diakonia* in BDAG (2000, 3rd ed.) has "service in an intermediary capacity" as its primary meaning and "service as attendant" only in its fifth meaning. The newer edition has taken Collins's research as determinative for its entry. For a brief history of the "lexicographical convention" (as Collins calls it), see John N. Collins, "A

the "daily distribution of food" (ἐν τῇ διακονίᾳ τῇ καθημερινῇ | *en tē diakonia tē kathēmerinē*) (Acts 6:1). This situation is described more fully in Acts 6:2: "So the Twelve gathered all the disciples together and said, 'It would not be right for us to neglect the ministry of the word of God in order to wait on tables [διακονεῖν τραπέζαις | *diakonein trapezais*].'" Compared to the ministry of the Word, to serve tables is a mundane, menial task.[5] However, since 1990, with the appearance of a thorough linguistic study of *diakon–* words from classical and Hellenistic Greek by John N. Collins, there has been significant debate and revision about the meaning of these important words in the New Testament.[6] Collins suggests that *diakon–* words "must be removed from the semantic field of caring service."[7] From extrabiblical Greek sources, Collins found some evidence that placed *diakon–* words within the semantic range of meaning for "servant" or "service," but most evidence supported their primary translation as an official representative or a "go-between" rather than "menial" servant.[8] Hence, Collins argues that this word group signified

---

Monocultural Usage: διακον– Words in Classical, Hellenistic, and Patristic Sources," *Vigiliae Christianae* 66 (2012): 287–309, esp. 288–95.

5. It may be noted that when the Twelve report the decision in Acts 6:4, they call their task related to the Word as "the service of the Word" or "the ministry of the word" (τῇ διακονίᾳ τοῦ λόγου | *tē diakonia tou logou*). Clearly, there is something more going on here than a contrast between menial table service and the proclamation of the Word of God, since both tasks are described as *diakonia*. Also see Craig S. Keener, *Acts: An Exegetical Commentary*, vol. 2, *3:1–14:28* (Grand Rapids: Baker Academic, 2013), 1264, especially for the historical context of what the "daily" distribution of food might have looked like. Keener also denies that this passage is to be connected directly with the later office of deacons, since *diakonos* elsewhere is used to describe Christ, Paul, and Paul's colleagues as ministers. The verb in Acts 6 (*diakoneō*) applies both to "administrators" of the daily food *and* the ministry of the Word. Keener, *Acts*, 2:1272.

6. John N. Collins has noted that to relegate lowly service or only menial tasks to the *diakonos* misaligns the word group. Instead, *diakon–* words refer to emissaries or agents sent to perform or carry out the orders of another person. See Collins, *Diakonia*, esp. 77–131, 169–76. I find much of Collins's argument convincing from a purely philological standpoint. Nevertheless, what I have offered in the main text above seems feasible, even while accepting Collins's research. At its base, the root *diakon–* has a servant idea behind it, but not perhaps solely of menial or mundane tasks. As Margaret Mowczko states, "Paul never uses any *diakon–* word for ordinary servants." See Mowczko, "What Did Phoebe's Position and Ministry as Διάκονος of the Church at Cenchrea Involve?," in *Deacons and Diakonia in Early Christianity*, ed. Bart J. Koet, Edwina Murphy, and Esko Ryökäs, WUNT, 2nd ser., 479 (Tübingen: Mohr Siebeck, 2018), 97.

7. John N. Collins, *Deacons and the Church: Making Connections between Old and New* (Harrisburg, PA: Morehouse, 2002), 15. In particular, Collins suggests that a redefinition of *diakonia* in the 1800s in Germany allowed the Lutheran churches there to posit the role of deacons or the diaconate as primarily caring service. Collins's argument is that this idea was based on the influence of Jesus being a servant in the Gospels and that it therefore ignored the extrabiblical linguistic evidence that expanded the range of meaning for these root words. Collins finds Beyer's article in *TDNT* (from 1935) to be marred with the assumption that *diakonia* and cognates refer solely to menial service.

8. Collins, *Diakonia*, 77–95.

activities more along the line of delivering messages or being an agent for someone.[9] Instead of meaning "slavish service at table," *diakon–* words were "freely applied to activities by people of eminence" and sometimes in connection with religion.[10] Most importantly for Collins, the term *diakonos* "always looks back to a person, persons, institution or physical dependency."[11] Collins believes that among Christians, the person to whom a *diakonos* always looks back is the bishop (ἐπίσκοπος | *episkopos*)—both in the New Testament and the early church.[12]

Without engaging in excessive discussion concerning the proposal of Collins's work, it remains important to demonstrate how this key concept of *diakonia* is related to the meaning of ministry in this chapter. Since *diakon–* words are fundamental for understanding "ministry" in the New Testament, I need to interact with some aspects of Collins's proposal. First, Collins has pressed for the semantic range of *diakon–* words in the New Testament to be expanded beyond menial service; he has not argued that *diakon–* words *never* have the meaning of service. He argues instead that they do not carry the primary meaning of *menial* service. Therefore, he proposes that the "lexicographical range for the words" is "much broader than the traditional one."[13]

Second, the preponderance of linguistic evidence that Collins presents from classical and Hellenistic Greek surely demands a broadening of the usual definition of *diakon–* words, but I would suggest it does not eliminate the narrower sense of serving at menial tasks. Each passage in the New Testament needs to be considered within its context. While I agree with Collins in his effort to expand the potential semantic range of these words, I am concerned that he does not acknowledge the legitimate role that the servanthood of Jesus Christ may have played in shaping the semantic range of meaning in the New Testament.

9. Collins, *Diakonia*, 194.

10. John N. Collins, "Ordained and Other Ministries: Making a Difference," *Ecclesiology* 3, no. 1 (2006): 11–32, here 23. Collins further argues that the range of meaning in English as it is used in the NT will need to land "along the spectrum of ideas like the following: messenger, spokesperson, representative, go-between, medium, agent, attendant, an attendant who is dispatched time and again by a diner to fetch the various dishes. And of course it is of interest that most of the instances of this table attendant occur in relation to banquets of a religious character" (24).

11. John N. Collins, "Re-interpreting *Diakonia* in Germany," *Ecclesiology* 5 (2009): 69–81, here 79.

12. Collins, "Re-interpreting *Diakonia* in Germany," 79.

13. These are the words of Paula Gooder describing Collins's proposal. See Paula Gooder, "*Diakonia* in the New Testament: A Dialogue with John N. Collins," *Ecclesiology* 3, no. 1 (2006): 33–56, here 48.

Third, the major criticism that I have of Collins's work comes mainly from his tendency to read into the New Testament the later role of deacon and allow that to determine the interpretation of several key passages where *diakon*–words occur. For example, Collins reads the third- or fourth-century idea that deacons were to serve the bishop as attendants and finds this suitable with the Hellenistic meaning of *diakonos* (namely, one who represents another in an important task). However, just because we find "attendant" or "representative of someone else" in the extrabiblical Greek literature does not mean that we can justify taking the third-century-CE bishop-deacon relationship and overlaying it back onto the range of meaning in New Testament contexts (e.g., at Phil. 1:1).

As I will show, it is extraordinarily difficult to discern precisely what was occurring in the first-century church in terms of leadership functions. To assume the way deacons operated in relation to the bishop at the beginning of the third century is the way they operated in Philippians 1:1 (where Paul greets the "bishops and deacons" [NRSV]) is to read too much back into the first-century text and situation. Collins's work allows us to understand broader dimensions of meaning in the term *diakonos*, but it cannot give us a definitive comprehension of the functional tasks assigned to the term in the New Testament itself.

Fourth, Collins desires to use the New Testament texts to determine a theology of ministry for today, especially in terms of bishops, priests, and deacons. Coming from a Catholic approach to the question, Collins suggests that ministry is *not* for everyone.[14] Along with Anglican scholar Paul Avis, I think that the logic of Collins's view leads to a result that "most Christians . . . do not or cannot have a ministry."[15] Such a view is opposite to my understanding of the New Testament and of the church today. When Collins moves from linguistic study to an attempt at theological assertion based on that study, something seems missing from the overall meaning of ministry.[16] One cannot help but feel this is a theological presumption imposing itself on his assessments of biblical texts with regard to *diakon*– words. For example, when interpreting 1 Corinthians 12:4–6, Collins notes that the phrasing in the NRSV is as follows: "There are varieties of *gifts*, but the same Spirit; and there are varieties of *service*, but

14. The title of a small book by Collins underscores this point precisely: John N. Collins, *Are All Christians Ministers?* (Collegeville, MN: Liturgical Press, 1992). He answers the question with a definitive no.

15. Paul Avis, *A Ministry Shaped by Mission* (Edinburgh: T&T Clark, 2005), 52. Avis calls such a view "unacceptable and unbiblical," noting that all Christians receive a "charisma of the Holy Spirit through their initiation into the body of Christ" (52).

16. For a response to this approach, see James Monroe Barnett, "Diaconate Defined Not by Word Study but by Early Church," *Diakoneo* 17, no. 5 (1995): 1.

the same Lord; and there are varieties of *working*, but it is the same God."[17] Collins describes several exegetes as understanding the emphasized terms to denote the same thing, that the terms are interchangeable.[18] They are heavenly gifts distributed by the one God so that the *charismata* = *diakoniai* = *energēmata* (χαρισμάτα = διακόνιαι = ἐνεργήματα) are open to the entire church.[19]

Against this view, Collins asserts that *diakoniai* in 1 Corinthians 12:5 is the same form of ministry that Paul uses of Apollos and himself as διάκονοι | *diakonoi* in 1 Corinthians 3:5. What is described in the earlier passage is that Paul and Apollos are ministers or "servants [*diakonoi*], through whom you came to believe—as the Lord has assigned [ἔδωκεν | *edōken*] to each his task" (1 Cor. 3:5). Not everyone was "given" or "assigned" this task of preaching the Word of God, through which the Corinthians came to believe. "This *diakonia* was not a 'ministry' given to the whole church but was in fact the privilege, responsibility and burden of those few chosen to deliver the Word in the name of God, Christ and Spirit."[20] When Collins adds to this interpretation the linguistic range of meaning for *diakon–* words, he brings a completely new slant to 1 Corinthians 12:4–6. For him it reads as follows: "There are varieties of gifts, but the same Spirit; both varieties of ministries and the same Lord, and varieties of workings but the same God." For Collins, the first clause is a general statement about gifts, and then the next two clauses (introduced by "both") are about two "species of gifts"—namely, "'ministries' (for the likes of Paul and Apollos) and secondly 'workings' (which are distributed church wide: as the passage goes on to say, 'it is the same God who inspires them all in every one')."[21] Therefore, *diakoniai* are relegated to specifically commissioned individuals within the church. These are not servants with menial tasks but messengers who have been given the task of the *diakonia* of the Word. Collins suggests that to describe "ministries" as a task for all believers is to misunderstand the word *diakoniai* here.

Is this the only way to interpret these words from 1 Corinthians? Paula Gooder has provided a critique of Collins's interpretation on this point.[22] She

17. My emphasis. The NIV translates these three phrases as "different kinds of gifts . . . different kinds of service . . . different kinds of working."

18. Collins, "Ordained and Other Ministries," 28.

19. Collins, "Ordained and Other Ministries," 28.

20. Collins, "Ordained and Other Ministries," 28.

21. Collins, "Ordained and Other Ministries," 29. Collins tries to support his reading from the Greek "both . . . and" (καί | *kai* . . . καί | *kai*).

22. Gooder, "*Diakonia* in the New Testament," 52. Gooder also engages Collins's interpretation of Eph. 4:11–12, where Collins attempts to understand the threefold result of Christ's gifts to the church as something *received by* the church, not *done by* the whole church. However, others read this as if the gifts "equip the saints for the work of ministry, for building up the

acknowledges that his approach is a possible way to read the Greek grammar but also admits that it has flaws, especially when attempting to prove that gifts are the genus and ministries and workings are the species of that genus.[23] Further, I would suggest that while these gifts, ministries, and workings may not be direct equivalents (as Collins proposes), they could be operating in something like a trinitarian manner—perhaps even *perichoretic*. When Paul says later that everyone receives something from the Spirit, he calls it a "manifestation" (φανέρωσις | *phanerōsis*). "Now to each one the manifestation of the Spirit is given for the common good" (1 Cor. 12:7). By the end of the chapter, Paul points to the fact that not everyone has *the same gift*, but God has "placed" (ἔθετο | *etheto*) various manifestations of the Spirit in the church for the benefit of all (1 Cor. 12:28). Within the context of chapter 12, this triplet expression in verses 4–6 seems to stress the *unity* of the giver of the gifts while noting the *diversity* of the ways these gifts may operate.[24] Three times Paul repeats that the giver of each gift, serving, or working is the same (Spirit, Lord, God). While the word "varieties" or "differing" (διαιρέσεις | *diaireseis*) is also repeated and emphasized three times in order to highlight the diversity, it may better be understood as "apportionings" or "allotments."[25] There is an emphasis in this variety on the *gifting* by God—the portion that has been allotted to the church. Behind the variety of activities is the unity of the source—the Triune God.

The theology of ministry that I propose represents a view that answers the question, Are all Christians ministers? with a resounding yes! I can agree with Collins's linguistic study of Hellenistic and classical Greek and yet disagree with his use of that information as requiring "ministry" (*diakonia*) to be fulfilled only through certain (ordained) individuals. When Collins uses his lexicographical evidence to underscore the fact that *diakon*– words require a meaning of some intermediary performing a task on behalf of another, he assumes that such a task must fit the ecclesial structure of a much later century. Why must the *diakonos* be representing the *episkopos*? Why couldn't the *diakonos* be an intermediary representing Christ himself? Could not this be a service *on behalf of Christ* that belongs to *all* believers instead of a few and therefore a derived authority?

---

body of Christ" (NRSV), which means that all the saints are doing the work of ministry. After carefully dissecting the grammar of this passage, Gooder rightly concludes that the Greek could read either way. Describing her assessment of both these passages, Gooder says, "Their meaning is at best opaque" (54).

23. Gooder, "*Diakonia* in the New Testament," 52.

24. Cf. Anthony C. Thiselton, *The First Epistle to the Corinthians: A Commentary on the Greek Text*, NIGTC (Grand Rapids: Eerdmans, 2000), 932.

25. Thiselton, *The First Epistle to the Corinthians*, 928. The word "varieties" or "allotments" is in the position of emphasis in Greek (the first word in each of the three phrases).

The emphasis in Paul's letters seems to be placed on the responsibility of the local congregation to regulate and engage in ministry. Such a theology of ministry I would call *pneumatic*. Paul speaks of the κοινωνία | *koinōnia* of the Spirit, which is usually described as "fellowship of the Spirit." However, instead of viewing it as the "common membership of a congregation," it may be more properly described as a "sharing" of the Spirit or even a "common experience of the Spirit."[26] Therefore, "participating in the Spirit" may be a better translation. The church, then, is "something which grows out of the shared experience of the Spirit."[27] Therefore, as a people who have been encountered by the presence of God in a direct manner, our shared experience of God contributes to our sense of community.

All of the people of God are given gifts, are called to serve—to minister—and are energized to work by the Spirit. "All these are the work [ἐνεργεῖ | *energei*] of one and the same Spirit [τὸ ἓν καὶ τὸ αὐτὸ πνεῦμα | *to hen kai to auto pneuma*], and he distributes [διαιροῦν | *diairoun*] them to each one, just as he determines" (1 Cor. 12:11). This is the basis for our theology of ministry. The one Spirit distributes a variety of gifts to each individual within the body of Christ, precisely as the Spirit determines the common need. All the people of God are to be engaged by the Spirit, equipped to do the "work of ministry" (εἰς ἔργον διακονίας | *eis ergon diakonias*) (Eph. 4:12 NRSV). James Dunn underscores this point regarding Paul's theology of ministry: "His understanding of the local church as the body of Christ necessarily implies each member having a function within that congregation, and a responsibility for its common life and worship. This presumably is the rationale behind his exhortations to *all* members of different churches to teach, admonish, judge, and comfort."[28]

The meaning of the *diakon–* words in some Pauline usage have surely been influenced by the story of Jesus as found in Luke 22:27. Without denying the lexicographic expansion of these words toward a higher role of an ambassador or emissary, surely the action of Jesus in serving at the table (Luke) and bending to wash the disciples' feet (John) held a potent sway over how the first-century church understood *diakonia*.[29] In the Lukan passage, we find the pertinent discussion comes directly after the Supper:

26. James D. G. Dunn, *The Theology of Paul the Apostle* (Grand Rapids: Eerdmans, 1998), 561–62.

27. Dunn, *Theology of Paul*, 561.

28. Dunn, *Theology of Paul*, 593 (his emphasis). He lists the following passages as support: Rom. 15:14; 1 Cor. 5:4–5; 2 Cor. 2:7; Col. 3:16; 1 Thess. 5:14.

29. I acknowledge that the Gospel of John does not use the word *diakonos* in its footwashing scene, but the story itself clearly has similar overtones to the statements made in the Synoptic Gospels regarding servanthood. Also, in John we are told by Jesus to follow his example and wash others' feet (John 13:14–15), so this is meant to be a pattern where the servant/slave

A dispute also arose among them as to which of them was considered to be greatest. Jesus said to them, "The kings of the Gentiles lord it over [κυριεύουσιν | *kyrieuousin*] them; and those who exercise authority over them call themselves Benefactors [εὐεργεται | *euergetai*]. But you are not to be like that. Instead, the greatest [μείζων | *meizōn*] among you should be like the youngest [νεώτερος | *neōteros*], and the one who rules [ὁ ἡγούμενος | *ho hēgoumenos*] like the one who serves [ὁ διακονῶν | *ho diakonōn*]. For who is greater, the one who is at the table or the one who serves [ὁ διακονῶν | *ho diakonōn*]? Is it not the one who is at the table? But I am among you as one who serves [ὡς ὁ διακονῶν | *hōs ho diakonōn*]." (Luke 22:24–27)

Jesus's point in this pericope is clear: lording it over others is inappropriate for Christians, especially those who lead. Instead, service is the hallmark of Christ and therefore of his followers. This is especially poignant since it appears within the event of the Supper. "I am among you as one who waits on tables." This seems to be the most natural way of understanding what is being said with *diakonōn* here. The translation of this word as "emissary" or "standing in the stead of a higher authority" seems less the case. Instead, this is a clear depiction of the way Christ wanted his own disciples to operate in the world.

The passage from Mark speaks similarly to that in Luke:[30] "Not so with you. Instead, whoever wants to become great [μέγας | *megas*] among you must be your servant [διάκονος | *diakonos*], and whoever wants to be first [πρῶτος | *prōtos*] must be slave [δοῦλος | *doulos*] of all. For even the Son of Man did not come to be served [διακονηθῆναι | *diakonēthēnai*], but to serve [διακονῆσαι | *diakonēsai*], and to give his life as a ransom for many" (Mark 10:43–45). In Mark, the comparison is between the following:

megas . . . diakonos	prōtos . . . doulos
great . . . servant	first . . . slave

In Luke, the comparison differs:

meizōn . . . neōteros	hēgoumenos . . . diakonōn
greatest . . . youngest	the one who rules . . . the one who serves/ministers

---

(*doulos*) washes the feet of guests. However, it is important not to mix the meanings of *doulos* and *diakonos* too much here. My point is simply that such a narrative about Jesus's actions among the disciples would have strong effect on first-century Christians. Here one may consider the rather early hymn of the first-century church as quoted by Paul in Phil. 2:5–11. There Christ Jesus is described as "being in very nature God" and taking on "the very nature of a servant [μορφὴν δούλου | *morphēn doulou*]" (Phil. 2:6, 7).

30. I. Howard Marshall, *The Gospel of Luke: A Commentary on the Greek Text*, NIGTC (Grand Rapids: Eerdmans, 1978), 811. Marshall notes that Luke's setting at the table is more likely to be original but that it is possible that Mark's saying is separate from Luke's.

In both texts, Jesus is pointing out the difference between the way rulers commonly govern and the way Christian leaders are to operate. If "lording over others" is the common way of the world, then being a servant or slave of all (Mark) or being the one who serves/ministers (Luke) is clearly the preferred manner for followers of Christ.[31] That seems to be the point in both passages. When Jesus said, "I am among you as one who serves" (ὡς ὁ διακονῶν | hōs ho diakonōn) (Luke 22:27), he established a precedent for believers (and especially leaders) to serve and not run roughshod over people. While rulers among the gentiles "lord it over" (κυριεύουσιν | kyrieuousin) those they govern, the disciples are not to be like that. Instead, they are to be like Jesus and serve (Luke 22:25).

It is this concept of service or ministry to others that the New Testament takes to be characteristic of genuine Christians and their leaders. Peter appeals to the elders of the congregation in ways entirely reminiscent of the Lord's words: Be "eager to serve; not lording it over [κατακυριύοντες | katakyriuontes] those entrusted to you, but being examples to the flock" (1 Pet. 5:2–3).[32] Paul readily speaks of himself and other workers on Christ's behalf as "servants" of Christ or the church—sometimes translated as "ministers" (1 Cor. 3:5; Col. 1:25; 2 Cor. 6:3; 11:23). Therefore, it seems clear that before an office of "deacon" developed in the first-century church, there was a manner of life for every Christian that matched their Lord—namely, that of service. The office that developed seemed to formalize particular aspects of community life through official "servants" that could give devoted attention to specific physical and spiritual needs. All believers were called to serve by virtue of their relationship with the Lord, who was the servant of all. How could Christians do otherwise? If we follow our Lord, then stooping with basin and towel to wash the feet of others is precisely where and when we live up to the full measure of the stature of Christ. Hence, we are all ministers—servants who represent one higher than us who has also called us into service.

It is my contention that all believers have been entrusted with "the ministry of reconciliation" (τὴν διακονίαν τῆς καταλλαγῆς | tēn diakonian tēs katallagēs) (2 Cor. 5:18). Collins and others want to limit ministry to particular positions or people: "A ministry is a charge put upon someone, and those who gave us the language took it originally from a broadly religious

31. As R. T. France has noted, "Leadership is characterized by service, by being under the authority of others, like a διάκονος or δοῦλος." See R. T. France, The Gospel of Mark: A Commentary on the Greek Text, NIGTC (Grand Rapids: Eerdmans, 2002), 419.
32. It should be noted that the verb "lord it over" is the same one that is used with Jesus's words in Luke 22, except this verb adds an intensifying preposition prefix (kata) to it.

background because they wanted to speak of churchly charges: for most, their ministries were commissions handed out by church authorities; for a few—very few—there was a sense of a ministry received instead directly from God."[33] This statement assumes too much. First, it speaks of "commissions handed out by church authorities." In the New Testament—especially in the Pauline congregations—there was very little of local church "authorities" as we would consider them today. As I shall demonstrate below, there were functional leaders (like overseers, elders, prophets, pastors, teachers, and servants/deacons), but "authority" is something relegated to Christ (as the head of the church) and to the whole assembled congregation (as people entrusted with the gospel and who will eventually be called upon to judge the world and angels) (1 Cor. 6:2–3). Again, this feels like Collins is reading the fourth-century ecclesial institution back into the first-century church.

Second, it describes *diakonia* as a "charge put upon someone." I have no qualms with this description—and Collins has provided all of us with a great service by demonstrating this broader semantical range of *diakon–* words. However, this description does not delineate precisely from whom the charge comes. My argument is that all Christians have been given this ministry of reconciliation and that God himself is the One who has commissioned them. Such an important task is not relegated to a chosen few—important as leaders in this ministry surely are!—but the commission is given to all who believe to share the message of reconciliation (τὸν λόγον τῆς καταλλαγῆς | *ton logon tēs katallagēs*) (2 Cor. 5:19).

Third, it downplays the "sense of ministry received . . . directly from God." Why? Is it because church offices are easier to manage than charismatic gifts? Is it because there is a disbelief that God can and does call people to fulfill a ministry—not just clergy? As I have argued previously, the people of God's presence are directly encountered by the Spirit of God, who "distributes" manifestations of the Spirit "to each one, just as he determines" (1 Cor. 12:11).[34]

God has reconciled *us* to himself through Christ and has given *us* the ministry of reconciliation (2 Cor. 5:18).[35] It is *our* task—not just Paul's—to serve

---

33. Collins, *Diakonia*, 258.

34. Collins aligns the ministry of reconciliation *first* with the apostles, prophets, and teachers of 1 Cor. 12:28, and *then* with "whoever has been entrusted with the word and commissioned to proclaim it." Collins, *Diakonia*, 259. If we are all priests before God, as Peter states, then are we not also *all* to "declare the praises of him who called you out of darkness into his wonderful light" (1 Pet. 2:9)?

35. Victor P. Furnish argues that the "us" here [ἡμῖν | *hēmin*] includes all believers, not just Paul or associates. See Victor P. Furnish, *II Corinthians: Translated with Introduction, Notes and Commentary*, Anchor Bible 32A (Garden City, NY: Doubleday, 1984), 317, 336.

the world as ambassadors on behalf of Christ (ὑπὲρ Χριστοῦ οὖν πρεσβεύομεν | *hyper Christou oun presbeuomen*), "as though God were making his appeal through us" (2 Cor. 5:20). Is only Paul an ambassador? Are only Paul's associates called into the task of representing Christ in this *diakonia* of reconciliation? The fact that the action of Christ on behalf of the world has already achieved reconciliation is the *message* of reconciliation (τὸν λόγον τῆς καταλλαγῆς | *ton logon tēs katallagēs*) (2 Cor. 5:19).[36] Christians are representatives of Christ's message and serve the ministry of reconciliation to the world on his behalf. Hence, *diakonia* here refers "not to an office but to a function of serving, the role of presenting for acceptance God's offer of reconciliation."[37] God has entrusted to us (θέμενος ἐν ἡμῖν | *themenos en hēmin*) this vital ministry of reconciliation. Surely this is a commission not only for Paul but also for the people of God.

Latre- *and* Leitourg- *Words*

In moving from *diakon–* words to the second and third sets of Greek words that help to define ministry in the New Testament, we move toward words that have a greater relation to religious activity. The second set of words has a root form of *latre–*. The first term to consider in this set is λατρεύω | *latreuō*, which means "to be a servant" or "to serve," especially in relation to a religious service or worship.[38] It is used twenty-one times in the New Testament.[39] The noun form of the verb *latreuō* is λατρεία | *latreia*, which is used five times in the New Testament.[40]

The third word group that clarifies our understanding of ministry comes from the verb λειτουργέω | *leitourgeō*, which means "to perform a public service at one's own expense" or "to minister, assist."[41] Its word origin arises from two Greek words, λαός | *laos* (people) and ἔργω | *ergō* (to work).[42] It is used three times in the New Testament.[43] The noun form of this word is

---

36. Murray Harris notes that the aorist tense of καταλλάξαντος | *katallaxantos* (who reconciled) in 2 Cor. 5:18 and the imperfect tense of ἦν καταλλάσσω | *ēn katallassō* (was reconciling) in 2 Cor. 5:19 point to the past nature of the achievement, probably the cross and resurrection of Christ. See Murray Harris, *The Second Epistle to the Corinthians: A Commentary on the Greek Text*, NIGTC (Grand Rapids: Eerdmans, 2005), 438.

37. Harris, *The Second Epistle to the Corinthians*, 439.

38. Hermann Strathman, "λατρεύω, λατρεία," *TDNT* 4:62–65.

39. As a representative sampling, see Matt. 4:10; Luke 1:74; Rom. 9:4; 12:1; Heb. 8:5; 9:9.

40. John 16:2; Rom. 9:4; 12:1; Heb. 9:1, 6.

41. Hermann Strathman, "λειτουργέω," *TDNT* 4:226–31.

42. More specifically, it is the word "public" (λήϊτος | *lēitos*), which is derived from λαός | *laos*, that gives the first part of the word λειτουργέω | *leitourgeō* here.

43. Heb. 10:11; Acts 13:2; Rom. 15:27.

λειτουργία | *leitourgia*, which is used six times in the New Testament.[44] From this last term we derive our English word "liturgy."

What is the meaning of these ministry terms of the second and third word groups? By examining some of their uses in context, we may be able to see connections for understanding first-century ministry as well as grasp something beneficial for our own cultural context today. Paul uses *latreia* to refer to "temple worship" (Rom. 9:4) and "true and proper worship" (Rom. 12:1). It is "in view of God's mercy" that the Romans are "to offer your bodies as a living sacrifice [παραστῆσαι τὰ σώματα ὑμῶν θυσίαν ζῶσαν | *parastēsai ta sōmata hymōn thysian zōsan*], holy and pleasing to God—this is your true and proper worship [ἁγίαν εὐάρεστον τῷ θεῷ, τὴν λογικὴν λατρείαν ὑμῶν | *hagian euareston tō theō, tēn logikēn latreian hymōn*]" (Rom. 12:1). Here *latreia* is used to remind readers of all of the rituals and aspects related to cultic worship in Israel. However, now it frames Christian worship in terms that are clearly non-Levitical—present your bodies on the altar of sacrifice and in so doing you will be involved in worship that is reasonable and proper for those who are in the new covenant.

The writer to the Hebrews uses *latreia* twice to speak of "regulations for worship" and the work of priests in the tabernacle to "carry on their ministry" (Heb. 9:1 and 9:6 respectively). The verb form, *latreuō*, is used also in Hebrews: "the gifts and sacrifices being offered were not able to clear the conscience of the worshiper" (Heb. 9:9), with λατρεύοντα | *latreuonta* being a participle referring to "the worshiper" or "those who worship." The verbal form is also used in Hebrews 8:5, where it describes the activity of all priests who "serve at a sanctuary that is a copy" of what is in heaven. Here λατρεύουσιν | *latreuousin* is translated "they serve," referring to the priestly activity in the sanctuary.

The group of words related to "liturgy" refers most commonly to ministry, especially those actions related to the priesthood. In Luke 1:23, this term *leitourgia* is used to describe the work of the priest Zechariah: "When his time of service [ἡμέραι τῆς λειτουργίας | *hēmerai tēs leitourgias*] was completed, he returned home." While Jewish priests "serve" in the sanctuary, "the ministry [λειτουργίας | *leitourgias*] Jesus has received is as superior to theirs as the covenant . . . is superior to the old one" (Heb. 8:6). In its verbal form it can be used to describe Christians worshiping or ministering to God, as in Acts 13:2: "While they were worshiping [λειτουργούντων | *leitourgountōn*] the Lord and fasting, the Holy Spirit said . . ." Yet this term can also refer to helping others with one's physical means, as Paul says in Romans 15:27: the

44. Luke 1:23; Phil. 2:17; Heb. 8:6; 9:21; 2 Cor. 9:12; Phil. 2:30.

people of Macedonia were pleased to share with those in need in Jerusalem, for "they owe it to the Jews to *share* with them their *material blessings*" (ὀφείλουσιν καὶ ἐν τοῖς σαρκικοῖς λειτουργῆσαι αὐτοῖς | *opheilousin kai en tois sarkikois leitourgēsai autois*).[45]

At the heart of the work of our High Priest, Jesus Christ, is ministry—service. Yet these words that describe such lofty service before God in the heavenly tabernacle are also used to describe our humble efforts at worship on earth. We cannot disconnect the concept of service from the concept of worship! Further, such service is not bound within the walls of the sanctuary or within the offerings we give to God. Worship in the new covenant is wrapped up in a vertical dimension of giving to God the praise and adoration due to him while at the same time is ineffective without the concomitant response in the horizontal dimension of serving others. In other words, God is not pleased with sacrifices arising only from our lips but demands the *service* of our lives. "Through Jesus, therefore, let us continually offer to God a sacrifice of praise—the fruit of lips that openly profess his name. And do not forget to do good and to share with others, for with such sacrifices God is pleased" (Heb. 13:15–16).

What Is the Purpose of Priests?

An inquiry into a theology of ministry that springs from the New Testament cannot proceed without engaging the issue of the priesthood in the former covenant. Why was there a priestly caste separated from the people of Israel? Answering this question will set the stage for understanding priests in the New Testament—and, by extension, for developing a theology of ministry today.

When the people of Israel were three months out of Egypt, they camped at the foot of Mount Sinai. Moses went up the mountain to speak with God. There he learned the reason why God had freed the Israelites from four hundred years of bondage: "You yourselves have seen what I did to Egypt, and how I carried you on eagles' wings and brought you to myself. Now if you obey me fully and keep my covenant, then out of all nations you will be my treasured possession. Although the whole earth is mine, you will be for me a kingdom of priests and a holy nation" (Exod. 19:4–6). God announced the goal for his people—to be his treasured possession, to be a kingdom of priests, and to be a holy nation. Of these three descriptions, let us consider for our purposes the phrase "kingdom of priests."

---

45. The words emphasized point to the NIV's translation of the words connected with the *leitourg–* stem.

Surely there were priests in the pagan world around the Israelites, especially in Egypt. Nonetheless, there were no priests for YHWH, as of yet; the Aaronic priesthood still had to be established. As the story unfolds, we realize that God desired *all of his people* to be in a relationship with him, a characteristic belonging to priests. In the ancient world, it was the priesthood that was allowed to commune with the gods on behalf of the common people. As the Israelites would discover from God's detailed description of the priesthood in the following chapters, priests were to be holy so that they might come into God's presence without fear; priests were to mediate between God and the people; priests were to enter designated areas in order to commune with God. I suggest that what would eventually become the Aaronic priesthood was—in principle—what God had intended for the *entire* community from the beginning. When God was ready to offer his covenant to this people, he explained his rationale for rescuing them—to create a people in relationship with him to the degree that they could commune with him face-to-face. If this was God's desire, why did a mediating caste of priests arise from Aaron's family and the tribe of Levi?

As Exodus 19 unfolds, it becomes clear why not all the people became priests. God told Moses that he would appear in a thick cloud and the people would hear him speaking from it (Exod. 19:9). The people were to prepare themselves by consecrating their lives and making themselves holy before God (Exod. 19:10–15). When they were ready, on the third day, God came down from Mount Sinai "in the sight of all the people" (Exod. 19:11). When God arrived, there was a fantastic light show: thunder, lightning, and a loud trumpet blast. "Everyone in the camp trembled" (Exod. 19:16). Moses then led the people to meet with God at the foot of the mountain—at the boundary God had set. Smoke billowed from Mount Sinai because God settled on it in the form of fire. The whole mountain trembled in God's presence, and the trumpet blasts grew louder. Then Moses spoke to God, and God answered. So intense was the voice of God that the people thought they were going to die. Only those God allowed could advance. At this point, God spoke the conditions of the covenant—what is commonly known as the Ten Commandments. When these were given and they heard God's voice and saw such divine pyrotechnics, the people trembled with fear. They said to Moses, "Speak to us yourself and we will listen. But do not have God speak to us or we will die" (Exod. 20:19).

There it is—the reason why a mediating class was needed to go between God and his people. Their overwhelming fear of God's presence made them not want to be with him face-to-face. Moses's response was intriguing: "Do not be afraid. God has come to test you, so that the fear of God will be with you to keep you from sinning" (Exod. 20:20). But the people stayed far back while God gave several specific commands concerning how the people would live in his covenant (Exod. 20–23).

In Exodus 24, God asked Moses, Aaron and sons, and the seventy elders of Israel to come up the mountain. Moses was to come the closest while the others were to remain at a distance. This representative group went up and "saw the God of Israel" (Exod. 24:10). Reminiscent of John's vision in Revelation, they all saw God with a pavement of sapphire under his feet. They ate and drank with God in order to fulfill the terms of the covenant.[46] The people stayed at a distance. Immediately after this description of the conclusion of the terms of the covenant, God gave Moses information on the tabernacle and priesthood. The people under this covenant were too afraid to come near to God, and also, God had set limits on their approach to him. Boundaries and mediators were necessary. Fear and trembling characterized the hearts of the people. The motive for abstaining from sin was fear of the Lord. As we shall see, all of this changes with the new covenant in Christ (Heb. 12:18–29).

The Role of Priests in the New Covenant

The cultic ritual of the former covenant is transformed in the new because of the work of Jesus Christ. One of the crucial changes is that a distinct class of priests is no longer required to assist worshipers coming before God. We do not need a "clergy class" to go between God and ourselves. We can come before God as priests in our own right. In the new covenant, God has removed the barriers, which created separation. However, his original intent—to have a people who would be a treasured possession, a holy nation, a kingdom of priests—still holds. Consider Peter's words: "But you are a chosen people, a royal priesthood, a holy nation, a people belonging to God, that you may declare the praises of him who called you out of darkness into his wonderful light" (1 Pet. 2:9). No one can mistake the clear reference to Exodus 19:6 here; God's purposes have not changed. While the new covenant drastically changed the form and essence of the former covenant, the purposes of God for his people remained the same. God still desires us to be a kingdom of priests before him. This is confirmed again in the Revelation to John: "To

46. The covenant at Sinai was similar to covenants made by suzerains and vassals in the ancient Near East during the fourteenth century BCE. In the Sinai covenant, God took the place of the conquering suzerain, and Israel took the place of the vassal, becoming subservient to him by this agreement. The specific aspects of these historical covenantal treaties are strikingly similar to the one at Sinai. God apparently used a form and language of covenant with which the Israelites were familiar. See K. A. Kitchen, *Ancient Orient and Old Testament* (Downers Grove, IL: InterVarsity, 1996), 90–102.

him who loves us and has freed us from our sins by his blood, and has made us to be a kingdom and priests to serve his God and Father—to him be glory and power for ever and ever!" (Rev. 1:5b–6).

God desires that no boundaries exist between him and us. We can come to God through Jesus Christ without the cumbersome mediation of an earthly priest. Why? Because we ourselves are priests unto our God in this new covenant. If the scene on Mount Sinai was terrifying for the people of God and the result was such fear that they did not want to get close to God, we must remember that we have come not to Mount Sinai but instead to Mount Zion. Consider these words from the writer to the Hebrews:

> You have not come to a mountain that can be touched and that is burning with fire; to darkness, gloom and storm; to a trumpet blast or to such a voice speaking words that those who heard it begged that no further word be spoken to them because they could not bear what was commanded. . . . The sight was so terrifying that Moses said, "I am trembling with fear."
>
> But you have come to Mount Zion, to the heavenly Jerusalem, the city of the living God. You have come to thousands upon thousands of angels in joyful assembly, to the church of the firstborn, whose names are written in heaven. You have come to God, the Judge of all, to the spirits of the righteous made perfect, to Jesus the mediator of a new covenant, and to the sprinkled blood that speaks a better word than the blood of Abel.
>
> See to it that you do not refuse him who speaks. (Heb. 12:18–25)

At Mount Sinai, the people trembled; at Mount Zion, the people rejoice. At Mount Sinai, boundaries were put up so that the people could not come too close to God; at Mount Zion, there are no boundaries—we can approach the very throne of God itself. At Mount Sinai, the people refused to listen to God's voice because of fear, and so demanded a mediator; at Mount Zion, we can listen to him who speaks without fear in our hearts because Jesus is the mediator of a new and better covenant. At Mount Sinai, fear was the motivation for obedience; at Mount Zion, love is the motivation. We have been brought nigh by the blood of Christ to the very throne room of God! In the old covenant, the high priest had to offer sacrifice yearly for the sins of the people. In the new covenant, Jesus is our High Priest, but not from Aaron's family; his priesthood is from the line of Melchizedek (Heb. 4:14–5:10). Since we are Christ's brothers and sisters, we are also priests in his line.

Christ, our High Priest, did not offer sacrifices in the earthly tabernacle but in the heavenly one (Heb. 9:11–12). He entered there not by the blood of bulls and goats, which could not cleanse one's conscience, but with his own blood, in order to obtain eternal redemption (Heb. 9:12–13). This sacrifice

was acceptable to God and therefore never needed to be repeated because of
its efficacy. As our High Priest, he also became a mediator of a new covenant.
The entire former covenant was fulfilled in Christ's work. There is no need
for the bloody sacrifices to continue; as priests in the new covenant, we do
not offer these kinds of sacrifices.[47] In the former covenant, the priesthood
was limited to a certain family and tribe. In the new covenant, the priesthood belongs to all believers (1 Pet. 2:9; Rev. 1:6).

The New Testament (Christian) Priesthood and Ministry

With these thoughts from the biblical witnesses in mind, I move toward the
crux of my argument for a theology of ministry. Allow me to note from the
outset that my interpretation of both Scripture and the historical development
of the clergy is not perhaps the "majority" position. It is, however, a major
part of the fabric for what follows as a proposal for ministry in the church
today. It may be stated simply: there is no separate "priestly" caste to do the
work of ministry; all God's people are to do the work of ministry. Now I turn
to support that conclusion further.

What is not in dispute by any historian, biblical scholar, or theologian of
whom I am aware is the fact that in the New Testament, the Greek word "priest"
(ἱερεύς | hiereus) (or later, the Latin equivalent sacerdos) is not used once to
refer to an individual Christian or "clergy."[48] Indeed, as we have come to use it,
the word "clergy" itself does not appear in the New Testament.[49] As Carl Armbruster states, "The most striking fact is the total absence of the term [hiereus]
from the pages of the New Testament in regard to the ministerial priesthood."[50]
Only Jesus Christ is described as a priest in the new covenant—indeed, as the
"apostle and high priest" of our confession (Heb. 3:1). Other terms are used to

47. As Albert Hauck has noted, only the Christian religion has no sacrifice (Opfer). See
Hauck, "Priestertum, Priesterweihe in der christlichen Kirche," in Realencyklopaedie für prot-
estantische Theologie und Kirche, vol. 16, Preger-Riehm, ed. Albert Hauck (Leipzig: Hinrichs'
Buchhandlung, 1905), 47.

48. Joseph Blenkinsopp, "Presbyter to Priest: Ministry in the Early Church," Worship 41, no.
7 (August–September 1967): 428–38, esp. 428. Blenkinsopp repeats this claim from an earlier
writing: Blenkinsopp, "On Clericalism," Cross Currents 17, no. 1 (Winter 1967): 15–23, esp.
17. Cf. also Raymond E. Brown, Priest and Bishop: Biblical Reflections (New York: Paulist
Press, 1970), 13. These two authors are Roman Catholic biblical scholars—the first of the OT,
the second of the NT.

49. This will be clarified and supported below.

50. Carl J. Armbruster, "Priesthood and Ministry from the New Testament to Nicaea," in
Proceedings of the Catholic Theological Society of North America: 24th Annual Convention
(Boston: Boston College, 2012), 63–74, here 66.

describe individual believers who do work on behalf of Christ for the sake of God's people, but not the word "priest." However, the clear direction of various parts of Paul's theology of the church (as well as Peter's and even John's to some extent) is to describe the whole people of God as a body of priests—a "holy priesthood" or a "royal priesthood" or "kingdom and priests" (1 Pet. 2:5, 9; Rev. 1:6; see table 1.1). Hence, the entire body of Christ is a holy priesthood under the High Priest, Jesus Christ, who intercedes for us in the heavenly sanctuary (Heb. 7:25; 8:1–2). The work of sacrifice has been completed by Christ once and for all time (Heb. 7:27–28). The primary role of the priests of the former covenant required the work of sacrifice; since that has been completed, the remaining work of the priesthood has morphed into other intercessory activities on behalf of fellow Christians and the people of the whole world.[51]

Sacrifices by the New Priesthood

Priests in the new covenant continue to offer gifts to God as their proper "sacrifice," but these are not sacrifices that atone for sin or dispense forgiveness. Priests in the new covenant offer their bodies "as a living sacrifice, holy and pleasing to God—this is your true and proper worship" (Rom. 12:1). In other words, priests in the new covenant offer themselves in entirety to God as spiritual worship to God. For Christian priests, sacrifice begins with laying down their entire lives.

Sacrifice continues with Christian priests offering a "sacrifice of praise" (θυσίαν αἰωέσεως | *thysian aiōeseōs*), which is described as "the fruit of lips [καρπὸν χειλέων | *karpon cheileōn*] that openly profess his [Christ's] name" (Heb. 13:15).[52] Further, it is not enough to praise God with lips; Christians must also "not forget to do good and to share with others" (Heb. 13:16a).

---

51. The assertion that a separate priesthood is required in Christianity is not supported in the NT. As H. Flatten has said, "Protestant theology rejects the concept of the clergy as unbiblical; over against the priesthood of all believers, there is no special priesthood." See H. Flatten, "Klerus," *Lexikon für Theologie und Kirche*, ed. Michael Buchberger, 7 vols. (Freiburg: Herder, 1934), 6:337 (my translation). Pierre Grelot expresses the same sentiment: "In the Jewish and pagan sense, there is not Christian priesthood, but a service to Christ in his Church and to the faithful of Christ. The specific functions of priestly mediation entrusted to those ministers were not raised again." *Dictionnaire des Religions*, ed. Paul Poupard, 2 vols. (Paris: Presses Universitaires de France, 1984), 1:1761 (my translation). The cultic role of priest in the old covenant has no counterpart in the new covenant. This will become clear as we develop these concepts in this chapter.

52. William L. Lane, *Hebrews 9–13*, WBC 47b (Dallas: Word Books, 1991), 550–51. Lane provides an excellent background on the use of these sacrificial terms in Hebrews. He notes that "sacrifice of praise" may be better rendered "sacrifice *consisting of* praise." Also, the "fruit of lips" has a rather rich history from Hosea 14:3 (LXX) and several passages from Psalms. It is used commonly in the context of voluntary offerings of praise for God's grace.

These priestly duties of the whole body of Christ begin with confession or acknowledgment (ὁμολογούντων | *homologountōn*) of the goodness of God as seen in the very Hebraic concept of "his name" (Heb. 13:15). They continue with the whole body of Christ "doing good" (εὐποιΐας | *eupoiias*) and "sharing physical goods with others" (κοινωνίας | *koinōnias*).[53] With these sacrifices God is pleased (θυσίαις εὐαρεστεῖται ὁ θεός | *thysiais euaresteitai ho theos*).

Since the tabernacle for Christians is no longer on earth but in the heavenly realms where our High Priest, Jesus, serves on our behalf, there is no ritual sacrifice or cultic performance by a priest needed in the historic and usual sense of that term. The priesthood in Christianity has been redefined.

Indeed, if the former roles of priests and the high priest have been taken over by the work of Christ himself, then what is left for a priestly labor among Christians? This seems to be the argument of Hebrews—and perhaps by inference, the rationale for not calling leaders "priests" in the Christian church of the New Testament era.

1 Peter 2:5, 9

Similar to these specific statements concerning sacrifice is Peter's declaration that believers are "like living stones," who are being "built into a spiritual house to be a holy priesthood [εἰς ἱεράτευμα ἅγιον | *eis hierateuma hagion*], offering spiritual sacrifices [πνευματικὰς θυσίας | *pneumatikas thysias*] acceptable to God through Jesus Christ" (1 Pet. 2:5). Here as well we see the *spiritual* nature of sacrifices and the fact that these are *acceptable* to God. All of this is done "through Jesus Christ" (1 Pet. 2:5; Heb. 13:15a).

A few verses after 1 Peter 2:5, Peter provides an expansion on the "holy priesthood" by retrieving the important words from Exodus 19:5–6.[54] Peter states, "But you are a chosen people [ὑμεῖς δὲ γένος ἐκλεκτόν | *hymeis de genos elekton*], a royal priesthood [βασίλειον ἱεράτευμα | *basileion hierateuma*],[55] a

53. Lane notes that *eupoiia* occurs only here in the Greek NT. Among other Hellenistic sources, there exists in this word a "tangible expression to concern for others," and it is frequently found in the context of "benevolence to the poor" (*Hebrews* 47b:552). Further, he underscores the probability of *koinōnia* here meaning more than sharing or participation, but even partnership where goods are shared with others (552).

54. There may also be a connection with Isaiah 43:19–21, where God states that he is doing a "new thing" whereby streams will rise up in the wasteland "to give drink to my people, my chosen [τὸ γένος μου τὸ ἐκλεκτόν | *to genos mou to elekton*], the people I formed for myself [λαόν μου ὅν περιεποιησάμην | *laon mou hon periepoiēsamēn*] that they may proclaim my praise [τὰς ἀρετάς μου διηγεῖσθαι | *tas aretas mou diēgeisthai*]." (The Greek inserts here are from the LXX so that we might compare the Greek phrasing in 1 Peter.)

55. Günther Bornkamm notes that *basileion* "means belonging to a king." Therefore, we can see this priesthood as one that is "royal" in the sense that it is the king's own. It serves the king. See Bornkamm, "ἱεράτευμα," *TDNT* 3:249–50.

Table 1.1
Descriptions of the People of God

Exodus 19:5–6 (LXX)	
"treasured possession," "chosen people"	λαὸς περιούσιος | *laos periousios*
"kingdom of priests"	βασίλειον ἱεράτευμα | *basileion hierateuma*
"holy nation"	ἔθνος ἅγιον | *ethnos hagion*
Isaiah 43:19–21 (LXX)	
"to my people, my chosen"	τὸ γένος μου τὸ ἐλεκτόν | *to genos mou to elekton*
"the people I formed for myself"	λαόν μου ὅν περιεποιησάμην | *laon mou hon periepoiēsamēn*
"that they may proclaim my praise"	τὰς ἀρετάς μου διηγεῖσθαι | *tas aretas mou diēgeisthai*
1 Peter 2:9	
"chosen people"	γένος ἐλεκτόν | *genos elekton*
"royal priesthood"	βασίλειον ἱεράτευμα | *basileion hierateuma**
"holy nation"	ἔθνος ἅγιον | *ethnos hagion*
"special possession"	λαὸς εἰς περιποίησιν | *laos eis peripoiēsin*†
"that you may declare the praises of him who called you"	ὅπως τὰς ἀρετὰς ἐξαγγείλητε τοῦ ὑμᾶς καλέσαντος | *hopōs tas aretas exangeilēte tou hymas kalesantos*‡

* This also may be translated as a "kingdom of priests," as the NIV has done with the same phrase in Exod. 19:6.

† This phrase may also be reminiscent of Isaiah 43:21: "the people I formed for myself" (λαόν μου ὅν περιεποιησάμην \| *laon mou hon periepoiēsamēn*).

‡ Clearly, this is an allusion to Isa. 43:21: "That they may proclaim my praise." Believers now are asked to speak forth a message of praise of the One calling them from darkness to light. See Paul J. Achtemeier, *1 Peter: A Commentary on First Peter*, Hermeneia (Minneapolis: Fortress, 1996), 166.

holy nation [ἔθνος ἅγιον | *ethnos hagion*], God's special possession [λαὸς εἰς περιποίησιν | *laos eis peripoiēsin*], that you may declare the praises [ὅπως τὰς ἀρετὰς ἐξαγγείλητε | *hopōs tas aretas exangeilēte*] of him who called you out of darkness into his wonderful light" (1 Pet. 2:9).

In order to see the origination of Peter's terminology, let us consider Exodus 19:5–6 from the Septuagint (LXX), the Greek translation of the Hebrew Bible that served as *the* Bible for the New Testament church. "'Now if you obey me fully and keep my covenant, then out of all nations you will be my treasured possession [λαὸς περιούσιος | *laos periousios*]. Although the whole earth is mine, you will be for me a kingdom of priests [βασίλειον ἱεράτευμα | *basileion hierateuma*] and a holy nation [ἔθνος ἅγιον | *ethnos hagion*].' These are the words you are to speak to the Israelites" (Exod. 19:5–6).

Peter moves from this imagery in Exodus and Isaiah to that of Hosea: "Once you were not a people, but now you are the people of God; once you

Figure 1.1
Peter's Holy Priesthood Imagery

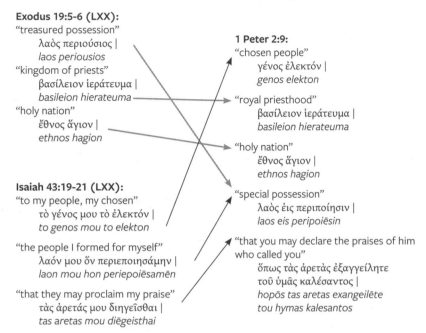

Exodus 19:5-6 (LXX):
"treasured possession"
λαὸς περιούσιος |
laos periousios
"kingdom of priests"
βασίλειον ἱεράτευμα |
basileion hierateuma
"holy nation"
ἔθνος ἅγιον |
ethnos hagion

Isaiah 43:19-21 (LXX):
"to my people, my chosen"
τὸ γένος μου τὸ ἐλεκτόν |
to genos mou to elekton

"the people I formed for myself"
λαόν μου ὅν περιεποιησάμην |
laon mou hon periepoiēsamēn

"that they may proclaim my praise"
τὰς ἀρετάς μου διηγεῖσθαι |
tas aretas mou diēgeisthai

1 Peter 2:9:
"chosen people"
γένος ἐλεκτόν |
genos elekton
"royal priesthood"
βασίλειον ἱεράτευμα |
basileion hierateuma
"holy nation"
ἔθνος ἅγιον |
ethnos hagion
"special possession"
λαὸς ἐις περιποίησιν |
laos eis peripoiēsin
"that you may declare the praises of him who called you"
ὅπως τὰς ἀρετὰς ἐξαγγείλητε
τοῦ ὑμᾶς καλέσαντος |
*hopōs tas aretas exangeilēte
tou hymas kalesantos*

had not received mercy, but now you have received mercy" (1 Pet. 2:10).[56] Believers—just like Israel—were an "elect race" (γένος ἐλεκτόν | *genos elekton*) or a group of people with a "common origin."[57] The people of God are priests belonging to the King and have a unity as a new race of people and as a nation whose "common customs are shared."[58]

Whereas in the past a priestly caste was required from the tribe of Levi and the house of Aaron, in the present we all are priests before God. Not one of us stands in the position of mediation; that place belongs to our High Priest alone. Yet there remains today a disturbing belief among God's people that they cannot approach God effectively for themselves, that they need a priest to mediate or at least someone who has been trained to pray for them. Such a mediator is unnecessary because of the work of Christ. The whole people of God may enter together into the heavenly holy of holies due to the work

56. Compare the names of the prophet Hosea's children: Lo-Ammi (not my people), Lo-Ruhamah (no mercy). See Hosea 1:6–10.

57. Paul J. Achtemeier, *1 Peter: A Commentary on First Peter*, Hermeneia (Minneapolis: Fortress, 1996), 163.

58. Achtemeier, *1 Peter*, 165.

that Christ has accomplished. Access has been granted to the body of Christ to function as a "holy nation" and a "kingdom of priests." And so, "in the Christian communities of the first century, there was no independent priestly function that was exercised by a special caste or minister."[59] Reflecting the fact of the completed work of Christ in offering a once-for-all sacrifice, the Christian priesthood was centered on the people of God themselves, ministering under their High Priest, who performed his priestly duties in the heavenly tabernacle.

A Matter of Functions Not Offices

To this point, there may not be strong disagreement with the basic trajectory I have described concerning priests in the New Testament. However, over the first few centuries in the history of the church, the prominence of this paradigm for a universal priesthood began to be replaced by a more hierarchical structure that focused on a Christian priesthood—not the universal priesthood of believer but the *institutional* priesthood of those authorized to perform certain functions on behalf of others in the church. Here we enter a historical realm whose waters are difficult to navigate. As one scholar notes, "Without any contest, the great difficulty for the interpreter in a liturgical task concerning the origins of hierarchy and ecclesiastical organization of the first centuries is the dearth of documents and the immense variety of hypotheses that are put forward."[60]

Perhaps a helpful way to enter this particularly complex historical development is by considering the etymology of the English word "priest." While there are a variety of possible ways the word came to us, the majority interpretation seems to be that it derived from the Greek word for "presbyter" (πρεσβύτερος | *presbyteros*). However, this Greek word means "elder," or one who is senior. As we shall see, it is used throughout the New Testament for a group of leaders in the church. The Greek word for priest (ἱερεύς | *hiereus*) was not the source for the English word "priest." Also, the Latin *sacerdos* was not the etymological source for "priest," even though it means that. How did we get from *presbyteros* to priest?

When considering an answer to this question, examining the titles used to describe leaders in the New Testament is one place to start. To describe these terms as "titles" or "offices" is anachronistic, since there was nothing like these in the New Testament church. The terms actually described *functions*

59. Alexandre Faivre, *The Emergence of the Laity in the Early Church*, trans. David Smith (New York: Paulist Press, 1990), 7.

60. Alexandre Faivre, "Quelques études sur la question des ministères," *Revue des Sciences Religieuses* 47, no. 1 (1973): 133–48, here 133 (my translation).

not titles.[61] How could "ministers" (in terms of what we call clergy today) be described in the New Testament? They could be called bishops, presbyters (elders), deacons, ministers, servants, apostles, prophets, evangelists, pastors, teachers, leaders, stewards, and more. It is the use of the more prominent of these functions in the New Testament that will assist us in understanding possible ways to reconsider shaping our lives together today in the local body of Christ. Yet this cannot be the entire story, since understanding what each function did in the New Testament church is still too sketchy to provide us with foundational elements on which to build our ecclesiology. Craig Keener offers a sobering comment in this regard: "In the first century, however, titles seem to have varied from one location to another, and their meaning often varied when the titles did not. For that matter, the churches no less pragmatically adopted different models of church government in different locations."[62]

Therefore, it is not merely the examination of functions that will assist us. We will also examine the New Testament for any hints as to how churches may have been structured in this early period and how ministry operated among the people of God. If I may offer a glimpse of my conclusion here, it is simply that great variety and even plurality of gifts and ministries prevailed in the first-century churches, due to the work of the Spirit among God's people. This focus on the gifts and various ministries did not foster chaos, because the leaders worked to guide the local congregation toward mission and spiritual growth.

The first-century church-governing structure is difficult to discern. As Karen Jo Torjesen has noted, "The Christian church, of course, did not spring up suddenly into a well-defined organization with buildings, officials, and large congregations. In its earliest stages it is best understood as a social movement like any other. It was informal, often counter-cultural in tone, and was marked by a fluidity and flexibility that allowed women, slaves, and artisans to assume leadership roles."[63] After twenty centuries of the development of

---

61. Consider the Pauline text of Phil.1:1, where Paul greets the saints at Philippi "with the overseers and deacons" (σὺν ἐπισκόποις καὶ διακόνοις | *syn episkopois kai diakonois*). While it may seem that these two terms refer to titles, such presumption places too much later understanding of positions in the church back onto these terms. These are clearly *leaders*, separated from the "saints" in Paul's greeting, but undoubtedly not the type who held formal offices from the third century CE. As Alistair Campbell states, "The words are sufficiently vague to mean no more than 'those who lead and serve,' or perhaps, 'those who serve by leading,' remembering the way in which Paul is happy to apply the term διάκονος to his own ministry and that of others." See Alistair Campbell, *The Elders: Seniority within Earliest Christianity*, Studies of the New Testament and Its World, ed. John Riches (Edinburgh: T&T Clark, 1994), 124.

62. Keener, *Acts*, 2:1273.

63. Karen Jo Torjesen, *When Women Were Priests: Women's Leadership in the Early Church and the Scandal of Their Subordination in the Rise of Christianity* (San Francisco: Harper-SanFrancisco, 1993), 11.

Christianity across the globe, we enter the world of the New Testament with preconceived understandings of how things operated then, often on the basis of how we perceive them to operate (or believe they should operate) now. Jesus did not leave his followers an organizational flowchart for his flock. Indeed, he did not appear to be interested in organizing the structure of the church in such a way that it would perpetuate itself. He had already seen what well-intended religious structures could do to the heart and spirit. Yet throughout the history of the Christian church, various groups have claimed that a particular governmental or leadership structure was God's intention for his people.

Jesus did leave guidelines for his followers related to their heart dispositions, but not their electoral processes. Further, Matthew records Jesus as responding to Peter's confession of faith by saying, "I will build my church" (Matt. 16:18). While Jesus did not establish a "church" as we would call it today, his ministry was replete with building *community* among his disciples. This "ecclesia" was the "little flock" that had been given to Jesus. The promise here is that Jesus will continue to build his flock—his assembly.[64] Paul and other New Testament writers gave hints of ecclesiologies that were nascent— barely developing and beginning to walk. Yet I submit that within the New Testament we can find plentiful resources for ways a church should operate. It is less about a particular style of governmental system whereby the congregations hold together their business and operating principles, and more about a style of living and acting together as God's people. It is a fallacy to think that we can return to the New Testament in order to retrieve a purer, less cultural-laden pattern of some transcultural form of church government that we can then transplant into the twenty-first century. We do not live in the cultural box of the first-century church. However, the patterns that they used for relationships and the principles that guided them still provide us a framework for our own churches today.

Our search into the New Testament for patterns will not produce simply *one* model. As Keener rightly notes with respect to elders, "Probably various

64. For a discussion that argues strongly for an understanding of the "rock" of Peter's confession as acknowledgment of Christ's messiahship, see Everett Ferguson, *The Church of Christ: A Biblical Ecclesiology for Today* (Grand Rapids: Eerdmans, 1996), 47–52. While some NT scholars find it implausible that the word "church" (i.e., *ekklēsia*) ever was spoken by Jesus, Ferguson points to a strong use of "community" and the building of community by Christ throughout his ministry. See esp. *The Church of Christ*, 47n67. It is also interesting to note that in the four Gospels, ἐκκλησία | *ekklēsia* occurs only in Matthew (three times) and never in Mark, Luke, or John. It occurs thirty-nine times in Pauline literature. For a discussion of this and its significance, see C. K. Barrett, *Church, Ministry, and Sacraments in the New Testament* (Eugene, OR: Wipf & Stock, 2005), 9–18.

forms of leadership existed in early Christianity. It is possible that 'elder' might include an overseer of local overseers in 1 Pet. 5:1 (which allows for later practice); but the emphasis there is egalitarian (5:1, 3–5), and church leadership in the New Testament remained primarily local, aside from the ministry of the apostles (and in the latter case sometimes both)."[65] What is clear from the New Testament is that there is a variety of descriptors used to label leadership functions in the church: apostles, prophets, shepherds, deacons, presbyters/ elders, stewards, bishops/overseers, ministers, and similar terms.[66] We will turn now to examine several of them in the first-century church in order to determine what value they might hold for us today.

Elders/Overseers/Pastors

First, let us consider the function of eldering, overseeing, and pastoring. I have placed these three terms together because in the New Testament it appears that these functions were used somewhat interchangeably. This claim requires some textual substantiation and explanation.

The term "bishop" or "overseer" (ἐπίσκοπος | episkopos) refers to someone who stands watching or looking over things. It is found in Acts 20:28, Philippians 1:1, and 1 Timothy 3:2. The last reference provides us with an insight into Paul's advice to Timothy about qualifications for a bishop/overseer.[67]

Here is a trustworthy saying: Whoever aspires to be an overseer desires a noble task. Now the overseer [ἐπίσκοπος | episkopos] is to be above reproach, faithful to his wife, temperate, self-controlled, respectable, hospitable, able to teach, not given to drunkenness, not violent but gentle, not quarrelsome, not a lover of money. He must manage his own family well and see that his children obey him, and he must do so in a manner worthy of full respect. (If anyone does not know how to manage his own family, how can he take care of God's church?) He must not be a recent convert, or he may become conceited and fall under the same judgment as the devil. (1 Tim. 3:1–6)

65. Keener, Acts, 2:3032.
66. Faivre, The Emergence of the Laity in the Early Church, 9.
67. From where did the early church get this term episkopos? Alistair Stewart's exhaustive research in this area provides substantial support for Edwin Hatch's thesis from 1880 that episkopoi were financial officers of pagan associations or collegia. Stewart presents the evidence from the Hellenistic context as well as from early church literature on church orders to demonstrate the financial leadership function of episkopoi. See Alistair C. Stewart, The Original Bishops: Office and Order in the First Christian Communities (Grand Rapids: Baker Academic, 2014), esp. chap. 2. Also see Edwin Hatch, The Organization of the Early Christian Churches: Eight Lectures, Delivered before the University of Oxford, in the Year 1880 (London: Longmans, Green, 1918). Later, I will engage more with Stewart's specific proposal about bishops, presbyters, and deacons.

In a similar description of qualifications for leaders of the church, Paul extends to Titus almost the same advice. However, here we see Paul calls these leaders *presbyteroi*—elders in Titus 1:5 and then overseers in Titus 1:7.

> The reason I left you in Crete was that you might put in order what was left unfinished and appoint elders in every town, as I directed you. An *elder* [πρεσ-βύτερος | *presbyteros*] must be blameless, faithful to his wife, a man whose children believe and are not open to the charge of being wild and disobedient. Since an *overseer* [ἐπίσκοπος | *episkopos*] manages God's household, he must be blameless—not overbearing, not quick-tempered, not given to drunkenness, not violent, not pursuing dishonest gain. Rather, he must be hospitable, one who loves what is good, who is self-controlled, upright, holy and disciplined.
> (Titus 1:5–8, my emphasis)

A comparison between this list to Titus regarding the overseer/elder and the previous one to Timothy reveals these qualifications are almost the same. The ἐπίσκοπος | *episkopos* of Titus 1:7 is also called an elder (πρεσβύτερος | *presbyteros*) in Titus 1:5.

Further evidence from the New Testament in this regard reveals an interchangeable usage as well. In Acts 20:17, Paul sent for the "elders" (πρεσβυτέρους | *presbyterous*) of the Ephesian church before embarking on his journey to Jerusalem. He addresses these elders in the following way: "Keep watch over yourselves and all the flock of which the Holy Spirit has made you overseers [ἐπισκόπους | *episkopous*]. Be shepherds [ποιμαίνειν | *poimainen*] of the church of God, which he bought with his own blood" (Acts 20:28). Here we see all three terms—elders, overseers, and pastors/shepherds—used to describe the one function of leadership in the congregation at Ephesus. Paul addresses this admonition to *elders* and speaks of them as *overseers* of the flock that the Spirit has given them; they are to "be shepherds" or, perhaps more literally (since it is a verbal expression),[68] they are "to shepherd" or "to pastor" the church of God. It seems clear here that elders and bishops were identical, and at least one of their functions was "shepherding" or "pastoring."[69] Another reference to elders underscores the interchangeability of terms.

> To the elders [πρεσβυτέρους | *presbyterous*] among you, I appeal as a fellow elder and a witness of Christ's sufferings who also will share in the glory to be

68. It is a present active infinitive, whereas the terms "elders" (20:17) and "overseers" (20:28) are nouns.

69. Eduard Schweizer, *Church Order in the New Testament*, trans. Frank Clarke (Eugene, OR: Wipf & Stock, 2006), 85.

revealed: Be shepherds [ποιμάνατε | *poimanate*][70] of God's flock that is under your care, watching over them [ἐπισκοποῦντες | *episkopountes*][71]—not because you must, but because you are willing, as God wants you to be; not pursuing dishonest gain, but eager to serve; not lording it over those entrusted [τῶν κλήρων | *tōn klērōn*][72] to you, but being examples to the flock. (1 Pet. 5:1–3)

All three terms are evident here as in Acts 20:28, but here "elders" is the noun while "be shepherds" and "watching over them" are verbal forms. Nevertheless, these terms continue to be used somewhat interchangeably here as functions of the leading elders.

One further study in the New Testament may assist us in ascertaining what these leadership positions might mean. Paul's pattern in church planting was to appoint elders (presbyters) in every town (Titus 1:5). When Barnabas and Paul went out on their missionary journey, they "appointed elders for them in each church and, with prayer and fasting, committed them to the Lord, in whom they had put their trust" (Acts 14:23). It appears, then, that a Pauline practice in the New Testament church was to appoint leaders who were called "elders"—not a single leader, not a bishop as would appear in the third-century church, but a plurality of leaders who would guide the local congregation with care and love.[73]

In Paul's list of qualifications for an overseer in 1 Timothy 3:4, 5, and 12, we find a verb used to describe how an elder (and in v. 12, a deacon) should "*manage*" or "rule" his household. "If anyone does not know how *to manage* [προστῆναι | *prostēnai*] his own family, how can he take care of [ἐπιμελήσεται | *epimelēsetai*] God's church?" (1 Tim. 3:5). The second verb, "take care of," is used in juxtaposition to "manage." Therefore, we may be able to understand more about this verb "manage" in terms of leadership if we consider how its synonym is used.

Elders/bishops/pastors are to "take care of" people and manage responsibilities just as the Good Samaritan took care of the man beaten and left for dead. This statement is supported by the fact that the only other place in the

70. This is also a verbal form, an aorist active imperative: "do shepherding" over God's flock.

71. As can be seen in this word, it is a verbal form of *episkopos* and here has the idea of looking out for or watching over.

72. This is the word from which we get "clergy" in English, but here it clearly is applied to God's flock.

73. After pointing to early Christian sources where shepherding and overseeing are connected, Wolfgang Nauck states, "These oldest ecclesial examples demonstrate that a concept from the stem [ποιμαν–] almost always is associated with a concept from the stem ἐπισκοπ–" (my translation). These were not separate offices or titles but functions of overseeing. See Wolfgang Nauck, "Problemes des fruhchristlichen Amtsverstandnisses (1 Petr. 5:2f.)," *Zeitschrift für neutestamentliche Wissenschaft und Kunde* 48 (1957): 200–20, here 201–2.

New Testament where this verb "to take care of" (ἐπιμελέομαι | *epimeleomai*) is used is Luke 10—the story of the Good Samaritan. "But a Samaritan, as he traveled, came where the man was; and when he saw him, he took pity on him. He went to him and bandaged his wounds, pouring on oil and wine. Then he put the man on his own donkey, brought him to an inn and *took care of him* [ἐπεμελήθη | *epemelēthē*]" (Luke 10:33–34, my emphasis).

What a powerful image of Christian leadership—management by taking care of the flock. This is meant to imply not that leaders must only bind wounds in their management but rather that when they tend over the flock, they are helping, assisting, and giving their lives for the lives of others. It would also be "taking care of" this individual if, when he is well, he would receive a warning from the Good Samaritan about how to travel when going down from Jerusalem to Jericho—travel in pairs; bring a dog; ride in a wagon with others. In any case, Christian leaders are marked by concern for those found along the way, especially those whose lives have been delegated to their responsibility. These are leaders with the heart of a servant—those who manage the affairs of the church by taking care of those under their charge.

In another Pauline passage, elders are described in a similar manner with the same verb: "to manage." "The elders who direct the affairs [προεστῶτες | *proestōtes*] of the church well are worthy of double honor, especially those whose work is preaching and teaching. For the Scripture says, 'Do not muzzle the ox while it is treading out the grain,' and 'The worker deserves his wages.' Do not entertain an accusation against an elder unless it is brought by two or three witnesses. But those elders who are sinning you are to reprove before everyone, so that the others may take warning" (1 Tim. 5:17–20).

Here is one of the clearer descriptions of elders' functions in the New Testament—and these are still very general. The elders who "direct the affairs of the church" or who "rule" the church well (προεστῶτες | *proestōtes*) are to be given special consideration.[74] What does it mean for elders to "rule"? The Greek word is a perfect active participle, προεστῶτες | *proestōtes*, from προΐστημι | *proistēmi*, which we saw already in 1 Timothy 3:4–5 means "to manage."[75] It means several things: (1) to stand before (in rank); (2) to preside; (3) to direct; (4) to manage; (5) to be concerned about, care for, or give aid.[76]

---

74. In this context, such consideration inevitably means that the financial or material needs of these elders is the issue, especially those who work at preaching and teaching.

75. A perfect active participle stresses the resulting state of affairs due to some past action. The emphasis of this tense in 1 Tim. 5:17 might be rendered as follows: "The elders who, having directed the affairs of the church so that their past actions have contributed to its present well-being . . ."

76. "προΐστημι," BDAG, 713–14.

The Origin of Christian Elders

From where did the position of elder come? Traditionally, the idea of an elder was thought to be borrowed from Judaism. Recently, however, scholars have debated whether Christian elders were so closely connected to Jewish elders.[a] A. E. Harvey makes a strong case that the Christian concept of elder was borrowed not from Hellenistic society (the word is almost never used of an "official" in society) nor directly from the Jewish synagogues or Sanhedrin, since the New Testament elder is very different in function and purpose from the Jewish counterpart. He states that the Christian use of "elder" "does not find such a ready explanation in Jewish institutions as is usually thought."[b]

It seems highly improbable that the early Jewish Christians would have used a Jewish term like "elder" and not given it some of the characteristics that the Jews had given it. Eldership in Israel was an institution of great significance; it began as part of the patriarchal and tribal system of the ancient world in the Middle East.[c] Eventually, elders became a class of men with control over local communities.[d] The Hebrew word *zaqin*, "elder," may come from the word for beard, which points toward older males. The Septuagint often translates it πρεσβύτεροι | *presbyteroi*. In Deuteronomy, the elders had "legal powers which are obviously based on ancient custom."[e] Even in exile, the elders led the community. After the exile, the elders were not so much a tribal college of leaders as an aristocratic class.[f] At some point in the Persian period, a council of elders became prominent. It was named the γερούσια | *gerousia*. (The Roman equivalent of *gerousia* is *senatus*.)[g] Its members seemed to be made up of priests and leaders, which in turn may have influenced the composition of the later Sanhedrin.[h]

Before the first century CE, synagogues were not so much places as people who organized and "managed the affairs of the local Jewish community."[i] In the first century CE, heads or presidents of synagogues were called *presbyteroi*, but by

Which of these possible meanings would be preferable here? From Jesus's words against pagan and religious leaders who "lord it over" their subjects, we can eliminate any kind of translation that would hint at such ungodly rule. However, it seems that elders/overseers were Paul's way of creating organization for new churches and of continuing the "tradition," the teaching handed down by the apostles. Elders offered stability and continuity for local bodies of the church. Therefore, the concept of directing the affairs of the church with a heart of care is the most suitable rendering at this point. Perhaps the second century, the word faded off the Jewish scene.[j] In addition, the "elders" of the synagogue do not have clearly marked duties in any ancient record of Jewish literature. The leader of the synagogue was held responsible for the conduct of worship and reading on the Sabbath. Harvey comments that elders of local synagogues were not "so much officials as counselors and leaders spontaneously recognized by the people."[k]

Did the early church take their cue from this kind of synagogue elder? We may never be entirely certain from where Christians in the first-century church obtained the term. In a more recent study by Alistair Campbell (1994), Harvey's suppositions receive detailed support and yet are extended far beyond them. Campbell argues that the term "elder" cannot be understood in terms of an "office" in the first-century church. Its usage in both Jewish and Greco-Roman settings was more imprecise, tending to be focused on honor given to a person of age or on position in the family.[l]

[a] See A. E. Harvey, "Elders," Journal of Theological Studies, n.s., 25 (1974): 318–32.

[b] Harvey, "Elders," 326.

[c] Lothar Coenen, "Bishop," in The New International Dictionary of New Testament Theology, ed. Colin Brown (Grand Rapids: Zondervan, 1975), 1:194. Also see Exod. 12:21; 24:1; and Num. 11:16 as representative samples of elders in ancient Israel.

[d] See 2 Sam. 19:11; 1 Sam. 4:3; 8:4; Coenen, "Bishop," 195.

[e] Gunther Bornkamm, "πρέσβυς," TDNT 6.657.

[f] Bornkamm, "πρέσβυς," TDNT 6:659. Also see Jack P. Lewis, "zaqen," TWOT 1:249–50.

[g] See Coenen, "Bishop," 196.

[h] Lawrence H. Schiffman, From Text to Tradition: A History of Second Temple and Rabbinic Judaism (Hoboken, NJ: Ktav, 1991), 68, 70.

[i] Schiffman, From Text to Tradition, 166.

[j] Coenen, "Bishop," 196–97.

[k] Harvey, "Elders," 325.

[l] See Alistair Campbell, The Elders: Seniority within Earliest Christianity, Studies of the New Testament and Its World, ed. John Riches (Edinburgh: T&T Clark, 1994), esp. 44–64 on elders in Jewish synagogues (and Qumran); and 106–40 for Pauline usage of the term.

a consideration of how this verb, *proistēmi*,[77] is used in several other relevant places in the New Testament will expand our understanding even further.

This word is used in Romans 12, where Paul lists different gifts in the church. Each is to perform the gift according to God's grace—if prophesying

77. The other NT citations are as follows: Rom. 12:8; 1 Thess. 5:12; 1 Tim. 3:4, 5, 12; Titus 3:8, 14. The Titus passage uses *proistēmi* in a slightly different sense from the others, and so we will not focus on it. Paul uses it to speak of "engaging" in good works, busying oneself with good deeds.

or serving or teaching or preaching or sharing, let it be done according to the measure of faith and grace given. One gift listed here is "leadership" (NIV) or "ruling" (KJV). This gift is to be used with diligence (Rom. 12:8). The word for leadership is ὁ προϊστάμενος | *ho proistamenos*—literally, "the one taking the lead" or "the one directing" the group. It is a participial form of the same word used in 1 Timothy 5:17. Here we see that "taking the lead" is a gift from God to the church; it is a necessary part of the body. In 1 Thessalonians 5:12, Paul offers one more glimpse into this word: "Now we ask you, brothers and sisters, to acknowledge those who work hard among you, who care for you [προϊσταμένους | *proistamenous*] in the Lord and who admonish you. Hold them in the highest regard in love because of their work" (1 Thess. 5:12–13). The phrase "who care for you" translates our word for "rule or direct the affairs." These literally are the "ones taking the lead." Again, the idea of "over/under" has no part in God's kingdom if what is meant by that is a "lording over" as the gentiles do (Luke 22:25). When humans "lord it over" someone, it is often because they presume that their position or function makes them a better person or gives them power to demand performance from those under them. Leaders in the body of Christ are not better than anyone else in the body merely because their function is leading or managing. In this light, it seems misleading to describe the leaders' relation to the flock in terms of "over/under." Christian leaders do not subjugate a class of people beneath them; rather, they elevate their brothers and sisters—they edify them, they build them up. Christian leadership does not "lord it over" but serves—it directs with care.

We have seen that elders rule, but not in a way similar to the common usage of that term. Because of its misleading connotations, "rule" should be replaced with "manage or direct with loving care." To do this, the elder/overseer is "ranked"—that is, placed before a brother or sister for the sake of leading them, not subjugating them. It is a matter of function—of duty. It has nothing to do with essence—with who we are.

A question might be asked: How can caring, servant-hearted leaders have authority to lead a group's life if they are not in some way "over" them? The answer itself is simple; it is an answer based on principles of God's kingdom, not those of this world. To put these principles into practice demands an intentional, moral effort on our part.[78] Christian leadership *begins* with rela-

---

78. In upcoming chapters, a fairly significant amount of space regarding Christian leadership will be devoted to sanctification. The character of leaders greatly shapes their leading and serving. Without decentering the self, ministry or leading will develop entropy—that is, will lose its energy and create disorder within the "system." Ministry and leading cannot arise from self-centered agendas, or they will become avenues for abuse of power.

tionships among people. Leaders build relational trust so that they are granted the right to lead and the respect needed to do so by followers.[79] As a leader, I can have authority in someone's life if my own life has been an example to them of loving concern and godly living. My authority rather naturally arises out of my relationship with God and others. People will listen to those who have served them, who have laid down their lives for them. Leaders do not need to lord it over anyone in order to be effective; rather, they should serve the flock by taking care of it with a heart of love as well as modeling how a thing is to be done. This is the initial step for putting the work of overseeing into practice today.

Leadership may be recognized by people when they give leaders the authority to lead due to their *role* or *position*. It may also be recognized when leaders have some expertise, education, or qualifying experience in a given area. In such cases, followers have confidence that the leaders know what they are doing.[80] However, I have found that in most congregations, these variations on granting authority to leaders are more shaped by culture or one's family than Christian principles. Without developing personal relationships, leaders whose authority is based on positional or educational leadership will soon find themselves facing fickle followers.

One dimension of authority needs to be added here. In addition to the *personal* authority described above, there is a *spiritual* authority that is necessary in ecclesial leadership. Within the realm of congregations, there is more to leadership than developing relationships. There is a spiritual dimension of authority, which is couched in the context of discipleship—of teaching and learning. This dimension seeks to provide spiritual accountability by teaching believers how to live as Christians and by overseeing their actions. As Paul encourages Titus while he is ministering in Crete, "These, then, are the things you should teach. Encourage and rebuke with all authority. Do not let anyone despise you" (Titus 2:15). This statement is at the conclusion of chapter 2, which is riddled with the commands "Teach!" or "Encourage!" or "Speak!" Paul advises Titus to "exhort" or "encourage" (παρακάλει | *parakalei*) and "rebuke" or "reprove with all authority" (ἔλεγχε μετὰ πάσης ἐπιταγῆς | *elenche meta pasēs epitagēs*). This final phrase

79. I owe the following discussion on power and authority to Joe E. Trull and R. Robert Creech, *Ethics for Christian Ministry: Moral Formation for Twenty-First Century Leaders*, 2nd ed. (Grand Rapids: Baker Academic, 2017), 94. Trull and Creech provide a description of three types of authority among leaders: authority based on position, authority based on expertise, and authority based on personal relationships.

80. Again, these three views about authority come from Trull and Creech, *Ethics for Christian Ministry*, 94.

gives us insight into Paul's understanding of spiritual authority. The word *elenche* speaks of testing something; it can refer to laying something bare, which in turn exposes its flaws. By way of inference, then, it can refer to speaking to someone when they are thinking or living incorrectly in order to help them change the way they think or act. Such language is operative throughout the New Testament (especially in Paul), but the last phrase, "with all authority," is unique. It refers to the authorization to carry out an order. Clearly, Paul wants Christian leaders to use *spiritual* authority with the flock of God when correction or rebuke is needed. Yet even (or especially) with carrying out the authority to rebuke, leaders cannot operate in an "over/under" manner like the world. Again, this is why the moral fabric of leaders' lives is such an important element in serving the body of Christ—because leading people demands that we relate to them personally yet also maintain some authority with them.

Spiritual authority can easily degenerate into carnal quests for power. This is one reason why God seems to prefer a plurality of leaders in local congregations and even national or international denominations. With such plurality, the leaders can be accountable to authority. The local church is not a democracy, to be sure, yet it is equally not an autocracy—or even an oligarchy. This is why styles of governance that simply take over models of leading from examples in business or politics miss the spiritual reality of the headship of Christ, the true leader of all ecclesial communities. Leaders in the body of Christ are called to their tasks by God and the congregation. In light of this, all authority in the church belongs to Christ, the head; every authority properly exercised in the church is "delegated authority"—that is, an authority exercised on behalf of the head of the church to fulfill his will and mission.[81] Abuse of ecclesial authority arises when humans attempt to establish their own authority in a congregation. Watchman Nee notes three warnings for those who lead Christ's church: (1) they must know that all authority comes from God (Rom. 13:11), (2) they must deny themselves, and (3) they must constantly keep in fellowship with the Lord.[82] Further, he provides the following excellent advice:

> Authority is established by God; therefore no delegated authority need try to secure his authority. Do not insist that others listen to you. If they err, let them err; if they do not submit, let them be insubordinate; if they insist on going their own way, let them go. A delegated authority ought not strive with [humans]. . . .

81. This idea of "delegated authority" comes from Watchman Nee, *Spiritual Authority* (New York: Christian Fellowship, 1972), 61–62.
82. Nee, *Spiritual Authority*, 61–62.

We should never say so much as one word on behalf of our authority; rather, let us give people their liberty.[83]

The attitude of humility shines through this statement—no coercion is needed. God establishes a person's authority by calling her to a place of leadership and demonstrating God's will through her leadership.

Given the biblical material that we have studied in this chapter concerning titles and functions in the first-century church, the question now must be asked, How did we get from New Testament eldering to a monarchical bishopric then to a Protestant pastorate today? This is a question whose answer awaits us in a study of the history of the church.

83. Nee, *Spiritual Authority*, 121.

2

A Historical Background to Ministry

Development in Functional Titles for Ministry from 100 to 300 CE

What happened to leadership in the church after the era of the New Testament? The evidence for early church government from 80 to 120 CE is scarce. Further, the evidence we do have is sometimes difficult to read with confidence because of the "fluid situation of the nascent ministry" during this time.[1] This makes it difficult to offer a clear or uniform picture of the manner by which early church leadership operated. Just because Antioch saw its bishop in one way does not mean Alexandria, Rome, or Corinth viewed their bishops similarly. In this critical apostolic and postapostolic period, cultural pressures and various influences began to shape church government so that by 200, leadership essentially resided in one person—the bishop. How did this come about?

Clement of Rome

Let us begin our investigation with Clement, an early church leader at Rome. In a letter to the Corinthian church dated between 96 and 98,[2] Clement

---

1. This description comes from Bart J. Koet, "Dreaming about Deacons in the *Passio Perpetuae*," in *Deacons and Diakonia in Early Christianity: The First Two Centuries*, ed. Bart J. Koet, Edwina Murphy, and Esko Ryökäs, WUNT, 2nd ser., 479 (Tübingen: Mohr Siebeck, 2019), 264. Koet was arguing in the context of the *Passion of Perpetua*, an early Christian martyr, that some scholars may see her as a Christian prophetess but that he would be hesitant to label such "titles" as prophet because of the fluidity of the ministry and use of titles, even in the 200s CE.

2. See Cyril C. Richardson, "Introduction to the Clement's First Letter," in *Early Christian Fathers*, ed. Cyril C. Richardson (New York: Macmillan, 1978), 34.

addresses a problem of rebellion against leaders in Corinth. Having reminded
the Corinthians of their long-held status as an early church founded by
Paul, Clement chastises the Corinthians for the schism some have created
by overthrowing the presbyters. He admonishes them to repent. What is the
problem? After displacing these elders, some of the young and "arrogant"
rebels "have set themselves up as leaders in abominable jealousy."[3] Clement
encourages everyone to "coalesce harmoniously and unite in mutual sub-
jection" under the previous, rightful leaders.[4] God established the order of
leaders when he said in Isaiah 60:17, "I will appoint their *bishops* in righteousness and their *deacons* in faith" (Clement's translation). At first this
appears to be a translation from the Septuagint (LXX), but both the Hebrew
and Septuagint read quite differently: "I will make peace your *overseer* and
righteousness your *ruler*" (Isa. 60:17, my literal Hebrew translation, my
emphasis). The Septuagint that has come down to us reads as follows: "I
will appoint your *rulers* [ἄρχοντάς | *archontas*] in peace and your *overseers*
[ἐπισκόπους | *episkopous*] in righteousness" (LXX, my emphasis). While
Clement may be using a Greek Old Testament of which we have no evidence
today, in comparison to the Septuagint (which he uses elsewhere), Clement
reverses the clauses and inserts the word "deacons" for "rulers."[5] Hence,
with the use of the terms "bishops" and "deacons," he seems to imply that
God prophesied the exact name and function of these future church leaders!
In whatever way he arrived at this translation, he used it to make his point.[6]
God established leaders both in Scripture and in Corinth. But who are these
leaders for Clement? Are they bishops? Deacons? Elders? What do these
terms mean to him and his readers at the close of the first century? Here
is a somewhat enigmatic passage that may give some light: "Our apostles

3. Clement, *Letter to the Corinthians* 14.1, in *AF*, 63. Richardson's edition translates this as
"who take the lead in stirring up loathsome rivalry." *Early Christian Fathers*, 50.

4. Clement, *Letter to the Corinthians* 37.5, in *AF*, 95. The Greek reads, "πάντα συνπνεῖ καὶ
ὑποταγῇ μιᾷ χρῆται εἰς τὸ σῴζεσθαι ὅλον τὸ σῶμα," in *AF*, 94.

5. Clement, *Letter to the Corinthians* 42.4–5, in *AF*, 101. A more literal translation of the
Septuagint would be as follows: "I will appoint your leaders [ἄρχοντάς | *archontas*] in peace
and your administrators [ἐπισκόπους | *episkopous*] in righteousness." Deacons were not even
mentioned.

6. For a thorough rehearsal of the various ways that scholars think Clement may have been
using Isa. 60:17, see Bart J. Koet, "Isaiah 60:17 as a Key for Understanding the Two-Fold Ministry
of Ἐπισκόποι and Διάκονοι according to First Clement (*1 Clem.* 42:5)," in Koet, Murphy, and
Ryökäs, *Deacons and Diakonia in Early Christianity*, 182–89. One recurring theme in Koet's
work is the idea that bishop-deacons represented a twofold ministry in the first-century church.
He points to Phil. 1:1 and *Didache* 15:1–2 as further support of his thesis. While I agree with
Koet's evidence and working of his discussion here, I find he does not note clearly enough the
collation of *presbyteros* and *episkopos* into one function in the NT itself and therefore is less
inclined to recognize the "eldering" and "pastoring" functions in the early *episkopos*.

likewise knew, through our Lord Jesus Christ, that there would be strife over the bishop's office [ἐπὶ τοῦ ὀνόματος τῆς ἐπισκοπῆς | *epi tou onomatos tēs episkopēs*]. For this reason, therefore, having received complete foreknowledge, they appointed the leaders [τοὺς προειρημένους | *tous proeirēmenous*] mentioned earlier and afterwards they gave the offices a permanent character; that is, if they should die, other approved men should succeed to their ministry [τὴν λειτουργίαν | *tēn leitourgian*]."[7] With these ideas in mind, how could the Corinthians rebel and overthrow their leaders? "For it will be no small sin for us if we depose from the bishop's office [τὰ δῶρα τῆς ἐπισκοπῆς | *ta dōra tēs episkopēs*] those who have offered the gifts blamelessly and in holiness. Blessed are those presbyters [πρεσβύτεροι | *presbyteroi*] who have gone on ahead."[8]

Here we see that Clement understands bishops and presbyters (elders) somewhat synonymously.[9] In this, Clement is in line with the New Testament and apostolic writings of the first century. "Elders" and "bishops" are names for the same or similar functions. The Corinthians have overthrown their bishops, their presbyters—this one office. They should "be at peace with [their] duly appointed presbyters [πρεσβυτέρων | *presbyterōn*]."[10] They should adopt "the attitude of obedience, to submit to those who are the leaders of our souls [ἀρχηγοῖς τῶν ψυχῶν ἡμῶν | *archēgois tōn psychōn hēmōn*]."[11]

In addition to bishops and elders appearing to have similar functions in Clement, there is no "monarchical" or single-ruling bishop present in his thought. Clement chastens the Corinthians for overthrowing their old leaders, not just a single bishop. This fact is critical in understanding Clement's era. The apostles did not leave a single bishop or elder in charge—they left several. These were their successors. As Patrick Burke has observed, the sources thus far "provide no evidence for a monarchical episcopate at the

---

7. Clement, *Letter to the Corinthians* 44.1–2, in *AF*, 103.

8. Clement, *Letter to the Corinthians* 44.4–5a, in *AF*, 105; Greek text, 104.

9. J. B. Lightfoot makes this equation of the terms "bishop" (ἐπίσκοπος | *episkopos*) and "elder" (πρεσβύτερος | *presbyteros*). See Lightfoot, *The Apostolic Fathers: Clement, Ignatius, and Polycarp*, part 1, *Clement*, 2nd ed. (Peabody, MA: Hendrickson, 1989), 2:129. Also see Richardson, *Early Christian Fathers*, 63–64n2. In addition, Eduard Schweizer notes that bishops in Clement's letter are "called presbyters or overseers (1.3; 21.6; 44.4; 47.6)." See Eduard Schweizer, *Church Order in the New Testament*, trans. Frank Clarke (Eugene, OR: Wipf & Stock, 2006), 149. To further support his union of these two titles, Clement chides the Corinthians' sedition against the "presbyters." See Clement, "Letter to the Corinthians," 47. Also, see A. E. Harvey, "Elders," *Journal of Theological Studies*, n.s., 25 (1974): 318–32, here 329. As we shall see, with Ignatius, the two titles appear distinct.

10. Clement, *Letter to the Corinthians* 54.2, in *AF*, 117.

11. Clement, *Letter to the Corinthians* 63.1, in *AF*, 129.

end of the first century, except in Asia Minor and Syria."[12] Burke adds that even Asia Minor and Syria only have priority on bishops in some embryonic form at this time.

The Didache

A second source for this period is the *Didache*, which operated as an instruction manual for church ministry. The date offered for this collected source ranges between 70 and 150 CE.[13] Recent studies suggest the *Didache* represents some early material but may have been codified later in the second century.[14] Some of its comments on church government may be descriptive of events and issues contemporaneous with the apostles of the New Testament era (50–100 CE). Therefore, the *Didache* offers a valuable glimpse into part of the church world in early Christianity. The section dealing with church leaders (chaps. 11–15) discusses apostles and prophets as one group and bishops and deacons as another group. The term "elders" does not appear, although the title "teacher" is prominent. The apostles and prophets are described as itinerant leaders.[15] The church is warned to take caution in receiving them—apostles should stay one day, three if necessary. If they press to stay beyond three days or if they ask for money, they are false prophets.[16] It seems clear that apostles and prophets are trans-local—that is, they travel with their ministries and do not stay in one place too long where there is already a church. Since apostles and prophets establish new churches, the description of their mobility here should not surprise us. If a prophet wants to "settle with you," he has a right to receive support; in the same way, a "genuine teacher" has a right to support.[17] From this source, we see that early churches experienced prophets as traveling ministers or as resident ministers similar to teachers.

In terms of local authorities, the *Didache* says this: "Therefore appoint for yourselves bishops and deacons worthy of the Lord, men who are humble and not avaricious and true and approved, for they too carry out for you the ministry of the prophets and teachers. You must not, therefore,

---

12. Patrick Burke, "The Monarchical Episcopate at the End of the First Century," *Journal of Ecumenical Studies* 7, no. 3 (Summer 1970): 499.

13. Richardson, *Early Christian Fathers*, 161.

14. See Maxwell Stamforth and Andrew Louth, *Early Christian Writings: The Apostolic Fathers* (New York: Penguin Books, 1987), 189.

15. Linwood Urban, *A Short History of Christian Thought* (New York: Oxford University Press, 1995), 319.

16. *Didache* 11.5, in *AF*, 363.

17. *Didache* 13.2, in *AF*, 365.

despise them, for they are your honored men, along with the prophets and teachers."[18]

Several issues arise from this passage. First, bishops and deacons are placed together as a grouping here, as were apostles and prophets earlier in the text. They were chosen by the people. For deacons, this is reminiscent of Acts 6. For bishops, this procedure seems awkward—surely bishops were appointed, not elected? Apparently in some communities, bishops were chosen; at least the desires of the congregation were expressed.[19] If we read into this office of bishop what would come later—namely, that of a monarchical episcopate—then "election" seems quite out of place. If, however, we see this bishop as an "elder" in a local congregation, it seems more reasonable that such local leaders could be chosen by the congregation.[20] Usually, the people of God can sense spiritual leadership and authority resident in someone among them. Informally, they will go to such an "adviser" for spiritual help; formally, they would choose such a helper as a leader for the entire congregation. This is not a bishop who "rules" over a region or group of cities, as would come later. This is a bishop/elder similar to the function in the New Testament; this person is someone who oversees local church affairs.

18. *Didache* 15.1–2, in *AF*, 367. See also Richardson, "Didache," in *Early Christian Fathers*, 178. Also see "The Didache," in *Early Christian Writings*, trans. Maxwell Stamforth and Andrew Louth (New York: Penguin Books, 1987), 197.

19. In Acts 14:23, Paul and Barnabas "appointed elders for them in each church." The marginal reading is, "Paul and Barnabas had elders elected" in every church. The two renderings are vastly different in their method and result. Which was it—appointed or elected? The verb, χειροτονήσαντες | *cheirotonēsantes*, has a literal sense of "to appoint by show of hands," as is found in Josephus, *Antiquities* 18.22. While admitting the word may have its origin in the electing process of the Greek cities, Craig Keener believes the literal idea of raising hands to take a vote is probably more figurative in Acts 14:23, where it may mean "select." See Craig S. Keener, *Acts: An Exegetical Commentary*, vol. 2, *3:1–14:28* (Grand Rapids: Baker Academic, 2013), 1281n331, 2183. Since Paul and Barnabas are the "implied subject" of this verb, Keener prefers the idea of installing or appointing elders (Keener, *Acts*, 2:2183). Nevertheless, it is possible that the term could refer to the people being instructed by Paul and Barnabas to vote. Perhaps it is more likely that it refers to Paul and Barnabas "voting" or "choosing" and thereby electing appointed elders. French Arrington suggests that it is impossible for this to mean a congregational election, but he does not offer a rationale. It seems either method is possible from the Greek. The *Didache* may reflect one way leaders were chosen—by election. See French L. Arrington, *The Acts of the Apostles: Introduction, Translation, and Commentary* (Peabody, MA: Hendrickson, 1988), 146–47.

20. Clayton Jefford proposes an interesting thesis in this regard. Since the imperative "appoint" here in *Didache* 15.1 is a command, then we would need to know the recipient of the manual in order to understand who is supposed to do the "appointing" or "choosing." Further, Jefford notes that he believes the recipients could be a *third* office—one that remains unnamed in the text—namely, that of "elders" (*prebyteroi*). It is odd that such an early manual on church function does not address the elders or even mention them. This may be a possible reason why. See Jefford, "Understanding the Concept of Deacon in the *Didache*," in Koet, Murphy, and Ryökäs, *Deacons and Diakonia in Early Christianity*, 207.

Second, the qualifications for these offices are similar to those in 1 Timothy and Titus. Their functions are not elaborated, only their character traits—gentle, generous, faithful, experienced. The church must have already been aware of what these men did as bishop and deacon, and therefore the writer does not discuss their function.

Third, "their ministry to you is identical with that of the prophets and teachers."[21] As mentioned above, prophets could be itinerant (with the apostles) or resident; teachers were always resident in a local body. Since the *Didache* has connected teachers with prophets in this statement, it must be referring to *resident* prophets and teachers. What is very clear is that the early church had a variety of ministries and authority functioning together in one local body. However, nowhere in this document is anyone given authority higher than another; each one was to do their part, working together for the good of the entire body and the cause of Christ. There is no one bishop overseeing the operation of all. Instead, the church has to be instructed to honor bishops and deacons with the prophets and teachers. Their ministries are identical in terms of honor. Surely this cannot mean they do the same things; rather, it must point to the level of respect these functions should have. Apostles, prophets, and teachers are listed by Paul as three of the fivefold gifts to the church (Eph. 4:11). Bishops and deacons are not listed there, yet this instruction manual requires its readers to respect them at the same level. Clearly, God has placed all four of these functions in the local church in order to accomplish his will.

In nothing that we have extant from the first century CE have we seen anything resembling two prominent models of church leadership today. One of these will develop in the second century, the other over several centuries up to the present (especially among Protestants). The first model is the "monarchical episcopate." The second prominent model of leadership today is the "pastor as leader," in which a single person becomes the professional who knows how to do ministry and leads the church spiritually. The church pays this individual to do the work of ministry, thereby forfeiting its responsibility to share in ministry. Such a pastor model is foreign to the first century, even though it is prominent among many Protestant churches today. The model that shouts to us from the earliest church is one with two facets: plurality of leaders and variety of gifts. Whatever else may be said or surmised from the evidence of the first century, plurality and variety seem to be the crucial components. How, then, did the church develop other models?

---

21. This is the rendering from the *Didache* 15.2, in Richardson, *Early Christian Fathers*, 178.

Ignatius of Antioch

The trend to develop one strong, centralized office of authority within the church depended on geography—and perhaps cultural proclivity. In Syria (especially Antioch) and Asia Minor, the focus of authority was located in one person—the bishop. This arose as early as the beginning of the second century. Ignatius was the bishop in Antioch, Syria.[22] Between 112 and 115 CE, Ignatius traveled under guard to Rome to be martyred for the faith. Along the journey, he wrote six letters to churches and one letter to a fellow bishop (Polycarp). In these letters, we see a clear depiction of a monarchical episcopate—that is, a one-ruler bishopric. However, in other regions at this same time, there is evidence of plurality of elders as the model of leadership.[23] Yet most historians of the church agree that by 150–200 CE, all "leading centres of Christianity would appear to have had their Bishops, and from then until the Reformation, Christianity was everywhere organized on an episcopal basis."[24]

How did this arise? We have seen that the terms "bishop" and "elder" were used in the New Testament but not with the meaning they had achieved in some regions by 150 CE. While they were somewhat interchangeable and fluid in the New Testament, they were not so in the late second century. Burke suggests that Ignatius was a major advocate for this change. Ignatius continually made a distinction between bishop and elders and made the latter subordinate to the former. While the idea of monarchical bishoprics may have existed before Ignatius's letters, it was Ignatius who spread it, gave terms for it, and offered it as a "system" for churches in all Christendom.[25] What does Ignatius say about bishops and elders that would cause Burke to point to him as the major cause for the shift from plurality of leadership to singularity? I will examine Ignatius's letters in order to understand his views of leadership.

First, Ignatius speaks of one bishop, several elders, and several deacons. For him, there is one bishop who is supported by the "presbyters" and deacons in

22. Ignatius was bishop of Antioch. Under the emperor Trajan, Ignatius was martyred in Rome. He was born around 35–50 CE and died between 107 and 115 CE. See Frank L. Cross, "Ignatius," in *Oxford Dictionary of the Christian Church*, ed. Frank L. Cross and Elizabeth A. Livingstone, 3rd ed. (New York: Oxford University Press, 1997), 676.

23. Frank L. Cross, "Bishop," in Cross and Livingstone, *Oxford Dictionary of the Christian Church*, 174. Cross notes that Egypt is one of these regions. Also, Robin Lane Fox states that the following regions had elders leading the churches rather than monarchical episcopates: Alexandria, Syriac-speaking churches (as opposed to Greek-speaking) of Syria, and churches in southern Gaul (France). See Robin Lane Fox, *Pagans and Christians* (New York: Knopf, 1987), 499.

24. Cross, "Bishop," 174.

25. Burke, "The Monarchical Episcopate at the End of the First Century," 517.

a region/city. Some have seen these distinctions as three orders of ministry.[26] Ignatius says, "Whoever does anything without bishop, elders (presbytery), and deacons, does not have a clean conscience."[27] Also, "Pay attention to the bishop and council of presbyters and deacons."[28] To Polycarp, the bishop of Smyrna, Ignatius says that he is committed to those who are submitted to the bishop, elders, and deacons.[29] From these passages it is obvious that for Ignatius, these three offices are the leadership of the church in a local area. Are they "orders of ministry"? Perhaps, but we may be reading too much back into Ignatius's words. Still, there is a "division of authority" here that will become long-lasting in the church.[30] As Eduard Schweizer states, "The co-existence of different spiritual gifts has become a gradation of offices."[31] While the people of God are still "bearers of God" and everything holy (*To the Ephesians* 9.2) and endowed with every gift from the Spirit (*To the Smyrnaeans*, salutation), the emphasis throughout is on obedience to the hierarchy of leadership, not on the charismatic authority in the gifts.

Second, Ignatius describes the single bishop as if he were "the Lord" in the midst of the church, saying, "We must regard the bishop as the Lord himself."[32] Just as the Father God is "bishop of all" and invisible, the bishop in the church is over all yet visible.[33] When we obey the bishop, we are obeying Christ; therefore we should do nothing without the bishop.[34] It is the bishop who is in charge of the affairs of the church. If someone wants to get married, the consent of the bishop is necessary.[35] Nothing is to be done without his approval. What, then, is the role of the elders? They are to support the bishop. Like a tuned harp, the elders are to be in harmony with the bishop so that leaders will make a harmonious chorus for God.[36] The elders are to cheer up the bishop; this is their duty.[37] The bishop presides in the place (τόπον | *topon*) of God while the elders preside after the type of the council of apostles.[38]

---

26. William R. Schoedel, *Ignatius of Antioch: A Commentary on the Letters of Ignatius of Antioch*, Hermeneia (Philadelphia: Fortress, 1985), 112.

27. Ignatius, *To the Trallians* 7.2, in *AF*, 219.

28. Ignatius, *To the Philadelphians* 7.1, in *AF*, 243. At the beginning of this epistle, Ignatius greets those who are united with the bishop, elders, and deacons (237).

29. Ignatius, *To Polycarp* 6.1, in *AF*, 267.

30. We shall examine below how presbyters (elders) come to be called priests.

31. Schweizer, *Church Order in the New Testament*, 154.

32. Ignatius, *To the Ephesians* 6.1, in *AF*, 187.

33. Ignatius, *To the Magnesians* 3.2, in *AF*, 205.

34. Ignatius, *To the Trallians* 2.2, in *AF*, 215.

35. Ignatius, *To Polycarp* 5.2, in *AF*, 267.

36. Ignatius, *To the Ephesians* 4.1, in *AF*, 187.

37. Ignatius, *To the Trallians* 12.2, in *AF*, 223.

38. Ignatius, *To the Magnesians* 6.1, in *AF*, 207.

To the same church, Ignatius adds this: "Therefore as the Lord did nothing without the Father, either by himself or through the apostles (for he was united with him), so you must not do anything without the bishop and the presbyters."[39] From these statements, it is clear that Ignatius regarded the elders (presbyters) as a supportive council to the bishop and that nothing could be done without them.[40]

The Smyrnaeans were to follow the bishop, "as Jesus Christ followed the Father, and follow the council of presbyters as you would the apostles; respect the deacons as the commandment of God. Let no one do anything that has to do with the church without the bishop. . . . Wherever the bishop appears [ὅπου ἄν φανῇ | hopou an phanē], there let the congregation [τὸ πλῆθος | to plēthos] be; just as wherever Jesus Christ is, there is the catholic church."[41] With Ignatius we find early evidence of a single leader among leaders. That one leader's decision was superior and his word final. Without these leaders, there was no church. They watched out for heretical wolves and led the flock. Nothing was to be done without them. While such an emphasis on a single bishop's authority was not universal among Christians, it became so.

How did the monarchical episcopate rise to such a level of use and acceptance? Who knows? Robin Lane Fox suggests a possible explanation—"bishops were born from conflict."[42] The evidence we possess from until about 100 CE points to churches operating with a variety of ministries in leadership. From this plural leadership, conflict could have been born that would have needed to be adjudicated. One of the elders may have settled the disputes best, or a leader outside the elders may have been chosen to handle conflict. Whatever

39. Ignatius, *To the Magnesians* 7.1, in *AF*, 207.

40. He also admonished the Magnesians to be diligent to follow God's command "with your most distinguished bishop and that beautifully woven spiritual crown which is your council of presbyters and the godly deacons." See Ignatius, *To the Magnesians* 13.1, in *AF*, 211. Also, in *To the Trallians* 3, the elders (presbyters) are to be respected as "God's council" and "as the band of the apostles" (*To the Trallians* 3.1, in *AF*, 217).

41. Ignatius, *To the Smyrnaens* 8.1–2, in *AF*, 255. It is reasonable to see how the later ecclesial concept may have been birthed from Ignatius's high regard for the bishop: *ubi episcopus, ibi ecclesia* (wherever the bishop is, there is the church). However, Tom Greggs has recently argued that Ignatius intended this statement about wherever the bishop is to be seen as a "statement of unity, not a statement of condition for the existence of the church." See Tom Greggs, *Dogmatic Ecclesiology*, vol. 1, *The Priestly Catholicity of the Church* (Grand Rapids: Baker Academic, 2019), 125n46. While I see this as a plausible interpretation of Ignatius's *To the Smyrnaens* 8.1–2, there remains so much focus on the single bishop throughout his letters that it seems just as likely that Ignatius meant the bishop's presence is required for the existence of the church. Further, if no one can do anything without the bishop, then can there be a church without the bishop present? Since Ignatius compares the bishop's presence to that of the risen Christ among the community, then perhaps *ubi episcopus, ibi ecclesia* is quite close to his viewpoint.

42. Fox, *Pagans and Christians*, 503.

the cause for a single bishop's rise in authority, throughout the second and third centuries this authority solidified, especially as challenges arose against the faith. Jerome, writing in the 400s, suggests one reason for the rise of the singular bishop's role. In a commentary on Titus he states,

> Before the attachment to persons in religion was begun at the instigation of the devil, the churches were governed by the common consultation of the elders; but after every one thought that those whom he had baptized were his own, and not Christ's, it was decreed that one of the elders should be chosen, and set over the rest, upon whom should fall the care of the whole Church, and all schismatic seeds should be removed. As the elders knew from the custom of the Church that they were subject to him who was set over them, so the bishops knew that they were above the elders, more from custom than from the truth of an arrangement by the Lord, and that they ought to rule the Church in common with them.[43]

What is amazing in this quotation is the admission that the monarchical episcopate is a matter of custom and that collegial eldership was at least the original pattern from which custom later strayed. Ignatius could speak of the unity of the church focused in the person or office of the bishop. Irenaeus, Tertullian, and Cyprian could speak of truth being handed down and kept pure from heresy by the bishop. The apostles passed down their authority to a duly authorized bishop.[44] Eventually, the gift of the Holy Spirit was seen to reside in the bishop and could be shared only through his hands.[45] Not until the Reformation does this model of the church undergo radical scrutiny, but even then it does not change substantially.

From "Presbyter" to "Priest"

One of the more surprising developments in both terminology and function in the late second to third centuries CE is found in the gradual redefinition of πρεσβύτερος | *presbyteros* (elder) as *sacerdos* or ἱερεύς | *hiereus* (priest). What seems clear about this development is that it does not arise from a priestly function of the *presbyteros* in the New Testament. As we have seen, bishop

43. As cited in The Second Helvetic Confession 5.162, in *The Book of Confessions and the Constitutions of the United Presbyterian Church in the USA*, 2nd ed. (New York: The General Assembly of the UPC, 1970).

44. See Jaroslav Pelikan, *The Christian Tradition: A History of the Development of Doctrine*, vol. 1, *The Emergence of the Catholic Tradition (100–600)* (Chicago: University of Chicago Press, 1971), 118.

45. See Fox, *Pagans and Christians*, 506. I might note here that after Christianity became legalized in the fourth century, the power, prestige, and role of the bishop was greatly enhanced.

or overseer (ἐπίσκοπος | *episkopos*) and elder (*presbyteros*) were used somewhat interchangeably in the New Testament. Indeed, any attempt to retrieve exact job descriptions of bishop, elder, deacon, apostle, prophet, and others seems quite impossible at this distance of two millennia. There are historical nuances and shadows that cloud our view as do our own twenty-first-century preconceptions about the meanings of these titles. However, we do know that the *presbyteros* is nowhere performing a priestly function in the New Testament, because no Christian ministerial position performed such a function.[46] The whole community of God's people, not just the leaders, were priests.

As the monarchical episcopate grew, there arose a "council of elders" or a "council of presbyters," whose task was to assist and support the bishop.[47] During the 100s—the era just after the apostles—a concern arose regarding the unity of the church in the face of alternative branches of Christianity. To safeguard against this onslaught, a rather strong focus on the role of bishop rose in some places. One can see this in the overwhelming amount of respect and obedience required by Ignatius for the bishop of a region. Opposing the bishop was equated with opposing God (*To the Ephesians* 5.3). The people were never to act independently of their bishop (*To the Magnesians* 7.1). Hence, the bishop "can serve as a powerful weapon against disunity and budding heresy."[48]

Moreover, during the 100s a second factor led to the rise of the bishop's role. There was concern in some circles that not just anyone should preside at a Christian worship service or oversee the ritual of the Eucharist. For almost all of this century, the bishop was also considered a presbyter (sometimes referred to as "presbyter-bishop"), probably because he rose out of the council of presbyters.[49] However, only the bishop—or one of the presbyters he appointed in his stead—could preside at the Eucharist. As the Eucharist gradually developed a more central position in the services of Christians in the second century, the position of the presider became more central as well. Further, near the end of the second century we have evidence that Christians increasingly understood the Eucharist as a sacrifice—not in opposition to Hebrews' claim that Christ's was the final sacrifice but in response to Jesus's

46. See Thomas F. Torrance, *Royal Priesthood: A Theology of Ordained Ministry*, 2nd ed. (Edinburgh: T&T Clark, 1993), xv; also Raymond E. Brown, *Priest and Bishop: Biblical Reflections* (New York: Paulist Press, 1970), 13.

47. We have seen this above in Ignatius's comments in *To the Trallians* 12.2.

48. Brown, *Priest and Bishop*, 39.

49. See Brown, *Priest and Bishop*, 34–40, on the "presbyter-bishop." This point is debated by Alistair C. Stewart, *The Original Bishops: Office and Order in the First Christian Communities* (Grand Rapids: Baker Academic, 2014), 6–7. Further, Stewart dislikes the title "presbyter-bishop" since it assumes the two terms are interchangeable (4).

Are Bishops and Elders the Same?

Historian Alistair C. Stewart has proposed that the terms "bishop" and "elder" are not synonyms but rather "perionyms" (partial synonyms). He suggests that the passages in the New Testament that we have already considered above (Acts 20:17–28; Titus 1:5, 7) do not show interchangeable words but from their context have a much more complex relationship. Stewart suggests that the apparent synonymy can be explained in terms of "federations," where individual church leaders may have gathered to deal with common issues. He believes that in their individual churches they may have been called *episkopoi*, but in the gatherings of the federation they would have been known as *presbyteroi*. Further, he uses Hellenistic "associations" and their "benefactors" to enlighten the concept of *presbyteros* in the church.[a]

While Stewart carefully engages documents and even inscriptions from the early church era (convincing me of the feasibility of such federations and the unusual use of titles), there seem to remain some gaps that he fills in with assumptions in order to make his theory workable. First, his interpretations of the key passages in Acts and the Pastorals demonstrate little that supports his thesis against synonymy. Second, his proposal regarding the economic function of *episkopoi* is interesting but does not always take into account the vast differences by which *episkopoi* operated according to region and cultural demand. Third, his argument that there was no collegial leadership (for example, the presbytery) in the early Christian communities

command to keep remembering him in this way. Consequently, the Old Testament Levitical priesthood became something of a template for the functions of church leaders. These factors, then, caused the "elder" to be one who was authorized through the laying on of hands by the bishop to preside at the eucharistic table of sacrifice. Hence, the *presbyteros* gradually became a *sacerdos*—the elder became a priest.

The term "priest" (ἱερεύς | *hiereus*) was first applied to a Christian minister in the extant literature by Polycrates of Ephesus in about 190. He referred to the apostle John as *hiereus*.[50] In the 200s, the idea of priesthood applied first

50. Carl J. Armbruster, "Priesthood and Ministry from the New Testament to Nicaea," in *Proceedings of the Catholic Theological Society of North America: 24th Annual Convention* (Boston: Boston College, 2012), 63–74, here 67. Cf. also Joseph Blenkinsopp, "Presbyter to Priest: Ministry in the Early Church," *Worship* 41, no. 7 (August–September 1967): 428–38, esp. 431. We learn this from the early church historian Eusebius, *The Church History: A New Translation with Commentary* 5.24.3, trans. Paul L. Maier (Grand Rapids: Kregel, 1999), 198.

is even less convincing. While these proposals are well researched and fascinating, they should be topics for further research. Stewart himself admits the provisional nature of his "hypothetical account" but argues that "a rather slender narrative is preferable to a confident narrative without foundation in the evidence."[b]

Dimitrios Moschos has put forward several similar challenges in his review of Stewart's book.[c] He sees Stewart as "over-interpreting" (*überinterpretierte*) in the passages of Scripture (e.g., 2 John 9) and early literature (e.g., *Didache* 15.1, where Stewart translates λειτουργοῦσι | *leitourgousi* as "to celebrate the liturgy"). Moschos says "the most important objection" against Stewart's influential scheme of interpreting "may be raised precisely with his functionalistic framework." Approaching the "offices" of the early church through the lens of organizational function limits some of his view. Moschos also notes that "other charismatic aspects like prophets, exorcism or healing are scarcely observed." What of the "charismatic authority" that prophets exercised?[d]

---

[a] See Alistair C. Stewart, *The Original Bishops: Office and Order in the First Christian Communities* (Grand Rapids: Baker Academic, 2014), 14–16.

[b] Stewart, *The Original Bishops*, 298.

[c] Dimitrios Moschos, "Rezensionen: Alistair C. Stewart, *The Original Bishops*," *Zeitschrift für Antikes Christentum* 20, no. 3 (2016): 524–27.

[d] Moschos, "Rezensionen," 527 (my translation).

---

to bishops and then eventually to a presbyter who presided at the Eucharist.[51] Tertullian (c. 155–after 230 CE) writes of the bishop as *sacerdos*—a priest.[52] A little later Origen (c. 185–254) writes that presbyters are priests, at least along the lines of a biblical typology.[53] Hippolytus of Rome (c. 170–235) writes of a *klēros* or clergy made distinct by ordination.[54]

By the middle of the 200s, the concept of the Eucharist as a sacrifice was prominent throughout the Christian church. Indeed, the analogy began to grow stronger between the ancient people of God (Israel) and the Christian church. The law of Moses had analogous components to the Christian

---

Polycrates wrote, "There is also John, who leaned on the Lord's breast and who became a priest wearing the miter."

51. Armbruster, "Priesthood and Ministry," 67.

52. Tertullian, *De exhortatione castitatis* 7.3; and *De baptismo* 17.

53. Blenkinsopp, "Presbyter to Priest," 431.

54. Blenkinsopp, "Presbyter to Priest," 431.

dispensation.[55] This was particularly true of the levels of leadership that had arisen in Christian churches. The deacons corresponded to the Levites; as such, they performed their work under the authority of the bishops and presbyters.[56] The presbyters corresponded to the priests, and the bishop corresponded to the high priest. From a Syriac document, *Didascalia*, which is dated about 235 CE, we find a clear statement of this connection. "The Apostles have also decreed that there shall be Elders in the Church like the holy Priests, the sons of Aaron; and Deacons, like the Levites . . . and an Overseer who should be leader of all the people, like Aaron the High Priest, chief and leader of all the Levites and priests and of all the camp."[57] This analogy contributed to the supreme position of authority that a bishop held within a city or area. It gradually made clear that only specially consecrated ministers were allowed to perform *priestly* functions, such as preside at the Eucharist.

A distinctive theology of a Christian priestly class was most clearly seen at this time in Cyprian of Carthage (d. 258). For Cyprian, Christ is a priest in the line of Melchizedek. This was prefigured in the types of gifts that Melchizedek offered—namely, bread and wine, the same elements as the Lord's body and blood.[58] Cyprian then builds the argument to this crescendo concerning Christian priests who offer sacrifices: "For if Christ Jesus, our Lord and God, is himself the high priest [*summus sacerdos*] of God the Father, and has offered his very own self as a sacrifice to the Father, and has instructed in advance that this is to be done in memory of him, then by all means that priest truly engages in the stead of Christ [*vice Christi*] who imitates what Christ did and then offers a true and complete sacrifice in the church to God the Father, if he begins to offer in this manner according to that which he sees Christ himself to have offered."[59]

As Joseph Blenkinsopp notes, by the early fourth century (300s), the "process of assimilation is complete in all basic essentials as far as the Roman Church is concerned: the distinction between *clerus* (*ordo*) and *laici* (*plebs*), the use of the term *laicus* (layman) in the restrictive and negative sense (as

---

55. Edwin Hatch, *The Organization of the Early Christian Churches: Eight Lectures, Delivered before the University of Oxford, in the Year 1880* (London: Longmans, Green, 1918), 141. While this source is quite old, I have found his essential points to be supported by evidence that is more recent.

56. Hatch, *The Organization of the Early Christian Churches*, 52.

57. *The Didascalia Apostolorum in English*, trans. Margaret Dunlop Smith Gibson (London: Clay and Sons, 1903), 19. This statement comes from the section titled "Commandments from the Writing of Addai the Apostle," 5. The entire document claims to be the teaching of the twelve apostles.

58. Cyprian, *Letter* 63.4, in CSEL 3.2, 703.

59. Cyprian, *Letter* 63.14, lines 11–17, in CSEL 3.2, 713 (my translation).

in fact it is defined in canon law), and the presbyter as a sacrificing priest."[60] While the universal priesthood of believers was still maintained during this period, it increasingly became muted, especially due to the widening division between clergy and laity. It is to an examination of this growing divide that we now turn.

Historical Developments from the Third Century Forward

Clergy-Laity Distinctions

In the New Testament, there is no clergy-laity distinction. We are all the people of God. Indeed, the word "clergy" as referring to a separate ministerial class does not even appear in the Scriptures. As we have already seen, the word λαός | *laos* describes the people of God in the New Testament. The Israelites were God's people, and now the Christian community has become the "new people" (λαὸς καινός | *laos kainos*).[61] However, the adjective λαϊκός | *laikos* (belonging to laity) does not occur in the New Testament. In order to understand the history of this division into two classes of Christians, we need to study the etymology of the words "clergy" and "laity." From the medieval Latin word *clerus*, the French and English developed their word "clergy."[62] "Clergy" comes into English from an Old French word, *clergie*.[63] It means either a clerk or someone ordained in the church—clergy. *Clerus* was used in classical Latin to describe its Greek equivalent—namely, an allotment of land or lot (κλῆρος | *kleros*).[64] In the Septuagint, the Greek translation of the Hebrew Scriptures, κλῆρος | *kleros* is used primarily of the inheritance allotted the Levites as their "portion" (cf. Deut. 18:1–2).[65] In the New Testament, Peter uses this term in admonishing elders to consider their motives for shepherding

60. Blenkinsopp, "Presbyter to Priest," 431.
61. Hermann Strathman, "λαός," *TDNT* 4:57.
62. A. Ernout and A. Meillet, *Dictionnaire Etymologique de la Langue Latine: Histoire des Mots*, 4th ed. (Paris: Librairie C. Klincksieck, 1967), 127.
63. S.v. "cham-creeky," *The Oxford English Dictionary*, ed. J. A. Simpson and E. S. C. Weiner, 2nd ed. (Oxford: Clarendon, 1989), 3:311. The *g* in English is apparently brought into the language from the pronunciation of the Old French understanding of the Latin word *clericatus*.
64. S.v. "clerus," *Oxford Latin Dictionary*, ed. P. G. W. Glare (Oxford: Clarendon, 1983), 336. For the development of the Greek term, see Werner Foerster, "κλῆρος," *TDNT* 3:758–69, esp. 763–64, for NT usage.
65. See R. E. Latham, *Dictionary of Medieval Latin from British Sources*, Fascicule II C (London: Oxford University Press, 1981), 360. Also, related Latin words are these: *clericalis*, which means "clerical" or referring to the order of office of clergy; *clericatus*, which means the order of clergy; and *clerica*, which refers to the tonsure of a priest or monk—a sign of the clerical office in the Middle Ages.

and then tells them not to lord over "those entrusted to you" (1 Pet. 5:3). Other ways of rendering the term *klēros* are as follows: "the people assigned to your care" (NLT); "God's heritage" (KJV); "those in your charge" (RSV); "flock committed to your charge" (Phillips); and "those who are allotted to your care" (NEB). There is nothing here in any possible translation of *klēros* that refers to a class of elders or leaders distinct from the people of God. Instead, the people of God themselves are the κλῆροι | *klēroi*—the clergy, as it were.[66] As Alexandre Faivre notes, the *klēros* of 1 Peter consists of the "flock itself," not "the elders appointed to oversee the flock."[67]

From where did the concept of clergy as a separate class of Christians arise? Most scholars agree that the idea of clergy as opposed to laity arose somewhere in the third century CE (i.e., in the 200s).[68] As Edwin Hatch has said, "Little by little those members of Christian Churches who did not hold office were excluded from the performance of almost all ecclesiastical functions."[69] Several writers and church documents in particular give us some insight into this growing division.[70] Writing in Latin between 196 and 212 in Carthage, North Africa, Tertullian offers several passages that provide insight into how Christian congregations were structured and operating in that region (and perhaps beyond). In an important passage from *De exhortatione castitatis* (Concerning an Exhortation to Chastity), Tertullian emphasizes the universal priesthood of all Christians, not just those within a specific order (*ordo*).

66. The *Oxford English Dictionary* (312) notes that Milton (*Church Government* 2.3) in 1641, Burroughes in 1652, and Chandler in 1736 all considered the idea that clergy should refer to God's people, not to a class of ordained ministers.

67. Alexandre Faivre, *The Emergence of the Laity in the Early Church*, trans. David Smith (New York: Paulist Press, 1990), 6.

68. Alexandre Faivre is one of the foremost scholars on the emergence of the laity. He has outlined a survey of the development of the distinct classes (clergy and laity) beginning with the third century CE. See Alexandre Faivre, "Clerc/laïc: Histoire d'une Frontière," *Revue des Sciences Religieuses* 57, no. 3 (1983): 195–220. The charts aligned with ecclesial titles as they appear in the documents around 200 CE in Rome, Carthage, Alexandria, and Syria are most helpful (197–200).

69. Hatch, *The Organization of Early Christian Churches*, 127.

70. David F. Wright, "Laity," in *New Dictionary of Theology*, ed. Sinclair B. Ferguson and David F. Wright (Downers Grove, IL: InterVarsity, 1988), 375. The greatest amount of information on the class distinction we have noted appears to be among German sources. See the following: H. Barion, "Klerus und Laien," in *Die Religion in Geschichte und Gegenwart: Handwörterbuch für Theologie und Religionswissenschaft*, 3rd ed. (Tübingen: Mohr, 1959), 3:1662–63; also B. U. Hergemoeller, "Klerus, Kleriker," in *Lexikon des Mittel Alters* (Munich: Artemis, 1991), 5:1207–10; and also Albert Stein, "Klerus und Laien," in *Evangelisches Kirchenlexikon: Internationale theologische Enzyklopädie*, ed. E. Fahlbusch, Jan Lochman, John Mbiti, Jaroslav Pelikan, and Lukas Vischer, 3rd ed. (Göttingen: Vandenhoeck & Ruprecht, 1986), 2:1306–10. The last two sources agree that the third century CE was the beginning of the clear division between clergy and laity.

"Are not even we laypeople [*laici*] priests?"[71] Using 1 Peter 2:9, he reminds his readers that we all have been called to the priesthood simply because we are Christians. Within the framework of his argument in this context, however, he presses the fact that the apostles gave specific instructions to the clergy (whom he calls the *ordo sacerdotalis*—priestly order) that they not remarry after their spouse dies. Since we are all priests, Tertullian applies this rule to all the *sacerdotes* (priests), including the laity. Thus, "if you have the right of a priest [*ius sacerdotis*] in your very own self whenever it is necessary, then you must also have the discipline of a priest [*disciplinam sacerdotis*] when it may be necessary to have the right of a priest."[72]

Behind this specific argument lies a clear statement regarding the two different levels in the church. He notes, "The authority of the church has established the difference between clergy [*ordo*] and laity [*plebs*]."[73] I have translated the last two words "clergy" and "laity," but it is clear that *ordo* and *plebs* need some explanation for such a translation. Somewhere in the past, Tertullian believed that the church in some deliberative meeting (*consessum*) delivered an authoritative split between those who were part of the order (clergy) and those who were the common people in the congregation (*plebs* or laity). This language is quite new to the theological world of the third century—at least in Latin.[74] It seems clear that in Carthage by about 200 CE there were already two levels for understanding how people were to function in the congregation: clergy (*ordo sacerdotalis*) and laity (*plebs* or *laicus*).

In his treatise *De praescriptione haereticorum* (Concerning Prescription of the Heretics), Tertullian chastises the heretics for their frivolous attitude toward the process of ordination for the clerical offices. The heretics have ordinations that are "reckless, capricious, and fickle."[75] Nothing is easier than rebellion in the camp where such things are promised. "And so someone today can be made bishop, tomorrow someone else; a deacon today can become a reader tomorrow;

71. Tertullian, *De exhortatione castitatis* 7.3–4, in *Exhortation a la chasteté*, ed. Claudio Moreschini, Sources chrétiennes 319 (Paris: Cerf, 1985), 92, line 16 (my translation).

72. Tertullian, *De exhortatione castitatis* 7.4, in Moreschini, *Exhortation a la chasteté*, 94, lines 24–26 (my translation).

73. Tertullian, *De exhortatione castitatis* 7.3, in Moreschini, *Exhortation a la chasteté*, 92, lines 17–19 (my translation).

74. One scholar suggests that Tertullian's use of this old Latin word, *ordo*, may have introduced the concept of clergy as a different "order" over against the laity in the Latin language. See Anni Maria Laato, "Tertullian and the Deacons," in Koet, Murphy, and Ryökäs, *Deacons and Diakonia in Early Christianity*, 246n16. This may be a hunch, but I think that so far the evidence agrees.

75. Tertullian, *De praescriptione haereticorum* 41.6, in *De la prescription contre les hérétiques*, ed. R. F. Refoulé and P. de Labriolle, Sources chrétiennes 46, 2nd ed. (Paris: Cerf, 2006), 147, lines 16–17 (my translation).

The First Use of the Word "Laity"

The first instance of the word "laity" is from Clement of Rome in his letter to the Corinthian church around 96–98 CE. I have not noted it earlier because I consider it to be related more precisely to the Old Testament order of things. Clement's point in *1 Clement* 40.1–5 is for his readers to obey the Master (ὁ δεσπότης | *ho despotēs*), who has commanded things to be done a certain way—in order. This was the case with the sacrifices of the Old Testament: "For to the high priest the proper services [ἴδιαι λειτουργίαι | *idiai leitourgiai*] have been given, and to the priests the proper office [ἴδιος ὁ τόπος | *idios ho topos*] has been assigned, and upon the Levites the proper ministries [ἴδιαι διακονίαι | *idiai diakoniai*] have been imposed. The layman [λαϊκὸς ἄνθρωπος | *laikos anthrōpos*] is bound by the layman's rules."[a] The "laity" here are not connected to the church in Corinth; they refer to the non-Levites who did not have special clothing or sacerdotal duties in the temple.[b]

[a] *1 Clement* 40.5, in *AF*, 99.
[b] For an extremely thorough exegesis of this passage in comparison with Isa. 29:13, as well as passages from Ezekiel, see Alexandre Faivre, "Préceptes laïcs (λαικὰ προστάγματα) et commandements humains (ἐμτάματα ἀνθρώπων). Les Fondements scripturaires de *1 Clement* 40,5," *Revue des Sciences Religieuses* 75, no. 3 (2001): 288–308.

a priest today will be a layperson [*laicus*] tomorrow. For they even yoke up [*injungunt*] the priestly offices [*sacerdotalia munera*] to laypersons [*laicis*]."[76] Can there be a much clearer statement concerning the expected differences between the function of the priestly caste and the layperson?

A final example from Tertullian will suffice. In his teaching *De baptismo* (On Baptism), we see some glimpses of the clergy-laity divide. Who can baptize? Tertullian makes the point that all Christians can baptize, but there should be unusual circumstances if a layperson were to perform this ritual. Baptism rightly belongs to the function of the bishop.

> The supreme right [*summus ius*] of giving it [baptism] belongs to the high priest [*summus sacerdos*], which is the bishop. After him, it belongs to the presbyters and deacons, yet not without authorization [*auctoritate*] from the bishop, for the sake of the church's dignity [*honorem*]; for when this is safe, peace is safe. Except for that, even laypersons have the right [to baptize], because what is

76. Tertullian, *De praescriptione haereticorum* 41.7–8, in Refoulé and de Labriolle, *De la prescription contre les hérétiques*, 148, lines 20–24 (my translation).

received on equal terms can be given on equal terms. Unless perhaps you are prepared to allege that our Lord's disciples were already bishops or presbyters or deacons, that is, as the word ought not to be hidden by any person, so likewise baptism, which is no less declared to be "of God," can be administered by all. Yet how much rather are the rules of humility and restraint incumbent upon laypersons—seeing they apply to greater persons—who must not arrogate to themselves the function of the bishop. Opposition [*aemulatio*] to the episcopate is the mother of schisms.[77]

This approach to baptism sounds strangely like Martin Luther's almost thirteen hundred years later. Tertullian catches his opponents off guard by asking if baptism was offered to the apostles due to the fact that they already held offices in the church! The absurdity of this claim makes his point more potent—namely, that all Christians have a birthright through baptism. Not even the apostles could say they came to the gospel and baptism due to their position in the church. The Word of God cannot be hidden by humans, and neither should baptism. Theoretically, every Christian can baptize. However, for the sake of the "honor of the church," we keep the order agreed upon by consensus among the churches.

Ordination

While Tertullian does not mention the track by which laypersons could become part of the clergy order, others in the third century do leave us some clues.[78] The distinction was brought about by ordination and the laying on of hands by the bishop. Special qualifications were required of those who were to preach or serve the Eucharist. In addition, special privileges were acquired by those so ordained. Thus, the division between clergy and laity became a permanent structure in the church—one that never had its roots in the New Testament.[79]

77. Tertullian, *De baptismo* 17.1–2, in *Tertullian's Homily on Baptism*, ed. and trans. Ernest Evans (London: SPCK, 1964), 35, 37 (alt.). The Latin comes from this text as well: 34 and 36. In the last sentence, the Latin word *aemulatio* has several connotations, including "imitation," or "envious emulation," or "unfriendly rivalry." It may be more in keeping with Tertullian's point to call this opposition something like taking on the role of a bishop and doing the episcopal actions yet without the authority of the office of episcopate (*episcopatum aemulatio*). It is easy to see how this could become the "mother of schisms" (*schismatum mater est*).

78. See John St. H. Gibaut, *The Cursus Honorum: A Study and Evolution of Sequential Ordination* (New York: Peter Lang, 2000), for discussion on the development of a path for clergy among the three orders.

79. See Stein, "Klerus und Laien," 1306. Besides noting the competition between charismatic gifts and regular "offices" in the early church, Stein suggests that the offices as prescribed by the bishops won out.

Laying On of Hands in the New Testament

While it may be argued that Luke shows some type of ordination to the "diaconate" (or a deacon-like group) in Acts 6 and to missionary work in Acts 13 and then to eldering in Acts 20, it seems more likely that we have placed our ideas of office and ordination onto the prayer and commissioning context of these events. In other words, ordination as we have come to know it—where the institutional church approves, sanctions, and ordains a candidate for ministry—is not happening in the first-century church.

Eduard Lohse portrays the tendency to read back onto the biblical text the later style of ordination. He suggests that in Acts 6:1–6, the "institution of the Seven is meant as Christian ordination."[a] Although the allusions to Numbers 27:18, 23 are appropriately noted by Lohse, his conclusion establishing "Christian ordination" for Acts 6 seems highly anachronistic. Moreover, the word "ordination" does not occur in the New Testament. In addition, the verb "to ordain" does not occur there—at least not in the "technical sense" that we use it today.[b] Furthermore, one must presume something like "offices" are operating in the Pastorals in order to suggest (as Lohse does) that a "divinely granted charisma" was needed to "discharge his [Timothy's] office."[c]

Why can this not be the straightforward concept of laying on hands for spiritual endowment? We do not know precisely what *charisma* was given to Timothy on this occasion, but the verses before and after it do not press us to view it as an "office" or even "leadership" (1 Tim. 4:14). A prophetic message was given when the elders laid their hands on Timothy. Therefore, he should not neglect this gift he received. To say as Lohse does that this is a "Christian transfer of office, as in Rabbinic ordination," seems to say too much.[d]

In response to this claim, one might assert that the later ordination ritual, which is clearly marked by the end of the fourth century CE, finds its basic structure within the New Testament concept of laying on of hands.[80] To be sure, the laying on of hands in the New Testament is closely connected to receiving something from the Spirit (e.g., *charisma*) or even the gift of the Spirit itself (e.g., in Acts). However, since I have been arguing that the "offices" in the New Testament were more like functional placeholders than titles of

80. Dieter Sänger, "Ordination, II. Neues Testament," in *Religion in Geschichte und Gegenwart*, ed. Hans Dieter Betz, 4th ed. (Tübingen: Mohr Siebeck, 1998–2007), 6:619.

Bradshaw, on the other hand, rightly notes that the imposition of hands in the New Testament in relation to ordination possesses an "inherent ambiguity" that "seems to preclude reaching any definitive conclusion as to its precise significance in those few New Testament instances where it might be connected with appointment, still less abstracting from them a fixed interpretation that can then be applied unequivocally to its use in later ordination rites."[e] Opposed to this is Everett Ferguson, who sees an ordination of a type ("properly understood") in the New Testament.[f] It is clear for Ferguson that the laying on of hands within the historical context of the New Testament had to mean something like the installation of a person for a particular office or function. Although there was variety in the ordination, there remains a basic process—prayer, laying on of hands, and (on some occasions) a prophetic message or approval.

While I agree with Ferguson's point, I would underscore the differences between the fourth-century ordination rituals and the first-century ordination procedures. Even more to the point, I would propose that the first-century procedures do not equate (for the most part) with ordination procedures today—especially if the minister is placed into a clergy class over against the lay class.

[a] See Eduard Lohse, "χείρ," *TDNT* 9:433n55.
[b] See Leon Morris, "Ordination," in *The New Dictionary of the Bible*, ed. J. D. Douglas (Grand Rapids: Eerdmans, 1979), 912.
[c] Lohse, "χείρ," 9:433.
[d] Lohse, "χείρ," 9:434.
[e] See Paul F. Bradshaw, *Rites of Ordination: Their History and Theology* (Collegeville, MN: Liturgical Press, 2013), 13.
[f] See Everett Ferguson, "Ordination in the Ancient Church: IV. Ordination in the First Century," in *The Early Church at Work and Worship*, vol. 1, *Ministry, Ordination, Covenant, and Canon* (Eugene, OR: Cascade Books, 2013), 109.

offices, I would further argue that ordination as it came to be practiced in the 300s CE was not the same as laying on of hands in 1 or 2 Timothy. Laying on of hands could connote a blessing or even provide a healing.[81] This act was used sometimes in receiving the gift of the Holy Spirit—but sometimes it was not. Paul reminds Timothy not to be neglectful of the gift (χαρίσματος | *charismatos*) "which was given you [ὅ ἐδόθη σοι | *ho edothē soi*] through

81. A classic source of information for the imagery and concepts involved in the biblical sources for laying on of hands is found in Everett Ferguson, "Laying On of Hands: Its Significance in Ordination," in *The Early Church at Work and Worship*, vol. 1, *Ministry, Ordination, Covenant, and Canon* (Eugene, OR: Cascade Books, 2013), 160–72.

prophecy [διὰ προφητείας | *dia prophēteias*] when the body of elders laid their hands on you [μετὰ ἐπιθέσεως τῶν χειρῶν τοῦ πρεσβυτερίου | *meta epitheseōs tōn cheirōn tou presbyteriou*]" (1 Tim. 4:14). While this may become a basis for later ordination rituals, there is nothing in the New Testament that clearly delineates this as "ordination" as we understand it today. Instead, this seems to demonstrate a close connection between spiritual gift (*charisma*) and perhaps a function assigned (*ministry*). This is *not* to suggest that the first-century church was without leaders specifically commissioned by either the church or God to perform certain tasks. It is to state that the *office of the ordained leader* taken from the reality of late third- and early fourth-century clergy as distinct from the people of God who are not ordained (the "laity") is not supported by the New Testament alone.

The third century also saw the rise of a division within the clergy class itself. In the previous century, the episcopal office had risen in most regions to the level of a single-person rule over area churches. Such a church "ruler" was the one person in charge of the affairs of the local church and eventually regional churches. The bishop had become the central focus of local churches. The presbyters were below him in rank. While called "presbyters," they were not elders as the New Testament had described, but instead their biblical name, "presbyters," changed in meaning to "priests." Below these priests were the deacons and a host of other *ordines minores*. For example, there were door-keepers, readers, *exorcista* or demon exorcisers, and other helpers; these were the "minor orders." The "major orders" were subdeacons, deacons, priests, and finally bishops.[82] The laity or non-clergy were simply on the bottom of this rigid hierarchy; they were not essential to the church. As Alexandre Faivre notes, "The difference between [clergy and laity] came inevitably to be seen in the distribution of powers within the eucharistic assembly, and this meant that all the Christians taking part in that liturgy were no longer equal."[83]

The *Apostolic Tradition* is a document on church order from Rome dated around 220–235 CE providing criteria for who belongs to the "clergy." The *Apostolic Tradition* undoubtedly holds some information from the second century, but it is primarily a third-century source from a Christian school in Rome that was attempting to fight against a different understanding of church order.[84] It presents the bishop, presbyters, and deacons as three distinct orders of ministry that belong to the "clergy." Beyond these three offices

82. Hergemoeller, "Klerus, Kleriker," 1207.
83. Faivre, *The Emergence of the Laity*, 70.
84. This is the thesis of Alistair C. Stewart in the introduction to Hippolytus, *On the Apostolic Tradition*, trans. Alistair C. Stewart, 2nd ed. (Yonkers, NY: St. Vladimir's Seminary Press, 2015), 48–50.

are a host of other suboffices: the confessors, the readers, the subdeacons, virgins, and widows. Each is distinguished from the clergy in this document primarily by what functions they are allowed to perform and by a difference of installation. While the bishop, presbyters, and deacons have hands laid on them (*cheirotonia*) in "ordination," the others do not. For example, "When a widow is appointed [*kathistasthai*] she does not receive laying on of hands [*cheirotonein*]."[85] Then a rather complex rationale is offered for why the widow is installed with the word only—namely, because "she does not lift up the sacrifice nor does she have a proper liturgy [*leitourgia*]."[86] The document continues in explanation: "For the laying on of hands [*cheirotonein*] is with the clergy [*klēros*] on account of the liturgy [*leitourgia*], whereas the widow is installed [*kathistasthai*] on account of prayer, which is for everybody."[87] Hence, even ministers who performed certain functions for the benefit of the whole church were not placed in the clergy class but that of the laity. "The result was that the laity, who belonged to the chosen people of priests, very soon became the people of their priests."[88]

From the document *Didascalia* (Syriac, ca. 235 CE), we learn that the presbyters have a place reserved for them in the eastern side of the "house," while in the midst of those elders is placed the "throne of the bishop."[89] On the other side of the house should sit the "laymen," and then the women.[90] The deacon is to make certain that everyone sits within their area.[91] The bishop "governs in the place of the Almighty," and therefore "should be honored by you as God."[92] The deacons, who serve the bishop and must do nothing without him, stand "in the place of Christ."[93] The deaconesses are to be honored as if "in the likeness of the Holy Spirit," and the elders (presbyters) are "in the likeness of the Apostles."[94] Hence, the laity must bring their tithes and offerings to the bishop, who is their high priest in the new covenant. Everyone should obey the bishop and stay within their rank.[95] The laity should never "thrust" themselves into the priesthood, since that dignity belongs to someone

85. Hippolytus, *On the Apostolic Tradition* 10.1, in Stewart, 113. Cf. Faivre, *The Emergence of the Laity,* 75, for the Greek.
86. Hippolytus, *On the Apostolic Tradition* 10.4, in Stewart, 113.
87. Hippolytus, *On the Apostolic Tradition* 10.5, in Stewart, 113.
88. Faivre, *The Emergence of the Laity,* 71.
89. *The Didascalia Apostolorum in English* 12, in Gibson, 65.
90. *The Didascalia Apostolorum in English* 12, in Gibson, 65.
91. *The Didascalia Apostolorum in English* 12, in Gibson, 66.
92. *The Didascalia Apostolorum in English* 9, in Gibson, 48.
93. *The Didascalia Apostolorum in English* 9, in Gibson, 48.
94. *The Didascalia Apostolorum in English* 9, in Gibson, 48.
95. As Everett Ferguson has noted, "The region of Syria and Palestine definitely shows a greater prominence by the clergy and a more marked monarchial tendency than the rest of the

who has been lawfully given that task as a priest.[96] Therefore, obedience and
honor are due to the bishop as to one's father and mother. The bishop is the
"mediator between God and you in the several parts of your divine worship."[97]
As Alexandre Faivre comments, "The logical consequence of this attitude is
that the laity came to be treated as inferior."[98]

Am I arguing against the practice of ordination today? Absolutely not. I
believe that the body of Christ must have leaders, some of whom have devoted
their lives and livelihoods to the cause of Christ. If churches or denominations
want to follow the ancient practice of ordination from about the late second
or early third century CE, then I see no reason to avoid that practice—as long
as they are clear about what ordination is and is not. Ordination today cannot be seen as a clear *biblical* practice. There are hints of it throughout the
Scripture, but nothing like the practice today. In other words, churches should
understand that ordination today is more a *cultural* practice than a *biblical*
mandate. There are obvious reasons why churches today should demand some
requirements for setting forth people to full-time service of ministry—reasons
such as the need to determine one's seriousness in taking up the task, the ethi-
cal and character qualifications that demonstrate an individual's potential for
dealing with people in a moral manner, the specific need for ministers who
are educated in Scripture (and perhaps in other areas), and a clear sense of a
calling from God that is not based on someone else telling the individual that
they should do full-time ministry. If churches recognize that laying hands on
someone in ordination does not make that human being better than someone
else in the congregation, then there is a reasonable purpose for such processes
for ordination today.

However, two caveats should be registered here. First, as we have seen, there
are no priests in the Christian church other than Christ, our High Priest, and

---

Church at this period." See Ferguson, "Ordination in the Ancient Church. III. Ordination in the
Second and Third Centuries," in *Ministry, Ordination, Covenant, and Canon*, 86.

96. *Constitutions of the Holy Apostles* 2.27, in ANF 7:410. This document is probably Syrian
in origin and its final compilation is dated around 375 CE. It holds within its pages the entire
Didache and other aspects of comparison on church order with the *Didascalia*.

97. *Constitutions of the Holy Apostles* 2.26, in ANF 7:410.

98. Faivre, *The Emergence of the Laity*, 90. The widening of this gap between clergy and laity
was ensconced in the fabric of ecclesial life by the eleventh and twelfth centuries. The priest-
hood became separate from the rest of lay society due to its task of celebrating the Eucharist.
Their function was "the divine function of celebrating the eucharist, of creating—or helping
in the work of creation of—the body and blood of Christ on the altar." Christopher N. L.
Brooke, "Priest, Deacon and Layman, from St. Peter Damian to St. Francis," in *The Ministry:
Clerical and Lay*, ed. W. J. Sheils and Diana Wood, Studies in Church History 26 (Oxford: Basil
Blackwell, 1989), 65–85, here 66. Further, "If the host was a peculiarly sacred object, so were
the hands, so was the person, who consecrated it" (69).

the entire people of God. The barrier requiring mediation between God's presence and God's people was rent in two at the cross. Jesus Christ has become the sole mediator between God and humans. This seems to be a New Testament principle that has become shrouded in historical development. God desires his people to come to him directly and experience his presence directly through the avenue of the Holy Spirit. To separate the people of God's presence between a priestly (mediatorial) caste and a lay caste is to denigrate the very desire for spiritual intimacy that our God has provided through Christ.

For this reason, I cannot understand why some Protestant theologians want to speak of two types of priesthood in Christianity—one being the whole body of Christ and another being the representative ordained priesthood who serves the whole body. Thomas F. Torrance, for example, argues, "The real priesthood is that of the whole Body, but within that Body there takes place a membering of the corporate priesthood, for the edification of the whole Body, to serve the whole Body, in order that the whole Body as Christ's own Body may fulfill His ministry of reconciliation by proclaiming the Gospel among the nations. Within the corporate priesthood of the whole Body, then, there is a particular priesthood set apart to minister to the edification of the Body until the Body reaches the fullness of Christ (Eph. 4:13)."[99] Torrance believes that there is a priesthood set apart from the layperson in order to perform special service to the entire body of Christ, especially in the ministry of the Word and sacrament. The need for an ordained priesthood today is based in part on the growing importance of the eucharistic celebration in the first few centuries of the church. This prominence required authorized persons to celebrate the sacrament. As this sacramental offering became central to Christian worship, the clergy began to separate from the laity, in particular on this point: clergy were the "priests" of God in the new covenant who could supervise the sacrifice of the Supper just as the priests of the former covenant supervised the ritual sacrifices of the altar. As long as this connection between priesthoods held, the priesthood of believers became an appendage—a hollow vestige of reality. Ordination, then, became a way to "mark" priests as special people who preside at the eucharistic table *in the stead of Christ*. It is no wonder, then, that leadership roles for women began to erode after the second century at the same time that the distinction between ordained clergy (priests) and laity became prominent. If a priest is necessary, then on the basis of the Old Testament Levitical system, only males who are specially set aside are allowed to represent Christ at the sacrificial table.

99. Torrance, *Royal Priesthood*, 81.

A second caveat must be observed. The division between clergy and laity produces an unhealthy community of believers. I have attempted to demonstrate some historical rationale for the development of an ordained priesthood separate from the laity in chapter 1. The result places a question mark over this development due to leaving behind some of the most fundamental principles of the body of Christ in the New Testament. One of the principles is that *all* the people of God's presence are the priesthood of God. It seems impossible to have a clergy-laity distinction without creating a separation in God's people. *Leaders* in the body of Christ are one thing; *priests* who are operating specific duties that the laity are forbidden to perform are quite another thing. Another principle is that the ministry of reconciliation belongs to *all* God's people, not simply to a priestly caste. It is my proposal in the remaining chapters to sketch a possible scheme for how we might have *leaders* who help the entire congregation of believers be priests unto God and the world, as well as to sketch how to equip the people of God to do the work of ministry that God intended.

Charismatic Gifts versus Institutional Authority

One other aspect must be noted regarding the development of the clergy-laity distinction in the 200s CE. Consider also the "interplay" in the New Testament between charismata and leadership functions. In their introduction to ecclesiology, Brad Harper and Paul Louis Metzger highlight this point rather strongly, concluding that giftedness was a key criterion for leadership in the first-century church. They conclude, "To connect church leadership primarily to giftedness rather than to office necessarily diminishes the gap between clergy and laity, since all members of Christ's church are gifted to represent him to minister his grace to the rest of the body."[100] While it seems clear that Paul (and probably most of the NT churches) expected congregations to be vibrant centers of spiritual giftedness,[101] the second and third centuries dem-

---

100. Bradley Harper and Paul Louis Metzger, *Exploring Ecclesiology: An Evangelical and Ecumenical Introduction* (Grand Rapids: Baker Academic, 2009), 188.

101. Robert Jewett has noted that first-century congregations were highly charismatic. While the Epistle to the Romans has not been viewed as one of Paul's more charismatic letters, Jewett highlights the fact that Paul considered the commonality between the Roman church and himself to be the charismatic way of life. In Rom. 1:11–12, Paul desires to give the Romans a "spiritual gift" (χάρισμα πνευματικόν | *charisma pneumatikon*). Jewett comments, "Paul obviously felt the need to communicate as a charismatic with charismatics, emphasizing the spiritual bond that linked all believers together with Christ who is 'the Spirit' (2 Cor. 3:17)." Robert Jewett, *Romans: A Commentary*, Hermeneia (Minneapolis: Fortress, 2007), 124. Jewett also notes that the term πνεῦμα | *pneuma* is used thirty times in Romans (73). Further, "Glossolalia was probably a typical aspect of most early Christian congregations" (73). In light of this, Rom. 8:9, where

onstrated a strong institutional response to eruptions of the Spirit, which were viewed as threats to the authority of the leaders. The result was a tamping down on spiritual gifts and an elevation of the bishop's office, through which the Spirit was mediated to the people. Was it possible for Christian congregations to have charismata *and* institutional authority side by side?

In 1953, the German scholar Hans von Campenhausen published his research about authority and spiritual power in the first three centuries of the church.[102] He offered a sustained argument that in the second century CE, the Spirit and gifts increasingly were placed in tension with institutional church offices (such as bishops).[103] Near the end of the second century, a group of enthusiasts following a prophet named Montanus spawned a "volcanic revival movement [*eine eruptive Erweckungsbewegung*]" that challenged the established authority.[104] Von Campenhausen notes that this prophetic movement caused "a widespread sensation by the energy of its activities and its preaching, the seriousness of its demands, and the passionate conviction of its eschatological expectations; and it was these things which first aroused

---

the believers are described by Paul as ἐν πνεύματι | *en pneumati* (in/among the Spirit), points "undeniably" to a "charismatic description of the community" (489).

102. Hans von Campenhausen, *Ecclesiastical Authority and Spiritual Power in the Church of the First Three Centuries*, trans. J. A. Baker (Peabody, MA: Hendrickson, 1997). For the German, see Hans Freiherr von Campenhausen, *Kirchliches Amt und geistliche Vollmacht in den ersten drei Jahrhunderten*, Beiträge zur Historischen Theologie 14, ed. Gerhard Ebeling (Tübingen: Mohr, 1953).

103. However, von Campenhausen nuances this proposal very carefully by building on this general thesis. He states, "To start in every case from a supposed opposition between two separate blocs, the official and the charismatic [*der amtlichen und der charismatischen Gruppen*], is a typical modern misunderstanding." Von Campenhausen, *Ecclesiastical Authority*, 178; von Campenhausen, *Kirchliches Amt*, 195. Yet when von Campenhausen pushes further into the second and third centuries, he describes the tension as solidifying into firm opposition. I am aware that von Campenhausen's thesis and methods have been called into question due to his imposition of "a developmental theory that the New Testament resists"—namely, that the two alternatives (charismatic and institutional) were "ideal types of social structuring" derived from Max Weber. Their "clear-cut" conceptualization does not fit with the fact that "the charismatic and the institutional existed side by side from the beginning." These quoted comments come from Kevin Giles, *Patterns of Ministry among the First Christians*, 2nd ed. (Eugene, OR: Cascade Books, 2017), 6. He also notes that the critique of Holmberg in 1978 brought an end to support for von Campenhausen's thesis. See Berndt Holmberg, *Paul and Power: The Structure of Authority in the Primitive Church as Reflected in the Pauline Epistles* (Lund: Gleerup, 1978). However, as I noted earlier in this footnote, it seems that von Campenhausen *does* acknowledge the rather interactive play between these two aspects in the first-century church without suggesting they are too "clear-cut" in their distinctions. It is in the second century that his thesis underscores the distinctions—and I think he is reading history appropriately here in relation to these two dimensions of church life.

104. Von Campenhausen, *Ecclesiastical Authority*, 181; von Campenhausen, *Kirchliches Amt*, 198.

opposition. The abstruse character of its revelations, its fanatical rigorism [*der fanatische Rigorismus*], and above all the raving frenzy of its ecstasies [*die rasende Wildheit ihrer Ekstasen*] made men mistrustful of the genuineness of its spirit."[105] At about the same time, there had been an enormous threat to traditional or received doctrine from Gnosticism. Notoriously difficult to define due to its wide popularity and divergent doctrines, Gnosticism was a second-century spiritual syncretistic movement that attempted to siphon the themes of Christian stories through the narrow funnel of specialized forms of Greek metaphysics. From the deserts of Egypt where the third-century Gnostic Nag Hammadi codices were found in 1945 to the plains of Judea and even to the streets of Rome, Christians waged war against the ideas of fellow Christians who held rather dearly to their Greek metaphysical predilections. The response of the church authorities was to march against such heresies by solidifying the "truth" in the person of its leaders, especially the bishop.[106] The effect of this fight against Gnosticism was to "intensify conservative trends" as well as to solidify "the authority of the church officials."[107]

As the church moved into the third century, trends against Montanism and spirit-movements became rigidly set as institutional policy. More and more, the stalwarts of the church came to think like Hippolytus of Rome (170–235), who viewed the delay of Christ's second coming as the reason for the need of institutional stability through a hierarchy. Akin to this motif was the idea that prophecy ended with the last living apostle (John).[108] Combine these two concepts—namely, a delayed parousia that required a church hierarchy and a cessation of prophecy in the living church—and the early church possessed a recipe for diminishment of both the Spirit's life-giving role in the body of Christ and any significant theological reflection on the doctrine of the Spirit. The view of Hippolytus became the accepted, default position of the church. Stanley Burgess provides this insight on the development:

> By the third century the free, spontaneous, uprushing spiritual life was giving way in a Church which was rapidly developing a fixed rule of faith and a closed canon of divine oracles, governed by an order of bishops established by an

105. Von Campenhausen, *Ecclesiastical Authority*, 182; von Campenhausen, *Kirchliches Amt*, 199–200.

106. While this may not have been the universal response of the church at this time to the threat of Gnosticism, it was a rather predominant voice.

107. Von Campenhausen, *Ecclesiastical Authority*, 186; von Campenhausen, *Kirchliches Amt*, 204.

108. Stanley M. Burgess, *The Holy Spirit: Ancient Christian Traditions* (Peabody, MA: Hendrickson, 1984), 52. Burgess notes that these ideas come from Hippolytus's *Treatise on Christ and Antichrist* and the *Commentary on Daniel*.

external rule of succession. The prophet ruling by revelation was giving way to the bishop ruling with authority. The free and spontaneous exercise of the charismata was being replaced by an inflexible system of form and ritual. In this environment it was impossible for the New Prophecy to exist side by side with the new order without experiencing great tension.[109]

One substantial result of the emphasis on hierarchy in the church was the downplaying of the role of the congregation of believers as the priesthood of God. As Tom Greggs has noted, "Accounts of the essential hierarchy of the church invariably tend towards accounts not of the corporate 'rule of the priests' or the whole body's priesthood but of the primacy of (or at best a preference for) a given polity as the (or a) marker of the true church."[110]

The Priesthood of Believers

Up to this point in my study, I have dealt mainly with the early centuries and the rather sharp turn by the institutional Christian church away from the universal priesthood of believers and the "radical egalitarianism" of the Spirit among them to ever-expanding eddies of institutional hierarchy. With Constantine, the late antique period of the Greco-Roman world also saw the folding of the Christian church under the wing of the empire. The changes from the simple congregations of house churches in the first century to the complex system of clerical offices and hegemonic power of a state church have been well documented. For our purposes, we can easily grasp that the system of the institution continued in its trajectory away from the gifts and operation of the Spirit among God's people to rather rigid legalities that would result in the medieval system of canon law.

Therefore, we move from the third century CE to the development in the sixteenth century that powerfully influences a Protestant theology of ministry and a Protestant ecclesiology. It is a biblical motif that I have already noted in the previous chapter. While the concept of a universal priesthood of believers is clearly depicted in the New Testament, the full ramification of its significance must wait until centuries later—indeed, until the Protestant Reformation, and in particular the theology of Martin Luther.[111] In his

---

109. Burgess, *Holy Spirit*, 52.
110. Greggs, *Dogmatic Ecclesiology*, 1:124.
111. For a general overview of Luther's view of the priesthood of believers, see Cyril Eastwood, *The Priesthood of All Believers: An Examination of the Doctrine from the Reformation to the Present Day* (Eugene, OR: Wipf & Stock, 1960), esp. 1–65. Eastwood attempts to trace Luther's concept beyond the Reformer through Calvin, Anglicanism, and Wesleyanism to the

early Reformation writings, Luther presented the rather novel view that all of God's people, not merely one particular class, are a kingdom of priests. "Therefore we are all priests [*sacerdotes*], as many of us as are Christians."[112] It is our Christian baptism that has given us this shared status of the priesthood with Christ, for "all of us that have been baptized are equally [*aequaliter*] priests."[113] Whoever is a Christian, therefore, must "be assured of this, that we are all equally priests."[114] The anointing oil of the Holy Spirit (*oleo sancti spiritus*) has been placed on every Christian, anointing and sanctifying (*unctus et sanctificatus*) them for the work of priests before God.[115] The Romanists have torn apart the people of God by setting the sacrament of ordination as the demarcation between clergy and laity, asserting that some indelible mark (*caracteris indelibilis*) has been eternally

---

present. While there are traces of this history, the universal priesthood of believers remains muted in Protestantism throughout the past five hundred years. For a succinct rehearsal of this history, see Greggs, *Dogmatic Ecclesiology,* 1:121–22. For one way to conceive how this universal priesthood may be restored to a primary position in the church, see Robert A. Muthiah, *The Priesthood of All Believers in the Twenty-First Century: Living Faithfully as the Whole People of God in a Postmodern Context* (Eugene, OR: Pickwick, 2009).

112. Martin Luther, *The Babylonian Captivity of the Church (1520)*, trans. A. T. W. Steinhäuser, Frederick C. Ahrens, and Abdel Ross Wentz, in *Luther's Works*, ed. Helmut T. Lehmann, vol. 36, *Word and Sacrament II*, ed. Abdel Ross Wentz (Philadelphia: Fortress, 1959), 113; for the Latin, see Luther, *De captivitate babylonica ecclesiae praeludium*, in WA 6:564, 11.

113. Luther, *Babylonian Captivity*, 112; Luther, *De captivitate babylonica*, in WA 6:564, 6.

114. Luther, *Babylonian Captivity,* 116. Luther expresses similar ideas throughout his writings. He says, "Christ is a priest, therefore Christians are priests." Martin Luther, *Concerning the Ministry (1523)*, trans. Conrad Bergendoff, in *Luther's Works*, ed. Helmut T. Lehmann, vol. 40, *Church and Ministry II*, ed. Conrad Bergendoff (Philadelphia: Fortress, 1958), 20; for the Latin, see Luther, *De instituendis ministris ecclesiae ad clarissimum Senatum Pragensem Bohemiae*, in *Varii Argumenti, Ad Reformationis Historiam (1521–1523)*, ed. Henricus Schmidt, vol. 6, *D. Martini Lutheri Opera Latina* (Frankfurt am Main: Heyderi et Zimmeri, 1872), 508. And again "All Christians are priests in equal degree [*aequo*]." Luther, *Concerning the Ministry (1523)*, 21; Luther, *De instituendis ministris ecclesiae*, 509. Also, the Scriptures "makes all of us equal priests." Luther, *Answer to the Hyperchristian, Hyperspiritual, and Hyper-learned Book by Goat Emser in Leipzig—Including Some Thoughts Regarding His Companion, the Fool Murner (1521)*, trans. Eric W. Gritsch and Ruth C. Gritsch, in *Luther's Works*, ed. Helmut T. Lehmann, vol. 39, *Church and Ministry I*, ed. Eric W. Gritsch (Philadelphia: Fortress, 1970), 154; Luther, *Auf das überchristlich, übergeistlich und überkünstlich Buch Bocks Emsers zu Leipzig Antwort. Darin auch Murnarrs seines Gesellen gedacht wird (1521)*, in WA 7:630, 10–11. Also in this work, "Nowhere is it [ministry] called 'priesthood' [*sacerdocium*] or 'spiritual' [*spiritualis*]." Luther, *Answer to the Hyperchristian*, 154; WA 7:630, 13–14; and "All of us in the whole mass of people [*mit dem ganzen Hausen*] are priests without the consecration of the bishop." Luther, *Answer to the Hyperchristian*, 157; WA 7:633, 16–17; and finally, "Yet all of us are in a common church [*ein gemeyn Kirche*]; we are all spiritual [clergy] and priests, to the extent that we believe in Christ." Luther, *Answer to the Hyperchristian*, 159; WA 7:634, 23.

115. Luther, *Babylonian Captivity*, 115; Luther, *De captivitate babylonica*, in WA 6:566, 16–17.

set upon them in ordination.[116] Luther makes the following sober judgment: "Here, indeed, are the roots of that detestable tyranny of the clergy over the laity."[117]

It was clear to Luther, however, that this was no simple semantic shift from laity to clergy or from laity to priesthood. Centuries of class distinction within the religious orders and worldly realms had taken root in the rich soil of medieval feudalism. Writing to the German nobles in 1520, Luther made clear that such class distinction in which the clergy were considered a separate status (the "spiritual estate") from the laity (the "worldly estate") was the "first wall" that Rome had built that needed tearing down. According to Rome, all bishops, priests, and monks belonged to the "spiritual or religious estate" (*der geistliche Stand*) while princes, lords, artisans, and farmers belonged to the "secular or worldly estate" (*der weltliche Stand*).[118] For Luther, such structures were a "piece of deceit."[119] Therefore, "all Christians are truly of spiritual status, and there is no difference among them except that of office."[120] We all receive one baptism, one gospel, and one faith; it is these three things alone that make us Christians and therefore make all Christians a part of the "spiritual estate."[121] "For whoever has crawled out of the water of baptism can boast that he is already a consecrated priest, bishop, and pope, even though it is not seemly that just anybody should exercise such an office."[122]

> Here even in the New Testament, the Holy Spirit carefully refrains from giving the name *sacerdos* or priest, or cleric [*pfaffe*] or still any other office to any apostle; rather, the Spirit only gives the name "the baptized" or "Christians,"

116. Luther, *Babylonian Captivity*, 117; Luther, *De captivitate babylonica*, in WA 6:567, 22–23.

117. Luther, *Babylonian Captivity*, 112; Luther, *De captivitate babylonica*, in WA 6:563, 31–33.

118. Martin Luther, *To the Christian Nobility of the German Nation concerning the Improvement of the Christian Estate* (1520), trans. Charles M. Jacobs, James Atkinson, and James M. Estes, in *The Annotated Luther*, ed. Hans J. Hillerbrand, Kirsi I. Stjerna, and Timothy J. Wengert, vol. 1, *The Roots of Reform*, ed. Timothy J. Wengert (Minneapolis: Fortress, 2015), 381. For the German, see Luther, *An den christlichen Adel deutscher Nation: von des christlichen Standes Besserung* (1520), in *Reformatorische Schriften I, Luthers Werke*, ed. Prof. Buchwald et al., 3rd ed. (Berlin: Schwetschke und Sohn, 1905), 208.

119. Luther, *To the Christian Nobility of the German Nation*, 381.

120. Luther, *To the Christian Nobility of the German Nation*, 381.

121. Luther, *To the Christian Nobility of the German Nation*, 382.

122. Luther, *To the Christian Nobility of the German Nation*, 383. Luther continues by adding that no one should "push himself forward and take it upon himself" to be placed in these offices in the church. They must be elected and given the consent of fellow believers in the congregation.

as a name, which exists from (new) birth and inherited from baptism. For in baptism none of us is born an apostle, a preacher, a teacher, or a pastor, but rather we all are born simply priests and clerics. We take some out of those who were born priests and call or select [*berüfft odder erwelet*] them to such offices so that they may manage [*richten sollen*] these offices on behalf of us all.[123]

Hence, the conclusion that Luther presses toward is this: there is no difference between clergy and laity in terms of status; people are not better or worthy of greater honor *simply* because they are members of the clergy. While those who are hard at work among God's people are to be respected and honored for their work, this is not merely due to their clergy status. There are different officeholders and different tasks among God's people, but there must not be a difference of position or cultural status.[124] "A cobbler, a blacksmith, a peasant—each has the work and office of his trade, and yet they are all alike consecrated priests and bishops, and everyone should benefit and serve everyone else by means of their own work or office, so that in this way many kinds of work may be done for the bodily and spiritual welfare of the community, just as all the members of the body serve one another."[125]

123. Luther, *Von der Winkelmesse und der Pfaffenweihe* [On the private masses and consecration of priests] *(1533)*, in WA 38:230, 13–20 (my translation).

124. I recognize that the Reformation scholar Brian A. Gerrish has argued that Luther has some apparent inconsistency in his writings regarding the priesthood of all believers and the "ordained ministers." He notes that Luther uses the universal priesthood in writings mainly to attack Rome's view of the priesthood. Hence, most of the early treatises and several others that I have quoted above argue for the leveling of the clergy class so that all believers stand equal in Christ. See Gerrish, "Priesthood and Ministry: Luther's Fifth Means of Grace," in *The Old Protestantism and the New: Essays on the Reformation Heritage* (London: T&T Clark, 1982), 92. However, in 1523, Gerrish notes, questions come to Luther concerning electing pastors and obtaining ministers when there is no bishop available in the usual sense. Luther responds that if a bishop does not make provisions for a ministry of the Word, then the congregation (as part of the common priesthood) should speak the Word. In response to a Bohemian church, Luther states something similar. Then in 1532, Luther speaks again regarding "furtive preachers" (*Winkelpredigern*) who do not respect the *Pfaher* (clergyperson) and the position of the *Leyen* (laity) but would allow any "drunk from the tavern" to chime in (Gerrish, "Priesthood and Ministry," 93). Yet in 1533, Luther returns to the fact that all Christians make up the priesthood—they are "born" priests, not made so. Gerrish explains these issues in context yet concludes that the apparent incoherency in Luther's discussion of priesthood and ministry is due to the various issues and parties he was addressing throughout his career. Hence, Luther maintains the need for a "professional minister" but does not support such ministers if they usurp the priestly rights of the people of God (Gerrish, "Priesthood and Ministry," 104). For my purposes, however, I do not find Luther's apparent inconsistency on these issues to diminish his strong statements on the priesthood of all believers. Instead, I find he tries to maintain some level of order in the church by having ministers recognize their position and function without creating a separate clergy class.

125. Luther, *To the Christian Nobility of the German Nation*, 384.

Luther challenged the concept of ordination to the priesthood as problematic because it tended to give priests a sense of qualitative difference between themselves and the laity due to the *indelibis caracteris*. For Luther, then, "this mask of ordination [*illa ordinationis larva*] is unnecessary."[126] In a sermon from 1525, Luther asserts, "Christ is a priest with all his Christians. This priesthood is not created or ordained [*nicht Machen odder ordenen*]. Here no one is made a priest [*ist gemachter priester*]. He must be born a priest and bring with him the inheritance [*erblich*] from his birth. I am thinking about the new birth from water and Spirit. There all Christians become such priests of the highest priest [*des höhisten priester*], children and joint-heirs with Christ."[127] Christian priests cannot be "made" but must be born anew by the Spirit. "For a priest, especially in the New Testament, was not made but was born [*non fit, sed nascitur*]. He was created, not ordained [*non ordinatur, sed creatur*]. . . . Indeed, all Christians are priests, and all priests are Christians."[128] Christians are "born to the ministry of the Word in baptism [*ad verbi ministerium natus e baptismo*]."[129]

What are the duties of a priest? In his treatise to the Bohemian church in 1523, Luther lists seven responsibilities:

1. ministry of the Word, which is common to all Christians (21),
2. to baptize (23),
3. to consecrate the bread and wine (24),
4. binding and loosing from sin (25),
5. to sacrifice (28),
6. to pray for others (29), and
7. to judge and pass on doctrines (31).[130]

126. Martin Luther, *Concerning the Ministry (1523)*, 20; for the Latin, Luther, *De instituendis ministris ecclesiae*, 508.

127. Martin Luther, "Warumb das?," in *Fastenpostille 1525*, WA 17^{11}:6, 30–35 (my translation).

128. Martin Luther, *Concerning the Ministry (1523)*, 19; for the Latin, Luther, *De instituendis ministris ecclesiae*, 507.

129. Luther, *Concerning the Ministry (1523)*, 37; Luther, *De instituendis ministris ecclesiae*, 527.

130. The page numbers after each of the seven responsibilities are from Luther, *Concerning the Ministry (1523)*. Later in this same text, Luther will state clearly the connection between the Word of God and the church: the church owes its "birth to the Word, is nourished, aided and strengthened by it" (*Nam cum ecclesia verbo Dei nascatur, alatur, servetur et roboretur, palam est, eam sine verbo esse non posse, aut si sine verbo sit, ecclesiam esse disinere*). Luther, *Concerning the Ministry (1523)*, 37; Luther, *De instituendis ministris ecclesiae*, 527. Hence, it is obvious that the church cannot be without the Word, because "if it [a church] is without the Word it ceases to be a church." Luther, *Concerning the Ministry (1523)*, 37; *De instituendis ministris ecclesiae*, 527.

All of these seven responsibilities belong to every Christian. Hence, "There is no other Word of God than that which is given to all Christians to proclaim."[131] No other baptism than "the one which any Christian can bestow."[132] There is no other sacrifice than "of the body of every Christian."[133] These responsibilities discharged to all Christians "make the priestly and royal office."[134] This is not an estate or order but only the office and function. There is no "indelible stamp" or "character" etched in the soul of an ordained priest forever, making some qualitative difference between the clergyperson and a layperson.[135] How, then, are we to have ministers or clergy? Luther states that the way to distinguish between the office of preaching/ministry and the general priesthood of baptized believers is that the preaching office is a "public service" that is conferred on someone "by the entire congregation," in which all the members "are priests."[136]

Luther underscores his preference for the use of the word "priests" in relation to Christians: "Therefore I would be very happy if this word 'priests' were just as common as that which they call us when they say 'Christians.' For it is all one and the same thing: priest, baptized, Christian."[137] In essence, what I propose in this book is a working out in practice what Luther has stated in theory.[138]

131. Luther, *Concerning the Ministry (1523)*, 34; Luther, *De instituendis ministris ecclesiae*, 524.
132. Luther, *Concerning the Ministry (1523)*, 35; Luther, *De instituendis ministris ecclesiae*, 524.
133. Luther, *Concerning the Ministry (1523)*, 35; Luther, *De instituendis ministris ecclesiae*, 525.
134. Luther, *Concerning the Ministry (1523)*, 35; Luther, *De instituendis ministris ecclesiae*, 525.
135. Luther, *Concerning the Ministry (1523)*, 35; Luther, *De instituendis ministris ecclesiae*, 525.
136. Martin Luther, *Predigten des Jahres 1535*, in WA 41:210, 25–27.
137. Martin Luther, *Epistel S. Petri gepredigt und ausgelegt (1523)*, in WA 12:317, 9–11 (my translation).
138. I use the words "in theory" in relation to Luther's doctrine of the universal priesthood of believers because his attempt to put it into practice seems limited. In *The People of God's Presence*, I mention that in Luther's early Reformation years he had made consideration for producing a small, pure band of devout believers, which he called an *ecclesiola* (little gathering), instead of *ecclesia* (the church). See Terry L. Cross, *The People of God's Presence: An Introduction to Ecclesiology* (Grand Rapids: Baker Academic, 2019), 22. As George H. Williams has noted, "The believers' church has some of the characteristics of an *ecclesiola in ecclesia*." See George H. Williams, "A People in Community: Historical Background," in *The Concept of the Believers' Church: Addresses from the 1968 Louisville Conference*, ed. James Leo Garrett Jr. (Scottdale, PA: Herald, 1969), 100. In one treatise, Luther provides a glimpse as to what such a small gathering of committed Christians might look like. See Martin Luther, *Liturgy and Hymns*, ed. S. Leupold, in *Luther's Works*, ed. Helmut T. Lehman (Philadelphia: Fortress, 1965), 53:53–55. He also provides a theology of ministry by noting *how* churches may elect representatives to do the work of preaching and sacraments. See *Daß eine christliche Versammlung oder Gemeinde Recht und Macht habe, alle Lehre zu Beurteilen und Lehre zu berufen, ein- und abzusetzen: Grund und Ursache aus der Schrift (1523)*, in *Martin Luther: Kirche und Gemeinde, Luther Deutsch: Die Werke Martin Luthers in neuer Auswahl für die Gegenwart*, vol. 6, ed. Kurt Aland (Göttingen: Vandenhoeck & Ruprecht, 1983), 52–55. Also, compare two sources on

Summary Points

The study in these two chapters on biblical and historical background to ministry has attempted to demonstrate several important points, which I will summarize. First, the concept of ministry in the New Testament is a descriptor used for leading and serving functions in the church. From the various words for ministry, we can see some sense of a commissioning for *all* believers to participate in sharing the message of reconciliation. To be sure, there are some "called" to serve as apostles, prophets, evangelists, pastors, and teachers; others as elders, overseers, and servers (early deacons). Yet the predominant theme of the New Testament is that all the people of God have been entrusted with the ministry of reconciliation, carrying the message of the good news of salvation to the world. Thus, the first crucial concept we can take from principles in the New Testament church for today is that ministry is for all God's people. To use Peter's language, all of the people of God are priests. To use Luther's language, all believers form the universal priesthood in Christianity.

Second, leadership in the congregations of first-century churches seemed to be plural. While I recognize that this remains only a hypothesis that cannot be proved beyond doubt, I do believe it is clearly demonstrated to an acceptable degree of feasibility in the texts themselves so that it can become a principle guiding the church today. All references to church leaders are cited in the plural—with the exception of 1 Timothy 3:2 and Titus 1:7. Yet even these singular terms can be explained as "apparent rather than real because the article is probably generic."[139] Leading God's people requires a plurality rather than a singularity.

Third, there remains for the people of God *no mediatorial priesthood*—no priestly caste over against a lay caste. Each person is brought into a relationship with God through Jesus Christ, our High Priest, so that we may have direct access to the presence of God, boldly coming to the throne of grace without the need of a human mediator. This principle shatters the human structures in the church today that tend to separate the whole people of God

---

Luther and ministry: Gerd Haendler, *Luther on Ministerial Office and Congregational Function*, ed. Eric Gritsch, trans. Ruth Gritsch (Philadelphia: Fortress, 1981), and Hellmut Lieberg, *Amt und Ordination bei Luther und Melanchthon* (Göttingen: Vandenhoeck & Ruprecht, 1962). Although old, the work of Gerhard Hilbert remains a classic: *Ecclesiola in Ecclesia: Luthers Anschauungen von Volkskirche und Freiwilligkeitskirche in ihrer Bedeutung für die Gegenwart* (Leipzig: Deichert, 1920), esp. 1–3. Hilbert argues that Luther wanted *ecclesiola* to be realized in practice but did not place it into the working embodiment of the church.

139. Hatch, *The Organization of the Early Christian Church*, 83. The point seems to be that "the bishop" or "the elder" in these passages is "generic" because the qualifications for becoming one such functionary is being lifted up. This makes perfect sense.

into clergy-laity—in effect, two classes with different responsibilities and re-lationships with God.

Fourth, the changes in the leadership structure from the first-century church to the third-century church are understandable, given the external pressures of strange doctrines circulating as truth. However, the changes morphed beyond the *regula fidei* of the apostolic teaching and into something more akin to monarchical control. Surely Paul would not have recognized the bishop of the *Didascalia*, whom Faivre wryly describes as "omnipotent."[140] Somewhere be-tween the second and third centuries, the *episkopos* had moved from a position of primacy among the circle of *presbyteroi* to a position of supremacy over them—and everyone else in his church.[141] There certainly are historical reasons for why some of this authority shifted, but the clear rationale for this historical movement is lost to us now. It is possible that Alistair Stewart has offered the best historical rationale for the position of a singular *episkopos* (monepisco-pacy) gaining supremacy within a large city among other *episkopoi* (who in their individual congregations were "bishops" but in the gathered group of bishops were called *presbyteroi*), but even he acknowledges the hypothetical nature of such a reconstructive history.[142] What we have established as the pressing need for a presiding officer over the eucharistic celebration seems to be an urgent force toward limiting those who could serve this capacity. When we combine the analogous relation of church offices with the Levitical system of the Old Testament, the idea of a priestly caste returns. This would play out in terms of the bishop as high priest, the presbyters as priests, and the deacons as the Levites serving in the temple, not as priests but as special servants. The dignity (ἀξία | *axia*) and honor that is given to those presiding over the Eucharist meant that no laypeople could grab this holy task on their own.[143] The history of the first five centuries of the Christian church should demonstrate that it is impossible to have a fully functioning priesthood of believers alongside a priestly caste. Hence, the question of how this could look today remains one task for the remainder of this book.

Fifth, the character traits of the leaders in the New Testament are clearly offered in several passages. I would suggest that these traits combine to form a leader who serves—that is, someone who guides the local congregation in their mission in the world by operating like a shepherd among the flock. Here

140. Faivre, *The Emergence of the Laity*, 89.
141. Hatch, *The Organization of the Early Christian Churches*, 91. The comparison between "primacy" and "supremacy" was Hatch's point.
142. Stewart, *The Original Bishops*, esp. chaps. 4 and 5.
143. Hatch, *The Organization of the Early Christian Churches*, 140. Hatch cites the *Constitutions of the Holy Apostles* 3.10, in *ANF* 7:429.

the example of Jesus Christ to his disciples is crucial: "I am among you as one who serves" (Luke 22:27). Such service is most evident in the entire mission of his incarnate life and his submission to the death of the cross (Phil. 2:6–8). If one is going to be a *Christian* leader, one must incarnate such reversal of worldly power and learn to serve others.

A final summary point lies in the historical development of an either/or response to spiritual leadership. What do I mean by this? Either the church allowed *charismata* to hold authority for its people or it required *institutional offices* to lead the people. What if the relation between the charismatic gifts of the Spirit and the institutional offices for leadership were not either/or but of dialectical tension? What if the people of God's presence were meant to walk together "in the Spirit" while following the lead of qualified individuals who were "full of the Spirit" (as were Stephen and Philip)?

I believe that the gifts of the Spirit to the church *include* leading or governing charismata. Gifts were meant to be not in opposition but complementary to each other—indeed, working *with* each other for the sake of the body of Christ and the mission of the church. It remains to be seen how and if such a pneumatic ecclesiology can work in today's world. I propose that only something this radical can resurrect the life of the people of God in gathered community. Our theology of the church requires a re-formation of a theology of ministry. It is to that task we now turn.

Toward a Theology of Ministry among God's People

Introduction to Ministry as Serving

Having established in the previous chapters that ministry belongs to all the people of God, we turn now to consider what such ministry might look like in practice today. Questions may rightly be asked about such a proposal. If everyone is a minister, does anyone lead? If all believers are engaged in ministry, what does that mean for "clergy" or ordained ministers? How do pastors fit in this scheme—if at all? Does not such a proposal open the church to chaos rather than order?

While I will try to answer these and other related concerns in the remainder of this book, I want to address several issues that can be settled here. To say that a pneumatic ecclesiology like the one I have proposed is without leaders is to miss the point of the previous two chapters. The people of God always need leaders—people gifted, called, and appointed by God and the people of God to serve a particular function among them. However, to allow for such leaders does not require that we create a distinct class of clergy who are considered "priests" before God on behalf of the people of God. The people of God's direct presence have experienced an encounter with God that has begun a transformation in their lives, inserting them into the body of Christ and gifting them with spiritual gifts to serve others (1 Pet. 4:10). Here they begin to learn the way of being Christian in today's world among other believers in the local congregation. In this context, they are *directly encountered* by God's Spirit and need no special mediator between God and them (other than

Christ). Therefore, leaders in the Christian congregation must not derogate the priesthood of all believers through any action or attitude that might call into question the full weight of that status. Leaders serve the local body of Christ in a manner that reflects their Lord's servitude among humans.

Frequently, when humans speak of leadership, they are referring to the authority or power of someone *over* others. Undoubtedly, this is because of the way humans experience authority or power. As we saw in the previous chapters, this was not the way of Christ. Followers of Christ are to recognize that they are to be servants of others because that was the way Christ operated while on earth (Luke 22:27). What kind of power or authority is *Christian* power? It is the power of the incarnate, crucified, and risen Lord.

Paul addresses the issue of power to the church in Corinth: "For the message of the cross is foolishness [μωρία | *mōria*] to those who are perishing, but to us who are being saved it is the power [δύναμις | *dynamis*] of God" (1 Cor. 1:18). The cross of Christ is senseless to unbelievers; they cannot grasp the fact that God has turned reality on its head so that now their wisdom is foolishness and God's apparent foolishness is truly wisdom. "Has not God made foolish the wisdom of the world?" (1 Cor. 1:20). Yet Paul does not simply make a contrast between foolishness and wisdom; he adds to God's wisdom the concept of *power*. Believers who are in the process of being saved (σῳζομένοις | *sōzomenois*)[1] acknowledge that the event of the cross-resurrection is the power that delivers from sin. As such it is also the wisdom of God. Hence, the power that saves us is not power in any usual human use of that term. This is a power whose strength is made perfect in weakness, whose might is measured not in terms of size or number but in terms of the "weakness" of the cross. It must have seemed like foolishness when Jesus told his disciples in the garden to put away their swords, but it was the power of God unto salvation. It must have seemed like foolishness when Jesus stood beaten and bruised in silence before his accusers, but it was the wisdom of God. It must have seemed like moronic obstinacy when Jesus refused to call a legion of angels to rescue him from the cross, but it was the wisdom and power of God. "Like nothing else, the event of the cross forever shatters the equation of divine powers of this world with oppressive rule and self-aggrandizing mastery over others."[2] For those of us who are

---

1. This verb is a present passive participle, laying emphasis on the progressive nature of the event of salvation (the present participle) and the passive nature of the action (passive voice): "are being saved."

2. Daniel L. Migliore, *The Power of God and the gods of Power* (Louisville: Westminster John Knox, 2008), 52. The comments before this quotation were spawned by Migliore's own presentation on the cross (52).

being delivered from the grip of the god of this age, Christ is "the power of God and the wisdom of God" (1 Cor. 1:24). To be sure, the power of God is also evident in the demonstration of God's might over death and the grave through the resurrection of Jesus Christ. Nevertheless, were it not for the reversal of power as seen in the incarnation and the cross, the triumphant power of the resurrection would have been muted. Indeed, salvation requires the incarnation, death, and resurrection of Jesus the Christ in order to deliver humans from the chains of the tyrannical power of sin. As Daniel Migliore states, "From the sickness of seeking mastery and control over others, God can save us only by the exercise of a wholly different kind of power—the power of suffering love."[3] By laying down his life like a lamb headed to the slaughter, Jesus "refuses to play the power games of this world. He turns away from the never-ending cycle of violence against violence."[4] The cross-resurrection event redefines for us what the power of God means. Sin's power is coercive and oppressive, but Christ's power demonstrates freedom over sin's tyranny, allowing us to dance joyfully together in God's fields of grace.

What does all of this discussion about power have to do with a theology of ministry and a re-formation of the structure of the church? It will come as no surprise that among Christians today, churchgoers have some harrowing stories where spiritual authority became abusive.[5] On some occasions, leaders have abused followers of Christ because of a structure that provided too much power in one person or a small group of people; on other occasions, leaders have fallen into a quagmire of thinking that the people of God somehow belonged to them. Whatever the reason for spiritual abuse of authority, when it occurs, the underlying theological pattern of Christ's reversal of power has been ignored or misunderstood.

Leading is a matter of serving, not of power over others. This is the radical dimension of Christian leadership. Leading the people of God's presence is not a matter of earthly power or authority by which those who rule the church are placed in an over/under relationship of domination. Leading the people of God's presence means serving God's people in ways of guiding, comforting, advising, directing, and managing the affairs of the gathered people of God. Paul asks the Thessalonians to acknowledge and respect "those who work hard among you [τοὺς κοπιῶντας ἐν ὑμῖν | *tous kopiōntas en hymin*], who

---

3. Migliore, *The Power of God and the gods of Power*, 75.
4. Migliore, *The Power of God and the gods of Power*, 53.
5. See especially in this regard David Johnson and Jeff Vonderen, *The Subtle Power of Spiritual Abuse: Recognizing and Escaping Spiritual Manipulation and False Spiritual Authority within the Church* (Minneapolis: Bethany House, 1991).

care for you [προϊσταμένους ὑμῶν | *proistamenous hymōn*] in the Lord and who admonish you [νουθετοῦντας ὑμᾶς | *nouthetountas hymas*]. Hold them in the highest regard in love because of their work. Live in peace with each other" (1 Thess. 5:12–13). The three aspects of leadership that are highlighted here are these:

1. those who work hard among you (τοὺς κοπιῶντας ἐν ὑμῖν | *tous kopiōntas en hymin*),
2. those who care for you (προϊσταμένους ὑμῶν | *proistamenous hymōn*), and
3. those who admonish you (νουθετοῦντας ὑμᾶς | *nouthetountas hymas*).

First, the Thessalonians were charged "to know" or "to acknowledge" (εἰδέναι | *eidenai*) those who "labor" (NRSV) or "work hard" (NIV) among them. Leading through serving is arduous, exhausting work.[6] It requires knowing well the people that one leads, which in turn means living with them in order to serve them. It is interesting that for each of these three actions, Paul couches them in terms of the brothers and sisters "knowing" or "acknowledging" those who perform them. While knowing the people one leads is a prerequisite for leading God's church, a corresponding knowing is required of the people in response. Moreover, the word "you" (plural) is iterated three times—one for each verb. The people of God know quite well when leaders are in their position for themselves instead of "for you all." They also sense when leaders lay down their lives for them by sharing their own lives with them in work, in caretaking, and in guidance. Therefore, holding leaders who perform these actions in "the highest regard in love because of their work" comes about because both leaders and the people know each other so well. Although such leading is wearisome work, Christ has called leaders and followers to "come to me, all you who are weary [οἱ κοπιῶντες | *hoi kopiōntes*][7] and burdened, and I will give you rest. Take my yoke upon you and learn from me, for I am gentle and humble in heart, and you will find rest for your souls. For my yoke is easy and my burden is light" (Matt. 11:28–30).

Second, the Thessalonians were to know those "who care for you" (NIV) or "have charge of you" (NRSV) or are "over you" (ESV; NKJV) or "preside over you" (NET), or "lead you" (HCSB; NCV) in the Lord. In chapter 1, we studied this word (προΐστημι | *proistēmi*) extensively in relation to the function of elders. While this word has the idea of "rank" or "rule" within its

---

6. S.v. "κοπιάω," BDAG, 444, where the first meaning is "become weary, tired."
7. Notice that the same word (κοπιάω | *kopiaō*) is used in Matt. 11:28 as in 1 Thess. 5:12.

semantic range of meaning, I posited earlier that a synonym used in 1 Timothy 3:5 (ἐπιμελήσεται | *epimelēsetai*, which means "to take care of") narrows the meaning away from "rule over" and toward "take care of." If candidates for ἐπίσκοπος | *episkopos* cannot "manage the affairs" of their own families, how can they "take care of" the church? The only other place where this synonym (ἐπιμελήσεται | *epimelēsetai*) is used in the New Testament is when the Good Samaritan bandaged the victim's wounds, put him on his donkey, brought him to an inn, and "took care of him" (Luke 10:34). Hence, to define this word used for leaders (elders and deacons in 1 Tim. 3) as meaning "rule" or "preside over" misses the context of first-century congregations in which leadership was not over/under but service to and care for those who are in the flock of God.[8] Within this verb for "rule" there is "management," to be sure, but it is management with care—not some roughshod rule over others. In this way, respect is due to the leaders of God's people because they lead the way in taking care of others in the congregation. This, too, is hard work that can create weariness.

Third, the Thessalonians were to know those who "admonish you" (NIV; NRSV) or "give you instruction" (NASB) or "teach you" (NCV). While each of these terms is a possible translation for νουθετέω | *noutheteō*, the seven other times it is used in the New Testament seem to lean toward the idea of warning, as it does immediately after the passage we are considering: "Warn [νουθετεῖτε | *noutheteite*] those who are idle and disruptive, encourage the disheartened, help the weak, be patient with everyone" (1 Thess. 5:14). An important task of leaders is to watch out for the flock, especially with regard to dangers the flock may not see themselves. Giving instruction that warns believers of the potential pitfalls to faith in the world where they live and work demands the wisdom of God to understand it and the grace of God to share it meaningfully.

While this is not an exhaustive list of leaders' functions in the church, it certainly provides a solid foundation for building such a list. From the language of this passage, it is clear that leaders should know their people and the people should know their leaders. Only in this reciprocal environment can there be genuine leadership that provides caring guidance for the work of ministry in the congregation. Leaders in the body of Christ are not "bosses," but rather are servants who manage the affairs of the church well by demonstrating their care for the flock of God (1 Tim. 5:17). Such leading through serving provides the local body of Christ a pattern for their own ministry to

---

8. S.v. "προΐστημι," BDAG, 713–14, where the first meaning is "to be at the head of, rule, direct," but the second meaning is "be concerned about, care for, give aid."

others. Service is at the core of *all* ministry, whether that of leaders or of all the people of God.

A Ministry of "Making Room" for the Other

What do I mean when I state that all God's people are to do the work of ministry? Since all believers are part of the corporate priesthood of Christ, all believers have functions to perform in the church and world on Christ's behalf. Ministry is birthed out of the regenerative operation of the Spirit in our lives and out of the gifts of the Spirit planted in us. Ministry is not relegated to a rarified number of specially called individuals in the church; ministry is the service of God's people that we were meant to perform. "For we are God's handiwork, created in Christ Jesus to do good works, which God prepared in advance for us to do [προητοίμασεν ὁ κρισθέντες ... ἵνα ἐν αὐτοῖς περιπατήσωμεν | *proētoimasen ho kristhentes . . . hina en autois peripatēsōmen*]" (Eph. 2:10).[9] At least one aspect of the "good works" planned by God for us to perform lies in the "works of service" or "work of ministry" (Eph. 4:12). In the body of Christ, no one is called to be a spectator; all are called to do the work of ministry (ἔργον διακονίας | *ergon diakonias*). How are we all to do this? Does not such "ministry" require training? Are not ministers supposed to be "called" into such work?

While I strongly urge all leaders in the body of Christ to receive academic and professional training, I do not presuppose that all ministry in a local congregation will need to be performed by such leaders. The leaders are to "equip the saints for the work of ministry" (Eph. 4:12 NRSV). The words translated "to equip" (πρὸς τὸν καταρτισμὸν | *pros ton katartismon*) have the sense of making perfect adjustments or adaptations so that something or someone is qualified for a purpose. The verb form is used in Matthew 4:21 for "mending their nets" (NRSV). Leaders repair the weaknesses or gaps in the lives of God's people so that they may be completely qualified to do the work of ministry, thereby building up the body of Christ as each part does its work (Eph. 4:16). Like the human body, the body of Christ grows through exercise. Such training of a congregation for ministry is not an easy task, especially since most places for educating pastors and leaders today do not provide training on how to teach the congregation to do the work of ministry. While I cannot provide a detailed plan for such an education here, I can

9. The verb περιπατήσωμεν | *peripatēsōmen* can mean "to walk" and as such is used in the NT to describe a way of life with a focus on one's conduct or behavior. Believers were created for good works in Christ so that they could walk them out—conduct their lives by doing them.

provide the rationale and some glimpses for what such a task may look like. It is to that task we now turn.

Christian Ministry Is an Extension of the Presence of God in Christian Worship

Training every believer to work together as the corporate priesthood of Christ has several components, the first of which is worship. As Hebrews 13:15 states, "Through Jesus, therefore, let us continually offer to God a sacrifice of praise—the fruit of lips that openly profess his name." In this statement, praise is connected to professing Christ's name; worship is connected with witness. Believers are priests whose central function is to worship God. The Spirit gathers God's people together for the purpose of worship or service of God.[10] When we enter God's presence together, united in praise and worship by the Spirit, we focus our attention on God; we *minister* or *serve* him. Our "common work," as Karl Barth calls it, is gathering for such worship (*CD* IV/2:638). As we magnify our God, God manifests himself in our gathering, doing things in the Spirit that can only be achieved by his power and presence. Believers learn to "make room for God's presence" among us. However, there is no formula to *make* God's presence show up among us. Worship cannot be a quid pro quo—an exchange of our gifts to God for the purpose of getting something in return. As Barth argued, "No human effort can ensure this divine encounter. But [humans] *can* clear the obstacles out of the way; and *this* is the purpose of church order."[11] Clark Pinnock offers this important point regarding presence: "Though present everywhere, Spirit can be more effectively present among those who know the risen Lord, can work there with greater intensity promoting human renewal."[12]

It is my contention that the ministry of bearing the presence of Christ to the world cannot be performed effectively without first ministering to God in the gathered presence of his people. To use Barth's trifold paradigm, the Spirit *gathers* the congregation together, *upbuilds* them in faith through worship and Word, and then *sends* them out into the world to do his bidding. However, it is Christian worship that is the "center" of Christian living and ministry.

10. The German word for worship is *Gottesdienst*, which in literal translation means "service of God." I have always found this comparable to the English phrase among Protestants of "worship service." However, I prefer the German nuance.

11. Karl Barth, "The Church—the Living Congregation of the Living Lord Jesus Christ," in *God Here and Now*, trans. Paul M. van Buren (New York: Harper & Row, 1964), 76 (his emphasis).

12. Clark Pinnock, *Flame of Love: A Theology of the Holy Spirit* (Downers Grove, IL: InterVarsity, 1996), 116.

From this center (*Mitte*), the community expands its influence to a "wider circle of the everyday life of Christians and their individual relationships" (*CD* IV/2:639; *KD* IV/2:723). If we bypass the "gathering" and "upbuilding" of the congregation by the Spirit and jump directly to the "sending," then our mission may become fraught with questionable motivations and priorities. Resting in God's presence and building each other up in the Lord establishes an intimacy with God and others that continually transforms us. We understand God's intentions and our own motivations better. "Responding to the Spirit, we move ever closer to God, shedding preoccupation with self and pursuing the true basis of our human life."[13] It is in the context of a community's praise and worship of God that it is "constantly reminded of the task or witness committed to it, and in which it prays constantly for the insight and strength with which to perform it, and for the world to which it has to direct it . . . by so doing" (*CD* IV/3.2:865–66).

By making room for God in worship, we are better posed to make room for God in service to others. Through the simplicity and profundity of worship, God adjusts our motivations to align more precisely with his. When we meditate, sing, pray, and offer intercession for others together in God's presence, we should not be surprised if we *hear* God together as well. The Spirit of God is at work in the community so that we learn how better to serve fellow humans by learning how better to serve God. W. A. Whitehouse has explained well how worship engages and changes believers:

> Faith expresses itself in worship, and worship is the surrender of human interests, in adoration, to a Lord whose influence upon the being and well-being of the worshippers they wholly accept and wholly trust. Because God blesses human beings in all acts of worship where self-preoccupation is lost in praise of His goodness, their "service to Him" is transmuted into a new experience of "being served." In this experience they are turned afresh towards neighbors on the other side, so to speak; towards their fellow [humans] whose cause God has made His own in Jesus Christ.[14]

In the context of gathered worship, the Spirit enlightens the community of believers so that it experiences "ongoing encounters with the source of its knowledge and confession, in its vitally necessary listening to the voice of the Good Shepherd" (*CD* IV/3.2:832). Such enlightenment by the Spirit

---

13. Pinnock, *Flame of Love*, 120.
14. W. A. Whitehouse, "Christological Understanding," in *Theological Foundations for Ministry: Selected Reading for a Theology of the Church in Ministry*, ed. Ray S. Anderson (Grand Rapids: Eerdmans, 1979), 224 (alt.).

is not unattached from the Word of God. Indeed, the Spirit works with and through the Word in order to enlighten, inform, and refresh God's people so that they may understand how better to speak the Word to humans they encounter. God's people must gather to hear the Word and encounter the Spirit in order to be built up in the faith. "The same Word which the community has to attest to the world will and must be continually heard afresh by it to its own constant gathering, upbuilding and sending" (*CD* IV/3.2:832).

Christian service to God (or worship) must have an inward direction before it can provide an outward ministry. Only as Christians are nourished in the Word can they provide adequate witness to it in the world. Therefore, edification in the Word through the Spirit among God's people is essential to any form of ministry. However, if such edification becomes the end goal, its service becomes "an institution for private satisfaction in concert, or a work of sterile inbreeding" (*CD* IV/3.2:833). The church must recognize that the goal of being nourished by God in worship and through the Word is so that it may be sent bearing Christ into the world.

Barth provides an apt metaphor to this situation, noting that both the "inward service" and "outward service" of the church are like the "circular motion of the heart which in order to pump blood through the whole organism not only goes out in the diastole but also has to return in the systole, yet only to go out again in the renewed diastole" (*CD* IV/3.2:833). This imagery offers a clear depiction of the people of God's presence—renewed and edified in their spirits through gathered worship, sent out and bearing Christ to the world, and returning again to the gathered community of believers to engage the cycle again.

Over time in repeated cycles of worship to God and service to humans, believers experience God's presence among God's people and among the people of the world. While our worship and prayer together do not guarantee God's presence will be among us in a transforming way, they can make the conditions ready "for receiving the divine self-communication."[15] The power of worship is found not in the experience of our feelings but in the transformation of our hearts by communion with God. In response to God's grace in Jesus Christ, gathered believers direct their attention God-ward, offering prayers of gratitude and thanksgiving; they rehearse the story of God's faithfulness to his people for generations; they intercede on behalf of others in the world. They are priests of the Lord God. The people of God wait on God's presence, making room for God to be with us. This simple act—repeated over and over

15. Don E. Saliers, *Worship as Theology: Foretaste of Glory Divine* (Nashville: Abingdon, 1994), 86.

throughout a congregation's life together—forges a depth of character that is open to transformation in the midst of God's presence and God's people. By making room for the presence of God, we begin to make room in ourselves for the presence of the Other.

As a pastor, I was able to have a front-row seat to the transformative potential of worship. One of the more profound discoveries I recognized was that repeated gathering for Word and worship with a local congregation creates patterns of living out the Christian faith in ways that seem not to be duplicated otherwise. On several occasions I have been asked by sincere individuals, "What is the point of gathering together weekly? I can do Bible study and worship by myself at home—and without all the fuss that comes with all these people." My response has been shaped by what I have seen: Christians who worship together with others on a consistent basis come to learn God's heart for their community and are more likely to be doing the work of God in the world around them. I have seen this attested repeatedly. In order to offer genuine love to others, one must be in God's presence among God's people engaged in worship and listening to the Word as the Spirit interacts with the church. Such consistency of worship brings about a consistency in living out the faith. The local congregation becomes a training ground for Christian living and serving—first in the body of Christ and then in the world. Such training may not produce instantaneous results. After all, "coming to love as God loves takes time to unfold."[16]

Christian Ministry Is an Extension of Christian Living

Training the Christian priests of God to live out the life of Christ in them is a second component of a ministry that makes room for the Other. Here the priestly action for Christians is described in Romans 12:1–2, where we are asked to lay our bodies on the altar as a "living sacrifice" and be transformed by the renewal of our minds. This is our reasonable, logical way of performing priestly work.

At its core, all Christian ministry is an expression of the life of Christ that resides within believers. How does one live out the Christian life? An answer to that question is essential for moving forward with understanding ministry in general. For ministry to be *Christian*, there must be a similarity of motivation, intention, and action to that of Jesus Christ. It is my proposal that this is precisely why ministry is an extension of Christian living. Becoming like Christ is a lifelong endeavor for believers. Christianity was not meant to be

16. Saliers, *Worship as Theology*, 37.

some stylized version of "self-help" groups. Christianity requires following Christ and opening up one's circle of living to others; such a lifestyle makes us "better" Christians for the purpose of serving God and other human beings. Churches that circulate their good intentions only within the walls of a building will soon find their experiences of church (and God!) to be lifeless and draining. God wants to make us more like the image of his Son, Jesus Christ, so that we may find joy and meaning in life by giving our lives to others.

The *missio Dei* (mission of God) is other-regarding—focused on sharing God's love to people who may not even know they need (or want) it. Christ's mission was to fulfill the *missio Dei* on earth, demonstrating the love of God in human form and establishing reconciliation "to God through the cross" (Eph. 2:16). Now, Christ has entrusted "to us the message of reconciliation" (2 Cor. 5:19) by which we implore people to be reconciled to God (2 Cor. 5:20). The focus of our lives is not inward, not on making us fit to enjoy living here and now; the focus of our lives is on God and on the neighbor—on others who need us to bring the presence of the risen Christ to them by the power of the Spirit so that genuine ministry can occur.

The crucial aspect of this point is that ministry requires a change of life for believers. This is not merely a result of the direct encounter with God that brings about conversion. The change of life, which we are considering, is a consequence of continual encounters with God that bring about transformation and holiness in our lives. Ministry thrives under the auspices of the Spirit's sanctifying work, making believers less self-centered and more other-centered. In *The People of God's Presence*, I describe the concept of the *eccentric* nature of God—one whereby God's being bends toward the Other so that the orbit of God's life looks more elliptical as it leans toward humans.[17] It is this type of eccentric, other-regarding life that is necessary for Christ's ministry to continue through God's people today. Sanctification, then, is a prerequisite for all priestly ministry that claims the name of Christ.

Believers need the local congregation as a training ground to practice their faith in a context of love. Here is where others can be truthful with us ("speaking the truth in love") and we can be truthful with them. Here is where leaders can assist us in overcoming our long-held grudges against family members or our deep-seated anger toward people who have harmed us. Sanctification makes us clean in our *position* with Christ, but the *process* of cleaning us up can last a lifetime. Sanctification requires intentionality on our part to discover "what pleases the Lord" and then to do it (Eph. 5:10).

17. Terry L. Cross, *The People of God's Presence: An Introduction to Ecclesiology* (Grand Rapids: Baker Academic, 2019), 91–92, 227.

When I speak of sanctification, I am not proposing a kind of perfectionism or legalism whereby others in the church can judge one's progress in sanctification according to some written rule or someone's idea of being perfect. Sanctification is primarily a realignment of our loves (as Wesley would say) so that we begin to love God and desire to do things that please God. However, not all of us may achieve such a lofty goal all the time in this life. As God's people, we must be genuine—authentic—in our lives. If believers and unbelievers do not see us as humans who are striving to please God but who sometimes fail in that endeavor, then the church will be viewed as a group of "plastic" religion followers, not as human disciples of Jesus Christ. The more a local congregation attempts to portray an image of perfection (when it is not perfect) or to offer a mask to the world that everything is just perfect (when it is not), the more the people witnessing our cover-ups will wonder if there is hope for them.

Such genuine openness to the reality of who we are (humans in need of God's grace and power in sanctification) has always been important for the church, but it is essential today. Leaders in particular must be vulnerable—open to displaying the process whereby God is at work in their lives—without fear of reprimand. As a pastor, I had many occasions to share such stories as illustrating points in my sermons, but none was as memorable as "the lawn furniture." On a Saturday morning, our family purchased a beautiful set of lawn furniture at half price. I had visions of sitting in sofa-like comfort in the shade of our backyard that afternoon, but it was not to be. Confidently, I told my wife that I would have it all set up for evening (thinking we could grill outside and eat at our new table with four swivel chairs and two chaise lounges—it was a great deal!). About ten minutes into getting all the right tools, I realized that the sketch with instructions was not matching the actual furniture pieces that we had. Of course, I thought I could put it together anyway. About ten minutes later, I decided to check the instructions again, just in case I had misread the sketches. I had not. It was an entirely different set. I began looking for the written instructions, and at the bottom of one of the boxes was a paper that had a sketch of what looked like our table and chairs along with written instructions—in Korean! And so I spent about six hours trying to make sense of where the nuts and bolts went—*for one chair*. I am not one who cusses, but I was getting close. I was not happy with the people who had mixed up the instructions, calling them "stupid" and asking, "How could they do such a thing?" Wisely, my wife and daughter stayed inside the house, far removed from the spectacle that was arising in the backyard. When it began to get dark, I came inside—defeated. While I am not a mechanic or carpenter, I am somewhat familiar with how things should go together, so this was not an example of my own ineptitude. It was not "user friendly." (Two weeks later, my handy father attempted to put one chair together, and it took him three hours to figure it out. Eventually, we got the entire set put together.)

As I was washing up that evening, I realized that the sermon I had prepared earlier in the week was not going to work the next day. I was too emotionally disturbed to put on a happy face and preach the blessings of God. I jettisoned that sermon and quickly wrote another one—on sanctification and the lawn chair. On Sunday morning when I rose to preach, I lifted parts of the unfinished lawn chair before the congregation and began telling them the story of how I had been reduced to a mumbling madman by lawn furniture. Of course, it was funny—until the weight of what the Scriptures had to say about my attitude came to bear on all of us. It was the most vulnerable I had ever been with that congregation. It was intimidating, but I knew unless I admitted my problem, I would not be able to preach any other message that day. To this day—about twenty-five years later—I still get more comments about that sermon than any other. Something happened that day—the preacher on a pedestal came down a notch for that congregation, and it was a good thing. In counseling sessions and pastoral moments with people after that sermon, I was treated to a barrage of similar stories and how hearing my struggle with frustration and anger over something so petty opened their own lives to receiving healing and help from God. While I am not "Mr. Transparency," I still try to live in the lawn-furniture moment of vulnerability.

We do not need to be perfect humans in order to be instruments in God's hands to share Christ's ministry with other humans. (Thank God!) Yet making us more like Christ—or causing holiness to become a part of our own nature—is the "will of God, even your sanctification" (1 Thess. 4:3 KJV). Since God calls us to live a holy life (1 Thess. 4:7), then surely we can be given the power to live more and more like Christ every day. To be sure, this comes about only as Christ is our "righteousness, holiness and redemption" (1 Cor. 1:30). There is an accent on Christ's gracious love that comes to us in order to change us. "For it is God who works in you to will and to act in order to fulfill his good purpose" (Phil. 2:13); yet to this gracious work in us *we must respond* in kind and "find out what pleases the Lord" (Eph. 5:10) and then do it. I suggest that the power for this changeover must begin with God's Spirit encountering us and continuing to encounter us directly among the gathered people of God; however, growth in grace also comes from our human response to God's movement toward us.

In other words, sanctification is not *all* God's work but is also human cooperation with God's action in us. In this respect, we need to be intentional about ways to place ourselves in God's presence and then respond to the Spirit's

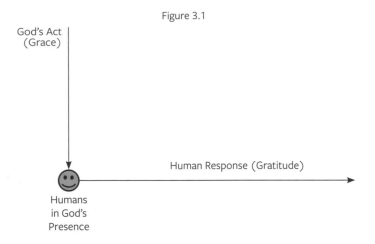

Figure 3.1

promptings. All ministry is God's ministry, but God has chosen to work with humans to deliver the message of salvation. This is not because God cannot do the work of ministry, but rather because God *chooses* to do ministry with us instead of without us. Therefore, we wait in God's presence—both privately and corporately—to learn from God and be transformed by the Spirit's work in us. Sanctification cannot be complete if we attempt to respond to God's work *by ourselves*. Sanctification requires all of us in the body of Christ to work together to hear what the Spirit is saying to the churches and to assist each other in growing up into Christ, who is the head. This corporate nature of sanctification has too frequently been lost on those of us in the believers' church tradition.[18] We have fallen into the subtle trap of pietistic individualism, thinking that God's presence need only be relegated to some interior part of the individual soul. How do we grow in Christ? We grow as a body, when *each part* does the work assigned to it (Eph. 4:16). "And we all, who with unveiled faces contemplate the Lord's glory, are being transformed into his image with ever-increasing glory, which comes from the Lord, who is the Spirit" (2 Cor. 3:18). The emphatic position of "we all" in this verse underscores Paul's belief that transformation into the image of Christ is possible when *we all together* contemplate (or reflect) that glory of the Lord's presence.

As a prerequisite for Christian ministry, sanctification is an act of transformation by God's Spirit that shifts the center of one's life from the self to God and others. Such movement toward the Other cannot be achieved by

18. For an excellent resource on the corporate nature of holiness within the believers' church tradition, see J. Ayodeji Adewuya, *Holiness and Community in 2 Corinthians 6:14–7:1: Paul's View of Communal Holiness in the Corinthian Correspondence*, Studies in Biblical Literature (New York: Peter Lang, 2003).

one's own efforts—it requires God's act of grace to change one's underlying disposition, one's love. However, sanctification does not end at this place of transformation; it continues in day-by-day experiences, where believers are confronted by powers and principalities of this world that are not in line with the holiness of God. In order to maintain a momentum toward sanctification, believers must also align themselves with God's will, finding out what pleases the Lord and doing it. This requires discernment with other believers as we walk through difficult areas of life. How should I handle the pressure from my boss to "fix" the books? How am I to deal with stem-cell research and the possible relief from hereditary diseases that it could bring my children? How am I to treat the person who harmed someone in my family? With all of these questions, we are asking, How does God want me to act? What would please God in this setting? To be sure, I may want to act very differently from God and therefore not engage these questions much, but if I am a follower of Christ, then at some point I will need to learn to submit my attitudes and actions to other believers in order to discern a way to live like Christ in this world. To mature in Christ, I need fellow believers who are committed to me and to whom I am also committed in love. As I will show in the final chapter, growing into a mature character as a disciple of Christ also requires participation in Christian practices together. Such *bodily* repetition of the truth of God's love and character as expressed through the life, death, and resurrection of Christ brings into our sinews the reality of Christ's own character.

At some point in our maturation in Christ, our character begins to take on the contours of Christ's own nature. The motivation for our actions is based on the quality time we have spent together in God's presence, perceiving the love that God has lavished on us that we should even be called children of God (1 John 3:1). The more we stand, sit, or kneel in the presence of God, the more we learn about our identity in Christ and the unconditional love that caused him to die for us. The more we learn about this love as we live in God's presence, the more we respond with actions motivated by gratitude for what we have received, causing our lives to revolve increasingly outward to others.

Waiting on God by paying attention to God in his presence is the first step toward maturation in Christ. We must learn what it means to be seated with Christ in the heavenly realms (Eph. 2:6). As Watchman Nee has noted, Christians must first learn to rest—to be seated with Christ (Eph. 2)—before they can walk with Christ (Eph. 4:1; 5:2) or stand with Christ (Eph. 6:13–14).[19] What we learn when we rest in Christ's presence is to lay our entire weight

19. Watchman Nee, *Sit, Walk, Stand* (Fort Washington, PA: Christian Literature Crusade, 1957).

on the grace of Christ. We are saved by *grace*—not by effort. If one does not sit in God's presence, one will attempt to walk before knowing the reason for walking! People who minister through the presence of Christ are those who have a firm grasp of their identity in God and their total reliance on the saving grace of Christ. Then, having a sense of grace, we can move on to *walk*. Out of an attitude of gratitude, we act. If this is ever reversed so that walking occurs before sitting, then our salvation (or ministry!) is based on what *we do* instead of what *Christ has already done*. Yet because of the grace of God, we walk—we live out our faith in response to such "great love" (Eph. 2:4). How do we walk? We walk (περιπατῆσαι | *peripatēsai*)[20] "worthy of the calling [we] have received" (Eph. 4:1). Therefore, we no longer walk as the gentiles do, "in the futility of their thinking" (Eph. 4:17), but we "walk in the way of love" (Eph. 5:2) as "children of light" (Eph. 5:8).

Sanctification requires both God's action and human response; it demands that we acknowledge God's great love toward us in his gracious action in Christ (sit) and that we move in relation to that prior action (walk). To be sure, it is God's "power that is at work within us," doing "immeasurably more than all we ask or imagine" (Eph. 3:20). Yet it is also necessary that we "work out [our] salvation with fear and trembling" (Phil. 2:12).

In Colossians 1:28–29, Paul brings together this relationship of God's work and humans' work in a clause that explains the reason he admonishes and teaches everyone that he can: "so that we may present everyone fully mature [τέλειον | *teleion*] in Christ" (Col. 1:28). Then he adds, "To this end I strenuously contend with all the energy Christ so powerfully works in me" (Col. 1:29). The phrasing is rather interesting and somewhat complex in Greek. First, Paul says that he labors hard (κοπιῶ | *kopiō*); this is the same word that we saw in reference to leaders who "work hard" (1 Thess. 5:12). However, here in Colossians Paul adds the word ἀγωνιζόμενος | *agōnizomenos*, which comes from the athletic realm in which a competitor strives or contends for a prize. So Paul says that he works extremely hard, straining every muscle toward this goal of making people fully mature in Christ. The remaining part of the sentence is the complex part: "according to Christ's active energy [ἐνέργειαν | *energeian*] energizing [ἐνεργουμένην | *energoumenēn*] in me with power [ἐν δυνάμει | *en dynamei*]."[21] Note that in this clause Paul uses three action-power terms to describe Christ's power in him; it is attached to the

---

20. This verb, περιπατέω | *peripateō*, means literally "to walk," but it came to be more figurative for how one conducted one's life, so it is frequently translated by modern versions as "live."

21. This is my literal translation from the Greek—purposefully awkward in order to show the meaning of these action-power words jammed together.

previous clause that contains words describing his own strenuous labor. The point seems to be this: I work extremely hard to achieve the goal of God for my life, but at the same time my hard work is based on (according to) the active energy of Christ activating power in me. Whether in ministry or Christian living (sanctification), the same basic pattern is necessary: God's grace activates his energy in us so that we operate with power that is not our own in order to labor strenuously so that we may achieve the goal of God for others and us.

Being steeped in the presence of God (what Nee might call "sitting") allows us to understand God's grace and power to such an extent that we begin walking in that presence and power to focus on the needs of others. The reason I have involved the biblical concept of sanctification here when speaking of ministry is that I see Christian ministry as an extension of Christian living. However, this means that we must be intentional together as God's people in order to engage in practices that help to shape our lives in the mold of Christ.[22]

In a later chapter, I will turn to a fuller discussion of Christian practices and their importance for Christian living and ministry. For now, however, it is enough to say that the people of God's presence learn how to live as Christians in the corporate context of a local church that engages in Christian rituals or practices. Christians are a people of God's presence who recognize the need for repeated activity in certain practices together in order to maintain healthy relationships with God.

Once again, here is my point: Christian ministry is an extension of Christian living. The demands of ministering / serving others are such that we cannot place our lives and needs ahead of the lives and needs of others. To be sure, everyone in ministry needs to learn boundaries and limits to giving priority to the Other, but that is why we must do ministry in the context of our community of faith—so that others can help us see when we need to provide "self-care" in order to recharge our own energy for service. The point here, however, is that if we attempt to minister to others without having first addressed the issue of our character (sanctification), we will discover that our lack of development in that area hampers our best intentions in service to others. Like the Corinthians in their congregational chaos, we, too, will become a "resounding gong or a clanging cymbal" (1 Cor. 13:1)—a sound that obscures rather than clarifies the gospel of Christ. It is through the daily

---

22. As I proposed in *The People of God's Presence*, the spiritual disciplines are important practices for us both individually and corporately. See Cross, *The People of God's Presence*, 193–97.

walking out of our lives as Christians that we learn how to "make room for" others in our congregations and in the world.

In *The People of God's Presence*, I proposed that the nature of our God should increasingly become our own nature.[23] One aspect of God's nature is that God is other-regarding—God "makes room for" the Other (Father, Son, and Spirit) in his own inner life and for others (creation and especially humans) in his expansion of the circle invited to join his own life. It is quite impossible for someone to minister to others with the presence of Christ if they are making room for no one else but themselves. To be self-centered rather than other-regarding is to engage in ministry without character. As the French philosopher Gabriel Marcel notes, we must exorcize the "ego-centric spirit."[24] If we are egocentric, we see others as objects to be used by our self-centered lives. Becoming other-regarding, we see others as a gift to us to be enjoyed and respected in their own right. How can we "exorcise the ego-centric spirit"? Marcel suggests that it begins with love—a disposition that is essential in opening our eyes to see others as a presence instead of an object. Marcel calls this *pure charity* or *availability* in which we make ourselves "available" to the Other.[25] When we start with the Other in mind, we begin to understand ourselves.[26] Such witness of availability requires relationships with others. As Frank Macchia has stated, "We are empowered by being changed and shaped into a person able to form and cultivate graced relationships with others in the image of God. The power for witness is the power of love at work among us."[27]

Sanctification is the process whereby we learn to "make room for" the Other—first God and then our neighbors. Among the community of believers in worship and living, we encounter God and show him love by paying focused attention in worship and offering him the service of our lips and lives. We learn here how to love God first (Matt. 22:37–38) and are filled with God's love for others so that we turn to love our neighbors (Matt. 22:39). Through loving God together we begin to learn how to love others—how to be "available" to the Other. We learn how to make room for God in our lives *and*

23. Cross, *The People of God's Presence*, chap. 2.

24. Gabriel Marcel, *The Mystery of Being*, vol. 2, *Faith and Reality*, trans. G. S. Fraser, Gifford Lectures (1949–1950) (South Bend, IN: St. Augustine's Press, 1950), 7.

25. Gabriel Marcel, "On the Ontological Mystery," in *The Philosophy of Existentialism*, trans. Manya Harari (New York: Citadel, 1956), 39. Also, Marcel, "Ego and Its Relation to Others," in *Homo Viator: Introduction to a Metaphysic of Hope*, trans. Emma Crauford (New York: Harper & Brothers, 1962), 23.

26. Marcel, *Faith and Reality*, 8.

27. Frank D. Macchia, *Baptized in the Spirit: A Global Pentecostal Theology* (Grand Rapids: Zondervan, 2006), 177.

make room in ourselves for others. Availability to others means a love that is open to the Other, allowing for a *reciprocal* relationship of giving over my person to the Other and receiving the Other into my person. It is "making room in oneself" for the Other.[28]

Christian Ministry Is an Extension of the Presence of Christ, the True Minister

Training the corporate priesthood in the local congregation to extend the presence of Christ to the world is the third component of Christian ministry. The ministry and mission of Christ continue through his body today. This is *not* to suggest that the church is an extension of the incarnation of Christ.[29] There is only the one Christ to whom the church points in witness. As Barth says, "Thus to speak of a continuation or extension of the incarnation in the Church is not only out of place but even blasphemous" (*CD* IV/3.2:729). The church is not a "second Christ" or even a "kind of extension of the one Christ," and therefore we must guard against thinking the church is an *alter Christus* (another Christ) or a *corredemptrix* (co-redeemer) or even a *mediatrix omnium gratiarum* (a mediator of all graces) (*CD* IV/3.2:729). The church is the people of God's presence who have been called by Christ into union with him and have been planted in the body of Christ through the power of the Holy Spirit. The people of God are called to bring the presence of Christ to the world through the proclamation of his Word and the humble bearing of his presence. The content of the church's task is simply Jesus Christ—that is, to witness *to him* and confess *him* before the world (*CD* IV/3.2:797).

However, to say that the church is not an extension of the incarnation does not mean that the church is without an incarnational ministry. While the church is not Jesus Christ, it is called to be like Christ in a manner analogous to his self-emptying (*kenosis*) in the incarnation. The actions and attitudes of the people of God open up their lives to correspond to the incarnational emptying of their Lord. Just as Christ entered the earthly sphere and became a human being, believers are asked to parallel that movement in their own living and ministry:

> In your relationships with one another, have the same mindset [τοῦτο φρονεῖτε | *touto phroneite*] as Christ Jesus:

---

28. Marcel, "On the Ontological Mystery," 40.

29. Ray S. Anderson, *Historical Transcendence and the Reality of God: A Christological Critique* (Grand Rapids: Eerdmans, 1975), 241.

Who being in very nature God,
>   did not consider equality with God something to be used to his own
>   advantage;
> rather, he made himself nothing [ἑαυτὸν ἐκένωσεν | *heauton ekenōsen*]
>   by taking the very nature of a servant,
>   being made in human likeness.
> And being found in appearance as a man,
>   he humbled himself
>   by becoming obedient to death—
>   even death on a cross! (Phil. 2:5–8)

What is often missed in frequent repetition of this early hymn is that the same attitude or mind-set that was in Christ, who "emptied himself" (ἑαυτὸν ἐκένωσεν | *heauton ekenōsen*) of what rightfully belonged to him, must now be repeated in the daily relationships of believers, or as Paul stated it more precisely, "among you" (ἐν ὑμῖν | *en hymin*). We miss the fact that the christological mode of kenotic divesting is a pattern for believers to follow in their relationships. Otherwise, in what way could we possibly fulfill the commands of the previous verses? "Do nothing out of selfish ambition or vain conceit. Rather, in humility value others above yourselves, not looking to your own interests but each of you to the interests of the others" (Phil. 2:3–4). The self-emptying of Christ in the process of becoming a human being now becomes a pattern for our own behavior in bearing the presence of Christ to others. In this way, we are more aware of the needs of others who are around us.

The church is not Jesus Christ. However, in a kenotic, self-emptying manner like Christ, the church can allow its actions to correspond (even if feebly) to the incarnational emptying of its Master. The greatest expression of God's love comes to us through the incarnation of God the eternal Son. In the execution of the Trinity's plan, Christ's attitude was one of subservience, even to the extent of death. Christ was in "very nature God . . . but made himself nothing." As disciples of this incarnate Christ, we, too, follow our Master's missionary pattern; we, too, reach out of our place of comfort and perhaps to people and regions that may not welcome us. But we obey because it pleases the Lord.

The people of God step into this mission not with arrogance, not lording it over those in need, but rather with humility and love. We follow the steps of Christ who became a servant among us because he "emptied Himself" (Phil. 2:7 NASB). We become one with the needy in order to minister Christ to them. Given the missionary nature of God and the extent to which God would go to reach humans, can the people of God do anything less?

The basis for this idea of incarnational ministry comes from the writing of Eldin Villafañe on theological education in an urban setting.[30] Incarnational ministry is ministry that takes in mind the *context* of living and sharing. It is ministry that "incarnates" or "takes on the flesh" of the local environment so as to understand its needs. In so doing, it is never paternalistic, never patronizing to the Other, but always respecting the Other by allowing him or her into one's own person. Barth provides probing words in this regard:

> Patronage means the human exercise of power by [people] against other [people] as though they were objects. It means treating of others, however benevolently, as so much material for one's own abilities. The community, however, has no power of its own to exercise in relation to others. It has not to cause them to experience its abilities. It has not to handle them. It has to attest to them the power of its Lord and the art of His grace. It has to call them unassumingly and without reserve to the freedom of faith and obedience. If it handles or patronizes them, it falsifies its task no less than when it neglects them. (*CD* IV/3.2:829, alt.)

For many of us, this is one of the more difficult parts associated with ministry today. How can we share the truth about God without sounding (or being!) arrogant—like we know more or have more than the person with whom we are sharing the good news (or good gifts) from God? How can we offer assistance to people in need without appearing to stand above them in some hierarchical meritocracy? At least part of the solution lies in the realm of a community's motivation, which must be continually aligned with God's own heart through gathered worship. We will see this more clearly in the next subsection. Another part lies in the realm of a ministry's contextualization. The context of Jesus's incarnation was humankind on earth; the context of our incarnational ministry might be young kids just hanging around the block, or the homeless we frequent on nearby street corners, or scarecrow-like humans under the spell of drug addiction. As Jesus came to this world to understand and save us in our human context—precisely where *we were*—believers go into the world of those who are starving or ostracized or oppressed and enter it with the love of God and the resources that we can garner in order to meet the pressing needs.

However, the important point for our consideration here is this: the people of God bring the presence of Christ to people and situations they encounter

---

30. Eldin Villafañe points out the central place for incarnational ministry: "Contextualization (or incarnation) is the *sine qua non* ('without which not') of all faithful and effective urban theological education." Villafañe, *Beyond Cheap Grace: A Call to Radical Discipleship, Incarnation, and Justice* (Grand Rapids: Eerdmans, 2006), 38.

in life. We are not Christ; we are the *bearers of Christ*. We are not better than those with whom we are sharing Christ simply because we have come to accept the good news of salvation through him. We understand fully that we are human beings in constant need of the grace and mercy of our God. Therefore, we share the One who brought us such grace and ministered to us. We announce to estranged, isolated, and alienated people everywhere, "Be reconciled to God" (2 Cor. 5:20).

The English name Christopher comes from two Greek words meaning "bearer of Christ" or "Christ-bearer" (χρίστος + φέρω | *christos + pherō*). It is precisely this bearing of Christ to others that I mean when I say that Christian ministry is an extension of the presence of Christ, the true minister. For theological reasons, the concept of "God-bearer" (θεοτόκος | *theotokos*) has been relegated to Mary, the mother of Jesus.[31] It refers literally to the "one who brings forth God," meaning the one who births God. In recent years, Kenda Creasy Dean and Ron Foster have discussed ministry (in particular, youth ministry) as "the Godbearing life"—that is, as people whom God calls to "become a Godbearer through whom God may enter the world again and again."[32] Using this term as a metaphor for how ministry can operate in the church and world today, the authors note that we cannot *be Christ* to youth—such confusion would lead to serious problems. However, we can *bring Christ* to them so that youth will follow *him*.[33]

How can we do this task of bearing Christ to people? Frankly, *we* cannot fulfill this task; *we* cannot become holy enough or powerful enough in our own strength to bring Christ to anyone. It is only through the power of the Holy Spirit that we bear Christ to people and situations so that *he* can minister to them. Christ is the *true* minister. Through the power of the Spirit, we bring Christ to people and people to Christ. As Dean and Foster note, "Only the power of the Holy Spirit makes ministry possible at all, and the presence of the Spirit transforms us into an 'incarnation' of another sort: the 'flesh and bones' of the church, the body of Christ."[34] As the community of believers who have been birthed into a new life in Christ, united with Christ through the Spirit, and joined together as his body, we can bring the presence of Christ with us wherever we go. In this way, ministry happens *as we go* in our everyday

31. For a clear, concise discussion of the history and theology behind the discussion of *theotokos*, see Roger E. Olson, *The Story of Christian Theology: Twenty Centuries of Tradition & Reform* (Downers Grove, IL: InterVarsity, 1999), chap. 14.

32. Kenda Creasy Dean and Ron Foster, *The Godbearing Life: The Art of Soul Tending for Youth Ministry* (Nashville: Upper Room Books, 1998), 18.

33. Dean and Foster, *The Godbearing Life*, 28. I find this entire program to be filled with excellent insight for all types of ministry, not only youth ministry.

34. Dean and Foster, *The Godbearing Life*, 28.

lives, not simply in a church building. We are the church, the body of Christ; *we* are the vessels through which God's presence is carried. As Ignatius of Antioch (d. 115 CE) described God's people, we are all "participants together in a shared worship, God-bearers [θεοφόροι | *theophoroi*] and temple-bearers [καὶ ναοφόροι | *kai naophoroi*], Christ-bearers [χριστοφόροι | *christophoroi*], bearers of holy things [ἁγιοφόροι | *hagiophoroi*]."[35] We are God-bearers; we are Christ-bearers.

Having been united with Christ by the Spirit, we gradually take on the nature of Christ's character. By being "in Christ," we discover that Christ is also "in us." As we are transformed into the image of Christ by participating in his presence through the Spirit, we learn to bring Christ's presence into our own lives and rather naturally then into the lives of others. *We* cannot minister life and peace to people; *Christ* can minister to them through us. We make room for Christ's presence among us wherever we are and with whomever we find ourselves. To be sure, such Christ-bearing ministry requires that we know the risen Christ is alive and ready to minister through the Spirit today. Barth is correct when he states that with all forms of ministry "there must be confidence in His continuing and lasting presence" (*CD* IV/3.2:861).

We witness to the presence of Christ by pointing to him, declaring that God has reconciled everyone to himself through Jesus Christ and now calls us to join in the abundant life available through him. We discover that Christ's mission and ministry have become *our* ministry and mission in the world. This is not a ministry exclusively for clergy. This is a ministry incumbent upon all believers. We all "bear witness" to Jesus Christ and also "bear Christ" to the world.[36] Thus, the ministry of the community is "orientated by [Christ's] ministry" (*CD* IV/3.2:831). We follow his pattern of service to God and to humans.

In a sermon from 1991, homiletics professor Thomas Long shared a story of his own initial "stirrings" to ministry.[37] When Professor Long was a teenager, his uncle Ed died while still quite young. Ed was well loved by all. As the family gathered for the funeral, it was learned that the minister at Ed's church was on vacation. Despite earnest pleas for him to stay on vacation, the minister drove a long way back to participate in the funeral. He arrived

---

35. Ignatius, *Ephesians* 9.2, in *AF*, 190–91.
36. For a full discussion of the NT term "witness," see Karl Barth, *CD* IV/3.2:611–12. For Barth, John the Baptist—with his "constantly pointing finger"—is the "prototype" of the NT witness (611).
37. Thomas G. Long, "Words, Words, Words: Baccalaureate Sermon, 1991," *Princeton Seminary Bulletin* 12, no. 3 (1991): 314–19, here 319.

at the house just before the family headed out to the church for the funeral. Long continues the story:

> The family was all together in Ed's home, and, through the big picture window, we saw the minister arrive. He got out of his stripped down Ford, all spindle-legged, wearing a cheap blue suit, clutching his service book like a life preserver. . . . What he did not know, could not know, is how the atmosphere in that living room changed that moment we saw him step out of his car. It was anticipation, but more than that. His arrival was, in its own way, a call to worship. This frail human being, striding across the lawn in his off-the-rack preacher suit, desperately trying to find some words of meaning to speak, brought with him, by the grace of God, the presence of Christ. In his presence and in his words . . . was the living Word.

It is that presence of Christ that all Christians bear with us wherever we go. Intentionally bringing Christ into situations and circumstances where the presence of Christ is needed requires a kenotic mind-set of service. This leads us to our next section—the role of the Holy Spirit in ministry.

Christian Ministry Is an Enablement with the Power of the Holy Spirit

Training the corporate priesthood of believers in the congregation to rely on the Holy Spirit to do the work of Christian priests in the world today is the fourth component of Christian ministry. Just as Jesus relied on the Holy Spirit to do his messianic work, the people of God's presence rely on the Spirit to continue Christ's mission. Lorelei Fuchs has pinpointed this continuance of mission well: "The Spirit forms the church as the continuing presence of Christ in the world, transforming it into the proleptic manifestation of God's eschatological reign."[38] The word "proleptic" here points to an anticipation of a future event; in terms of the Christian faith, we live in the constraints of human history but also with a measure of the future eschaton in the here and now. The powers of the age to come invade our present age because of the cross-resurrection event, where the power of the future age folded back onto the present age and raised Christ from the dead. As Christians, we experience the presence of God as a presence from

38. Lorelei Fuchs, "The Holy Spirit and the Development of Communio/Koinonia Ecclesiology as a Fundamental Paradigm for Ecumenical Engagement," in *The Holy Spirit, the Church, and Christian Unity: Proceedings of the Consultation Held at the Monastery of Bose, Italy, 14–20 October 2002*, ed. D. Donnelly, A. Denaux, and J. Famerée (Leuven: Leuven University Press, 2005), 164–65.

out of this world—or at least, out of this age. In this sense, the Christian church is becoming a "proleptic manifestation" of God's reign in the age to come.

This is why ministry that is truly *Christian* cannot arise entirely from one's own strength, mental acuity, psychological perception, or any of the possible human traits that may naturally show concern for the needs of others. The church "must live not out of its own resources but by the power of the indwelling Spirit, which breathes, strengthens, inspires and guides."[39] The new life given to the new humanity within the Christian community derives its potency from the presence of God. The daunting task of continuing the ministry and mission of Christ by bringing his presence into the midst of our broken world and pointing to him as the "wounded healer" is one that requires—no, demands—more than human initiative, motivation, or skill. This task demands the same anointing from the Spirit of the Lord that rested on Christ, who said,

> "The Spirit of the Lord is on me,
>   because he has anointed me
>   to proclaim good news to the poor.
> He has sent me to proclaim freedom for the prisoners
>   and recovery of sight for the blind,
> to set the oppressed free,
>   to proclaim the year of the Lord's favor."

> Then he rolled up the scroll, gave it back to the attendant and sat down. The eyes of everyone in the synagogue were fastened on him. He began by saying to them, "Today this scripture is fulfilled in your hearing." (Luke 4:18–21)

This was the ministry of the Messiah; it remains the ministry of the risen Christ through the church by the power of the same Spirit who anointed Jesus. Hence, the church is truly "the instrument of Christ, called to carry on his mission in the power of the Spirit."[40] This means that the church is anointed with the Spirit in order to make room for the presence of Christ to continue his work among people today. Only God the Spirit can exchange beauty for ashes and praise for despair through the continued work of the "Anointed One."[41] To be clear, however, I must underscore the fact that our task is *not* to

39. Pinnock, *Flame of Love*, 115.
40. Pinnock, *Flame of Love*, 116.
41. The Hebraic title of "Messiah" when translated into Greek is ὁ Χρίστος | *ho Christos*, which means "the smeared one" or "the anointed one."

save or transform the world. Our task is to allow the same Spirit who anointed Jesus the Christ to anoint us so that through our obedient witness the risen Lord can save, heal, and transform people and structures of the world ravaged by the alienation and harm of sin.

How does the Spirit of God "anoint" us today to continue Christ's work in the world? The Spirit who gives each individual believer new life is also the Spirit who binds us to each other in the community of faith. "The Spirit embraces us or fills us with the divine presence in order to sanctify us and empower us to be living witnesses to Christ as the Son of God and the Spirit Baptizer. When God surrounds and fills us with the divine presence, it is so that we can give of ourselves back to God in worship and witness."[42] Within the context of this local community, God's Spirit distributes gifts to whomever he will. "Now to each one the manifestation [ἡ φανέρωσις | hē phanerōsis] of the Spirit is given for the common good [πρὸς τὸ συμφέρον | pros to sympheron]" (1 Cor. 12:7). After this statement, Paul lists several of these manifestations and then states, "All these are the work of one and the same Spirit, and he distributes them to each one, just as he determines" (1 Cor. 12:11). The Spirit of God is in charge of the distribution of the gifts. Yet what are these manifestations, these gifts?

In 1 Corinthians 12 alone, Paul uses several different terms to describe these gifts as a whole:

πνευματικόι | pneumatikoi	"spiritual gifts"
χαρίσματα | charismata	"grace gifts"
διακονίαι | diakoniai	"ministries"
ἐνέργματα | energmata	"workings"
φανέρωσις | phanerōsis*	"manifestation"

* I have placed all these in the nominative plural forms except for φανέρωσις | phanerōsis, which is nominative singular. Paul uses the *plural* forms for the other four, so I try to reflect that usage.

The point of the diversity of words here matches Paul's point of diversity of gifts in the body of Christ. There is *one* Spirit who determines the distribution of these gifts, but there are *many different gifts* that are distributed throughout the body of Christ. All gifts are "for the common good" or for what would profit everyone.

Therefore, gifts "are divine actions that build up the community and advance its mission. They demonstrate the power of the Spirit, who is at work in the

42. Macchia, *Baptized in the Spirit*, 159.

church. They are manifestations of the Spirit's presence (1 Cor. 12:7)."[43] Wherever the Spirit operates among God's people, there exists the power, ingenuity, and wisdom to accomplish what God asks. When God set the instructions for building the tabernacle in the wilderness, he called Bezalel and filled him with the Spirit of God "in wisdom, in understanding, and in knowledge, and in every task, to devise plans, to work in gold and in silver, in bronze and in stonecutting for settings, and in wood carving to do every task of devising, and He has given in his heart to instruct" (Exod. 35:30 Alter).[44] God fills people with his Spirit, giving them skill and inspiration to devise the entire craftwork as well as administer the project. When Moses needed help in judging the people, some of the Spirit that was on Moses was shared with the seventy elders. "As the spirit rested upon them, that they prophesied, but did it no more" (Num. 11:25 Alter). Two elders were not with Moses and the others, but were in another part of the camp, yet they also prophesied (Num. 11:28). When Joshua protested, Moses responded, "Are you jealous on my part? Would that all the LORD's people were prophets, that the LORD would place His spirit upon them" (Num. 11:29 Alter). As Robert Alter comments, Moses points to an ideal of "what we might call radical spiritual egalitarianism."[45] Everyone can receive something from the Spirit of God. Christians may see this egalitarianism fulfilled on the day of Pentecost (Acts 2), when the sons and daughters of God responded in a similar prophetic manner.[46] And so it is today. When the church faces the Herculean task of bearing the presence of Christ to a people frequently hostile, or perhaps indifferent, to the gospel, it is the Spirit of God who showers gifts on his people so that the body of Christ will rise to the occasion with different divinely enabled skills and talents to fulfill the work of God in the world.

A key part of the Spirit's gifts in the New Testament is that *all* God's people may receive gifts from the Spirit. "Through the powers of the Spirit, the one Spirit gives every individual his specific share and calling, which is exactly cut out for him, in the process of the new creation."[47] Just as every believer is to be a priest with God, so, too, every believer is to be endowed with spiritual gifts—perhaps we could even say that every believer is to be a *prophet* of God, if we make clear that we are using the term "prophet" in its broader sense, as someone upon whom the Spirit falls with grace-filled gifts to tell forth the

43. Pinnock, *Flame of Love*, 130.
44. Alter 1:355.
45. Alter 1:517.
46. The idea of "to prophesy" in both Num. 11 and Acts 2 seems to point to speaking forth the glory of God along with some type of ecstatic behavior. This is described by Robert Alter as "dancing, writhing, emitting vatic speech." Alter 1:516.
47. Jürgen Moltmann, *The Church in the Power of the Spirit: A Contribution to Messianic Ecclesiology*, trans. Margaret Kohl (Minneapolis: Fortress, 1993), 295.

glories of God. The gifts of the Spirit are for everyone in the body of Christ. "The charismata are by no means to be seen merely in the 'special ministries' of the gathered community. Every member of the messianic community is a charismatic not only in the community's solemn assemblies but every day, when members are scattered and isolated in the world."[48]

As I have noted, in Western societies the church in the twenty-first century faces the prospect of irrelevance. People in the West want some form of spirituality, but many do not desire such spirituality to come through the structure of the institutional church. In relation to the gifts of the Spirit, I would suggest that the reason some people are walking away from institutional churches (yes, even Pentecostal/charismatic ones!) is the fact that we have asked people to come to a lecture hall and sit, listening passively rather than participating actively in the Spirit's work in the church. We have asked them to join us in worship but have not opened up our worship in a meaningful way, where they can participate in it by bringing something to the community. We have asked them to commit an hour (or so) a week to hearing from a select group of leaders, but we have not asked them to commit their entire lives to a radical openness to God's Spirit whereby the core of their being is confronted and transformed in God's presence so that *they* have something to offer the people of God and the world. In other words, a select few are priests before God while the rest of the congregation is the non-Levitical laity. When we gather as the body of Christ in the local congregation, we must remember that we are all priests engaged in worship and service to our God.

As an enablement of the Spirit, Christian ministry is *paracletic*. We have seen already that ministry is *kenotic*—following the incarnational self-emptying of our Lord into the human realm of need. Now we can also say that ministry is paracletic—following the spiritual mode of the work of the Spirit. This adjective, "paracletic," comes from the Greek word παρακλήτος | *paraklētos*, which means "advocate" or "one called alongside to help." It is used in John 14:16, 26, to speak of the Holy Spirit whom Christ would send—the "paraclete" as is sometimes used in English. It is also used of Jesus Christ, who is our "advocate with the Father" (1 John 2:1 ESV). By using this word to describe ministry in the power of the Spirit, I am pointing to the Holy Spirit as the empowering presence of Christ's own ministry while here on earth but also to his continued ministry through the church in the power of the Holy Spirit.[49] Our priestly ministry corresponds to the ministry of

48. Moltmann, *The Church in the Power of the Spirit*, 246.
49. I take this phrase and the ideas surrounding it from Ray S. Anderson, *The Shape of Practical Theology: Empowering Ministry with Theological Praxis* (Downers Grove, IL: InterVarsity, 2001), 195.

Christ in that it is both kenotic and paracletic. However, just as with kenotic or incarnational ministry, we are not Christ, so with paracletic ministry, we are not the Holy Spirit. The people of God's presence bear with them the presence of the risen Christ through the power of the Spirit. As the Spirit led and empowered Jesus's ministry, so the Spirit continues Christ's ministry through us. The Spirit shaped the mode of Christ's ministry as paracletic—that is, as someone called alongside people to help up close and personal. It was a ministry of encouragement and exhortation.[50] It is to such a priestly ministry that we have been called. As Ray Anderson describes such a paracletic ministry, God "wants to live in my place and my situation" in order to bring his healing and hopeful presence; therefore, God "enters my situation in its concrete historical reality and appears in it for that very purpose."[51]

In practical terms, what does such paracletic ministry look like from the side of human beings who perform ministry to other human beings? Paracletic ministry is service to humans who are in need of God's presence. It is the practical outcome of being Christian priests in the new covenant. It means coming alongside humans with our physical presence in order to encourage and support them with our own presence, but primarily with the presence of Christ to whom we bear witness. When hurting people experience human beings living alongside them in grief, despair, or pain, there is a mutual sharing of another's burden. The gaping abyss of despair cannot so easily swallow someone who has other humans holding on to them in their desperate situation. It is here that paracletic ministry begins—bringing one's own person, one's own physical presence, into the pain of another first, so that the presence of the risen Christ through the power of the Spirit can be channeled in that human presence. Caregivers must *participate* in some way in the pain, grief, or despair, so that hurting humans can *feel* a human touch of love and thereby be opened to experience the presence of Christ. Ministers (and here I mean everyone in the body of Christ!) cannot simply sit by as sad-faced counselors objectively distanced from the pain of it all. They must dive into the mess alongside the person who is overwhelmed, experiencing the context and content of their pain firsthand. Such personal attention from those who minister to hurting people opens the way for them to experience God directly and personally. As Anderson notes in this regard, "When God comes to me in the mode of paraclesis, it dawns on me: 'God has come and he wants to live in my place and my situation.'"[52] Christ takes up my cause "as his own."[53]

50. Anderson, *The Shape of Practical Theology*, 196.
51. Anderson, *The Shape of Practical Theology*, 197.
52. Anderson, *The Shape of Practical Theology*, 197.
53. Anderson, *The Shape of Practical Theology*, 197.

And here it is important to note that the presence of Christ that comes to us is not only the risen Lord but the One whose presence is "clothed with human misery," so that through his own experience of the vicissitudes of human life and death he comes with "unutterable compassion" to sustain and uphold those who are ravaged by the curse of sin.[54] Once those in pain realize this—whether they are believers or unbelievers—such a reality is no small thing. God is present *in my hurt* in order to help me. This is the paracletic ministry of Christians, which in reality continues the paracletic ministry of Christ. This is the ministry of Christians through the enablement of the Spirit's presence and power. This is the new priesthood of God.

54. These quoted words and ideas come from Thomas F. Torrance, "Service in Jesus Christ," in *Theological Foundations for Ministry: Selected Readings for a Theology of the Church in Ministry*, ed. Ray S. Anderson (Grand Rapids: Eerdmans, 1979), 729.

The *Praxis* of Leading the People of God in (Their) Ministry

Introduction

One practical result of taking the universal priesthood of believers seriously is to acknowledge that leading God's people requires a *re*-formation of some structural elements as well as the mind-set of believers in the local congregation. If readers were expecting a typical book on leadership theory, then the previous chapters filled with theology and history undoubtedly have been disappointing. Yet I remain convinced that a biblical-theological foundation is crucial for leadership of God's people today so that we neither mindlessly replicate the leadership models of our past nor thoughtlessly mimic models of the business world in the present. The critical situation of the contemporary church in Western society today means that we cannot simply continue to use whatever structural models worked for us in the past. Moreover, the church is not a business. To be sure, it has business dimensions to its life, but the reason for the church's existence and the priorities we place on our mission mean that the primary mode of our existence is as the people of God's presence who serve God and the world. We are a people called to bear witness to Christ, bringing his presence with us through the Spirit's power into all areas of life. This is why we exist—and our structures must reflect that priority. What would the church look like if we took seriously the universal priesthood of believers? It is to the practical outcome of that proposal we now turn—again with a *theological* basis for the *practical* endeavor.[1]

As noted in the introduction to this book, the church is both a human institution and a miraculous creation by God. Therefore, the church is both visible and invisible. As Karl Barth remarked in his trademark dialectical fashion, "It is not improper but proper to the Christian community to be visible," but "it is also not improper but highly proper to it to be also invisible" (*CD* IV/3.2:722–23). As such, the church is more than a human organization because "God is at work in it by His Holy Spirit" (*CD* IV/2:616). Yet it is also more than a merely invisible fellowship of the Spirit, since as such it would succumb to "ecclesiological docetism" (*CD* IV/3.2:723). Hence, I am proposing a pneumatic ecclesiology, but one with "skin on." What I mean by this is that the people of God's presence live with both charismata and organizational structure side by side. Indeed, the work of governing or leading (Rom. 12:8) is one of the charisms of the Spirit! Being filled with and led by the Spirit does not mean we cease being embodied humans. In the same way, churches are filled with God's presence yet do not become invisible, phantom-like operations. God delights in using *human* instruments. We, however, sometimes feel the tension between the Spirit and our own human bodies. In the same way, the church lives with such tension between the organizational structure that is necessary for accomplishing our mission in the world and the spontaneous flow of the Spirit's presence that is necessary for motivating, clarifying, and empowering our mission. This is one reason the church prays—in order to discern the appropriate balancing act of the Spirit's life within our very human institutions.

However, as I noted in a previous chapter, the outer, visible structures of the church must reflect the invisible, spiritual nature of the body of Christ so that our witness before the world is genuine. How might we attain ecclesial structures that reflect the God we serve? Some have suggested that we use only leadership and polity structures that are found in the New Testament. While the sentiment behind this approach may be laudable, the reality of ferreting out such structural elements is difficult at best.[2] I have already demonstrated that the "titles" of the

---

1. Throughout this chapter, I will argue for viewing the interrelatedness of theory and practice through an ancient philosophical term that has been vibrantly renewed in contemporary theology—namely, *praxis*. While theology in the West has mainly been left to the realm of theory in Christian thought, it has seldom left those rarified realms to make any demonstrable difference in the way we *do* the Christian life and ministry. I will propose another way of considering the theory-practice divide, and that is through *praxis*—a theory-laden practice that involves doing, learning, and doing again. More will be said later in this chapter concerning such *praxis*.

2. William H. Willimon, *Pastor: The Theology and Practice of Ordained Ministry* (Nashville: Abingdon, 2002), 29. Willimon states, "We search the New Testament in vain for much stress on continuity of *structures* of Christian leadership" (his emphasis).

first-century church may not supply us today with clarity regarding their precise function for both the New Testament and today. How are we to understand "apostle," for example? It is one who is commissioned for a task, to be sure, but are the Twelve (apostles) different in kind from the numerous "apostles" who also saw the risen Lord (1 Cor. 15:7)? What did apostles do in the first century? If one were called an apostle today, how would we know what he or she should do? The same type of questioning would be necessary for bishop, elder, deacon, pastor, and others. We cannot teleport these functions from the first century to our century without some distortion in the meaning.

Moreover, there does not seem to be one polity—that is, a single governmental style that is sanctioned by the New Testament. There is an episcopal (bishop) style of leading provided in some of Paul's later letters as well as an apparent presbyteral (elder) style of leading in some of his earlier letters. Others see a more congregational style in various parts of the New Testament. While I believe that the Spirit speaks to us through Scripture, there seem to be some things in the Word that remain open for our determination. Governmental style in churches appears to be one of these. I would submit that in part this may be due to the various cultural ways of organizing and leading groups of people. The Scriptures give us some *principles* by which to operate within whatever governing structure our culture finds most suitable and most fitting to the gospel. To claim divine revelation of one particular governmental style for the church seems to claim more than is asserted in Scripture. While we are to be obedient to the Scriptures, such obedience cannot equal "slavish imitation of the forms and order presented in the Bible" (*CD* IV/2:683).

What are such biblical principles clearly offered in the Bible? One of the foremost principles runs something like a mantra through this book. Barth says it best: "To be a Christian, and therefore a saint in the communion of saints, is to serve in and with the Christian community" (*CD* IV/2:693). *Service* or *ministry* is the responsibility of all Christians as the priesthood of believers. Thomas Torrance has noted, "Christian service is not accidental to being a Christian, but essential—rooted in being a slave of Jesus Christ."[3] Beyond this essential principle of service/ministry, we have seen several others, such as the idea that functions in the body of Christ are related to gifts, that functions are more important than titles, and that love and respect of the Other must shape all our actions toward fellow believers and the world. It is more important for the church to get the biblical principles concerning

3. Thomas F. Torrance, "Service in Jesus Christ," in *Theological Foundations for Ministry: Selected Readings for a Theology of the Church in Ministry*, ed. Ray S. Anderson (Grand Rapids: Eerdmans, 1979), 715.

the operation of the body of Christ right than simply to use the exact titles for positions of leadership found in the New Testament. For example, it is more important that a church operate with loving service to God and others than call leaders by a particular title such as bishop or overseer or whatever.

Such fluidity gives the church of every era and culture some freedom to operate according to local customs within the various strictures of time and place. Therefore, my proposal concerning the structure of the church argues not for current titles or positions in the churches necessarily to be changed but rather for the attitude of servanthood to infuse the work of whatever position we may hold. With whatever title one has—or does not have—we must engage what Christ asks us to do; namely, we must work together as co-laborers with God and with each other. Even within a titled position, one may change the atmosphere within the local community of believers by not insisting on the title as a part of one's appellation—that is, what others call us—since such labels tend to separate rather than unite the body of Christ.

Further, our polity and organizational structures must reflect the God we serve together. Jürgen Moltmann makes this clear with regard to structures: "Through its order, its ministries and its organizations the church either confesses or denies the thing that it has to represent."[4] In a small-print section on church law (*Kirchenrecht*) and the universal nature of the priesthood of believers, Karl Barth urges Christian communities to "avoid the fatal word 'office' and replace it by '*service*' [*dem fatalen Begriff 'Amt' zum Verschwinden . . . des* 'Dienstes']" (*CD* IV/2:694; *KD* IV/2:787).[5] He continues by asserting that "either all are office-bearers [*Amtsträger*] or none; and if all, then only as servants [*Dienstleute*]" (*CD* IV/2:694; *KD* IV/2:787). Hence, church structure "will have to be all the more vigilant against practical clericalism [*allem praktischen Klerikalismus*] . . . against every separation into the ruling and the ruled, the teaching and the hearing" (*CD* IV/2:695; *KD* IV/2:787). Finding ways to avoid such pitfalls and engage in such a leveling practice with the Christian community is a goal of this chapter on practical application.

Making Room for the Ministry of Others

Leaders in the body of Christ make room for the ministry of others. Indeed, this is their *primary* responsibility—namely, to encourage believers to live

---

4. Jürgen Moltmann, *The Church in the Power of the Spirit: A Contribution to Messianic Ecclesiology*, trans. Margaret Kohl (Minneapolis: Fortress, 1993), 290.

5. This word "service" (*Dienstes*) is emphasized by Barth in the German text but not in the English translation. I have added the emphasis here.

as priests of God. This *begins* by making room for the ministry and gifts of others in the congregation.

This does not mean the church is simply another training ground where certain skills of performing are provided and practiced. Leading God's people requires more than transmitting information to them—it demands loving and serving them within the context of God's gathered people. Leading God's people demands that we *know* them so well that sometimes we are aware of their gifts (and weaknesses?) before they are. Leading God's people demands that we help to make them whole persons, filling up any deficiency by living life together in close proximity. This is one potent message that comes from Ephesians 4: the gifts of apostles, prophets, evangelists, pastors, and teachers are given to the body of Christ *by Christ* for the purpose of "equipping the saints." The Greek word καταρισμός | *katarismos* is a participle that comes from a verb (καταρτίζω | *katartizō*) with three basic meanings: to "mend" or "repair"; to "equip so that (something) is fully furnished or ready for use"; and "to make (someone) fit or ethically prepared." What a graphic description of the leaders' daunting task: to help refurbish believers' lives to make them fully equipped or fit to do the work of ministry themselves (εἰς ἔργον διακονίας | *eis ergon diakonias*). Leading the people of God's presence is less about *one's own* preaching, teaching, ministering, counseling, and administration than making room *for others* to preach, teach, minister, counsel, and administrate.[6] Leadership among the people of God's presence is about making room for *them* to be trained and released into *their* ministry as we all work together with God.

What are the practical ramifications of the theological principle of the priesthood of all believers? If all are priests before God, then what is the purpose of an "ordained" ministry? It seems probable that any ecclesial system that fosters a division between "clergy" and "laity" will undermine in some way the universal priesthood of believers. Does this mean that God's people are meant to be without leaders? Absolutely not. Anytime a group of humans gathers for some common purpose, there is a need for leaders. The Scriptures provide plenty of reference to this truth. Nonetheless, we need to understand the place of ordination then and now among the priesthood of believers.

6. I am not suggesting that leaders simply "hand over" the pulpit to anyone who wants to speak—or share counseling duties with anyone who appoints themselves as qualified to counsel. I am pointing to the idea of discovery of the gifts and strengths that God has placed in members of the local body of Christ over which leaders tend with care and responsibility. Finding others in the body to engage in the ministry of their gifts and callings is one of the most important legacies any leader of a congregation can give to it. Discovering such gifts and callings then requires disciplined training so that whatever may be deficient in them can be repaired and they can move toward ministry out of wholeness rather than out of their gaps.

Ordination?

Where does the practice of ordination fit? Thomas Torrance suggests we look to the Old Testament: "In order to understand the New Testament teaching about consecration and ordination we have to examine the rites and language of the Old Testament tradition."[7] While I appreciate much of what Torrance has to say about ministry and service, I cannot agree with this assertion. Indeed, much of the development of Torrance's theology of ministry appears to be a theology of priesthood in the mode of the Old Testament.[8] Torrance assumes much of his own tradition of ministry when he reads the New Testament (and Old Testament). "Ordination is in order to minister the Word and Sacraments."[9] This is a common point among churches requiring ordination. Given the fact that only ordained individuals are authorized to preach the Word *and* celebrate the sacraments, it seems highly unlikely that people in the pew will get the notion that *they*—not just the ordained clergy person at the altar or pulpit—are the priests. Does this mean that I think just anyone can share communion or preach the Word? Yes and no.

First, it is important for the people of God to understand that the role of leaders is not to be priests before God on their behalf but to train fellow believers how to be Christian priests themselves. If only the lead pastor preaches from the pulpit or shares anything that is important in the life of the church when the congregation gathers, then the impression is that no one else is authorized to speak or share. This is not my understanding of the gifted people of God's presence both in the New Testament and today. Everyone comes with a hymn, a word, a testimony, a message—something with which to glorify God and edify fellow Christians. So yes—any believer should be able to share with the gathered body of Christ. Leaders should work hard to encourage believers to participate in the gathered meeting in some way. What are the gifts God wants to use through them? Yet my answer is also no—not everyone is designed, trained, or gifted to fill a pulpit. Guarding who speaks to the whole church and who shares the Word is an important task for leaders. While openness in the worship service is important for every local body of Christ, exercising care in who preaches and teaches is also important.

Second, am I suggesting that any believer can celebrate the sacraments? Yes and no. These practices are participatory rituals in which we all engage

7. Thomas F. Torrance, "The Ordering and Equipping of the Church for Ministry," in Anderson, *Theological Foundations for Ministry*, 405.

8. See especially T. F. Torrance, *Royal Priesthood: A Theology of Ordained Ministry*, 2nd ed. (Edinburgh: T&T Clark, 1993). Also, see chap. 2 above for a more thorough discussion of the historical dimension of ordination.

9. Torrance, "The Ordering and Equipping of the Church for Ministry," 424.

as believers within a local congregation.[10] Does one need to be ordained in order to perform baptism or serve communion? If the answer to that question is yes, then it is probable that there is a priestly conception of the pastor or church leaders in which the presider of the communion is "taking place in Christ."[11] What I mean is as follows: if sacraments or ordinances are to be done only by a select group in order to be legitimate, then will not the congregation understand by this limitation that *they* are not the priests of God but that the ordained clergy are? In theory, is there a biblical reason for not allowing any dedicated believer to baptize someone whom they have led to Christ? Is there a biblical reason for not allowing believers to lead in the Lord's Supper? I think not. However, this cannot open the congregation to disorder. Since the sacraments involve the whole local congregation, it seems appropriate for there to be order instead of chaos. Leaders must attend to this order, ensuring that actions are done with theological understanding as well as appropriate decorum for such events.

As noted in the first two chapters of this book, the development of a priestly caste for Christianity came many years *after* the first century. Determining who would be the "president" or "presider" over the Eucharist set the stage for the select group of people to be ordained in order to preside over the sacrificial table. Indeed, in this position, the priest *represents* Christ to and for the congregation, thereby removing any claim for women to hold such a role—or indeed anyone who is not ordained. Such distinction severs clergy and laity in ways that are notable, yet almost imperceptible now because of the long duration and tradition. As the Second Vatican Council emphasized, priests are "promoted [*promoventur*] to the service of Christ" where they "are given a share in his ministry [*cuius participant ministerium*]."[12] When priests are ordained, they are "signed with a special character [*speciali character*] and so are configured to Christ [*sic Christo configurantur*] the priest in such

10. The specific participatory practices that many Christians call "sacraments" will be treated below in chap. 6.

11. Tom Greggs, *Dogmatic Ecclesiology*, vol. 1, *The Priestly Catholicity of the Church* (Grand Rapids: Baker Academic, 2019), 243. Greggs views the "presidency" of communion in ways quite similar to mine. He notes that the presider is not acting in Christ's stead as priest but also that a doctrine of the church does not need to declare one person to preside in the community. On the other hand, he notes the need "for structure and order." It is the Lord who is the Head of the Supper—and the remainder of us in his community are his guests.

12. *Decree on the Ministry and Life of Priests (Presbyterorum Ordinis)*, §1, in *Vatican Council II: The Conciliar and Post Conciliar Documents*, ed. Austin Flannery (Collegeville, MN: Liturgical Press, 1975), 863. For the Latin see *Decretum de presbyterorum ministerio et vita* (December 7, 1965), in *Dogmatic Constitutions, Declarations, Decrees of the Second Vatican Council, 1962–1965* (Latin and English), compiled by Kevin Simmons (Morrisville, NC: Lulu, 2012), 620.

a way that they are able to act in the person of Christ the head."[13] Priests, then, are "sharers in a special way in Christ's priesthood [*participes Sacerdotii Christi speciali ratione effecti*]."[14] Does not this create two classes of believers in the church—those who may preside at Eucharist and those who may not?

What, then, am I trying to say concerning ordination? Is it necessary or not? To be sure, it is important for the church to have full-time, committed leaders providing instruction, preaching, and pastoral care on behalf of the whole congregation. Do leaders need to be ordained in order to perform these roles? It does seem that some leaders were "installed" by the laying on of hands by other leaders in New Testament congregations as the will of both God and the congregation.[15] However, does this procedure relate to ordination today? Perhaps it does, but only in some very preliminary fashion.[16] Robert Muthiah puts the poignancy of the question clearly: "Ordination is normally associated with installation into a ministerial priesthood. But if such a priesthood is not justified, what is the nature of ordination?"[17] Miroslav Volf points us in a helpful direction with respect to leadership in the community of believers. The people of God's presence are a "polycentric community."[18] By this phrase, Volf refers to a community where the whole people participate in ecclesial life to such a degree that the "center" is found not in *one* of its leaders or even *several* of its leaders but in *all* the people who are called and gifted to be priests before God. There is no hierarchy in such a community, just as there is no hierarchy in the triune community of God. Father, Son, and Spirit live in perichoretic union, which produces a "polycentric and symmetrical reciprocity of the many."[19] Reflecting the nature of our God, the people of God's presence need or require not a hierarchical leadership structure but rather collegial and reciprocal leaders who do not lord it over the flock (1 Pet. 5:1–3). Ordained leaders serve a role in the body of Christ—namely, guiding

13. *Presbyterorum Ordinis*, §2, in *Vatican Council II*, 865; Latin: *Decretum de presbyterorum*, 622.

14. *Presbyterorum Ordinis*, §5, in *Vatican Council II*, 870; Latin: *Decretum de presbyterorum*, 628.

15. Everett Ferguson, *The Church of Christ: A Biblical Ecclesiology for Today* (Grand Rapids: Eerdmans, 1996), 311–16.

16. Kevin Giles suggests that ordination "cannot be demanded of Christian leaders/pastors" because it is "not prescribed by the Bible." Giles, *Patterns of Ministry among the First Christians*, 2nd ed. (Eugene, OR: Cascade Books, 2017), 235.

17. Robert A. Muthiah, *The Priesthood of All Believers in the Twenty-First Century: Living Faithfully as the Whole People of God in a Postmodern Context* (Eugene, OR: Pickwick, 2009), 74.

18. Miroslav Volf, *After Our Likeness: The Church as the Image of the Trinity* (Grand Rapids: Eerdmans, 1998), 224.

19. Volf, *After Our Likeness*, 217.

the flock lovingly and "*telling* the members of the church about their ministry and also of *doing* that ministry among them."[20]

Ordination has become a default mechanism by which Christian churches can validate the spiritual callings of their leaders. The requirements for ordination vary from denomination to denomination, but the legitimacy of someone's calling and preparation (sometimes education) to fulfill that calling is what the church tries to certify in ordaining its ministers. While I do not think it is inappropriate to require such qualifying criteria for leaders in the body of Christ, I recognize that it is more of a cultural tradition than a biblical one. I have made the case earlier in chapter 2 that the style of ordination we work with today is not biblical—that is, it is not clearly established in the ritual of laying on of hands in the New Testament. To be sure, some spiritual gifts may have been either recognized or given during the laying on of hands, but this action by the elders most likely occurred when people were being sent forth from the congregation to do a specific task (like the "deacons" in Acts 6 or Paul and Barnabas in Acts 13). As Robert Muthiah has stated clearly, in the New Testament nowhere "is the laying on of hands tied to installation into a hierarchical office."[21]

Whatever we think of ordination today, it must not become an obstacle to the universal priesthood of believers. If ordination places a barrier between "clergy" and "laity," then church leaders must carefully consider how to overcome this divide. Unfortunately, attempts to maintain an "ordained ministry" within the more general ministry of the entire congregation of believers seem to result in the elevation of ordained persons over the priesthood of believers. As Lutheran theologian Philip Hefner states when comparing the two ministries, "The ordained ministry is preeminent."[22] How can equity within a congregation be maintained when ordained ministry is "preeminent"? To be sure, commitment to full-time ministry as a career deserves genuine respect and honor from the church. Finding ways to provide honor without placing more weight on the potential division between clergy and laity is a unique problem for the church of the future. The language one uses for describing ordination as well as the titles employed by the local congregation for

---

20. Philip Hefner, "Ninth Locus: The Church," in *Christian Dogmatics*, ed. Carl E. Braaten and Robert W. Jenson (Minneapolis: Fortress, 2011), 2:224 (his emphasis).

21. Muthiah, *The Priesthood of All Believers*, 77. In *The Babylonian Captivity of the Church*, Luther argues that ordination is not mentioned in the NT. See Luther, *The Babylonian Captivity of the Church (1520)*, trans. Erik H. Herrmann, in *The Annotated Luther*, ed. Hans J. Hillerbrand, Kirsi I. Stjerna, and Timothy J. Wengert, vol. 3, *Church and Sacrament*, ed. Paul W. Robinson, (Minneapolis: Fortress, 2016), 111. For the Latin, see *De captivitate babylonica*, in WA 6:650, 20–23.

22. Hefner, "Ninth Locus: The Church," 225.

addressing people who have been ordained needs to be monitored with wisdom and insight. Obviously, leaders in a local congregation will need to be convinced of the detriment that such a laity-clergy divide will cause, or the divide will simply be widened.

In this regard, Volf is not helpful. He steers readers throughout his text toward a "free church" model in which believers *together* shape the direction of the church and reflect the equanimity in God's triune life within their own ecclesial lives. Yet at the point of ordination, Volf raises the specter of a clergy-laity divide (despite his protests to the contrary). Volf argues that offices in the church are "a particular type of charismata."[23] While there is no difference in principle between a priest or ordained minister and laypeople, there is a distinction between the "general and the particular priesthood."[24] However, Volf insists this distinction does not "divide the church into two groups."[25] While Volf's assertion may be reflective of the *theoretical* reality of his mind regarding church life, it is not very reflective of the *empirical* reality. The history of the church for the past two thousand years has taught us that if we create a clergy caste (priests or otherwise), we also create a second group—those who are not as privileged as the first group is. Are they "fundamentally equal," as Volf wants to argue?[26] I think not.

Muthiah notes that the problem for Volf begins with his idea that the charismata of offices are different from other charismata.[27] For Volf, charisms of office are different mainly because they serve the entire congregation. Apparently, Volf thinks that the other charisms do *not* serve or represent the whole congregation.[28] He recognizes that he is swimming against the current of his own logic when he states, "If one's premise is the equality of all ministries in the church, then the necessity of (ordained) office is not apparent."[29] Indeed, for one who has so eloquently and vigorously defended the equanimity of the Triune God and that of ecclesial relations, it is surprising to see Volf move toward ordination of offices in this way.

Muthiah chooses to "reconceive" ordination as a rite that is a validation for all believers' gifts and therefore is open for *all* believers.[30] While I do not go that far in my reconsideration of ordination, I do believe that ordination may be necessary for leaders in the church today. Moreover, I understand why the

---

23. Volf, *After Our Likeness*, 246.
24. Volf, *After Our Likeness*, 246.
25. Volf, *After Our Likeness*, 246.
26. Volf, *After Our Likeness*, 246.
27. Muthiah, *The Priesthood of All Believers*, 78–79.
28. Muthiah, *The Priesthood of All Believers*, 79.
29. Volf, *After Our Likeness*, 246.
30. Muthiah, *The Priesthood of All Believers*, 74.

practice of testing one's calling and qualifications to lead local congregations is part of many denominations' and churches' orders. However, my concern lies not in the practice of ordination itself but in the practice of some ordained ministers who assume the ritual of ordination gives them a right to domineer over a local congregation (or elsewhere). My concern also lies in the practice of congregations that lift up ordained ministers to a level unhealthy for any mere mortal, let alone one whose livelihood is the messy business of being in other people's lives! Surely the church of this century cannot repeat the arrogance of the past, when ordained clergy expected preferential treatment from the entire community (unbelievers too); yet we also cannot leave the church without leaders who wield some spiritual authority and guide the church in directions that follow their Master. Somewhere between these two extremes lies the potential to strike the balance of church leaders—one for which I am arguing in this book.

This is *not* to suggest the church is leaderless. As Otto Weber states, "The community requires leadership."[31] It is also *not* to imply that leaders in the church will no longer need to be full-time. From among the body of Christ, some are called "particularly to provide oversight, rule, discipline, teaching, and care."[32] For some leaders, this means that God calls and the congregation confirms that they should be employed to be of service to the local body of Christ in a full-time capacity. Having personally worked as a bivocational pastor (my other job was teaching high school) and eventually as a full-time pastor in the same congregation, I can testify to the abundant sense of clarity of mind and organization of time for the purpose of the church in the full-time position. However, were I to use that full-time calling to do all the work of ministry myself, I would be missing the point of training a universal priesthood of believers to do the work of ministry. One advantage that the church had when I was a bivocational pastor was the need for others in the congregation to pull their weight when I was not available. When I became full-time, it was vitally important that I not lose sight of that valuable lesson, which we all experienced.

Authority?

At this point, I can imagine readers asking important questions. Is it not important for a minister to have training and credentials in order to do the

---

31. Otto Weber, *Versammelte Gemeinde: Beiträge zum Gespräch über Kirche und Gottesdienst* (Neukirchen: Buchhandlung des Erziehungsverein, 1949), 83 (my translation). Weber reminds us that this leadership is one of a shepherd who leads the flock beside still water and into green pastures. Hence, the leading of the church consists of "concrete service."

32. Greg Ogden, *The New Reformation: Returning the Ministry to the People of God* (Grand Rapids: Zondervan, 1990), 150.

work of ministry? Yes, in one sense it is very important. However, if such ministers take on the work of the whole body for themselves, the task becomes Herculean and burnout is likely. To be sure, training is certainly necessary (as I will make clear below), but in addition to knowledge of the Bible, theology, preaching, history, and leadership, training must show others how to do ministry in their own settings.

People follow leaders who love and guide them in the way of being Christian in this world. If I assert my authority in a local congregation through flashing my credentials, demanding a title be used when I am addressed by them, and requiring an over/under relationship from believers under my care, then my authority will be based on those items. As Greg Ogden has said, "When leadership gifts are exercised in a manner consistent with a Christlike character, spiritual authority is the result."[33]

Making the Priesthood of All Believers "Work"

How might the local church implement the priesthood of all believers? Understanding the role of leaders and followers is essential as a foundation for building this participatory structure. While there may be many ways to implement such a priesthood, I offer the following principles to undergird the authentic functioning of such a corporate priesthood.

Equity among Believers

Equity among believers in the congregation is *the* essential prerequisite for the priesthood of all believers. Such equity is not to be confused with uniformity of gifts or functions, yet there can be nothing that hints of a clergy-laity divide. All God's people are ordained to be ministers by virtue of their union with Christ in salvation and baptism. Obstacles to equity must be torn down in the new age of Christ. The biblical basis for this is the fact that in Christ there is "neither Jew nor Gentile, neither slave nor free, nor is there male and female, for you are all one in Christ Jesus" (Gal. 3:28). The God we serve does not show favoritism, nor should we (James 2:9). Every member of the body of Christ in a local congregation must ardently work to esteem others above themselves and to press for a spirit of egalitarianism among God's people. Without such a spirit of mutual submission to each other out of reverence for Christ, there can be no effective priesthood of all believers. "The Church is called to convey to the world the image of a new

33. Ogden, *The New Reformation*, 142.

humanity."[34] We all must make room for others by respecting them as equals, created in the image of God and re-created in the image of Christ.

Some views of the church attempt to hold fast to the idea of equality of its members while simultaneously placing an "ordering" within the community of believers in which leaders are given a ministry of oversight. In such views, this "ordering (*taxis*) is called to reflect the quality of ordering in the divine communion of Father, Son and Holy Spirit."[35] By using the "ordering" in the Triune Godhead, some have proposed that we understand this ordering reflected in the church through the pope, bishops, priests, and laity (Joseph Cardinal Ratzinger) or through the bishops, who reflect the monarchy of the Father in such a ranking (John Zizioulas).[36] However, these views of hierarchy within the life of God attempt to minimize the apparent subordinationism within the Godhead and by extension within the church itself. Nevertheless, the claim made by this style of ordering within God's being has concomitant effects on the ordering of the church. While these views claim that the body of Christ is made up of "co-responsible persons,"[37] one or several leaders are differentiated from other persons and given the task of oversight. In this case, statements such as this appear disingenuous: "Such an ordering which reflects divine communion cannot imply domination or subordination."[38]

One difficulty I find with this proposal is that the Trinity appears to be *eternally* hierarchical in it. It seems that within the nature of God's being, there is a *taxis*—a ranking of over/under. Even if this were true in the eternal realm in God's life, when it is transferred to a sin-ridden world—even in the church—the system of "domination/subordination" simply becomes the way of life. If we are to pattern our lives together after some supposed hierarchy in the Trinity's essence, then as Volf has shown, we end up with a church structure that is hierarchical and dominative over other believers. If one of the persons of the Trinity is "dominant," then patterns of church life reflecting this dominance will construct a hierarchy that demands submission.[39] Volf points out that if one holds to a "symmetrical understanding of the relations"

34. *Baptism, Eucharist and Ministry*, Faith and Order Paper 111 (Geneva: World Council of Churches, 1982), 23.

35. *The Nature and Purpose of the Church: A Stage on the Way to a Common Statement*, Faith and Order Paper 181 (Geneva: World Council of Churches, 1998), 47.

36. Indeed, this was the point of Volf's book *After Our Likeness*. Volf analyzes the writings of Joseph Ratzinger (later Pope Benedict XVI) and John Zizioulas (Metropolitan in the Greek Orthodox Church) with regard to how their views of the Trinity shape their understanding of the hierarchy in the church.

37. *The Nature and Purpose of the Church*, 47.

38. *The Nature and Purpose of the Church*, 47.

39. Volf, *After Our Likeness*, 247.

between Father, Son, and Spirit, then the reflection of that understanding will be a church structure that is more collegial in leading and polycentric in structure.[40] As Volf says, "Universal distribution of the charismata implies *common responsibility* for the life of the church."[41]

Some evangelicals have taken this concept of hierarchy in the Triune Godhead into their understanding of male-female relations.[42] If we are to reflect the nature of God, there must be over/under in our human relations. This is why male and female are dealt with as a hierarchy of roles. However, this approach suggests that both within the Trinity and within male-female relations there is no hint of domination or inequality *in essence*—there is simply a difference *in function*. The difficulty with this argument should be obvious.[43] First, it implies an *eternal subordination* of the Son to the Father. Ontologically, there is a distinction between the Son and Father. In centuries past, this would have been heralded as heresy. Second, it makes a false division between essence and function. Can one have essential equality yet functional inequality? Are roles so removed from essences? One of the points of God's holiness is that his being is *perfectly represented* by his acting. There is no division between what God does and who God is.[44] Third, even if there were some magical way that the eternal God could allow a hierarchy within his life, thereby maintaining functional inequality with essential equality, the history of humankind has shown that such domination of over/under authority usually results in a devaluation of the person on the "under" side. Fourth, God created the human as male and female; they were both made in the image of God and are equal in this regard. Only after the fall and curse (Gen. 3) did dominion and ruling over another human being get started. Therefore, positing a hierarchy in God's ontological, essential nature is dangerous to our view of God and can be harmful to the equity among believers.

40. Volf, *After Our Likeness*, 247.

41. Volf, *After Our Likeness*, 230 (his emphasis).

42. The major weight of this argument has been taken up by Wayne Grudem, *Systematic Theology: An Introduction to Biblical Doctrine* (Grand Rapids: Zondervan, 1994); and John Piper and Wayne Grudem, "A Vision of Biblical Complementarity: Manhood and Womanhood Defined according to the Bible," in *Recovering Biblical Manhood and Womanhood: A Response to Evangelical Feminism*, ed. John Piper and Wayne Grudem (Wheaton: Crossway, 1991), 31–59.

43. See Kevin Giles, *Jesus and the Father: Modern Evangelicals Reinvent the Doctrine of the Trinity* (Grand Rapids: Zondervan, 2006); Giles, *The Rise and Fall of the Complementarian Doctrine of the Trinity* (Eugene, OR: Cascade Books, 2017); Giles, *The Trinity and Subordinationism: The Doctrine of God and the Contemporary Gender Debate* (Downers Grove, IL: InterVarsity, 2002).

44. Colin E. Gunton, *Act and Being: Towards a Theology of the Divine Attributes* (Grand Rapids: Eerdmans, 2002), 117.

The Role of Leaders in the Congregation

If there is equity among all believers, what is the place for leaders? As we have seen, God has not left the church leaderless. Yet what does it mean to be a leader among God's people? I prefer this rather generic term of "leader" for someone who is "taking point" or "directing" aspects of ministry within a local church. The New Testament uses this more generic term to refer to guides, chiefs, Roman governors, and even princes. It is the term ἡγεμών | *hēgemōn*. In its noun form it is used twenty times to speak of such leaders.[45] In its various verbal forms it is used twenty-eight times to speak of "leading the way," "presiding," or "governing."[46] The use in Hebrews 13:7, 17, and 24 is most clearly tied to leading in the church. "Remember your leaders [ἡγουμένων | *hēgoumenōn*], who spoke the word of God to you" (v. 7). Also, "Have confidence in your leaders [ἡγουμένοις | *hēgoumenois*] and submit to their authority, because they keep watch over you as those who must give an account" (v. 17a). And finally, "Greet all your leaders [ἡγουμένους | *hēgoumenous*] and all the Lord's people" (v. 24a).[47] The word "leader" seems to connote someone who guides and directs others toward a goal. It does not contain in its essential meaning the idea of over/under dominating authority. Otto Weber rightly states that "there is only one 'over' in the church of Jesus Christ—the sovereignty of the one Lord who becomes concrete in the spoken and responsive Word."[48] Indeed, there is no "*earthly* 'over' and 'under,'" in the church.[49] Leaders speak the Word of God to the people of God and keep watch over them like shepherds who care for the flock.

What does it mean to be a leader of God's people? I shall try to sketch a response to this question in detail below. First, however, it is essential that we view Christian leading as untethered to issues of power or over/under authority structures. Anything in Christian leadership that smacks of domination owes its life to the powers and dominions of this *kosmos*.[50] We saw in chapter 1 how Christ turned upside down the expectation of the world system for power by requiring his followers to be servants, not those who are served. Leaders in the communities where Christ is the head must remember that they

45. For example, see Matt. 2:6; 10:18; 27:2; Luke 20:20; Acts 23:24.
46. For example, Matt. 2:6; Acts 14:12; Heb. 13:7, 17, 24.
47. All three of these examples in Hebrews are participles—that is, verbal adjectives that act like nouns. Leaders are "the ones who lead."
48. Weber, *Versammelte Gemeinde*, 89 (my translation).
49. Weber, *Versammelte Gemeinde*, 83 (his emphasis).
50. This point about the "powers" and the "domination system," which equals the *kosmos* in the NT, comes from the insightful trilogy of Walter Wink, but especially *Engaging the Powers: Discernment and Resistance in a World of Domination* (Minneapolis: Fortress, 1992), esp. part 1, "The Domination System."

are "servants [ὑπηρέτας | hypēretas] of Christ" and "stewards [οἰκονόμους | oikonomous] of the mysteries of God" (1 Cor. 4:1 NASB). The two words Paul uses here are rather unusual descriptors in the New Testament for leaders. They are "servants," but not the expected term "slaves, servants" (δοῦλοι | douloi; διάκονοι | diakonoi), but "attendants who wait on others" (ὑπηρέτης | hypēretēs). This term can also refer to a rower on a ship—or even an "under-rower." This worker serves on a ship as one of the crew. He is not the captain of the ship but one who makes it operate in unison of movement. This is how Paul wants to be regarded by the Corinthians—as an "under-rower." In addition, he speaks of being a "steward" or "manager of a household" or even "treasurer" (οἰκονόμος | oikonomos). People in such a position of trust "must prove faithful" (1 Cor. 4:2). Both words remind the hearers that Paul is not in charge of the church but is a leader who is *serving in a working capacity* for the united function of the "ship" and who is *guiding the actions of the people in God's house faithfully on behalf of the Master.* How can leaders of this type dominate the people with whom they are serving? Christian leaders are not power mongers. Indeed, leaders in the church are Christ's gifts to his people (Eph. 4:11). Leaders are set apart by Christ and the congregation to "lead and help the rest of the church in doing that which is the task of everyone."[51]

Daniel Migliore has argued that among Christians the use of any kind of power that does not take into account the great reversal of power in Christ is illegitimate. He asks a provocative question for all God's people, especially leaders in the body of Christ: "What would the exercise of power look like in a church reformed and renewed in the light of the power of God made known in the crucified and risen Christ?"[52] Christian leadership is service to our God and to our fellow humans. Certainly one dimension of leadership in the light of the incarnation is that followers of Christ must be willing to humble themselves in order to do the work of ministry. Another dimension of leadership in light of the cross-resurrection event is that followers of Christ must find ways to deal "non-coercively with issues of the exercise of power in community."[53] Christian leadership serves the people of God's presence by engaging all the participants in the local congregation as a team of equals. Leaders understand that every believer is a "member of the messianic people of God," and therefore all members of the community "have the gift of the Spirit and are therefore 'office-bearers.'"[54] We must ask ourselves, "Do we equate

51. Ferguson, *The Church of Christ*, 317.
52. Daniel L. Migliore, *The Power of God and the gods of Power* (Louisville: Westminster John Knox, 2008), 69.
53. Migliore, *The Power of God and the gods of Power*, 69.
54. Moltmann, *The Church in the Power of the Spirit*, 290, 298.

power with the kind of control and mastery over others that characterizes the power plays of secular institutions?"[55] Decision-making must not belong to someone who takes over the control stick and maneuvers it beyond the reach of other believers. Decision-making must be a reflection of shared giftedness and shared authority. It operates with confidence that God's Spirit can and will bring consensus to the questions that confront the church. We must ask ourselves, "How does the everyday government of our churches reflect our view of the power of God whom we worship?"[56]

Yet we also know that leaders are necessary in the local body of Christ so that God's mission for the world remains the centerpiece of our agendas. There are *functional* differences of calling and gifts spread out among God's people, but this does not imply any leveling in God's eyes. The community of believers does not understand equality "in the sense of uniformity."[57] It honors a diversity of gifts, just as it honors the Triune God, who disperses such variety through the Spirit. Migliore states a necessary reminder of the need for leadership: "Some form of order and leadership is necessary in every community, including the community called the church. It is sheer romanticism to think it can be otherwise."[58] This is true. Nevertheless, it is essential for leaders of the people of God to recall that such positions may have authority, but not an over/under structure of power.

What is it that leaders are to do in the local congregation? Essentially, the role of leaders in the congregation is twofold: providing biblically based vision and equipping the saints for the work of ministry. Readers will notice that I did not mention preaching, teaching, or even pastoral care. These aspects of the ministry of the church may not always be resident in a church's group of leaders. Hopefully, the Spirit of God will gift some members in leading who also have the gift to teach or preach or offer counsel, but the greater concern here is that the *entire* body of Christ in one location be equipped to do the work of ministry, both within the church and outside of it. Too many times, we have asked one person to do the work of ministry that God intended to be handled by a plurality of gifted people. Just because one has pastoral gifts does not mean she or he is good at administration, bookkeeping, or organizing special occasions for the whole church. Further, those who are gifted in administration and leadership may not also have the gifts needed to preach or teach. It should be clear from this explanation that *leading* the people of God's presence does not necessarily mean *pastoring* as it is usually defined today.

---

55. Migliore, *The Power of God and the gods of Power*, 70.
56. Migliore, *The Power of God and the gods of Power*, 70.
57. Moltmann, *The Church in the Power of the Spirit*, 298.
58. Migliore, *The Power of God and the gods of Power*, 70.

How do leaders provide vision and equipping for the saints? They cast a vision of where they believe God wants to lead that congregation in the future. In order to do this, they will need to preach and teach the Word regularly, thereby striking the imagination of hearers to begin building a realm of faith and spirituality that spills over into their everyday lives. Helping to craft this vision is an essential task of leaders because, without such common goals and imaginative structures in place, the people of God's presence will become individualistic and spin off into their own spirituality without others in the body of Christ.

In addition to providing vision, church leaders train believers to know who they are in Christ, what gifts God has distributed to them, and how they are to bear the presence of Christ to the world. Leaders "equip" believers or "mend the gaps" they may have so that they can be effective in their own ministry/service to Christ and others. Volf underscores this by saying, "The task of leaders is first to animate all the members of the church to engage their pluriform charismatic activities, and then to coordinate these activities."[59] Leaders are *not* priests doing ministry on behalf of the congregation, thereby exempting other believers from doing ministry. Leaders continue to do ministry themselves, to be sure, but not as some specialized caste of privileged people in the church. In effect, all the people of God's presence are ministers together; we are "co-workers [συνεργοί | *synergoi*] with God" and each other (1 Cor. 3:9). Leaders work to bring out the evidence of God's gifts and coordinate them for the edification of the whole community of believers.

Leaders Help Believers Discern Their Gifts and Release Them into Ministry

Since a prominent centerpiece of my pneumatic ecclesiology is the gifts of the Spirit, I need to clarify what I mean by these and how discernment of them is a process of the whole church in which leaders can guide believers. I do not see a need for the either/or dualism that usually confronts ecclesial practice—namely, either a one-sided stress on institutional structures or a one-sided stress on charismatic gifts. The pneumatic ecclesiology that I envision sees these aspects of church life working together and informing each other. On the one hand, as Muthiah warns, "These structures must have the flexibility to allow for the free moving of the Spirit."[60] On the other hand, the movement of the Spirit among us must also respect and work alongside the institutional structures in order to save the people of God's presence

---

59. Volf, *After Our Likeness*, 230.
60. Muthiah, *The Priesthood of All Believers*, 84.

from being a chaotic Corinthian church where attenders cannot always see the movement of the Spirit because of the rather selfish movement of gifted people.

Howard Snyder provides us with an excellent starting point: "Spiritual gifts are not 'things' that God gives, like presents or bonuses. Rather they are *manifestations of his grace* in the church."[61] Spiritual gifts are given to God's people in order to build up the local community and to fulfill God's mission in the world. As Clark Pinnock notes, "Gifts are divine actions that build up the community and advance its mission. They demonstrate the power of the Spirit, who is at work in the church. They are manifestations of the Spirit's presence (1 Cor. 12:7)."[62]

It is important to note that "every member is a charismatic"[63]—that is, every believer in the congregation is endowed with spiritual gifts (*charismata*) from the Holy Spirit. "The community which lives in the power of the Spirit will be characterized by a variety of charisms. The Spirit is the giver of diverse gifts which enrich the life of the community."[64] As Peter tells his readers, "Each of you should use whatever gift [χάρισμα | *charisma*] you have received to serve [διακονοῦντες | *diakonountes*] others, as faithful stewards [οἰκονόμοι | *oikonomoi*] of God's grace in its various forms" (1 Pet. 4:10). "Each of you"—every single one of you—should serve in ministry to others as stewards or household managers of the spiritual gift entrusted to you. Notice the word "serving" or "ministering" (from διακονέω | *diakoneō*) and the word "stewards" (from *oikonomos*) are used in conjunction with *using the gifts given to each one*. Since every member of the local body of Christ has at least one gift,[65] there must be leaders in the congregation who are able to assist with the management or stewardship of such gifts. This means that leaders recognize the interdependence of all members since the manifestation of *each gift* in the local congregation was meant by the Spirit to help equip the saints for the work of their ministry. "The Holy Spirit bestows gifts on every member of the Body of Christ for the building up of the fellowship of the Church and for the faithful fulfilling of the mission of Christ. All have received gifts and all are responsible."[66] Ideally, this makes the community of gifted believers one that is active, not passive.

---

61. Howard Snyder, *Radical Renewal: The Problem of Wineskins Today* (Houston: Touch Publications, 1996), 133 (his emphasis).
62. Clark H. Pinnock, *Flame of Love: A Theology of the Holy Spirit* (Downers Grove, IL: InterVarsity, 1996), 130.
63. Moltmann, *The Church in the Power of the Spirit*, 296.
64. *Baptism, Eucharist and Ministry*, 27.
65. Snyder, *Radical Renewal*, 144; cf. Volf, *After Our Likeness*, 228, 230.
66. *The Nature and Purpose of the Church*, 41.

If one refuses to use one's gift or one does not recognize it, then the whole congregation is diminished by this lack of input. Clearly, giftedness in the body of Christ cannot mean chaos where individuals do whatever they want when they want. Giftedness must be submitted to the Holy Spirit and to leaders, whose responsibility it is to recognize gifts and then release God's people into the functioning of these gifts "in a fitting and orderly way" (1 Cor. 14:40).

How can leaders help a congregation recognize their spiritual gifts? In order to know people's gifts, leaders must be "in" their lives. Christian leadership is rarely about leading people from a distance. It is about living with people in the nitty-gritty of life and helping them to see how they relate their faith to the vagaries of existence. It is helping them to apply the Word of God to their situations so that they can help others in the same way. It is bringing the presence of Christ to them in crisis so that they can do the same with those to whom and with whom they share ministry. In this context of living, discerning and wise leaders will point to actions or attitudes that individuals may exhibit and will begin working with these individuals to determine whether the Spirit is working through their lives with a manifestation of his grace. However, Pinnock is correct in stating, "Leaders should not be trying to control everything but foster life and discern gifts of those under their care."[67] It is the Spirit who distributes gifts, not leaders.

It does little good solely to *recognize* gifts in people without *releasing* them in their gifts. What do I mean by release? Once someone's spiritual gift has been recognized (by the leaders and perhaps the congregation as well as the individual), the first step is to make room for them to use their gift in ministry. Some gifts become obvious as to when they should be released; others may be slower to release simply because we are not comfortable with them or because the church may not know that they need them at this point. Whatever the case, gifts were not given to lie dormant in the recesses of the soul. They are for the body of Christ to use in its ministry/service to the world.

Helping the congregation recognize and then release its gifts in the calling of the church to provide ministry to the world is a crucial dimension of leadership. I should like to illustrate the role of leaders in helping others discern the place for their gifts with the large stained-glass window at the front of the church where I worship. Facing east, the stained glass of red, blue, yellow, green, and purple rises from the baptistery to the ceiling behind

67. Pinnock, *Flame of Love*, 140.

the choir area and pulpit. On bright Sunday mornings, it becomes a glowing kaleidoscope filtering the various small translucent pieces of glass into an arrangement of a unified theme—it is a tall cross (which is actually the crossbeams of the structure) around which are the mosaic pieces of colored glass forming a yellow circle whose beams radiate outward from the center of the cross. Each piece of glass is different in size, color, and translucence. However, when arranged in the right places by the artist, they combine to form a *whole* picture. By itself, each piece means nothing—its meaning only comes clear when the piece is set within the whole and the light shines through it.

Leaders are like the artistic arrangers of God's masterpiece within a local church. They neither make the pieces of glass nor design the overall project. Instead, leaders work with each piece to determine how it fits in the portrait that God has planned for that congregation. The beauty of this stained-glass mosaic is found in its diversity of colors and skilled placement. The beauty of the mosaic of our gifts within the congregation is also found in its diversity. Leadership teams engage in the lives of God's people in order to discern where each person fits in the overall portrait that a local body displays. Rather than depicting some individualistic piety that only displays one's own religious spirituality to the world, the mosaic of the church depicts the unity of the Spirit that is not sameness but unity in difference.

In order to achieve this goal of ministry among the body of Christ, leaders must learn to operate in plurality (where feasible). In the New Testament, leaders are almost always mentioned in the plural—even in local congregations. Paul established a policy of appointing "elders in every town" (Titus 1:5) and "elders for them in each church" (Acts 14:23a). Plural leadership in a local congregation limits the tendency toward ruling with over/under authority by one person. Plural leadership allows a check-and-balance system for decisions that must be made on behalf of the church. Plural leadership reflects in some way the polycentric operation of the Trinity in which there is consensus of will and unity of action. If leaders operate as a team, there is greater likelihood that the church as a whole will operate as a team in its mission.

It seems improbable that each believer will discover, discern, and develop in their spiritual gifts within a hierarchical system of leadership. This does not automatically mean that gifts will flourish under an egalitarian system, but the prospects are greatly enhanced. Why is this the case? The Spirit gives gifts to those whom the Spirit wills. Where there is openness for God to distribute gifts throughout the local body, there will be greater openness to receive and utilize these gifts in the local congregation.

Practices of the Universal Priesthood of Believers

Since this chapter is designed to demonstrate a more practical side of the implications for leading God's people as a universal priesthood, I need to portray more clearly what the Christian priesthood does. In this way, it will be clearer how leaders are to "equip the saints" to do their work of priestly ministry. This description will lead us into an investigation of structural issues.

The various tasks that Christian believers perform together as priests may be summarized in this essential concept: priests serve God and others. As we have seen, this verb "serve" may easily be substituted with "minister to." We minister to God with our worship and deeds, bringing honor and glory to God with both lips and lives. We minister to others by serving them and sharing our lives with them. Indeed, the word "sharing" seems to act as something of a synonym for "serving" as a priest. Demonstrating their active participation in ministry, Christian priests serve God by ministering to him and serve humans by representing them to God and God to them. The essential aspect of priestly ministry is *sharing* our lives with others by *serving* them. This is no small task. As W. A. Whitehouse has rightly noted, when serving people "the point is to serve; and usually this means to be imposed upon without imposing."[68] This is the first and most foundational truth to understand about being a minister for others. Other aspects of the priestly task that involve sharing are described below.

Christian priests share the presence of Christ with others. The New Testament term κοινωνία | *koinōnia* means "sharing" or "participation" or "fellowship." Reflecting something of the trinitarian intimacy, our fellowship on earth is due to our common Lord. We *share* Christ's presence by the Spirit *together*. In the midst of the congregation, we demonstrate our love for Christ and our love for each other. However, this fellowship is not only for the people of God; it is given to us so that we might witness to this rich spiritual union with Christ to those who do not know him. Fellowship in the Spirit is not about chicken dinners, homecoming, and good times in the church fellowship hall. To be sure, it may include those things, but these are pale reflections of the reality underlying the fellowship in the Spirit. God the Spirit binds us together in peace, harmony, and unity. The people of God are not drawn together because we all have similar tastes, likes, or dislikes. Homogeneity, where the congregation looks alike and possesses similar class structures, does not genuinely characterize the people of God's presence. As Migliore states, "Homogeneity in the Christian community is therefore a contradiction

---

68. W. A. Whitehouse, "Christological Understanding," in Anderson, *Theological Foundations for Ministry*, 226.

of the gospel of God's omnipotent love, which frees us to accept as brothers and sisters those considered strangers and enemies."[69] God draws his people together from various races and cultures, from various regions and places, in order to experience and share the love of God that overcomes our categories and divisions. When it happens among God's people, it is a testimony to all who experience it that God is greater than our differences and that the shalom of the future eschaton can be experienced to some extent in the here and now. In this sense, the church "is to be a sign, symbol and forerunner of the Kingdom of God."[70]

Christian priests share their lives and substance with others. It is a central task of Christian priests to "share with others" (Heb. 13:16). The terminology here is the word for "fellowship" or "sharing" (κοινωνίας | *koinōnias*). A companion term used just before this is "doing good for others" (εὐποιΐας | *eupoiias*). Both of these terms have a technical meaning of "benevolence to the poor" and a partnership where goods are shared with others.[71] These are sacrifices with which God is well pleased.

Christian priests share their story with others. Central to the task of priesthood is the testimony—the witness—that we bring to others on behalf of Christ. Christian priests share the story of Christ and how that story intertwines with their own story. Narrative is a viable way to speak to the truth of God in one's life. Moltmann points out that the Christian community is a "story-telling fellowship."[72] As priests within that fellowship, we bear witness to the good news of Christ within the various contexts of our societies. The writer to the Hebrews describes well this task of bearing witness: we continually offer to God "a sacrifice of praise—the fruit of lips that openly profess his name" (Heb. 13:15). Therefore, we perform the priestly task of witness by *acknowledging* or *professing* (ὁμολογούντων | *homologountōn*) the character of our God as demonstrated in his name. From our lips arises a continual sacrifice consisting of praise—voluntary eruptions from our inner being in thanksgiving for God's grace.

Christian priests share their faults with one another. "Therefore confess your sins [ἁμαρτίας | *hamartias*] to each other and pray for each other so that you may be healed" (James 5:16). While Christian priests *profess* the goodness of God in praise (ὁμολογούντων | *homologountōn*), they also *confess* their sins to each other (ἐξομολογεῖσθε | *exomologeisthe*). Notice that the two Greek words have the same root word with different prefixes. We *profess* aloud and publicly

---

69. Migliore, *The Power of God and the gods of Power*, 106.
70. Snyder, *Radical Renewal*, 118.
71. William L. Lane, *Hebrews 9–13*, WBC 47b (Dallas: Word Books, 1991), 552.
72. Moltmann, *The Church in the Power of the Spirit*, 225.

the character of our God; we *confess* to one another (perhaps individually and less publicly?) the shortcomings that afflict us. Christian priests listen to each other and share their own ways of missing the mark so that the members of the body of Christ may be healed—made whole. Christian priests are under no illusion of perfection due to their own abilities. They do not need to wear a mask of pretention that deflects any probing of their lives. They model such openness and vulnerability in ways that honor God's grace in them.

Christian priests share joys with others. Christian priests exhibit delight in their God, rejoicing over the smallest things in life that reflect God's goodness. Their celebratory spirits are contagious—even for unbelievers. "Is anyone happy? Let them sing songs of praise" (James 5:13b). Despite outward circumstances, joy runs like a deep river below the crust of the earth, springing forth in geysers of expansive joy. Christian priests learn to share this joy with others.

Christian priests pray one for another. Christian priests intercede on behalf of others to their Lord through the power and presence of the Holy Spirit (Rom. 8:25). The universal priesthood of believers is a corporate body made up of "intercessors, who believe the future into being."[73] Christian priests recognize the importance of prayer on behalf of others through intercession before Christ, who is praying for all humans in the throne room of God. It is the heart of our High Priest in the heavens that dictates the empathetic urges in his priests on earth to pray for others. In this way, "our prayers on earth are the echo of his prayers in heaven."[74] As the Spirit brings the presence of the risen Lord among his assembled people, we begin to plead for the needs of fellow believers as well as fellow humans. Frequently, we do not know what to pray for, so the Spirit prays for us and through us (Rom. 8:26). Thus, as Tom Greggs has poignantly stated, "The event of the Spirit's intensive and active presence in the life of the believer moves the believer within the movement of God."[75]

Indeed, all of the priestly ministries of the local congregation have their beginning and goal in such intercessory prayer. "The practice of Christian prayer, however, cannot be separated from service and work for God's reign. Praying is always to be accompanied by working."[76] "But action is also no substitute for prayer."[77] "The Church does not minister through the power of its own action but only through the power of its Lord, and therefore it cannot fulfil its *diakonia* on earth without continuous engagement in intercession

73. Wink, *Engaging the Powers*, 301.
74. These words are from James Torrance, quoted in Greggs, *Dogmatic Ecclesiology*, 1:277.
75. Greggs, *Dogmatic Ecclesiology*, 1:280.
76. Migliore, *The Power of God and the gods of Power*, 110.
77. Wink, *Engaging the Powers*, 306.

through its great High Priest at the right hand of God Almighty."[78] While too few congregations may engage this corporate work of prayer, it is the lifeblood of maintaining ministry through humble service. Agendas and programs that tend to replace prayer simply confuse action with true Christian service. As Torrance has reminded us,

> The frantic attempts of the Church in modern times to find ways and means of making its message relevant to [humans], of clothing its ministries with worldly power, or of evolving methods and instruments which will ensure the popularity and success of its enterprise, are open admission that the Church has ceased to believe that the Gospel is really able to effect what it proclaims and of tragic disbelief in the power of intercession, i.e., in the active intervention of the Church's heavenly Mediator which is echoed through the Spirit in the Church's stammering prayers on earth.[79]

The *Praxis* of Leading God's People in (Their) Ministry

How can the universal priesthood of believers be implemented in a local congregation? I suggest one practical way is by doing ministry together and then reflecting on it together. The word πρᾶξις | *praxis* is an ancient Greek word used by Aristotle to refer to how humans live together in the city (πόλις | *polis*) with a type of reason he calls "practical reason" (φρόνησις | *phronēsis*). How do humans guide the life of the *polis* by making necessary judgments in various situations?[80] By way of contrast, ἐπιστήμη | *epistēmē* was a knowledge related to θεωρία | *theōria* (science and contemplation), while τέχνη | *technē* was a knowledge related to ποίησις | *poiēsis* (production of human artifacts).[81] *Praxis* is the third realm of human life and thought related to *doing* or living together.

Praxis *and Church Leadership*

How am I using *praxis* in relation to leadership of the church? Following the lines of Paulo Freire's approach, I use *praxis* to describe a dialectical process with which humans may operate in life—namely, in action and reflection. *Praxis* is *theory-laden action*.[82] Theory is frequently pitted against practice, thereby

---

78. Torrance, "Service in Jesus Christ," 731.
79. Torrance, "Service in Jesus Christ," 731.
80. Rebecca S. Chopp, "Praxis," in *The New Dictionary of Catholic Spirituality*, ed. Michael Downey (Collegeville, MN: Liturgical Press, 1993), 756–64, here 758.
81. Chopp, "Praxis," 758.
82. Paulo Freire, *Pedagogy of the Oppressed*, trans. Myra Bergman Ramos (New York: Continuum, 2002), 125.

separating the two. My use of *praxis* is an attempt to hold in tension these two sometimes polar aspects of theory and practice. Leaders train believers to engage in Christian *practices* without divorcing them from *theory* (or theology). In the process of *doing* ministry arise theological questions that propel our *thinking/reflection* on ministry, which in turn helps to reshape our *doing*, which again continues to provide input into our *reflecting*, which comes around again to shape our *doing*. In the past, theology has too frequently been separated from the life of the church, thereby diminishing the role of reflection on our churchly action. However, when theology is placed in the middle of the *praxis* of the church, it provides stability and vigor to our action. Rather than a vicious cycle out of which the church can never rise, this cycle represents a life-giving, dialectical process, which refuses to allow the Christian faith and practice to be housed in one particular mode of either reflection or action. Instead it forces our *theōria* to engage our *praxis* and vice versa. Christian theology seems to be better suited to this type of *phronēsis* or practical reason.[83]

How does this apply to leading the people of God into fulfilling their mission? Leaders are aware that theology must be learned *on the ground*, so to speak. Theology will forever remain amorphous and detached until it engages the challenges to the faith in all the variations of human existence. Understanding people's gifts within a congregation, leaders should begin to train believers to do ministry through experiencing ministry. Allow me to provide an example. It is extremely difficult to learn how to do ministry in a classroom. Of course it can be done, but it ends up being something like a brain surgeon who knows how to deliver a baby because she has learned about it in medical school but has never had to do so. However, if we put the brain surgeon in a classroom, providing the necessary techniques and information for deliveries, and then ask the surgeon to spend a few days in the hospital obstetric (OB) ward helping to deliver babies, her knowledge is likely to increase greatly. Why? Undoubtedly, it is because her *practice* or *experience* has clarified the *theory*. Now if we add to that a return to the classroom to follow up on what was learned and to reflect on the birthing process, we would discover that even more learning would occur. Then, every time the surgeon might return to that OB ward to help deliver babies, she would be engaging in a *praxis* of delivering babies. *Praxis* is a theory-laden action whose continued action and reflection build a type of practical reasoning (*phronēsis*) on the practice itself.

It is this cyclical, dialectical process, in which theory and practice are held together, that undergirds the training of all Christians in the local church to

83. Chopp, "Praxis," 764.

be ministers of Christ in the world. Believers *go out* into the world in order to bear witness to Christ and to bring his presence to those in need. In that process of going out there is a theological-laden practice to fulfill the mission of Christ. However, such a going out must be followed by a *coming in*, where believers gather to worship together, hear God's Word together, pray together, and receive clarity and motivation for further ministry together. They go out, come in, go out again, and come back again. As mentioned earlier, Karl Barth offers a potent image for this by reminding us of the diastole and systole process of the heart pumping blood throughout the body. Service to God (or worship) must have an *inward direction* before it can provide an *outward ministry*; such movements must also be *continual*. The inward and outward service are like the "circular motion of the heart which in order to pump blood through the whole organism not only goes out in the diastole but also has to return in the systole, yet only to go out again in the renewed diastole" (*CD* IV/3.2:833).

The concept of *praxis* is beneficial for our proposal not simply because doing always informs thinking but also because it is in this dialectical, cyclical space of doing-thinking, thinking-doing, that we make room for the presence of God's Spirit to engage God's people so that their actions have resonance with the true *missio Dei*. Such an approach to leading and ministry recognizes the necessity of a "holy pause" in which space is given to the Spirit and the Word of God to inspire our movements or even correct them so that we may bear the presence of Christ to others faithfully. We do not arrive at any task solely with a theory (theology) that needs to be enacted. Instead, we come to tasks acknowledging that our theories are experience-laden and our experience in performing the task at hand is theory-driven. The cycle of theory-*praxis* provides a paradigm for knowledge-action that seems to fit the Christian life and ministry best.

It is God's presence that we experience in the participatory nature of Christian worship and Christian practices that draws us out of the purely cognitive realm of theory and propels us into the practical realm of action. It is the presence of God in the participatory nature of Christian ministry, action, and service that draws us out of the purely active realm of doing and propels us back into the reflective realm of theory (theology). There is a "marriage of action and reflection."[84] This cycle continues in Christian life and ministry so that our thinking and action are shaped by our reflection and doing, thereby remaining "open" to the movement of the Spirit and to instruction of the Word of God within our different contexts of ministry.

84. Rebecca S. Chopp, *The Praxis of Suffering: An Interpretation of Liberation and Political Theologies* (Eugene, OR: Wipf & Stock, 1986), 37.

Spheres of Leadership

While many profiles and visions for church leadership exist, I have chosen to interact with one offered by Mark Lau Branson, who describes three spheres of church leadership.[85] The first sphere he labels *interpretive leadership*. This refers to the realm of leadership in the church whereby the entire community is taught and challenged to interpret various "texts" in their lives. Interpretive leadership "creates and provides resources for a community of interpreters who pay attention to God, texts, context, and congregation."[86] Leaders help to build an interpreting community of learners in the local congregation. This is true with every sermon or teaching when the texts of Scripture are presented in gathered community. How leaders interpret these fundamental texts trains the community in the art of interpretation. Leaders also train believers in how to apply the truths of Scripture to the contexts of their lives. Who are our neighbors? How is the church to respond not only to the spiritual needs of a community but also to the physical needs? Interpretive leadership "provides the resources, the inspiration, the perceptions that form a people who own the biblical and historical narratives, renarrate their own personal and corporate stories, and become aware of the numerous forces that shape their context."[87]

Relational leadership, the second sphere labeled by Branson, "creates and nourishes all of the human connections in various groups, partnerships, friendships, and families."[88] Recalling that our God is *relational* in the very core of his being, this style of leadership calls forth the heart of connections between human beings in the covenant community. It reminds us that our ministry is one of reconciliation (2 Cor. 5:18–21) between God and people as well as people and people. If leaders do not possess "emotional intelligence" to foster such relationality among God's people, then they will need to find ways to engage and improve such capacities.[89]

Implemental leadership, the third sphere, "develops strategies and structures so that a congregation embodies gospel reconciliation and justice in

85. It was while working through Muthiah's book on the priesthood of believers that I was introduced to Branson's work on leadership. See Muthiah, *The Priesthood of All Believers*, 167–70. The story of how Branson used these spheres in revitalizing a church is found in Mark Lau Branson, "Forming Church, Forming Mission," *International Review of Mission* 92, no. 365 (April 2003): 153–68.

86. Mark Lau Branson, "Forming God's People," *Congregations* 29, no. 1 (Winter 2003): 23–27, here 24.

87. Branson, "Forming God's People," 25.

88. Branson, "Forming God's People," 24.

89. Branson, "Forming God's People," 25. Branson refers to the book by Daniel Coleman, *Emotional Intelligence* (New York: Bantam, 1995), but there are also numerous sources related to church work that discuss these important themes.

a local context and in the larger world."[90] This third arena is necessary for any spiritual endeavor (like a church), since it gives skeletal structure to (frequently) amorphous ideas. Leaders help to craft meaningful structures for the congregation so that room is made for the goals of mission in the church and world. Utilizing the interpretation of texts and fostering the relational networks in the local congregation must be combined now with "concrete forms and practices."[91] With such implemental leadership, structures *serve the purpose of the congregation*, not simply provide rigidity for our lives together. Administrative work is probably the least appreciated aspect of pastoral ministry today. However, when it is part of a broader leadership plan (as in these three spheres of leadership), it can be a way to revitalize a discussion of how the church is set up and why.

To these spheres I would add two more dimensions of leadership: the active-reflective dimension and the spiritual dimension. *Active-reflective leadership* takes its cue from the writings of Freire, who underscores the fact that action and reflection are "interactive."[92] So, perhaps this hyphenated form of leadership can help to emphasize what we learn through *praxis*. Praxis helps us interpret texts and contexts, to be sure, but it also helps us live the Christian life *in the world* and then return to the community to engage in prayerful reflection on the action. We open the Scriptures together to learn what there is about this experience of serving other humans in the world that pushes us further into understanding the Christian faith—*our own individual* Christian faith. Through our actions together, we learn the faith and learn how to do the ministry of bearing Christ's presence to the world.

Allow me to clarify a bit more what I mean by the role of *praxis* in Christian ministry and life. Ministry is learned while doing it, but Christian ministry relies on a starting point that may be considered theoretical/theological. We do not necessarily arrive at a Christian ministry by engaging in action before understanding what God wants from us. Christian ministry must be rooted in God's revelation to us of what we are to do on Christ's behalf. It must have some tendrils sunk deep in the Word of God in order to nourish it along the journey. Without such nourishment, ministry will become some type of service only tangentially related to Christian love. However, once the task has been clarified and ministry engaged, the theoretical and practical dimensions become a learning cycle in doing the service of God. In other words, we do

90. Branson, "Forming God's People," 24.
91. Branson, "Forming God's People," 26.
92. Freire, *Pedagogy of the Oppressed*, 125. He states, "Human activity consists of action and reflection: it is praxis; it is transformation of the world. And as praxis, it requires theory to illuminate it. Human activity is theory and practice; it is reflection and action."

not need to obtain formal training in order to *do* ministry, since all God's people are expected to do so by the power and leading of God's Spirit. Yet we do need leaders who have formal training in nurturing all members of the body of Christ to be equipped to do works of service (ministry). Leaders must lead God's people in the direction of what God wants them to do. They must train believers in knowing and interpreting the Bible; they must live alongside believers in order to encourage them to use spiritual gifts that may presently lie dormant; they must provide instruction in Christian growth and sanctification; and they must "make room for" fellow believers to *do* the work of ministry among God's people and in the world.

Finally, I would also add *spiritual leadership* to the spheres of leading a church. What I mean in this sphere is the importance of guiding a group of people into hearing God for themselves without needing a mediator who is a professional clergyperson. Further, spiritual leadership focuses on developing the whole human being in order to make room for God to make them whole. Guidance and mentoring in prayer, Bible reading, group Bible study, and spiritual disciplines all help to lead believers into a spiritual state of readiness to be used by God.

Implications for the Training of Future Church Leaders

If what I have portrayed in this chapter is to come about in our churches, there will need to be a paradigm shift in the way we train future leaders of the church. Instead of focusing solely on training ministers to know *a certain set of information* (e.g., the Bible, theology, church history, ethics), we will need to broaden the knowledge set to include more than information about the Christian religion. Future leaders in our churches will need to know *how to perform certain tasks* within our communities of faith. Allow me to suggest a few of these. I see these areas as concentric circles, moving from the centermost to the outermost, revolving around the five spheres of leadership mentioned above.

1. *Spiritual leadership.* Future leaders will need to know how to equip the saints to do the work of ministry. Christian priests do not simply happen as a result of the new birth in Christ. Christian priests need to be equipped (restored to wholeness) and made ready to do service to the church and world. In the future, leaders must know how to discern people's callings and gifts. Training in recognizing such spiritual gifts needs to be an essential aspect of leaders' education.

Figure 4.1
The *Praxis* of Ministry

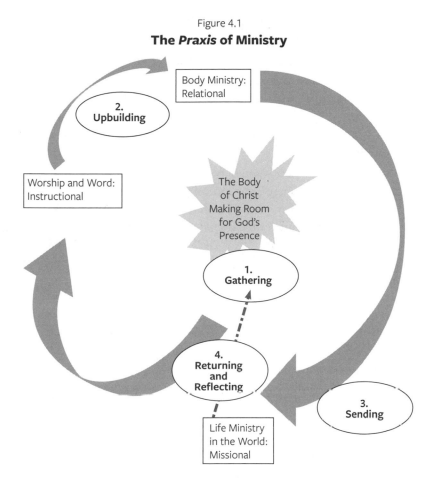

2. *Interpretive leadership*. Future leaders will need to know how to read Scripture and how to teach others to read Scripture in the congregation. They will need to teach by example ways to understand and probe the Scripture *together*. Leaders will need to provide a clear understanding of Scripture in order to teach how it can be applied in differing contexts.

3. *Implemental leadership*. Future leaders will need to know how to build teams of leaders and teams of members in groups. Education for this style of leadership must engage leaders in group dynamics and team management. How are decisions to be made in a team-leadership situation? What do structures look like that operate coherently with the universal priesthood of believers? How is leading a church different

from (or similar to) running a business? How can a local congregation discover and fulfill its mission in the world?

4. *Relational leadership.* Future leaders will need to know how to motivate people to be active, not passive, in the community of faith. How can we get others involved in the cause of Christ in this place? How do we teach people to live with each other in community? How do we build fellowship within a congregation? How do we release people into ministry? How do we teach believers to serve others?

5. *Action-reflective leadership.* Future leaders will need to understand the dynamics of learning in a congregation, especially the role of *praxis* in action-reflection of ministry. Leaders will need to know how to train believers in the reciprocating process of doing-thinking, thinking-doing. Leaders will need to make clear the role of worship for the purpose of mission. They will need to provide leadership in the very process of making room for the Spirit in ministry.

Given the complexities embedded in these tasks of leaders, why would we assume that just anybody without training would want to handle such a job? Perhaps uneducated leaders could conjure up enough spiritual energy in a congregation to get people to follow *them*, but in my experience it is highly improbable that these leaders will make room for others to use and develop their own gifts as God intends. In other words, leaders who have no biblical or theological education may founder on the shoals of defining appropriately the *mission* of the people of God. Leaders who have no knowledge of psychology or human relationships may fall short of the goal of building confident men and women ministers of *all* God's people. Leaders who have no skill set for showing people how to discern what God has gifted them may not recognize (let alone nourish) gifted believers. Leaders who have no training in communication may assume their own cobbling together of sermons or lessons is sufficient to build the local body of Christ on their own self-taught skills. Leaders who have no exposure to engaging intellectual challenges to Christianity may discover their church ripped apart by someone's challenge to the resurrection of Christ. Leaders who have no training in philosophy may find themselves dumbfounded when facing the senseless death of a ten-day-old baby and questions about God's fairness. Leaders who have no acquaintance with history may find their church moored on the rocks of some newfangled (yet ancient) heretical ideas without even realizing it. Leaders who have no experience with attempting to understand and read culture may find their people swept away by the latest fads or pulled down by some cultural eddy that is spinning in the opposite direction of the Christian faith.

The people of God deserve leaders who have been thoughtfully trained in all of these areas. This is not to say that education alone will resolve all issues in the local body of Christ. Clearly there are different levels of maturity and understanding operating at various times in any local congregation—among both leaders and followers. Yet given the immense complexity of navigating through today's anti-Christian society in the West, and given the even greater complexity of helping believers come to full function in their ministries, leaders ought to be prepared in all aspects of ministry to unleash the body of Christ into its gifts. To do less is to lead the church toward even more irrelevance in the future.

I realize that some churches do require formal education—perhaps even seminary training—for their leaders. However, my experience and exposure to such training is that it is long on disseminating information and short on training leaders to make room for the ministry of others. Therefore, even those churches that do require training for leaders may need to rethink their entire enterprise. Instead of teaching leaders to be *the* ministers in the form of a professional clergy themselves, these churches may want to train leaders in the task of making room for every person in the local congregation to be fully functional in their ministries. Instead of furthering the clergy-laity divide, this might begin to provide a legitimate platform for all God's people to do ministry.

For those churches that do not require any formal education, I understand some of the rationale behind this. My own denomination has only minimal training required for ministerial licensure. Perhaps one reason is that as a people of the Spirit, we understand that God's Spirit can "anoint" anyone to do ministry—educated or not. I honor that openness to the Spirit's radical intervention. One does not need to be educated in order to be used of God! The twelve disciples are evidence of that. I also have known many older ministers from previous generations who offered to God what they had—which often was a grade-school education. These individuals had a thirst for knowledge, especially the Word of God.

My own grandfather was called to preach, yet he had only a fourth-grade education. He read the Word constantly and studied and read quality books on history, doctrine, and biblical interpretation. His own experience of God's transforming power and his desire to preach the gospel so that people would hear the good news made him one of the most beloved and powerful speakers in our area. When he turned eighty-five, a stroke damaged part of his memory. When I came to visit him several months later, I found him in his living room with a makeshift table propped up with all of his history books opened to Darius and Cyrus and the Persians. I asked him to tell me what he was doing. He calmly looked at me, smiled, and said, "All the memory I had of the Scriptures and history vanished with the stroke, so I'm studying several hours a day to relearn what I used to know. I started with Genesis, and I'm up to Daniel now." I sat stunned. To think of starting his learning all over at such an advanced age out of love for God's Word was amazing to me. I was in seminary at the time, and to be sure, I did not have the discipline or passion to start all over again. My grandfather—and many like him whom I have known over the years—prized all learning and education that could make a person a vessel fit for the Master's use.

However, my point regarding formal education for leaders today can be summarized in this question: Given the complexity of leading God's people in today's world, why would anyone who feels called by God into leading the church not find a way to receive formal education for that purpose? It is undoubtedly true that churches could be more forthcoming in helping potential leaders financially so that they could avail themselves of such an education, but my point is prior to financial consideration. Why is it in some circles that if someone feels called to ministry today, the first thought is *not* about formal education? It may be that this is a symptom of a greater problem—namely, the bifurcation of the heart and head among people who have encountered the Spirit. For too long, Spirit-filled people have preferred sensing and feeling God as opposed to thinking about God. By splitting the two dimensions, we have missed the point of what God was really doing in the encounter with him. As I have noted earlier, the Spirit of God confronts humans at a pre-reflective, precognitive level of their being (perhaps their "spirit"), and this encounter is transformative of our orientation in the world. We may reflect on this encounter and even write theology about it, but we should not *split* the experience of God from the reflection on this God of the encounter. Both the heart and mind are essential for Christian living and ministry.

The Role of Women in Leading God's People

Introduction

Having established that Christian leading is serving, and that as priests all of God's people are called to minister to others and serve God and others, I turn now to a question that arises in our ecclesial context regarding women in leadership positions. Among Christians who attempt to take seriously the authoritative nature of Scripture for life, doctrine, and practice today, there is disagreement concerning women in leadership over two major areas: (1) the created "order" in Genesis 1 and 2, particularly as it relates to "headship"; and (2) several passages in the New Testament that seem to require women to remain silent and/or not teach men. Hence, the issue of women in leadership among God's people has been most strident in some evangelical and Pentecostal circles.

A crucial point that I have been trying to establish in this book is the principle of equity among all believers in terms of ministry. *All* believers—male and female—are "ordained" into ministry of the universal priesthood of believers in the new covenant. *All* are a kingdom of priests before our High Priest, the risen Christ. In this model of the church, leaders are placed in the church in order to "equip the saints for the work of ministry" (Eph. 4:12 NRSV). Leaders in the new covenant are not patterned on the Levitical priesthood of the old covenant but belong to the priestly line of Christ. Unlike the Levitical priesthood, Christ's priests are both male and female. Leaders in the new covenant may be male or female because either can serve in God's kingdom. Indeed, the New Testament seems to establish rather clearly that women are to be involved in ministry; that is not the question here. The question is whether women are to be *leaders* in the body of Christ. Given what I have argued thus far in terms of equality among believers, readers could anticipate my positive response to that question. However, in this chapter I would like to engage the Scriptures and theology carefully in order to allow readers to think through with me a rationale for women in leadership and ministry in the church.

What is leadership anyway? Is it a *power* position or a *servant* position? Christian leadership is shaped by the contours of the cross; therefore, leaders serve the body of Christ selflessly. What I mean by this is that Christian leadership reverses the concept of power, standing the notion of "over/under" authority on its head. Christian leaders "make room for others" by nurturing their callings and gifts. Christian leaders guide all believers to do ministry regardless of their social status, gender, or race. The Spirit distributes gifts to whomever he wills. There is not a hint that the Spirit limits gifts according to cultural standards or gender expectations. Indeed, Joel 2 seems to bust apart all such limitations of culture and gender, when sons and daughters have the Spirit poured out on them. And this is underscored by Peter on the day of Pentecost—this is that spoken of by the prophet Joel:

> In the last days, God says,
>   I will pour out my Spirit on all people.
> Your sons and daughters will prophesy,
>   your young men will see visions,
>   your old men will dream dreams.
> Even on my servants, both men and women,
>   I will pour out my Spirit in those days,
>   and they will prophesy. (Acts 2:17–18)

Given the foundation of the church in such rich gender equity in the Spirit, how can we deny that women are gifted and called by God to leadership in the body of Christ—and not just to women's ministry or children's ministry? Does the structure of over/under, which I have shown should be no part of Christian leadership, still reside in our mostly patriarchal, male-centered positions of ecclesial power?

In approaching this issue, we will examine the following questions:

1. Are there women in ministry and leadership in the New Testament?
2. Is there a created order of male headship and female submission?

3. How are we to understand difficult passages in the New Testament on women's roles?

I hold no illusion that merely working through these questions will satisfy all readers—or even settle the question. When it comes to issues related to male and female roles in society and in the church, so much of how we think will already be set by embedded understandings of cultural expectations. Therefore, a simple engagement with difficult passages of Scripture will not resolve the question for everyone. So why engage in such a task? There may be some readers who will appreciate how the various interpretations stack up against one another. Each "side" in this discussion has reasons for their interpretations. Therefore, my task is to lay out the reasoning of each position's interpretation so that readers may assess their worth in relation to each other. Along the way, I will provide a rationale for my own support of women in church leadership and for why this discussion is vital for the church to undertake today.

Are There Women in Ministry and Leadership in the New Testament?

While several approaches to answering this question could be taken—including a discussion of the radical way that Jesus allowed women to hear his teaching—I have chosen to begin by focusing on Paul's writing to the Romans. Since Paul is often labeled misogynistic, understanding his very positive remarks about women in ministry and leadership will provide ballast for those passages that appear more limiting. In the "farewell" chapter of the Epistle to the Romans, Paul offers greetings to various people. For my purposes, I shall consider Phoebe (Rom. 16:1), Priscilla (16:3–4), and Junia (16:7). What is not debated in the historical record of the first-century church is that women opened their homes for meetings of those coming to the Christian faith.[1] What becomes more debatable is the role that such women—particularly the women on whom we will focus our attention—played in church leadership. We begin with Phoebe.

Phoebe

I commend to you our sister Phoebe, a deacon of the church in Cenchreae. I ask you to receive her in the Lord in a way worthy of his people and to give

1. For a balanced discussion of this topic from a historical perspective, see Carolyn Osiek and Margaret Y. MacDonald, *A Woman's Place: House Churches in Earliest Christianity* (Minneapolis: Fortress, 2006), esp. 10–12, 144–63.

her any help she may need from you, for she has been the benefactor of many
people, including me.

Romans 16:1–2

It is probable that Phoebe was a *gentile* Christian, because her name was
prominent in Greek mythology.[2] In this list of notable people and groups,
Phoebe is introduced first to the churches at Rome with the phrase, "I rec-
ommend to you Phoebe, our sister." It is probable that she bore the letter to
Rome and thus was acknowledged in this special way by Paul.[3] Some think
that as the bearer of the letter, she would have been called upon to explain any
ambiguity on Paul's behalf. In order to show that she is well suited to perform
such an explanation, Paul notes her qualifications relating to the church at
Cenchreae—a coastal town about eight miles southeast from Corinth.[4] Paul
uses the familial term "sister" (τὴν ἀδελφὴν | *tēn adelphēn*) to describe his
kinship with her in the Lord.[5]

The next phrase describing Phoebe is one that remains somewhat shrouded
in the ancient past: "a deacon of the church [διάκονον τῆς ἐκκλησίας | *diako-
non tēs ekklēsias*] in Cenchreae."[6] As I have noted earlier, offices in the New
Testament church were not yet fully formed. Frequently, titles referred to *functions* within a congregation rather than the more official *positions* that would
develop by the third century CE.[7] The word here is διάκονος | *diakonos*, which
because of its ending in *os* refers to a *male* person who ministers or serves.
Phoebe is clearly a female, so why is Paul applying a masculine-gendered term
to Phoebe? At times in ancient Greek, a masculine noun can serve to point
to a function or position that is owned or operated by a woman.[8] Thus, such
an usage may have meant nothing in particular. However, its usage for both
men and women who operate in this mode is significant.

---

2. James D. G. Dunn, *Romans 9–16*, WBC 38B (Nashville: Thomas Nelson, 1988), 886; also
Douglas J. Moo, *The Epistle to the Romans*, NICNT (Grand Rapids: Eerdmans, 1996), 913.

3. Robert Jewett, *Romans: A Commentary*, Hermeneia (Minneapolis: Fortress, 2007), 942;
also Moo, *Romans*, 913.

4. Jewett, *Romans*, 943; also Richard N. Longenecker, *The Epistle to the Romans*, NIGTC
(Grand Rapids: Eerdmans, 2016), 1065. See as well Craig S. Keener, *Paul, Women, and Wives:
Marriage and Women's Ministry in the Letters of Paul* (Grand Rapids: Baker Academic, 2013),
238.

5. Longenecker, *Romans*, 1064.

6. Lee Roy Martin, a colleague, pointed out to me that this phrase, "deacon of the church,"
is unique in the NT. There are similar structures that parallel this, but none exactly like this (e.g.,
elders of the church [Acts 20:17; James 5:14]; and Christ the head of the church [Eph. 5:23]).

7. Moo, *Romans*, 914. Moo also notes (n. 11) that the term διακόνισσα | *diakonissa* (deacon-
ess) was not used until a later date, probably between 250–300 CE.

8. Dunn, *Romans 9–16*, 886.

Is Paul simply describing the fact that Phoebe is a "servant" or "helper" of the church at Cenchreae? While the word *diakonos* is applicable to every Christian,[9] most scholars view it here as something more than service. First, Paul uses the noun *diakonos*, not the more general noun for ministry or service, διακονία | *diakonia*. When matched with the participle οὖσαν | *ousan*, this means that Paul is specifying that Phoebe "lives" as a deacon at the church in Cenchreae.[10] This implies more than generalized service but points to a "recognized ministry" or a "position of responsibility within the congregation."[11] Second, if Paul meant to speak of Phoebe as "one who serves," he would have expressed it with a verb, διακονέω | *diakoneō*, not the noun *diakonos*.[12] This fact points toward seeing the action as a regular function or position. Whatever the specific nature of Phoebe's work in the church, it was clear that she was a leader of some sort.[13] It seems possible that she could have opened her house to the church at Cenchreae or even supplied hospitality to visiting Christians at this important layover seaport.[14]

In the final clause of Romans 16:2 lies a subtle expression that has given rise to many theories: "for she has been the benefactor of many people, including me." What does this mean? The term προστάτις | *prostatis* is translated "benefactor" by the NIV and NRSV, but "helper" or a similar variant in the RSV, NIV (1984), and NJB. This term was a notable title for a woman who provided support—financial and otherwise—for any endeavor. In the Roman world, patrons were individuals who provided support for *collegia* or associations. Patrons who were men were called προστάτης | *prostatēs* (*patronus* in Latin), and patronesses who were women were called προστάτις | *prostatis* (*patrona* in Latin).[15] Such individuals were usually wealthy and willing to gain honor in a community by sponsoring clients or associations for the

---

9. Moo, *Romans*, 913.

10. The precise wording in Greek is a participle phrase with οὖσαν | *ousan*, which means "being" or "living" or "existing." Jewett suggests that the phrase should be translated as an explanation: "since she lives as a deacon of the church in Kenchreia." In this way, it points to her "position or occupation in life." Jewett, *Romans*, 944.

11. Dunn, *Romans 9–16*, 886–87. Also Jewett, *Romans*, 944, on *ousan*. Cf. also Longenecker, *Romans*, 1064.

12. Dunn, *Romans 9–16*, 886. Dunn also notes that he would have used *diakonia* for service or ministry that is more general. The previous edition of the NIV (1984) has "servant" as a translation, but the 2011 NIV changed it to "deacon." Cf. Philip B. Payne, *Man and Woman, One in Christ: An Exegetical and Theological Study of Paul's Letters* (Grand Rapids: Zondervan, 2009), 61.

13. Jewett, *Romans*, 944. "Although earlier commentaries interpret the term *diakonos* as a subordinate role, it now appears more likely that she functioned as the leader of the congregation."

14. Dunn, *Romans 9–16*, 887.

15. Payne, *Man and Woman*, 62–63; cf. Dunn, *Romans 9–16*, 888.

common good.[16] They could also be responsible for finances of an endeavor or represent clients in legal disputes.[17] Historical records demonstrate that women could be such patronesses, even of public clubs or private groups. A patron/patroness would build necessary facilities for the community or group they supported. In the case of private religious groups, the patron might build a statue devoted to the god involved or even a temple for the group to gather in worship. They might provide free meals to those in need or hold banquets for civic celebrations. In return for such lavish support, patrons/patronesses would be thanked with flattering inscriptions on these buildings and would be placed in a seat of honor at the official gatherings.[18]

Robert Jewett surmises that Phoebe may have been a hostess of a house church in Cenchreae, since to be such a host or hostess required being a wealthy person with high social standing and with a residence large enough to hold a small gathering. Such a person might also preside over the meetings as well as lead in organizing the congregation.[19] Jewett states, "The fact that Paul mentions Phoebe as a patroness 'to many, and also to me' indicates the level of material resources that would support this kind of leadership role. In light of her high social standing, and Paul's relatively subordinate social position as her client, it is mistaken to render προστάτις as 'helper' or to infer some kind of subordinate role."[20]

It is important to pause at this word προστάτις | *prostatis* to see the potent language Paul uses for Phoebe as a leader. This noun is related to the verb προΐστημι | *prohistēmi*, which is used at various places in the New Testament to speak of leaders. The overwhelming majority of usages for this word group in the New Testament refers to leadership.[21] Therefore, whatever the specific meaning and function for προστάτις | *prostatis*, it holds some level of leadership in it. And the crucial point here seems to be that Paul himself benefited from Phoebe's leadership (or patronage).

Priscilla and Aquila

Greet Priscilla and Aquila, my co-workers in Christ Jesus. They risked their lives for me. Not only I but all the churches of the Gentiles are grateful to them. Greet also the church that meets at their house.

Romans 16:3–5

16. In classical Athens, a *prostatēs* was a "required citizen patron of a *metoikos*, a resident alien." See Osiek and MacDonald, *A Woman's Place*, 196.

17. Jewett, *Romans*, 946–47.

18. Osiek and MacDonald, *A Woman's Place*, 198. The description in this paragraph of the role of such patronage comes from Osiek and MacDonald.

19. Jewett, *Romans*, 947.

20. Jewett, *Romans*, 947.

21. Payne, *Man and Woman*, 62n6.

Paul asks the Romans to "embrace" fellow Christians sixteen times in this passage.[22] The first persons he asks to be greeted are his friends and co-workers (συνεργοί | *synergoi*)[23] from Corinth and Ephesus—namely, Prisca[24] and Aquila. They had fled Rome during the ban of Jews when Claudius was emperor in 49 CE (Acts 18:2). We know that Aquila was a Jew from Pontus, but it is unclear whether Prisca was Jewish (Acts 18:1). Apparently, they had come back to Rome and had a church gathering in their house (Rom. 16:4).[25] There are six references to this couple in the New Testament, four of which list Prisca first (Acts 18:18, 26; Rom. 16:3; 2 Tim. 4:19).[26] This reversal of name placement (that is, the woman first and the man second) may imply that Prisca held a higher status in the Roman context[27] or that she "was for some other reason considered more important."[28] When Paul left Corinth (where they met and worked together), Prisca and Aquila went with him to Ephesus, where they stayed and worked with the church there (Acts 18:18–21).

It was in Ephesus that the couple heard Apollos, a Jew from Alexandria who was a "learned man" (NASB, marginal reading) or an "eloquent man" (KJV; ESV) (ἀνὴρ λόγιος | *anēr logios*) who was "mighty in the Scriptures" (KJV) (δυνατός | *dynatos*) (Acts 18:24). The problem was that he only understood the baptism of John and so Prisca and Aquila took him and "explained to him the way of God more accurately" (Acts 18:26 ESV). Here we see that Luke again names Prisca first in the narrative. Could this imply that she took the lead in teaching Apollos? Whatever the case, it is clear that this woman was involved in teaching this man. Some interpreters suggest that this teaching (ἐξέθεντο) is not the same as the more traditional

---

22. Jewett, *Romans*, 952; also Moo, *Romans*, 919. For a thorough accounting of the list of names throughout this chapter, see Jewett, *Romans*, 952–54. He notes there are fifteen personal friends and coworkers residing now in Rome, as well as the leaders of five house or tenement churches in Rome.

23. This word means "fellow laborers" or "coworkers." It is used by Paul numerous times to denote those who worked with him in ministry. See Dunn, *Romans 9–16*, 892; Moo, *Romans*, 920; and Jewett, *Romans*, 957. Jewett says this is "technical language for missionary colleagues" (957). The fact that Paul's list of greetings begins with a woman (Phoebe) and continues with a woman (Prisca) is quite amazing in the ancient world. "It appears that Paul is aware of the prejudice against women's contributions in his society, and therefore works all the harder to make sure that the praiseworthy among them receive their due." Keener, *Paul, Women, and Wives*, 240.

24. Priscilla is the "diminutive" name for Prisca. It is the same person.

25. The ban on Jews in Rome expired when Claudius died in 54 CE.

26. Jewett, *Romans*, 955n29. I recognize that the Textus Receptus and the Majority Text have the word order with Priscilla first in Acts 18:18 and Aquila first in 18:26. I follow the manuscripts of earlier dating that have the order with Priscilla first in these passages.

27. Jewett, *Romans*, 955; also Longenecker, *Romans*, 1067. Some suggest that she was from a wealthy family and therefore her social status would elevate her above her husband.

28. Longenecker, *Romans*, 1067.

form of teaching (διδασκεῖν | *didaskein*) that Paul specifically admonishes women not to do (1 Tim. 2:12). Is there a difference in these two words, one denoting an informal, more private explanation (*exethento*) and the other denoting a public, more official teaching (*didaskein*)? This can be easily cleared up by noting that Luke uses the same term here as in Acts 28:23, where Paul preaches or teaches the Jews in Rome: "When they had appointed a day for him, they came to him at his lodging in greater numbers. From morning till evening he expounded [εξετίθετο | *exetitheto*] to them, testifying to the kingdom of God and trying to convince them about Jesus both from the Law of Moses and from the Prophets" (ESV). It appears Paul was involved in teaching the Jews from the Law and Prophets about Christ when he expounded or explained to them the way of Christ; it is the same word used in Acts 18:26, where Prisca and Aquila explain or teach Apollos the way of God.[29]

Junia

> Greet Andronicus and Junia, my fellow Jews who have been in prison with me. They are outstanding among the apostles, and they were in Christ before I was.
>
> Romans 16:7

Who is this team of apostles? More particularly, who is the second one listed, Junia? Since the time of the 1300s CE, manuscripts and translations have considered this to be a man named Junias[30] or Junius (e.g., NIV 1984, RSV, NASB, GNT, and NJB), as opposed to a woman named Junia (NIV 2011, NRSV, REB). The difficulty in discerning the difference comes in the form we have in this verse—namely, the direct object (accusative case) of the verb "Greet . . . Junia" (ἀσπάσασθε . . . Ἰουνίαν | *aspasasthe . . . Iounian*). If the name were a man's name, it would appear like this: Ἰουνιᾶν | *Iounian*; if the name were a woman's name, it would appear like this: Ἰουνίαν | *Iounian*. If one looks closely at the difference, one will see that the only difference is in the accent—the female name has an acute accent placed above the letter *i*, and the male name has a circumflex accent above the letter *a*. Without the

29. Linda L. Belleville, "Women in Ministry: An Egalitarian Perspective," in *Two Views on Women in Ministry*, ed. Stanley Gundry, Counterpoints: Exploring Theology, ed. James Beck (Grand Rapids: Zondervan, 2005), 59. In contrast to this point, Craig L. Blomberg states, "Even if their home was a house church, nothing in the text suggests this was some kind of formal, public instruction, though we cannot exclude the possibility." See Craig L. Blomberg, "Women in Ministry: A Complementarian Perspective," in Gundry, *Two Views on Women in Ministry*, 147.

30. Junias is considered to be a contracted form of the name Junianus. Longenecker, *Romans*, 1060.

accents, they are written exactly the same in Greek. From historical evidence, we know that early (and even some later) Greek manuscripts were written without any accents. Indeed, not until the sixth century CE did accent marks begin to surface on Greek manuscripts,[31] and from these manuscripts we find the feminine form Ἰουνίαν | *Iounian* accented.[32]

So, what can we determine about Junia's gender? First, the early church almost universally understood Junia as a woman.[33] Second, the reading of the Middle Ages and later, where *Iounian* was understood to be a man, can be attributed to the difficulty of that era understanding a woman to be an apostle.[34] Third—and perhaps most decisive—we find the female Latin name *Junia* occurring more than 250 times in Greek and Latin inscriptions in Rome itself, but *not one time* was the male name *Junias* found anywhere.[35]

What can we determine about the meaning of the phrase who "are outstanding among the apostles" (Rom. 16:7)? Does this mean "they are well known to the apostles" (ESV) or are "esteemed by the apostles" (NIV variant reading)? Or does it mean "they are prominent among the apostles" (NRSV)? The reason this is important is that if they are *among* the apostles, then we have an example of a woman who is an apostle in the New Testament. However, if they are only *esteemed by* or *well known to* the apostles, then their ministry is simply being acknowledged *by* the apostles. The argumentation becomes a little complex at this point, since it is based on grammatical aspects of the Greek language. It seems clear enough, however, that this is a statement that describes Andronicus and Junia as *outstanding apostles*, not as *esteemed as outstanding by the apostles*.[36]

31. Longenecker, *Romans*, 1060.

32. Bruce M. Metzger, *A Textual Commentary on the Greek New Testament*, 2nd ed. (Stuttgart: Deutsche Bibelgesellschaft/German Bible Society, 1994), 475.

33. The exception is Epiphanius (315–403 CE), who thought Junia was a man. However, he also thought Prisca (Priscilla) was a man who worked with Aquila, so his determination of gender is not very reliable. See Moo, *Romans*, 922n31.

34. As Craig Keener notes on this discussion, "The only reason someone would deny that Junia is a woman here, against the otherwise plain reading of the text, is the assumption that Paul cannot describe a woman as an apostle." See Keener, "Women in Ministry: Another Egalitarian Perspective," in Gundry, *Two Views on Women in Ministry*, 213.

35. Metzger, *A Textual Commentary on the Greek New Testament*, 475; also Jewett, *Romans*, 961. Jewett provides the analyses and searches by various individuals in nn. 104 and 105 on p. 961. For a summary of this textual discussion that is clear and readable, see Payne, *Man and Woman*, 65–67.

36. Those who argue that Andronicus and Junia were *not* apostles suggest that the grammatical construction of "outstanding among" (ἐπίσημοι ἐν | *episēmoi en*) with a dative case (as here with τοῖς ἀποστόλοις | *tois apostolois*) is used only "for impersonal objects—things, not people." See Daniel B. Wallace and Michael H. Burer, "Was Junia Really an Apostle?," *Journal for Biblical Manhood and Womanhood* 6, no. 2 (2001): 4–11. Cf. for a response Osiek

What does Paul mean here by "apostle"? Titles like these in the New Testament always remain somewhat shrouded in the mist of the first century, but we can infer by Paul's usage elsewhere that Paul can speak of the Twelve as apostles. Further, he can speak of apostles beyond the Twelve as having been appointed by the risen Christ (1 Cor. 15:7).[37] Since they were "in Christ" before Paul was, it is quite possible that Andronicus and Junia had seen the risen Christ.[38] According to this view, Andronicus and Junia were apostles of a "higher status."[39] They had functioned as apostles possibly for two decades before Paul wrote this letter to the Romans.[40]

However, other interpreters suggest that the term "apostles" here is used by Paul to "denote a 'messenger' or 'emissary' and sometimes to denote a 'commissioned missionary.'"[41] Thus, Douglas Moo concludes that "apostle" here simply means "traveling missionary."[42] It is true that Paul uses "apostle" to speak of itinerant preachers or an emissary of the church.[43] Yet the fact that Andronicus and Junia were "outstanding" apostles and were "in Christ before" Paul seems to point to their status of apostle as something more than regular missionaries (whom Paul calls "fellow workers" in this text).

The final question, then, is whether Andronicus and Junia held a leadership position in the church. In other words, does "apostle" here refer to a leadership function? We do know that "apostle" is usually the first in a list of functions and gifts operating in the body of Christ. Also, in Ephesians 2:20, Paul speaks of the household of God "built on the foundation of the apostles and prophets" (ESV). While we cannot be certain of the authority of apostles in the various settings of house churches scattered throughout the Roman world in the first century, it seems clear that for Paul the role of apostle was special in terms of leadership of the church.

---

and MacDonald, *A Woman's Place*, 304n19. If the object were to be personal, then, they suggest the pattern would require a genitive construction here (τῶν ἀποστολῶν | *tōn apostolōn*). However, numerous grammarians disagree with this assertion. The adjective for "outstanding" or "remarkable" here (ἐπίσημος | *episēmos*) "lifts up a person or thing as distinguished or marked in comparison with other representatives of the same class, in this instance with the other apostles." Jewett, *Romans*, 963. Jewett offers numerous examples from Greek to substantiate this claim.

37. It should be noted that Paul "repeatedly defines an apostle as one who encounters the risen Christ (1 Cor. 9:1; 15:8; Gal. 1:1, 15–17)." Payne, *Man and Woman*, 66.

38. Dunn, *Romans 9–16*, 894–95; Jewett, *Romans*, 964.

39. Dunn, *Romans 9–16*, 895.

40. Jewett, *Romans*, 964.

41. Moo, *Romans*, 924.

42. Moo, *Romans*, 924.

43. Osiek and MacDonald, *A Woman's Place*, 226.

Is There a Created Order of Male Headship and Female Submission?

Before addressing several difficult Pauline passages regarding women in church leadership, there is a fundamental theological concern, which can influence one's reading and interpretation of Scripture. It is the concept of "headship," especially in relation to God's intention in creation. There are many assumptions that influence the reading of the creation narrative (Gen. 1–2), especially with respect to what God intended the relation of male and female to be, both in the home and in life. For some, this relationship is perfectly conceived under the title "headship." Although the word "headship" does not appear in the Bible, the concept of "head" is certainly there.[44] Whether "head" has the connotations that we associate with that English word in modern society is a crucial question in this discussion.[45] However, even deeper than the inquiry into the linguistic meaning of "head" in the Scriptures is the *theological* understanding of what God intended by creating human beings as male and female. As we shall see, how one approaches this latter issue of theology will shape how one views the entire question of women in the role of leadership in the church. In order to clarify my position and its importance for the church today, I shall consider several assertions from supporters of male headship and offer a response to them.

Is Male Headship Part of the Created Order?

Some people assert that Genesis 1 and 2 provide us ample evidence that God has given the man primary responsibility for the spiritual and moral

44. See Philip B. Payne, *Man and Woman*, 285. Payne notes that the word "headship" never occurs in the NT. It also does not occur in the OT.

45. The word "head" (κεφαλή | *kephalē*) seems straightforward enough in English—it refers to a literal head or it can be used figuratively as a "chief" or "first place in a line of things." Gordon D. Fee, *The First Epistle to the Corinthians*, NICNT (Grand Rapids: Eerdmans, 1987), 501. Fee notes that the meaning of "head" as the Corinthians might have heard it is not "immediately clear" to English readers. There are two basic ways to translate this word, *kephalē*, in the figurative sense: one is "head = authority over" and another is "head = source or origin." First, a traditional way of understanding the word "head" in English is to associate it with the meaning of "authority over" or "leader" in charge of something. Wayne Grudem has led the way in attempting to establish this interpretation as better supported by the Greek literary evidence of the ancient world. See Wayne Grudem, "Does *Kephalē* Mean 'Source' or 'Authority Over' in Greek Literature? A Survey of 2,336 Examples," *Trinity Journal* 6 (Spring 1985): 38–59. Cf. also Grudem, "Appendix 1: The Meaning of *Kephalē* ('Head'): A Response to Recent Studies," in *Recovering Biblical Manhood and Womanhood: A Response to Evangelical Feminism*, ed. John Piper and Wayne Grudem (Wheaton: Crossway, 1991), 425–68. Opposed to this study is the work of Richard S. Cervin, "Does Κεφαλή Mean 'Source' or 'Authority Over' in Greek Literature? A Rebuttal," *Trinity Journal* 10 (1989): 85–112; and Payne, *Man and Woman*, 118–39. The evidence that "head" in classical and Koine Greek does not mean a leader with authority over someone is

direction of the home.[46] They view male headship not as a result of the fall (Gen. 3) but as a result of the created order established in Genesis 1 and 2 by several aspects in the narrative. One of these is the fact that God made the man first and the woman second. Further, while we find in Genesis 1 that both male and female are made in the image of God and both are intended to rule over the earth,[47] in Genesis 2:18–25 we find another dimension of complexity layered over the male-female relationship—namely, the fact that God "made the male the head and the female the helper."[48] It is this Hebrew phrase, "helper suitable for him" (*'ēzer kənegedô* | עֵזֶר כְּנֶגְדּוֹ), that demonstrates the intention of God to establish male headship over the woman before the fall. According to this view, to be a "helper" clearly indicates a supportive role for the woman. The man was not created to help the woman, but the reverse.[49] While women are created equal before God (in their essence) as described in Genesis 1, they stand differently in relation to each other in Genesis 2, where the male is the leader and the female the helper. Their roles are part of what differentiates them at the moment of their creation.[50] Therefore, we may infer from the fact that man was created first that God intended him to lead. Moreover, the woman came *from* the man and *for* the man, thereby placing her in a dependent, subordinate position in terms of leadership.[51]

In contrast to this view, I must ask whether the title "helper suitable for him" implies subordination of the woman to the man. The word "helper" (*'ēzer* | עֵזֶר) does not automatically imply that a helper is a servant or subordinate. "In no other occurrence in the OT does this noun refer to an inferior, but always to a superior or an equal."[52] Indeed, God is declared to be our helper—our savior, rescuer, protector, or strength.[53] God "comes alongside us in our helplessness."[54] Instead of implying subordination or an over/under

---

quite compelling. It seems certain that this is *not* how first-century readers or hearers of Paul's letters would have understood it. "Source" or "origin" seems to be a better-illustrated fit here.

46. Raymond C. Ortlund Jr., "Male-Female Equality and Male Headship: Genesis 1–3," in Piper and Grudem, *Recovering Biblical Manhood and Womanhood*, 95.

47. Ortlund, "Male-Female Equality and Male Headship," 97.

48. Ortlund, "Male-Female Equality and Male Headship," 99.

49. Ortlund, "Male-Female Equality and Male Headship," 102.

50. Ortlund, "Male-Female Equality and Male Headship," 102.

51. Thomas R. Schreiner, "Women in Ministry: Another Complementarian Perspective," in Gundry, *Two Views on Women in Ministry*, 290.

52. Payne, *Man and Woman*, 44.

53. All of these terms are clearly portrayed in the context of various OT examples, such as Josh. 1:14; 2 Sam. 8:5; 1 Chron. 12:17; Ezra 8:22. See Payne, *Man and Woman*, 44.

54. Alice Matthews, *Gender Roles and the People of God: Rethinking What We Were Taught about Men and Women in the Church* (Grand Rapids: Zondervan, 2017), 39. Matthews notes that there are sixteen references in the OT to God as our help.

hierarchy to which the female submits, the word "helper" points to someone who is in the yoke of life *together*, working toward the same goal. The preposition, which follows this word, underscores the point: a helper who is "suitable for him" or comparable to him or "in front of" him or "helper corresponding to" him (*'ēzer kənegedô* | עֵזֶר כְּנֶגְדּוֹ).[55]

Another argument to establish male headship, according to the complementarian view of male-female relations,[56] notes that Adam was given the task of naming all the creatures. He extends that task to giving the woman a name as well: the man (*'ish* | אִישׁ) declares that "she shall be called 'woman' [*'ishâ* | אִשָּׁה]" (Gen. 2:23). By naming the creatures, Adam brings "the earthly creation under his dominion."[57] This act of naming, in which he exercises his rule over the creatures, is reflective of Adam's headship.[58] This would also make clear to Eve that Adam was her head. As Thomas Schreiner states, "The naming of the woman occurs in 2:23, suggesting that Adam had the responsibility for leadership in the relationship."[59] Therefore, John Piper insists that a wife is to submit to her husband as a "divine calling" to honor him, "not in an absolute surrender of her will," but with a "disposition to yield to her husband's guidance and her inclination to follow his leadership."[60] In summary, then, "male-female equality and male headship, properly defined, are woven into the very fabric of Genesis 1–3."[61]

In contrast to this interpretation, I find that most of the arguments from this view rest on assumptions and invalid inferences from the text.[62] Where in Genesis 1–2 does the text speak of "headship" or, more precisely, of submission on the part of the female to her husband? To arrive at this conclusion, one must do extensive rereading *into* the meaning of the text from outside of it. Where in Genesis 1–2 is the instruction that the man holds the "primary responsibility" for the "spiritual and moral direction" of the home?

55. Richard S. Hess, "Equality with and without Innocence: Genesis 1–3," in *Discovering Biblical Equality: Complementarity without Hierarchy*, ed. Ronald W. Pierce and Rebecca Merrill Groothuis, 2nd ed. (Downers Grove, IL: InterVarsity, 2005), 86.

56. There are two definite "sides" in this discussion: (1) complementarians, whose views argue for equality of essence but difference in function; and (2) egalitarians, whose views argue for equality in both essence and function. While these titles do not always accurately portray the views within each group, I will use them for the sake of brevity.

57. Ortlund, "Male-Female Equality and Male Headship," 102.

58. Schreiner, "Women in Ministry," 291.

59. Schreiner, "Women in Ministry," 295.

60. John Piper and Wayne Grudem, "An Overview of Central Concerns: Questions and Answers," in Piper and Grudem, *Rediscovering Biblical Manhood and Womanhood*, 61.

61. Ortlund, "Male-Female Equality and Male Headship," 111.

62. Craig S. Keener, "A Response to Thomas Schreiner," in Gundry, *Two Views on Women in Ministry*, 338.

Does the process of Adam "naming" the animals really demonstrate his "rule" over them? Does that extend to the naming of the woman? Such a claim reads *into* the narrative something that is not there. Is there any hint in the text that "naming" is to be equated with "exercising authority over," as Schreiner and others claim? Other than simply declaring it to be so, the scholars supporting this idea cannot establish any "obvious way in which the man exercised any authority over either the animals or the woman" in naming them.[63]

Further, does the Genesis narrative really provide substance for the claim that wives are to be submissive to their husbands?[64] Nowhere in this text do the words "headship," "authority," or "submission" occur. There is nothing that can be inferred from the story to substantiate this claim that wives are to be subject to their husbands. It may be possible to see the curse in Genesis 3 as outlining a "rule over" the female by the male, but this is a result of sin not of God's intention in creation. As Kevin Giles asserts, "Nothing in the Bible suggests that in creation God established an unchanging and unchangeable hierarchical social order in which the man ruled over the woman."[65]

"Submission" is not a dirty word for Christians, but over/under domination that creates servitude through subordination is. Submission cannot mean domination—though it has throughout much of the history of the church and civilization. Servanthood is the attitude we all (male and female) must bring to life as taught us by the Master. Rebecca Merrill Groothuis makes clear that there is a difference between functional subordination and female subordination. *Functional* subordination applies to an individual's abilities (or lack of them) for completing a specific task. Coworkers working on a task given to a committee may illustrate this. One worker is the chair of the committee for the given duration of the task; the other is a member of the committee under the supervision of the coworker who is the chair. This is functional subordination, which differs from female subordination as supporters of male headship have described it. "Unlike functional subordination, female subordination is not contingent. Because a woman is always and necessarily female, she is always and necessarily subordinate. No condition or context in this life nullifies her subordination to male authority."[66] How does this apply

63. Hess, "Equality with and without Innocence," 87.
64. Keener, "A Response to Thomas Schreiner," 338. In his words, "Where is subordination implied here?" in reference to the term "helper" or in naming the animals.
65. Kevin Giles, *Patterns of Ministry among the First Christians*, 2nd ed. (Eugene, OR: Cascade Books, 2017), 205.
66. Rebecca Merrill Groothuis, "Equal in Being, Unequal in Role: Exploring the Logic of Women's Subordination," in Pierce and Groothuis," *Discovering Biblical Equality*, 317.

to the situation of women in church leadership today? Lisa P. Stephenson has noted that the forbidding of certain roles—such as preaching, teaching, or leadership—results in limiting women's roles in the church on the basis of their very being as women, *not* on some supposed functional limitation. It may seem that supporters of male headship are differentiating between what women *do* and who women *are*, but in reality limiting what they can do *as females* automatically makes them perceived as inferior in their being (not simply in their function).[67]

Can a Female Be Equal in Essence to a Male, Yet Different in Function?

The assertion of supporters of male headship denigrates the idea that equality must involve an "equality of *function*."[68] According to them, one can be equal in essence yet distinct in function. As the Danvers Statement from the Council on Biblical Manhood and Womanhood proposes, "Distinctions in masculine and feminine roles are ordained by God as part of the created order, and should find an echo in every human heart."[69] This is illustrated by the fact that priests in the old covenant could only come from the tribe of Levi. While all the Israelites had equal worth in God's sight, only Levites could perform the duties of priest. In a similar vein, "the pastoral role is reserved for men only."[70] Differences in function in the Bible do not necessitate differences in worth before God, they claim. Eve was Adam's *spiritual* equal in that she bore the image of God. "But she was not his equal in that she was his 'helper.'"[71] What emerges from Genesis 2 is that "male-female equality does not constitute an undifferentiated sameness."[72] God created "male and female in His image equally, but He also made the male the head and the female the helper."[73]

Further, in this view, differentiation of roles and functions in the home must also be applied to the church—God's family. The church is called "God's household" (1 Tim. 3:15), and therefore the structures of the Christian household

---

67. Lisa P. Stephenson, "Made in the Image of God: A Theological Apologetic for Women Preachers," in *Toward a Pentecostal Theology of Preaching*, ed. Lee Roy Martin (Cleveland, TN: CPT, 2015), 143–44.

68. Schreiner, "Women in Ministry," 288.

69. Affirmation 2 in "The Danvers Statement (1987): The Council on Biblical Manhood and Womanhood," in Piper and Grudem, *Recovering Biblical Manhood and Womanhood*, appendix 2, 470.

70. Schreiner, "Women in Ministry," 289.

71. Ortlund, "Male-Female Equality and Male Headship," 102.

72. Ortlund, "Male-Female Equality and Male Headship," 99.

73. Ortlund, "Male-Female Equality and Male Headship," 99.

become the structures of the church. Since God established male headship in the family, he certainly requires male headship in the church. This means that "the fundamental principles regarding the structures of the human family are to be applied to the church as God's household (1 Tim. 3:15)."[74] As is clear from Ephesians 5:22–6:4 and Colossians 3:18–21, families have a "God-ordained structure of leadership and authority" that now must be applied to the church.[75] Wives are told to submit to their husbands, and husbands are told to love their wives the way Christ loved the church. Indeed, marriage itself is a picture of the mystery of the relation between Christ (the head) and his church (the body). Furthermore, the fact that God is called Father "demands the observance of household order" in the church.[76]

The logical conclusion of this connection between family and the church is that the pattern of leadership (male) and submission (female) must remain in effect in the household of God. As George W. Knight remarks, "Paul is not insisting that every relationship between a woman and a man is one of submission and headship, but that where leadership is an ingredient of the situation, as in marriage, the woman should submit to that leadership (headship) of the man. Similarly, for example, in the family of God, the church, where leadership is involved, Paul insists that women not take on that role but submit to the leadership of men."[77]

The notion that a "woman is equal *in* her being yet unequal *by virtue of* her being is incoherent."[78] Two proponents of such a view, John Piper and Wayne Grudem, admit that the key to understanding their perspective is to focus not only on "behavioral roles of men and women" but also on the "underlying nature of manhood and womanhood themselves."[79] Therefore, they assert that equality exists in the *nature* of being human for both male and female. Nonetheless, they also assert that inequality exists in the *function* of being male and female. It is not just about the different "behavioral roles of men and women" but the "underlying nature of manhood and womanhood." Thus, they make a distinction in terms of *roles based on* the nature of who they are—male or female. According to their view, if you are born female,

74. Vern S. Poythress, "The Church as Family: Why Male Leadership in the Family Requires Male Leadership in the Church," in Piper and Grudem, *Recovering Biblical Manhood and Womanhood*, 239.

75. Poythress, "The Church as Family," 238.

76. Poythress, "The Church as Family," 241.

77. George W. Knight III, "Husbands and Wives as Analogues of Christ and the Church: Ephesians 5:21–33 and Colossians 3:18–19," in Piper and Grudem, *Recovering Biblical Manhood and Womanhood*, 169.

78. Groothuis, "Equal in Being, Unequal in Role," 310 (her emphasis).

79. Piper and Grudem, "An Overview of Central Concerns," 60.

the very nature of your femaleness demands that you operate in a role that is subordinate. This is what makes their argument incoherent.

The doctrine of male rule "presupposes that woman is uniquely designed by God *not* to perform certain distinctively human activities."[80] This sounds more like Aristotle than the Bible: "The male is by nature superior, and the female inferior; and the one rules, and the other is ruled; this principle, of necessity, extends to all mankind" (*Politics* 1254.b.7).[81] Further, Aristotle notes that "household management" has three parts—the rule of a master over the slave, the rule of a father over children, and the rule of a husband over the wife (*Politics* 1259.a.13).[82] The rule of the husband over his wife is "constitutional"—that is, it is established by the *nature* of being a male versus female, for "the male is by nature fitter for command than the female, just as the elder and full-grown is superior to the younger and more immature" (*Politics* 1259.b.1–5).[83] Although supporters of male hierarchy claim that they believe in the intelligence and giftedness of females, their proposal that God has placed the male in position of leading and the female in the position of *not* leading (by virtue of her being born a female) ends up sounding like Aristotle's constitutional reasoning. The very fact that males are "made" by God to be leaders in their nature makes them better fit for command than the females, who by nature are better fit for submission to that command.

Where in Scripture is it revealed that the male is the sole (or even primary) spiritual leader of the home? Where is the concept of the priest of the home in Scripture? Groothuis is correct when she says, "Despite popular evangelical teaching, the New Testament never says the man authoritatively represents God as the priest of the home."[84] Why is this not the case? It is because the Levitical priesthood has been replaced with the direct priesthood of Christ, our High Priest after the order of Melchizedek (Heb. 7:16–17). The entire community of faith—the body of Christ—makes up the universal priesthood of believers now. There is no caste system of priests or clergy required for mediation between Jesus Christ and us. Every believer is an ambassador for God, representing Christ to the world (2 Cor. 5:18–20). Because of the work of the cross-resurrection and the ascension of Christ, we all have equal access to God through him.

Does the case of the Levites in Israel shed any light on the new covenant priesthood? Clearly, the priests of the new covenant are *everyone*, not simply

---

80. Groothuis, "Equal in Being, Unequal in Role," 308.
81. Aristotle, *The Politics of Aristotle*, trans. Benjamin Jowett (Oxford: Clarendon, 1885), 8.
82. Aristotle, *Politics*, 22.
83. Aristotle, *Politics*, 22.
84. Groothuis, "Equal in Being, Unequal in Role," 313.

one tribe (as if such could be identified today among Christians!), not one race over another, not even ordained clergy versus laity. The priesthood belongs to *every* believer as part of the total priesthood of believers described in the New Testament.[85] As I have attempted to maintain in this book, in the new covenant there is no Levitical priesthood. The only priest is our High Priest, who is in the heavenly tabernacles making intercession for us. We do not need another mediator—we may go together directly to Jesus Christ. "The New Testament portrayal of the church as a priesthood of believers implies that the parallel to the Levitical priesthood is not the ordained office (or leadership function) but the church as a whole."[86] In this regard, women are priests in the new covenant just as much as men. Whatever was "prefigured" in the Levitical priesthood has "now been fulfilled forever in Jesus Christ."[87]

The priesthood of believers cannot coexist with a male hierarchy of spiritual command because the relationship that Christians (male *and* female) have with Jesus Christ, our High Priest, is one that is *direct*. If female Christians in the church (or home!) are required to go through a male head in order to have communion with God, the very nature of New Testament Christian faith is dismantled. Those supporting male headship "assign women a permanent inferior status in a hierarchy of spiritual authority, calling, responsibility and privilege."[88]

Is Male Headship a Result of the Fall or Part of the Created Order?

Schreiner argues that "male leadership is not the result of the fall, but it is God's good and perfect will for man and woman."[89] The Danvers Statement supports this thesis: "Adam's headship in marriage was established by God before the Fall, and was not a result of sin."[90] Supporters of male headship agree that sin perverts God's original order and causes strife between men and women, but the role differences were God's intention *at creation* and therefore are meant to be permanent in the created order of things. While they assert that sin and the curse have caused disruption in male-female relationships, this is only because the male either dominates or leads passively (as did Adam) and the female constantly attempts to usurp the male's authority (as did Eve).[91]

85. Stanley J. Grenz, "Biblical Priesthood and Women in Ministry," in Pierce and Groothuis, *Discovering Biblical Equality*, 273–77.
86. Grenz, "Biblical Priesthood and Women in Ministry," 275.
87. Groothuis, "Equal in Being, Unequal in Role," 313.
88. Groothuis, "Equal in Being, Unequal in Role," 314.
89. Schreiner, "Women in Ministry," 298.
90. Affirmation 3 in "The Danvers Statement," 470.
91. Ortlund, "Male-Female Equality and Male Headship," 99.

The Danvers Statement attempts to clarify these issues related to the results of sin: "In the home, the husband's loving, humble leadership tends to be replaced by domination or passivity; the wife's intelligent, willing submission tends to be replaced by usurpation or servility."[92] The distortions of God's plan as a result of sin create tension both in the home and the church. "In the church, sin inclines men toward a worldly love of power or an abdication of spiritual responsibility, and inclines women to resist limitations on their roles or to neglect the use of their gifts in appropriate ministries."[93] Both the home and the church suffer today from the sinful effects of the curse on Adam and Eve. Supporters of male headship argue that we cannot resolve the problem of the curse simply by announcing equality between male and female in terms of function. We must return to the created order of things that God intended. "Christian redemption does not redefine creation; it restores creation, so that wives learn godly submission and husbands learn godly headship."[94]

However, I would argue that over/under headship authority is a result of the fall and the curse in Genesis 3. Only at the point of the narrative in Genesis 3 does the language of "rule" and "dominion" have a newfound home in the human realm itself. While rule and dominion are used in Genesis 1:28 for the human care for the earth, it is after the curse of sin that the husband will rule over the wife—one human being over another human being (Gen. 3:16). Such dominion of one human over another *was not God's plan in creation* (as is made clear by Gen. 1 and 2).

In support of male headship, Raymond Ortlund states, "Christian redemption does not redefine creation; it restores creation." I would agree with this statement—but with an important difference. I do not see dominance (or headship) of males over females *until the fall*. In other words, *sin* produces the over/under scheme of living from which Jesus Christ came to redeem us. His own life and words announce this truth with clarity. So yes, we are to "restore creation" in the new age ushered in by Christ. We live between the ages now—between the age to come (heaven) and this present age, but we are to live according to the standards of the freedom brought to us in Christ and the vision of justice/righteousness that was God's original intention in creation and is the goal in the eschaton. Through the redemption we have received in Christ, believers have experienced a change in status before God and therefore have a responsibility to reflect that change in how we operate toward others as humans made in the image of God. Why should churches

---

92. Affirmation 4 in "The Danvers Statement," 470.
93. Affirmation 3 in "The Danvers Statement," 470.
94. Ortlund, "Male-Female Equality and Male Headship," 109.

today try to place on families the constraints of headship/subordination patterns that are clearly imposed due to sin?

The Danvers Statement suggests, "Redemption in Christ aims at removing the distortions introduced by the curse," but then goes on to describe things in the family and in the church as if they hardly experienced any change at all.[95] In the family, the statement simply notes that Christian husbands should "forsake harsh or selfish leadership and grow in love and care for their wives."[96] Wives should "forsake resistance to their husbands' authority and grow in willing, joyful submission to their husbands' leadership."[97] So this is the only result of salvation and the "new humanity" created by the in-breaking of the new age through the cross (Eph. 2:15 NRSV)? Is there no removal of the potential for domination and harm in the *structures* of over/under authority? Where is the attitude of Christ, who became a servant of all? Stephenson makes a crucial observation: "God did not create male and female within a dualistic relationship in creation. And even though sin distorted this original equality, with the advent of new creation persons are called and empowered through Christ and the Spirit to overcome the sinful tendency to continue to perpetuate a hierarchical anthropology."[98]

Is Male Headship Required in the Home and Therefore in the Church?

Bringing together an understanding of Genesis 1 and 2 with Ephesians 5:21–33, supporters of male headship point to the leadership role of the male in marriage as supportive of their reading of the divine institution of marriage as described in Genesis 2. Further, by implication this view of leadership in the home is carried over to the church. This view argues that the responsibility for the home lies with the male, who is the head.[99] Only the male is told to leave his home and cleave to his wife. She does not leave her family to start a new household, but he does. In marriage, "the man heads the home for God and the wife helps him to fulfill the divine calling."[100] When the husband fulfills his leadership role as established by God, he "does so as a servant of God, and the leadership given to him in this role expresses God's authority in the marriage."[101] For this reason, wives are to submit to their husbands "as you do to the Lord" (Eph. 5:22).

95. Affirmation 6 in "The Danvers Statement," 470.
96. Affirmation 6 in "The Danvers Statement," 470.
97. Affirmation 6 in "The Danvers Statement," 470.
98. Lisa P. Stephenson, "A Feminist Pentecostal Theological Anthropology: North America and Beyond," *PNEUMA: A Journal of the Society for Pentecostal Studies* 35 (2013): 47.
99. Ortlund, "Male-Female Equality and Male Headship," 103.
100. Ortlund, "Male-Female Equality and Male Headship," 103.
101. G. Knight, "Husbands and Wives as Analogues of Christ and the Church," 174.

Moreover, this view of male headship also sees Ephesians 5:21–33 as bringing further clarity to the importance of marriage for illustrating the relationship between Christ and the church. In this passage, the husband is given the leadership role, and the wife is told to submit to him. Just as Christian wives are to "respect" Christ, they are also to "respect" their husbands (Eph. 5:33). Christian husbands are to love their wives as "Christ loved the church" (Eph. 5:25) by giving himself up for it. Paul quotes Genesis 2:24 here in Ephesians and then declares, "This is a profound mystery—but I am talking about Christ and the church" (Eph. 5:32). Whatever this mystery might mean, in the view of supporters of male headship, it points to the headship of the man as analogous to the headship of Christ. Male headship, then, was established by God in creation and has been reinforced by Paul in the new creation as the analogous reference to the headship of Christ over the church. Therefore, role differences in the family were also meant to exist in God's family, the household of faith.[102]

Does the structure of the home really apply to the church? According to Vern Poythress it does. First Timothy 3:15 speaks of "God's household, which is the church of the living God," thereby connecting the home and the church. The church is God's family. Therefore, "the structure of family leadership is to be carried over into God's household: qualified men are to be appointed as overseers, that is, fathers of the church. A woman, however capable and gifted she may be, can never become a father of a family. As a woman, she is simply not so constituted. Likewise, a woman may never become a father in God's household."[103]

Does leadership transfer from the home to the church—and therefore only males can be leaders? The only verse that is used by the supporters of male headship here is 1 Timothy 3:15, which I find strangely silent on the transferal of male headship in the home to male headship in the church. Thus, even if one were to believe that there should be godly male headship of a husband over a wife *in the home* (and that is a big *if*), does that automatically mean that there must be male headship over women *in the church*?

Is the fact that the church is called a household of God in the New Testament strong enough evidence for using whatever patterns we may presume should exist in the home to exist in the church? How much of our patterns of life in the home are determined by our culture to begin with? Often our assumptions about cultural patriarchy are simply applied to church leadership with the presumption that such patterns are God's will, but they may simply

102. Schreiner, "Women in Ministry," 291.
103. Poythress, "The Church as Family," 239.

be our own culture's preference. In addition to the family of God, the church is the "bride of Christ," the "people of God," the "called-out ones," the "assembly," and so forth. To raise one metaphor (family) to the level of primacy in order to allow for the family systems in our homes to become the systems of leadership in our churches is to do a disservice to the rich meaning of who the church is. Moreover, it is taking the metaphor of household or family too literally. There is no clear expectation in Scripture that how things are done in the home should be precisely how things are to be done in the church.

Further, as I have already noted, it is not evident that male headship is established in the divine order of things at creation. While there is an order of precedence—Adam first, then Eve—Genesis does not make this into an order of authority at all. Further, since an over/under authority system is established clearly only *after* the fall, it seems more likely that such a system was due to sin and is part of the effect on our lives due to the curse. Does the church really want to preach that we have been forgiven, redeemed, washed, sanctified, and baptized in the Spirit, but at the same time that we do not point with our lives toward the day when everything will be as God originally intended? To be sure, we cannot say that it has come here and now in its fullness: that would be the mistake that some Corinthians made in their over-realized eschatology. Yet at least part of the task that lies before the church today is to model in front of the world what heaven will be like *after* the curse is fully lifted. Surely we have received the *spiritual* benefits of the curse being lifted through the cross as well as *some* of the *physical* benefits (Gal. 3:13–14). It seems that one task that the church as a whole should do in this hour is to discern just what aspects of the shalom of God's future should be struggled for in this period between the two ages. In other words, if a husband has authority over a wife, is that to be understood because of sin and the curse and consequently their relationship now is to be handled differently because of the redemption from sin? Or are we to continue in our marriage relationships to reflect the curse instead of the pure love and obedience to Christ and the mutual submission to one another that is the "mystery" between Christ and his church?

Engaging the text of Ephesians 5:21–33 (and its corollary text, Col. 3:18–19) is important for our understanding of Paul's point on the relation between marriage and the church. Paul begins this section in Ephesians 5:18, where we are urged to be "filled with the Spirit." Aligned with this statement are participial phrases (using "-ing" endings in English) that conclude with "submit[ting] to one another out of reverence for Christ" (Eph. 5:21).[104] Then

104. The participles are (in English): "*speaking* to one another with psalms, hymns, and songs from the Spirit. *Sing* and *make music* from your heart to the Lord, always *giving thanks*

Ephesians 5:22 continues in the Greek by stating (literally), "the wives to their own husbands, as to the Lord."[105] The verb "submit" is not in verse 22, because it is to be filled in from verse 21 ("submitting . . ."). Mutual submission to one another precedes any familial obligation for submission from wives to husbands. This is no small point. It levels the playing field, so to speak. Yet it also should be noted that all of the participles from verse 18 onward are connected to the command "Be filled with the Spirit." Submitting to one another is one of the ways offered by Paul as a means to fulfill that command.[106]

The concept of "head" here in Ephesians 5:23 also needs clarification. "For the husband is the head of the wife as Christ is the head of the church, his body, of which he is the Savior." Paul uses an analogy to speak to the meaning of Christ as head of the church. He engages this concept of the head in more detail in 1 Corinthians 11. In relation to "head" it is crucial to note that the understanding of the Greek word that readers would have grasped was that it did not connote "authority over" but rather meant "origin" or "source."[107] As Cynthia Long Westfall demonstrates, first-century culture was interested in the origins of a person's family. "Head" was often used to signify these "important kinship relationships" in terms of a "source" for the family.[108] It is difficult for twenty-first-century people to grasp even this important tidbit of the semantic range of "head" in the first century, because we tend not to prize family origins as markers of our identity. Therefore, we must do the hard work of understanding the cultural intent of the word "head" (κεφαλή | kephalē) for Paul's readers.[109]

However, the metaphor of head here is an *organic* one—the head attached to the body, which signifies the real relationship between Christ and the church. Christ is the source of the body's sustenance—he is the source of its nutrition

---

to God the Father for everything, in the name of our Lord Jesus Christ" (Eph. 5:19–20). Then verse 21 begins, "*Submit* to one another . . ."

105. The Greek from verses 21–22 reads as follows: Ὑποτασσόμενοι ἀλλήλοις ἐν φόβῳ Χριστοῦ, αἱ γυναῖκες τοῖς ἰδίοις ἀνδράσιν ὡς τῷ κυρίῳ | *Hypotassomenoi allēlois en phobō Christou, hai gynaikes tois idiois andrasin hōs tō kyriō*.

106. I. Howard Marshall, "Mutual Love and Submission in Marriage: Colossians 3:18–19 and Ephesians 5:21–33," in Pierce and Groothuis, *Discovering Biblical Equality*, 196.

107. Philip Payne makes a persuasive argument for "head = source" here in Eph. 5. See Payne, *Man and Woman*, 286–87.

108. Cynthia Long Westfall, *Paul and Gender: Reclaiming the Apostle's Vision for Men and Women in Christ* (Grand Rapids: Baker Academic, 2016), 80.

109. For a more detailed discussion and exegesis of key NT passages related to "head," see two documents that I prepared for the Church of God Doctrine & Polity Committee in 2019: Terry L. Cross, "Headship and Women in Leadership: Part I, 1 Cor. 11:2–16," and "Headship and Women in Leadership: Part II, A Study on the Created Order of Male-Female Relationships," https://churchofgod.org/doctrine-and-polity-papers.

and life. In Colossians 2:19, the body must not lose connection with "the head," from which it is "supported and held together by its ligaments and sinews, grows as God causes it to grow" (Col. 2:19). Further, Paul notes that the body of Christ must "grow up in all things into Him who is the head—Christ" (Eph. 4:15–16 NKJV). God has appointed Christ "to be head over everything for the church, which is his body, the fullness of him who fills everything in every way" (Eph. 1:22–23). All of these speak to the reliance on the head (Christ) for the life and nutrition of the body (the church). Instead of an over/under authority, then, the point here in Ephesians 5 is that "the husband is the person on whom the wife depends just as the church depends on Christ, and therefore submission is appropriate."[110]

Moreover, the explanation by Paul at the end of Ephesians 5:23 makes clear the way "head" is to be understood. The husband is the head of the wife as Christ is the head of the church—of which "he is the Savior." In what way can the husband in this analogy be the wife's "savior"? Clearly, this is a point of dissimilarity since no human husband can "save" a wife as Christ saved the church. Still, the word for "savior" (σωτήρ | *sōtēr*) is one that can mean a "provider."[111] Instead of Paul saying, "Christ is the head of the body, *the authority over it*," he makes "savior" the explanatory apposition to clarify who Christ is. Therefore, the meaning of "head" here must mean something other than "leader."[112] It seems very probable that Paul is creating a new metaphor, enhancing the meaning of "source" with the apposition "savior."[113] This is how a husband is to treat his wife—by loving her, by "nourishing" (ἐκτρέφει | *ektrephei*) her, and by "keeping her warm"[114] or "cherishing" (θάλπει | *thalpei*) her (Eph. 5:25, 29 NKJV). The word for "nourish" has the sense of "nurturing or feeding to bring someone to maturity." The word for "cherishing" comes from a word that means "to keep warm," as a mother hen keeps her chicks warm by brooding over them. The head described in Ephesians 5 is one who loves (the church / the wife) by nurturing her so that she reaches the full potential that Christ intends and by brooding over her—keeping her close to assist in her health and state of well-being. Westfall notes that in Greco-Roman society, a man would not be described as doing something honorable if he were performing such "feminine tasks." Such a

110. Marshall, "Mutual Love and Submission in Marriage," 198. Marshall notes that this idea is from Gordon Fee.

111. Marshall, "Mutual Love and Submission in Marriage," 198–99, esp. n. 41.

112. Payne, *Man and Woman*, 285.

113. Payne calls it an "original living metaphor." See Payne, *Man and Woman*, 287.

114. This meaning for θάλπω | *thalpō* is from *Thayer's Greek Lexicon*. The words "nourishing" and "cherishing" are from the NKJV but are matched to our participial usage in this sentence.

reversal of roles breaks down the world's philosophy about "hierarchy and the separation between the genders in favor of an organic unity and biological interdependency."[115] It also underscores the emphasis by Jesus on reversing power through serving. As we have noted, the primary characteristic of Christian leaders is service. This must be the content that fills the Christian understanding of "head."

How Are We to Understand Difficult Passages in the New Testament on Women's Roles?

As we move into a discussion of several difficult biblical texts, my goal is not to convince readers of one particular interpretation but rather to raise viable alternatives to understanding what is going on in the contexts (culturally and linguistically) that may align with the rest of Scripture and our theological direction about women in leadership thus far. If there is a legitimate way to grasp the meaning behind Paul's words about women and silence (other than the plain reading of the text), then perhaps there needs to be more generous approaches to dealing with these texts and this issue in the church.

1 Timothy 2:11–12

A woman should learn in quietness and full submission. I do not permit a woman to teach or to assume authority over a man; she must be quiet.

A Woman Should Learn in Quietness and Full Submission

Taken by itself (and out of context), this sounds like a universal, general principle applied to all Christian settings.[116] However, I shall describe below the *particular* situation that Paul is addressing related to teachers of heretical notions in the church at Ephesus. This is not a universal command. If we take it as universal, then we have difficulty in understanding other passages where Paul allows women to speak in public settings in the church. "Pressing even this more specific prohibition to mean all it could mean, however, women should not even teach Sunday school classes in which men are in attendance."[117] What, then, is Paul attempting to say?

Women are to learn in silence (ἡσυχία | *hēsychia*). Douglas Moo notes, "ἡσυχία is the only word in his [Paul's] known vocabulary which could clearly

115. Westfall, *Paul and Gender*, 94.
116. Blomberg, "Women in Ministry," 167.
117. Keener, "Women in Ministry," 230.

denote silence."[118] In other words, Paul means "silence" here (that is, cessation from speaking) because ἡσυχία | *hēsychia* is the only word in his writings that could come close to meaning silence. Philip Payne notes the error of this assertion. Paul could have used another word from his own vocabulary, σιγή | *sigē*, to mean "silence."[119] Therefore, the most appropriate way to translate *hēsychia* is as "quietness" or "peace." As opposed to the "useless wrangling" and controversies over words that characterize the false teachers, women are to learn in quietness and in full submission. Perhaps some false teachers who were women had stepped up in the public worship setting in Ephesus in order to teach others in the congregation their "truth." The entire purpose of 1 Timothy is to "command certain people not to teach false doctrines any longer" that are associated with "myths and endless genealogies" (1 Tim. 1:3b–4a). While the women are not the focus of attention as teachers of false doctrine, they are "criticized directly and indirectly for repeating influential narratives . . . and spreading gossip and slander from house to house."[120]

The false teachers apparently had dominated the scene of public communication in the church so that slander (1 Tim. 5:14), old wives' tales (4:7), malicious talk (3:11), and talking nonsense (5:13)[121] had taken over. By contrast, Paul encourages God's people to live a "tranquil and quiet life" (NASB) when praying and interceding for all humans (2:1). The truth is a matter not of endless controversies over words but of order where tranquility is the basis for learning truth and teaching truth. The content of the false teaching is clarified later in the letter. False teachers encourage the people of God:

1. to abstain from certain foods (1 Tim. 4:3; 6:17),
2. to argue over controversies that produce constant friction (1:4; 6:4–7),
3. to speak arrogantly about things they know nothing about (6:4),
4. to engage in "endless genealogies" (1:4),
5. to promote "doctrines of demons" (NASB) whereby they forbid marriage (4:1, 3), and
6. to believe in "myths" or "old wives' tales" (1:4; 4:7).[122]

118. Douglas J. Moo, "The Interpretation of 1 Timothy 2:11–15: A Rejoinder," *Trinity Journal*, n.s., 2 (1981): 199.
119. Payne, *Man and Woman*, 315. Payne especially has in mind the opinion of Douglas Moo.
120. Westfall, *Paul and Gender*, 302.
121. This list owes a great deal to a chart by Philip Payne where he compares the statements of "false teachers" with similar statements concerning women. See Payne, *Man and Woman*, 300.
122. This list is adapted from Payne, *Man and Woman*, 295.

I Do Not Permit a Woman to Teach or to Assume Authority over a Man; She Must Be Quiet[123]

Two key issues are found in this verse—both related to the Greek text. The first issue is located with the verbs "to teach" (διδάσκειν | *didaskein*) and "to assume authority over a man" (αὐθεντεῖν | *authentein*). While it seems clear what "to teach" might mean, the verb "to exercise/assume authority over" is more difficult. It is used only here in the New Testament Greek text, so we cannot easily compare it to other passages in Paul or elsewhere. Some scholars believe the best way to understand *authentein* is "to exercise authority."[124] According to this view, Paul is telling Timothy that women are not to exercise authority over a man.[125] However, the use of this term in classical and Hellenistic Greek up through the first century CE (Paul's era) is entirely negative. It has a variety of meanings: "to murder, to take one's life in his own hands, to usurp authority, to act independently of authority, to domineer."[126] The evidence is very clear—only three hundred or so years *after* Paul does the word αὐθεντεῖν | *authentein* begin to have a positive meaning of "have authority" or even "exercise authority over."[127] Why is this important? Surely Paul felt his readers could readily grasp the meaning of the key verb he used in this verse, and the evidence overwhelmingly shows that *authentein* is negative in meaning until centuries after Paul died.[128]

The second issue is found in the complex structure of the sentence, which uses a phrasing like "neither . . . nor" (οὐκ . . . οὐδέ | *ouk . . . oude*). The grammar in this sentence is one of the most complex in all of the New Testament. Scholars are quite divided on how to resolve this issue, presenting comparative

---

123. The NKJV translates this, "And I do not permit a woman to teach or to have authority over a man, but to be in silence."

124. Schreiner, "Women in Ministry," 310. Schreiner notes the studies of George W. Knight III, Leland E. Wilshire, and H. Scott Baldwin as providing definitive proof and agreement about this word's meaning.

125. David M. Scholer, "1 Timothy 2:9–15 and the Place of Women in the Church's Ministry," in *Women, Authority and the Bible*, ed. Alvera Mickelsen (Downers Grove, IL: InterVarsity, 1986), 205.

126. See various discussions in Payne, *Man and Woman*, 364–74; 361, esp. nn. 1, 2, 4; also, Keener, *Paul, Women, and Wives*, 108–9. For a contrary view of the literary evidence, see Al Wolters, "The Meaning of Αὐθεντέω," in *Women in the Church: An Interpretation and Application of 1 Timothy 2:9–15*, ed. Andreas J. Köstenberger and Thomas R. Schreiner, 3rd ed. (Wheaton: Crossway, 2016), 65–115.

127. Keener, *Paul, Women, and Wives*, 108. Keener notes that some of this evidence is from patristic literature.

128. Payne provides the most convincing discussion of this with clear manuscript evidence in *Man and Woman*, 362–73. Payne notes, "Not even one instance of the later ecclesiastical use of αὐθεντεῖν with the meaning 'to have authority over' or 'to exercise authority' has been established before or near the time of Paul" (373).

analyses of various Greek texts in an attempt to establish a clear sense of what this verse might mean. Some scholars view *ouk . . . oude* as requiring either both verbs to be "positive" or both verbs to be "negative."[129] Others suggest that is incorrect—one can be positive and one negative. Since this debate dissolves into a very detailed inquiry into the Greek language, I will leave its explanation to the footnotes. However, for my purposes, whether this line means two *distinct actions*, as in "neither teach nor exercise authority over" (as two equally positive verbs with the two distinct actions), or it means a *single action*, as in "I am not permitting a woman to teach and [in combination with this] to assume authority over a man,"[130] is quite difficult to determine.

A decision regarding women in ministry or leadership *cannot* be based on the linguistic or grammatical evidence alone. There is more involved than simply words. There are ideas behind the words—sometimes ideas that we cannot know clearly at this distance from the first century. The question that moves us forward from this passage is as follows: Is this a universal principle for the church so that "women are prohibited from teaching or exercising authority because of the creation order"?[131] I think not. It is a *particular* situation that Paul addresses in Ephesus related to false teachers. "If anyone teaches otherwise [ἑτεροδιδασκαλεῖ | *heterodidaskalei*] and does not agree to the sound instruction of our Lord Jesus Christ and to godly teaching, they are conceited and understand nothing. They have an unhealthy interest in controversies and quarrels about words that result in envy, strife, malicious talk, evil suspicions and constant friction between people of corrupt mind, who have been robbed of the truth and who think that godliness is a means to financial gain" (1 Tim. 6:3–5).[132]

1 Corinthians 14:34–36

Women should remain silent in the churches. They are not allowed to speak, but must be in submission, as the law says. If they want to inquire about something,

129. Andreas J. Köstenberger, "A Complex Sentence Structure in 1 Timothy 2:12," in *Women in the Church: A Fresh Analysis of 1 Timothy 2:9–15*, ed. Andreas Köstenberger, Thomas R. Schreiner, and H. Scott Baldwin (Grand Rapids: Baker, 1995), 81–103; this chapter appears in revised form as "A Complex Sentence: The Syntax of 1 Timothy 2:12," in Köstenberger and Schreiner, *Women in the Church*, 117–61.

130. Payne, *Man and Woman*, 358.

131. Thomas R. Schreiner, "An Interpretation of 1 Timothy 2:9–15: A Dialogue with Scholarship," in Köstenberger and Schreiner, *Women in the Church*, 163–225, here 225. Cited also in Philip B. Payne, *Man and Woman*, 319.

132. Two of the more comprehensive and sophisticated arguments for each side in this debate may offer more detailed information on each of the points given here—and more. This is especially true with respect to understanding the notoriously difficult passage 1 Tim. 2:12–15. See Giles, *Patterns of Ministry among the First Christians*, 195–216; and Schreiner, "An Interpretation of 1 Timothy 2:9–15," in *Women in the Church*, 163–225.

they should ask their own husbands at home; for it is disgraceful for a woman
to speak in the church.

Or did the word of God originate with you? Or are you the only people it
has reached?

Is Paul Quoting the Corinthians?

The issues involved in this text are also difficult.[133] I will examine several
proposals for understanding it. Is Paul (perhaps) quoting the Corinthians here
in verses 34–35 and then refuting them in verse 36? Or if not, then what are
we to do with an apparent contradiction between 1 Corinthians 14:34–35 and
1 Corinthians 11:2–16 (where women can prophesy and pray in church)?

One group of interpreters understands these verses as Paul quoting some
of the Corinthians' sayings in order to refute them.[134] Charles H. Talbert proposed this idea, noting that the rhetorical form of 1 Corinthians 14:34–35 and
36 is dialogical.[135] According to this interpretation, Paul quotes the Corinthian
"slogans" (as he has done three times previously in the letter) and then rejects
their argument (v. 36). When Paul rebuts the Corinthian quote, he uses a dis-
junctive particle in Greek both times in verse 36: ἤ | ē, which means "or." He
does this twelve times in 1 Corinthians to argue against a Corinthian view.[136]
However, why did Paul not introduce these words in verses 34–35 as some
false teaching or slogan of the Corinthians? Talbert suggests that instead of
such introduction, the strange and "discordant note may be regarded as the
position of Paul's opponents."[137] Moreover, the fact that Paul has addressed
Corinthian "slogans" on previous occasions in the letter lends support for
the idea that he may be doing it again here.[138] As Marion Soards states, while

133. Textually, for example, some scholars view these verses as an "interpolation" or "inser-
tion" by a later scribe so that vv. 34–35 are placed at the *end* of v. 40. A few of these manuscripts
are from the 300s CE, but most follow a "Western" tradition and end up being a rather minor
branch. These are manuscripts from about the late 300s CE to about 600 CE. They are D, F,
G, 88*, a, b, d, f, and g. One strong supporter of this interpolation theory is textual critic Fee,
Corinthians, 701.

134. While Anthony Thiselton does not entirely land on this "slogan" approach, he does
state that such a view is not "farfetched." Anthony C. Thiselton, *The First Epistle to the Corinthians: A Commentary on the Greek Text*, NIGTC (Grand Rapids: Eerdmans, 2000), 1150.

135. Charles H. Talbert, *Reading Corinthians: A Literary and Theological Commentary on
1 and 2 Corinthians* (New York: Crossroad, 1987), 92.

136. See Payne's succinct argument for and against this view in *Man and Woman*, 224; cf.
also the discussion of this in Keener, *Paul, Women, and Wives*, 75.

137. Talbert, *Reading Corinthians*, 92.

138. See Jerome Murphy-O'Connor, "Corinthian Slogans in 1 Cor 6:12–20," *Catholic Biblical Quarterly* 40, no. 3 (1978): 391–96; also see David W. Odell-Scott, "Let the Women Speak
in Church: An Egalitarian Interpretation of 1 Cor 14:33b–36," *Biblical Theology Bulletin* 13
(1983): 90–93; also J. E. Smith, "Slogans in 1 Corinthians," *Bibliotheca Sacra* 167 (2010): 68–88.

there is not a clear signal that this section is dialogical, the rebuttal proposal remains nonetheless "sensible and attractive."[139]

According to this view (the "slogan hypothesis"),[140] the Corinthians were not allowing women to speak ("women should remain silent in the churches") and were requiring them to "be in submission," as the law says (1 Cor. 14:34). This is the first "slogan." The second is similar but with a different basis: they should not ask questions in church but should learn at home from their husbands, for it is "disgraceful for a woman to speak in the church" (14:35). In verse 36, Paul begins with an extremely abrupt challenge: "*Or* [ἤ | *ē*] did the word of God originate with you?" And again, "*Or* are you the only people it has reached?" This proposal suggests that the "adversative" use of "or" here is a strong statement against the Corinthians' views as proposed in verses 34–35. However, Walter Liefeld argues that Paul was adversarial because of the Corinthians' disobedience of the requirement in verses 34–35, not because of some adversative "or."[141] Also, Craig Keener observes that when Paul deals with the "slogans" elsewhere in 1 Corinthians, they are "at least partly affirmed, though seriously qualified."[142] One would have expected Paul to continue with that pattern here, but he does not.

Is Paul Contradicting His Permission for Women to Pray or Prophesy?

This brings us to our next approach to understanding what Paul meant—namely, the apparent contradiction between women praying/prophesying and women being silent in the churches. A number of proposals have been offered to ameliorate this apparent tension. Let's consider them.

First, some have seen the meetings described in 1 Corinthians 11 and 14 as different in terms of type. For example, some see the meetings in 1 Corinthians 11 as *private meetings*—that is, informal gatherings for worship and perhaps teaching[143]—while the meetings in 1 Corinthians 14 are formal, "official" worship services for the church. Therefore, women are allowed to prophesy in small, informal meetings but not when the congregation officially

---

139. Marion L. Soards, *1 Corinthians*, New International Biblical Commentary, ed. W. Ward Gasque (Peabody, MA: Hendrickson, 1999), 304.

140. This phrase is from Jill E. Marshall, *Women Praying and Prophesying in Corinth: Gender and Inspired Speech in First Corinthians*, WUNT, 2nd ser., 448 (Tübingen: Mohr Siebeck, 2017), 206n56.

141. Walter L. Liefeld, "Women, Submission and Ministry in 1 Corinthians," in Mickelsen, *Women, Authority and the Bible*, 149.

142. Keener, *Paul, Women, and Wives*, 76.

143. Fee, *Corinthians*, 703.

meets. However, there is nothing in the texts that makes such a demarcation between the locations of the worship settings.

Second, some have viewed the *kind of speech* of the two passages as different. Perhaps Paul was addressing a type of "chatter" in 1 Corinthians 14 that is different from "inspired speech" in 1 Corinthians 11. Perhaps Paul was providing admonition on a *specific* practice in Corinth that the readers understood, but from which we are too distant now to grasp.[144] This could be supported by verse 35 where Paul tells the women to "ask their own husbands at home" (1 Cor. 14:35). It appears, then, that some of the talk was disruptive of congregational worship. While the word here for "speak" (λαλεῖν | *lalein*) could mean "chatter" in ancient classical Greek, it rarely held that meaning in the Koine Greek of the New Testament.[145] Whether or not it was "chatter," it was certainly disruptive.[146] Perhaps some of the talking "may have been questioning out loud about what the last speaker said or meant."[147] There seems to be some support in the text for this proposal, which I will consider more carefully later.

Third, some scholars suggest that Paul is addressing women in general in 1 Corinthians 11 and wives in particular in 1 Corinthians 14.[148] When the Greek word for "male" or "husband" (ἀνήρ | *anēr*) is in close proximity to the Greek word for "woman" (γυνή | *gynē*), the latter term (*gynē*) can mean "wife." It is suggested that this proximity is the case here in 1 Corinthians 14 but not in 1 Corinthians 11, where the context suggests male and female in general. C. K. Barrett reminds readers that married women in ancient Greece and Rome were frequently required to be silent—it was the custom that would reflect best on one's husband in the culture.[149] Romans, Greeks, and Hellenistic

144. Soards, *1 Corinthians*, 304–6.
145. Soards, *1 Corinthians*, 306; also Fee, *Corinthians*, 703. However, Graydon Snyder suggests it could mean "prattle." See Graydon F. Snyder, *First Corinthians: A Faith Community Commentary* (Macon, GA: Mercer University Press, 1992), 186. For a good discussion of this see Westfall, *Paul and Gender*, 238–39, on first-century women and conversational styles, esp. n. 88.
146. Fee, *Corinthians*, 703.
147. William F. Orr and James A. Walther, *1 Corinthians: A New Translation*, Anchor Bible 32 (Garden City, NY: Doubleday, 1976), 313.
148. Richard A. Horsley, *1 Corinthians*, Abingdon New Testament Commentaries, ed. Victor Paul Furnish (Nashville: Abingdon, 1998), 189; also Orr and Walther, *1 Corinthians*, 12; cf. also Soards, *1 Corinthians*, 302.
149. Charles K. Barrett, *The First Epistle to the Corinthians*, Black's New Testament Commentary, ed. Henry Chadwick (Peabody, MA: Hendrickson, 1968), 331. Barrett notes Aristophanes's comedy titled *Ecclesiazusae*, where women take over the Athenian assembly and create chaos (and apparently a rip-roaring comedy that played on the fact that women should not and could not take part in such political work).

Jews cited such cultural values.[150] Perhaps the Corinthian women (the "enthusiasts" or the "spiritual ones"—*pneumatikoi*) were beginning to "blur distinctions" between men and women, so Paul called them back to a more Jewish
expectation of public behavior for women in the synagogue.[151] However, once
again, we simply do not know which group Paul was considering here—
and the linguistic evidence does not always give us the certitude we might
desire.

Finally, some scholars suggest that women are allowed to pray and prophesy
in 1 Corinthians 11, but in 1 Corinthians 14 they may not participate "in the
oral weighing of such prophecies."[152] In 1 Corinthians 14:29, Paul tries to place
order on the delivery of prophecy by saying, "Two or three prophets should
speak, and the others should weigh carefully [διακρινέτωσαν | *diakrinetōsan*][153]
what is said." Hence, in this view women are allowed to exercise their ecstatic
gifts but are banned from weighing or "sifting" the prophets' messages.[154] Perhaps this was due to the rather universal belief in Greco-Roman society at
the time that women were "softer of mind than a man and more subject to
being flooded with emotion."[155] Women were designated as an inferior spe-
cies, similar to the male but less capable of intellectual or difficult work. For
centuries before and after Paul's time, medical descriptions of women had

150. Talbert, *Reading Corinthians*, 91–92. Talbert cites Livy (concerning Cato's words),
Juvenal (*Satires* 6), Philo (*Hypothetica* 8.7.14), and Josephus (*Against Apion* 2.201). The word-
ing in some of these citations and the underlying mentality toward women speaking in public
seems to coincide rather nicely with vv. 34–35.

151. Raymond F. Collins, *First Corinthians*, Sacra Pagina, ed. Daniel J. Harrington (Collegeville, MN: Liturgical Press, 1999), 513–14.

152. D. A. Carson, *Showing the Spirit: A Theological Exposition of 1 Corinthians 12–14*
(Grand Rapids: Baker, 1987), 129. Carson notes that Thrall, Grudem, and Hurley opt for this
usage in 1 Cor. 14. See James B. Hurley, "Did Paul Require Veils or the Silence of Women? A
Consideration of 1 Cor. 11:2–16 and 1 Cor. 14:33b–36," *Westminster Theological Journal* 35,
no. 2 (Winter 1973): 190–220.

153. Anthony Thiselton prefers the translation "let them sift." The idea is to "differentiate"
or "distinguish between," so it probably refers to distinguishing between God-given prophecy
and that which is not ("self-generated rhetoric," as Thiselton calls it). See Thiselton, *The First
Epistle to the Corinthians*, 1140.

154. Wayne Grudem suggests that since weighing prophecies would have verged into "teaching" territory and governing authority, in his opinion this could not be allowed by Paul. See
Grudem, "Prophecy—Yes, but Teaching—No: Paul's Consistent Advocacy of Women's Participation without Governing Authority," *Journal of the Evangelical Theological Society* 30
(March 1987): 20. It seems that Grudem limits his interpretation here in 1 Cor. 14 by how he
has understood 1 Tim. 2:12.

155. This statement comes from Chrysostom in the early 400s CE, but it had been the domi-
nant belief since the days of Aristotle, about three hundred years before Christ. See Chrysostom,
"Homilies on the Epistles of Paul to the Corinthians," 37.1, in *1–2 Corinthians*, ed. and trans.
Gerald Bray, Ancient Christian Commentary on Scripture, ed. Thomas C. Oden (Downers
Grove, IL: InterVarsity, 1999), 143.

been along these lines: women are different from men in that they are loose and spongy in their flesh; their bodies soak up moisture because they are porous. A man's body is firm and compact, not loose and spongy, and therefore is capable of greater intellectual and physical activity. Thus, it is proven that the female cannot do the same jobs as a male.[156] And so went the ancient line. These views of women certainly influenced the way people thought about public female participation in any aspect of society.

When limitations on women's roles in the church are raised by Grudem and others, they seem to continue the problematic myth of female inadequacy. The effect of their teaching is that women cannot be trusted to discern truth or weigh the evidence of spoken prophecies. Therefore, silence is required only concerning such "weighing carefully" what was said, not the ecstatic delivery itself. The difficulty in this position is severalfold:

1. there is nothing in verses 34–35 that says anything about the women's speech being focused only on weighing the prophecies just given;
2. the admonition in verse 29 is located too far away for readers to make a clear connection with verses 34–35 (especially without any words pointing to it);
3. the presupposition (of Grudem and others) is that women cannot teach and such evaluating of prophecy would be equivalent to teaching (people who recognize the gifts of the Spirit, however, would find this limitation odd: if the Spirit can fill a woman so that she overflows with prophetic utterance, then why can the Spirit not do the same by inspiring her to evaluate the words of others?); and
4. hovering over this argument is an air of suspicion (if not inferiority) concerning women's capacity to discern and evaluate prophecy.

Whatever the prohibition against women speaking here, it cannot be a universal command against Spirit-filled women participating in worship (since 1 Cor. 11 allows for that). Paul is not contradicting himself only a few chapters removed from his previous statement in support of women praying and prophesying. How can believers today support a woman being used of the Spirit to speak in tongues or prophesy in public worship and then deny a woman being used of the Spirit to weigh the inspired speech of others? Such thinking is incoherent.

156. An excellent article on this is by Lesley Dean-Jones, "The Cultural Construct of the Female Body in Classical Greek Science," *Women's History & Ancient History*, ed. Sarah B. Pomeroy (Chapel Hill: University of North Carolina Press, 1991), 114–15.

In looking elsewhere in these verses for an explanation that makes sense of both 1 Corinthians 11 and 1 Corinthians 14, one fact remains central: various forms of speech had created disruption in the worship services at Corinth. Church gatherings were not in large arenas or even halls that could seat a few hundred people. First-century worship took place mainly in houses where anywhere from ten to seventy-five people might gather. The context of 1 Corinthians 14 describes a worship service that was out of order—and hence Paul's admonition that God is a God of peace (εἰρήνης | eirēnēs), not disorder (ἀκαταστασίας | akatastasias) (1 Cor. 14:33a). Tongues were flying everywhere—both heavenly and (apparently) earthly. If prophets rose to speak, they were interrupted by others rising to share their own most recent revelation. Gifts of the Spirit were operating with full force in Corinthian worship, but the fruit of the Spirit (especially love) was absent. Moreover, believers could not make much sense of what was happening, and unbelievers walked away saying, "You are mad!" (1 Cor. 14:23 NASB).

Therefore, for the cause of Christ and his body of believers, Paul harnesses the chaos with orderly rules—one of which relates precisely to the cause of chaos—namely, disruptive speech. How do we know this is the case? Verse 35 explains that women should be silent and "inquire about something" from their husbands at home. The imperative verb here for "let them inquire" (ἐπερωτάτωσαν | eperōtatōsan) is used in Mark 14:60–61 of the high priest "interrogating" Jesus. It can even mean "to accost one with an inquiry."[157] Within the church at Corinth it seems likely that there were multiple people (men and women) speaking out ecstatically and somewhat randomly. While tongues, interpretation, and prophecy were operating in a rather confusing manner, there were also women (in particular) who were probing their husbands for answers to questions that arose from what was being said. The din of voices must have been so cacophonous that Paul attempted to rope the entire process into a corral of order. Women in such a specific setting are to be silent—to stop speaking (σιγάτωσαν | sigatōsan). It is the disruptive speech that is being clamped down by Paul, not ecstatic speech or prophecy or even judgment on the prophecy. He has already described that tongues/interpretation should occur in an orderly fashion with two or "at the most three" speaking "one at a time" (1 Cor. 14:27). In addition, "two or three prophets should

157. Thiselton, *The First Epistle to the Corinthians*, 1159–60. In Mark 14:60, the high priest "questioned" (ἐπηρώτησεν | epērōtēsen) Jesus (NASB), but he remained silent. In 14:61, again the high priest "was questioning" (NASB) (ἐπηρώτα | epērōta) Jesus. The first instance of the verb is an aorist active indicative, pointing either to a completed action or observing the action as a whole; the second instance is an imperfect active indicative, noting the process of continually asking in the past. This latter one could be translated, "the high priest kept on questioning him."

speak" in a similar orderly manner with the "others" weighing what is said (1 Cor. 14:29). Finally, if a spontaneous revelation "comes to someone who is sitting down, the first speaker should stop. For you can all prophesy in turn so that everyone may be instructed and encouraged" (1 Cor. 14:30–31). There must be *control* of the spiritual impulses, because the "spirits of prophets are subject to the control of prophets" (1 Cor. 14:32). All of this is because God is a God of peace, not disorder or confusion. Paul seems to be crafting a manual for spiritual speech in the congregation that is specifically addressed to the situation in Corinth. It is here that the problem created by women in the worship service is discussed. He addresses the *particular* disturbance in Corinth and the contribution that women were making to it. For the sake of the gospel, it must cease. For the sake of the common edification of the body, it must cease.

Moreover, it is crucially important to note that Paul does not deny women or wives the information needed to grow as a Christian. A wife can learn at home from her husband. In the Greco-Roman world of the first century CE, this was an extremely progressive idea—that women could and should learn from their husbands.[158] Paul's admonition for silence among the women in Corinth was offered not to stifle their opinions or views but rather to limit their questioning speech in public worship so that the body may be edified. The needs of the *whole* community override the concerns of *part* of the community—that is the universal principle here, not that all women everywhere for all time should be silent in worship. In this crucial text, it is necessary to see that a hermeneutic of "just reading the plain sense of the words" will not procure a clear understanding of what Paul is talking about. It is important that order be maintained in worship, so wives may learn from their husbands in the privacy of their own homes rather than interrogating their husbands (or the prophets) in the public arena of an already confused worship setting. It appears that a careful reading of the context clarifies that this is a *specific* command to a *specific* problem in Corinth.

Concluding Thoughts

When considering relations among the people of God, leadership structures are a pivotal aspect of how we relate to each other as human beings. However, a leadership that follows Christ must be marked by its service, not by the trappings of power. Among Christians the idea of authority too frequently

158. Keener, *Paul, Women, and Wives*, 84.

has held to the sin-filled notion of dominance—what we have called an over/
under mentality. Given the fact that the New Testament clearly outlines the
manner and character of Christian leaders as ones of service and love, such a
predilection for mastery over others—even (or especially?) in the church—is
baffling. Nowhere has this grab for power had more denigrating effect than
in the hierarchy of males over females in church leadership and ministry.[159]

The pneumatic ecclesiology that I have presented is not a leaderless people.
It functions effectively because of the presence of the Holy Spirit, who creates
a "new humanity" in Christ (Eph. 2:15 NRSV). It moves purposefully because
the Spirit moves it according to the Spirit's own direction; it works efficiently
because the Spirit energizes it to fulfill the *missio Dei* in this world. The Spirit
gives spiritual gifts to the people of God's presence so that the impossible
mission assigned to the church becomes possible. Among the distribution of
spiritual gifts, those of leading, governing, and administrating are crucial for
accomplishing the will of the Triune God. Since the Spirit did not exclude the
gift of his own presence from women on the day of Pentecost, why should we
expect the Spirit to limit the distributions of spiritual gifts (charismata) to
males only? In other words, leading, administrating, and governing are gifts
of the Spirit for the betterment of the church; how can we say to God's Spirit
that only males need apply for any one gift? If the Spirit has been poured out
on all flesh—sons *and* daughters—then at what point does the church have
the authority to restrict God's promise or action?

The people of God who have been encountered directly by the presence of
God must sense the Spirit drawing us to equitable relations, especially among
males and females. Men and women are not the same, to be sure, but before
God we are equal. Gifts, not gender, are the calling cards of the Spirit. The
question among the people of God's presence concerning leadership must
never be, "Does God call a female?" but rather, "What is in your hand?" What
is it that God has given to you so that you may fit into this local body and
advance the mission of Christ in the world, regardless of gender?

159. Westfall, *Paul and Gender*, 259–60.

The People of God's Presence
Participate in Practices
Ordained by Christ

Christian Practices

The people of God make room in our gatherings to participate in corporate practices that set the stage for God's presence among us and inculcate habits that trace the features of Christ's life within our own lives. This statement will need clarification and explication. Perhaps the way to clarify this thought most directly is by underscoring the nature of the church as the people of God's presence who are continually being transformed to become more and more like God in this world. How does this happen? I have proposed that this begins with a direct encounter with God—one that engages the precognitive, prereflective core of our being. It is here that the beginning of a reorientation to the world takes place—one that causes us to walk by faith not sight.

One difficulty with this model, however, is that it feels somewhat internal and disconnected with the reality of our physical lives. While I have tried to avoid such caricatures by suggesting that God confronts the *entire* person—the physical and spiritual dimensions—there remains something rather aloof in my ecclesiology, something almost disembodied perhaps. Salvation and sanctification in Christ are not merely spiritual, invisible realities that affect the "soul." They are the effects of the transforming presence of God's Spirit in the divine-human encounter. This transformation engages the *whole human being*—physical and spiritual.

The entire Christian life may be summed up as a human life that has been encountered by God's presence, "conformed to the pattern of [Christ's] life."[1] In some mystical yet real way, our earthly lives come to parallel our Lord's way of living on this earth through tracing our Lord's steps (1 Pet. 2:21). To be sure, there is only correspondence, not identity—Christ's life, death, and resurrection in human history, not our tracing of it, is *the* salvific event.[2] Yet, as Karl Barth points out, in the event of sanctification there is "the life-movement of the Christian" (*CD* IV/2:602).

It is here that I propose the idea of participatory Christian practices. As noted previously, I believe that the church in the twenty-first century will be challenged on a variety of issues by the increasingly post-Christian, secular societies in the West. One that I have not fully addressed is as follows: Can a spiritual experience with God be translated into the practical, embodied life of real human beings in this century? One important answer to this challenge is the communal aspect of participating in Christian practices through *bodily* actions.

For too long, Protestant churches have been heavy with words, tilting toward the cognitive side of the faith to such a degree that any experiential dimension becomes suspect. Christianity became a religion of the intellect, as if what ones *does* in life is solely the outcome of what one *thinks*.[3] In whatever way we may understand the origin and nature of sin in the world, surely we have learned in this last century that *thinking* a certain way—even an "improved" way—does not entirely resolve the sin problem. To be sure, sin warps our thinking, but the remedy is not simply sitting and listening to sermons so our thinking is repaired. Sin also affects the noncognitive aspects of human life—the aspects that shape our dispositions and affections, giving orientation to our predispositions. It is not just our minds that are marred by sin; it is our entire being—dispositions, emotions, affections, passions, and perceptions. The people of God's presence cannot simply gather in a lecture hall in order

1. Beth Felker Jones, *Practicing Christian Doctrine: An Introduction to Thinking and Living Theologically* (Grand Rapids: Baker Academic, 2014), 139.

2. Perhaps no one holds this line of nonidentity more fiercely than Karl Barth. When Christians take up their cross, it "is not a re-enactment of His crucifixion" but a correspondence to it (*CD* IV/2:600). See also Kimlyn J. Bender, *Karl Barth's Christological Ecclesiology*, Barth Studies Series, ed. John Webster, George Hunsinger, and Hans-Anton Drewes (Burlington, VT: Ashgate, 2005), 147–51.

3. James K. A. Smith, *Imagining the Kingdom: How Worship Works*, Cultural Liturgies 2 (Grand Rapids: Baker Academic, 2013), 34–35. Smith calls the approach that I have described above the "intellectualist paradigm" (34).

to have their *minds* changed, but they must meet God in the midst of their community in order to have their *hearts* transformed and their minds renewed by the Spirit.

This means, then, that the church "is not primarily an idea or a concept but praxis."[4] The people of God's presence are an *active* community of believers who serve God in their various pathways of living by engaging in their priestly ministry to God, other believers, and the people of their world. We are a *doing* people.[5] Therefore, "the church is not primarily a place to exchange ideas but a place for the practice of prayer and song, praise and worship, and celebrating the Lord's Supper. It is a place for sanctification, for being shaped by the Word of God, for learning to listen to God."[6] Our behavior as the people of God's presence is to reflect God's own nature and action. Our entire being must be encountered by God's Spirit so that the character of God gradually becomes our own character. As embodied beings, we require shared activities in which to participate—activities that can shape our habits and dispositions in the world.[7] Following the concepts inaugurated by Alasdair MacIntyre in the early 1980s, I choose to call these activities "practices."[8]

What do I mean by Christian practices? Craig Dykstra provides us with a useful definition: "A *practice* is an ongoing, shared activity of a community of people that partly defines and partly makes them who they are."[9] Further, Dykstra and Dorothy Bass provide the following explanation: "Christian practices are things Christian people do together over time in response to and in the light of God's active presence for the life of the world."[10] There are a number of examples that could clarify this term: corporate prayer, fasting, benevolent acts, reading Scripture together, and so forth. Practices have a way of shaping our "affective dispositions" and thereby orienting our "way of

---

4. Cornelius van der Kooi and Gilbert van den Brink, *Christian Dogmatics: An Introduction*, trans. Reinder Bruinsma with James D. Bratt (Grand Rapids: Eerdmans, 2017), 580.

5. As Dykstra and Bass have noted, "People-at-practice do things. They make gestures and touch one another." See Craig Dykstra and Dorothy C. Bass, "Times of Yearning, Practices of Faith," in *Practicing Our Faith: A Way of Life for a Searching People*, ed. Dorothy C. Bass (San Francisco: Jossey-Bass, 1997), 8.

6. Van der Kooi and van den Brink, *Christian Dogmatics*, 580. I would add that it is a place where we learn to make room for God's presence.

7. It will be clear that much of my discussion on the sanctifying nature of practices owes a great deal to Smith, *Imagining the Kingdom*, esp. 33–38.

8. Alasdair MacIntyre, *After Virtue: A Study in Moral Theory* (Notre Dame, IN: University of Notre Dame Press, 1981), esp. 175–81.

9. Craig Dykstra, *Growing in the Life of Faith: Education and Christian Practices* (Louisville: Geneva, 1999), 48n16.

10. Dykstra and Bass, "Times of Yearning, Practices of Faith," 5.

being" in the world.[11] Jamie Smith highlights what I am driving toward here: "Educating for *Christian* action will require attending to the formation of our unconscious, to the priming and training of our emotions, which shape our perception of the world. And if such training happens through narratives, then educating for Christian action will require an education that is framed by participation in the Christian story."[12]

In the sanctifying education of our dispositions, *participation in the Christian story* is vital. What does this mean? Our bodies "learn" through acquiring habits that involve them in participation. By participating *bodily* in the various Christian practices, we place meaning in our lives by tracing the life of Christ in the midst of our own lives together. The repeated action of participating in Christian rituals speaks *beyond* our intellectual dimensions of being human and drives deeply into our very being—precisely where the Spirit of God encounters us. There are essential dispositional postures and practices that place us in a position where God's holy presence may encounter us. In this regard, Dykstra offers further insight: "The practices of Christian faith turn out in the end not primarily to be practices, efforts. They turn out to be places in the contours of our personal and communal lives where a habitation of the Spirit is able to occur. And it is this that is the source of their power and meaning."[13]

However, one difficulty with thinking of Christian living in terms of its practices is that the performance of these can give the impression that mere repetition of a practice can bring God's presence to us. The grace of God's presence cannot be "earned" by *doing things*—even Christian things. As theologian Shirley Guthrie has said, "There is nothing we can do to force the Spirit of God to come to us and give us faith, hope and love. . . . He is free to work when, where and how he chooses. He takes the initiative and not we. . . . Although we cannot control his coming and going, we can at least place ourselves in the kind of situation in which we know he accomplishes his work."[14] What extraordinary insight! We cannot control the free, sovereign Lord, but we can place ourselves in "the kind of situation" where we know God shows up and works his will. God's presence among us is not our doing; it does not come about from our willing it so. Yet somehow these practices "can be shaped in response to God's active presence" among us.[15]

11. Smith, *Imagining the Kingdom*, 34–35.
12. Smith, *Imagining the Kingdom*, 38 (his emphasis).
13. Dykstra, *Growing in the Life of Faith*, 64.
14. Shirley C. Guthrie, *Christian Doctrine* (Atlanta: John Knox, 1968), 299–300.
15. Dykstra and Bass, "Times of Yearning, Practices of Faith," 5.

Practices, then, are essential habits for the people of God's presence. This may sound like a strange statement from a pneumatic ecclesiology, but the believer's *body* is also affected by the Spirit's work. Further, our bodies are essential aspects of our humanity; "bodies are not just vehicles for our minds."[16] Through living in the world, "we build up a habitual way of being-in-the-world that is carried in our body."[17] Our bodies "know" at a preconscious level and carry memories of that knowing through the way we approach the world, thereby helping to shape our "perception" of the world and our response to it even before the cognitive dimension of our lives "kicks in." Smith rightly notes that this "habitual body with a preconscious knowledge" is the "locus for a way of life."[18] Thus, how we are fundamentally oriented toward existing in the world is shaped in so many ways by how our body is habituated. For the people of God's presence, this type of "embodied knowledge" is learned by the habits (practices) that establish what it means to live a Christian way of life (and death) in the world.[19] The Spirit's presence helps to shape us to the contours of Christ's way of life through our bodies and minds.

How does this relate to the doctrine of the church? The central question for much of our ecclesiology has engaged the matter of God's presence among and in God's people. Since the issue of divine presence has often been associated with the so-called sacraments—in particular, with that of the Eucharist or Lord's Supper—this chapter will examine the several practices that have special significance because Jesus Christ instituted them, telling us to do them repeatedly until he comes. In religious language, we call the repetition of these prescribed actions "rituals." These religious practices can be meaningful in the lives of believers because they remind us to make room for God's presence among us through them. However—and perhaps more importantly for our point here—these practices are also vital for shaping our lives through

16. Smith, *Imagining the Kingdom*, 50.

17. Smith, *Imagining the Kingdom*, 44. Smith relies here on the work of Maurice Merleau-Ponty, a twentieth-century French philosopher. However, Smith's narration of this connection does not lose us in the philosophical depths; he helps us understand phenomenology without having to learn the entire system first. Further, he moves us forward with implications derived from Pierre Bourdieu and Mark Johnson with regard to how habits can play a role in Christian formation. It is a stunning display of absorbing the importance of philosophical study for the benefit of theology without desecrating the philosophical tool or limiting it to that of a "handmaid." See Maurice Merleau-Ponty, *Phenomenology of Perception*, trans. Donald A. Landes (New York: Routledge, 2014), esp. 132–48; Pierre Bourdieu, *The Logic of Practice*, trans. Richard Nice (Stanford, CA: Stanford University Press, 1990), esp. chap. 5, "Logic of Practice." See also Mark Johnson, *The Meaning of the Body: Aesthetics of Human Understanding* (Chicago: University of Chicago Press, 2007), esp. 1–15, 54–71.

18. Smith, *Imagining the Kingdom*, 44.

19. Smith, *Imagining the Kingdom*, 45.

kinetic action that attempts to parallel the life, death, and resurrection story of Jesus Christ on earth. It is the work of the Holy Spirit to bring our own human participation in the movement of Christ's life, death, and resurrection through these practices into a mystical union with our Lord and other believers. In the history of the Christian church, these activities have been called "sacraments." Due to the complex development and use of the term "sacraments," some groups prefer to describe these rituals as "ordinances," in reference to Christ "ordaining" them. As will be made clear in this chapter, we have reason to set aside the traditional language of both terms in favor of a more neutral yet descriptive phrasing of "participatory Christian practices."

In this chapter, I will inquire about the nature of the sacraments and attempt to determine the purpose for them among God's people, especially in relation to the divine presence. In order to arrive at an understanding of how these practices are to be understood within the context of the people of God's presence, I will present some limited theological and historical context regarding the sacraments and the general concept of "means of grace," and then turn to individual practices (baptism, Lord's Supper, and footwashing).

The Idea of Sacraments and Means of Grace

While "sacrament" is the term most often used to describe specific Christian rituals in Western churches, it is interesting to note that this word itself is not used in the Bible to denote the Lord's Supper or baptism. Indeed, there is no single biblical term that points to the common aspect of "sacrament" as we would use it today.[20] How, then, did it come to be used?[21]

Is the Category of Sacrament Helpful?

The term *sacramentum* was used in the Latin Bible to translate the New Testament Greek term *mystērion* (μυστήριον).[22] However, as Otto Weber correctly

20. Wolfhart Pannenberg, *Systematic Theology*, trans. Geoffrey W. Bromiley, 3 vols. (Grand Rapids: Eerdmans, 1998), 3:340.

21. In his recent ecclesiology, Tom Greggs offers an extended discussion on the "genus" of the term "sacrament." He asks, "So what if we simply removed the category? . . . Simply remove the *genus* 'sacrament'? What would be lost from the excision of this ambiguous and unbiblical genus?" I think this question is precisely on target and heads in the direction of my own proposal. Tom Greggs, *Dogmatic Ecclesiology*, vol. 1, *The Priestly Catholicity of the Church* (Grand Rapids: Baker Academic, 2019), 151–59, esp. here 153–54. Later Greggs states that he prefers "sign" over "sacrament" (164–65).

22. Otto Weber, *Foundations of Dogmatics*, trans. Darrell L. Guder (Grand Rapids: Eerdmans, 1983), 2:587. The NT passages that use this term are Eph. 1:9; 3:3, 9; 5:32; Col. 1:27; 1 Tim. 3:16; Rev. 1:20; 17:7.

notes, "that term never refers to the activities which later came to be called sacraments."[23] The New Testament references using *mystērion* (μυστήριον) are associated with genuine "mysteries" of the faith made clear to us in Jesus Christ (e.g., Col. 1:27; 2:3).[24] In the East, where Greek was spoken, the church used the term "mysteries" instead of "sacraments" to describe these rituals. By keeping the biblical term for the mysteries related to salvation, the East was able to connect the rituals more closely to the Scriptures as well as to salvation. In the West, by utilizing a secular concept (*sacramentum*), early Latin Christians borrowed a term that was well known in the ancient Roman world—especially the army. "A *sacramentum* was the oath of fidelity and obedience to one's commander sworn by a Roman soldier upon enlistment in the army."[25] The idea in the West connected *sacramentum* with an oath of fidelity.[26] In classical usage, *sacramentum* referred either to money deposited in the temple treasury for religious purposes or to military oaths of allegiance by recruits. Whether it referred to money held in reserve or a person, both the "thing or the person were consecrated" (*res aut persona consecrate*).[27] However, the history of the development of this doctrine is much more complex than this linguistic analysis portrays.[28]

Protestant Reformers pressed to see the Word of God connected to the sacraments, although there tends to be a scent of the medieval *ex opere operato*[29] still remaining in their views. For Martin Luther, there had to be a promise

---

23. Weber, *Foundations of Dogmatics*, 2:586. Weber mentions that other religions contemporary with Christianity used *mystērion* to refer to a mixture of myth and cult that was secretive and usually "not available to the non-initiated" (586). This is clearly not the Pauline usage of the term, but it also does not match the Johannine usage in Revelation.

24. In one of his small-print sections, Barth provides a two-page description of "mystery" as it appeared in the NT, noting that the original meaning denoted "an event in the world of time and space [*ein solches inmitten der raumzeitlichen Welt Ereignis*] which is directly initiated [*unmittelbar sein Initiant*] and brought to pass by God alone [*weil Gott allein . . . und Veranstalter ist*], so that in distinction from all other events [*Geschehen*] it is basically a mystery [*Geheimnis*] to human cognition in respect of its origin and possibility." See Karl Barth, *CD* IV/4:108; *KD* IV/4:118.

25. Stanley Grenz, *Theology for the Community of God* (Grand Rapids: Eerdmans, 2000), 513. Grenz says that it also could mean bond money put in escrow in the temple while a legal suit was waiting settlement.

26. S.v. "Sacrament," by Ann Loades, *The Oxford Companion to Christian Thought*, ed. Adrian Hastings, Alistair Mason, and Hugh Pyper (Oxford: Oxford University Press, 2000), 634–37, here 634.

27. John B. Payne, *Erasmus: His Theology of the Sacraments*, Research in Theology, ed. Dietrich Ritschl (Atlanta: John Knox / Bratcher, 1970), 275n1.

28. I do not have space to engage with that history here, but there are surveys and in-depth materials related to the sacraments from the early church through the modern era.

29. This is a phrase that essentially means that by the performance of the ritual the deed to which it points is accomplished.

from Scripture within the sacramental act: "Sacraments are promises attached to visible signs, and those promises are contained in Scripture."[30] Further, while the Word of God was important in combination with the performance of a sacramental ritual, so, too, was the *faith* of the recipient. "Everything, then, depends on this faith, which alone makes the sacraments accomplish that which they signify, and everything that the priest says comes true. For as you believe, so it is done for you (Matt. 8:13; 9:29). Without this faith all absolution and all sacraments are in vain and indeed do more harm than good."[31] John Calvin viewed sacraments as an external symbol (*externum symbolum*) of God's promises and a witness to God's grace reinforced by the outward sign.[32] Through the outward sign, God "seals on our consciences [*conscientiis obsignat*] the promises of his good will toward us in order to sustain the weakness of our faith [*ad sustinendam fidei nostrae imbecillitatem*]."[33] The sacraments without the Word are useless—"idle and unmeaning shadows" or "pure corruptions" and "delusive signs."[34] However, with the Word they are nourishment for every believer. They become, indeed, the Word made flesh—word pictures, as it were.

As a Reformed pastor and theologian, Karl Barth administered and supported the traditional view of the sacraments. From about 1943 onward, however, he shifted his thinking regarding the sacraments. He questioned whether the word "sacrament" should be used at all within theology and the church. Further, he carefully examined whether these rituals are actually conveyors of God's grace or are simply human acts in response to grace. His conclusion was that they do *not* convey grace but instead are human actions that respond to God's grace. By reconfiguring the sacramental rituals in this way, not only did he conceive of baptism and Eucharist in more Zwinglian terms but he

30. Martin Luther, *The Babylonian Captivity of the Church (1520)*, trans. A. T. W. Steinhäuser, rev. Frederick C. Ahrens and Abdel Ross Wentz, in *Luther's Works*, ed. Helmut T. Lehmann, vol. 36, *Word and Sacrament II*, ed. Abdel Ross Wentz (Philadelphia: Fortress, 1959), 124.

31. Martin Luther, *The Sacrament of Penance (1519)*, trans. E. Theodore Bachmann, in *Luther's Works*, ed. Helmut T. Lehmann, vol. 35, *Word and Sacrament I*, ed. E. Theodore Bachmann (Philadelphia: Muhlenberg, 1960), 11. The same is said in the sermon *The Holy and Blessed Sacrament of Baptism (1519)*, trans. Charles M. Jacobs, in *Luther's Works*, ed. Helmut T. Lehmann, vol. 35, *Word and Sacrament I*, ed. E. Theodore Bachmann, 30, where he states there are three things to pay attention to in this sacrament: "the sign, the significance of it, and the faith."

32. Calvin, *Inst.* 4.14.1 (1277). For the Latin, see Calvin, *OS* 5:259.

33. Calvin, *Inst.* 4.14.1 (1277); Calvin, *OS* 5:259.

34. Ronald S. Wallace, *Calvin's Doctrine of the Word and Sacrament* (Grand Rapids: Eerdmans, 1957), 136. The quotations arise from his commentaries on Matt. 28:19, Isa. 6:7, and Exod. 24:5, respectively. This highlights a value to Wallace's approach. He does not rely solely on the *Institutes* for information regarding the sacraments in Calvin's work.

also went beyond Zwingli by not continuing to support the practice of infant baptism—something that most branches of the Reformed tradition hold in a cherished position as a sign of initiation into the covenantal community.[35]

One of the reasons why I am highly suspect of using the term "sacrament" is that in this term linger these historical shadows. Barth has made a strong case that God's presence is promised in the rituals and that God commands us to perform them, but in the end God is free to choose not to be there. Perhaps a more precise way to say this is that God has freely chosen to be present to the church when his people perform these rituals. God's promise of his presence gives us hope that God will be there when we are obedient to his command. In other words, for Barth the "sacraments" are *human acts*, not acts of God's revelation or any conveyance of grace. They are obedient responses to God's gift in Christ and his promise to be present in these actions when we perform them corporately. In response to the *divine* action, humans respond with "an action which copies and reflects, but it is still an action" (*CD* IV/4:130). I would add to Barth's thoughts here the role of the Holy Spirit in allowing our human action to *participate* in some measure with the action of Christ, thereby embedding in us some aspect of Christ's own character.

The presupposition for our *human* action is the previous action of God in Jesus Christ. In response to God's grace in Christ, we obey his command to perform and participate in these practices in community. There is no grace conferred or transferred, only a promise of God's presence in response to our obedience. When members of the body of Christ are present at baptisms, they also remember their own baptism and commitment to Christ. In some way, watching another's baptism encourages all God's people to recall and renew their own oath or act of commitment to follow Christ in obedience—to live up to their baptism, as it were.

Hence, participating in the sacraments is not simply obeying a command that Christ gave when instituting these practices, but it is also *participating together* in our union with the fellowship of Christ's suffering and *being made conformable* to his death and resurrection (Phil. 3:10). This is not only for those who believe; it is also a sign of witness to those who do not believe. By reenacting the Last Supper, where Christ voluntarily offered his body and blood for the sins of the world, we *participate* in an act of ingesting spiritually the sacrificial life of Christ into our own lives as followers of Christ. We participate in actions

35. Barth makes clear his agreement and disagreement with Zwingli, admitting that his view of the sacraments in general is similar. He would not disagree, therefore, if someone wished to call his view of the sacraments "Neo-Zwinglian," with the provision that Barth did not derive his rationale from Zwingli. See Karl Barth, *CD* IV/4:130. Barth also notes that Zwingli supported infant baptism, which he thinks the logic of the argument requires one to preclude.

that thrust us into the very heart of our faith—namely, the self-surrendering, self-sacrificing love of Christ for the unlovable. We rise from partaking together with greater intention to carry our own cross for the cause of Christ. Our action demonstrates our unity with Christ and other Christians concerning the cross-resurrection event, marking us as followers of the Master's sacrificial, other-regarding love. By so doing, we witness to the world that we have been encountered by this Savior's love and that others can be as well.

Are the Sacraments a Means of Grace?

Perhaps the most frequent descriptor used for the sacraments is the phrase "means of grace."[36] What is meant by this? Among the Reformers, Zwingli most clearly wrote against this view of the sacraments as a means of grace. In 1530 Zwingli wrote *Fidei Huldrychi Zwinglii ratio* (*An Account of the Faith of Zwingli*), in which he stated "that all the sacraments are so far from conferring grace that they do not even convey or dispense it."[37] Only the Spirit can deliver grace to humans—and the Spirit is "the virtue and energy whereby all things are borne, and has no need of being borne."[38] In this way, Zwingli argued that a "channel or vehicle is not necessary to the Spirit."[39]

Previously, I have argued that God uses "media" from the finite realm as instruments in which God's very presence may reside so that humans may encounter the thing (the medium), yet within or beyond it may also experience the presence of God directly. If I do not have difficulty with God using media, then why should I have hesitation to use "means of grace" as a descriptive phrase for these special practices?

There are several reasons for my concern. First, the language itself seems to elevate the role of the medium to something sacred instead of pointing merely to something beyond the sign. The idea of a channel or vehicle to impart life and salvation to humans becomes more than a sign of grace; for

36. As an example of this usage, I quote two sections from Reformed theologian Donald M. Baillie, *A Theology of the Sacraments and Other Papers* (New York: Scribner's Sons, 1957), on both baptism and communion as sacramental means of grace. On baptism he states, "The point is that a person's baptism should be to him a means of grace, not merely at that moment but ever afterwards; and the faith which appropriates the grace offered in that sacrament includes the faith by which all his life long he looks back to his baptism" (88). On the Lord's Supper he states, "Thus the sacrament of the Lord's supper is indeed a means of grace, an instrument of salvation" (101–2).

37. Huldreich Zwingli, *An Account of the Faith of Huldreich Zwingli (1530)*, in *The Latin Works of Huldreich Zwingli*, trans. Samuel Macauley Jackson, ed. William J. Hinke (Philadelphia: Heidelberg, 1922), 2:46.

38. Zwingli, *Account of the Faith*, 2:46.

39. Zwingli, *Account of the Faith*, 2:46.

many humans, it becomes that grace. I find this to be a dangerous direction theologically, because it may set up the physical medium in ways that do not allow for God's sovereignty (on the one hand) and that may usher in human confusion (on the other). If the sacraments are necessary for salvation and can only be received through the church, then the church becomes the primary means for salvation. This seems to downplay the work of the Spirit in salvation and enhance the possibility that grace is viewed "as the church's inexhaustible pantry, from which it is doled out by careless hands without hesitation or limit."[40]

Second, I do not conceive that God needs to channel grace through material avenues, as if these were crafted to supply humans with some infusion of a substance (such as grace). The phrase "means of grace" tends to imply a rather crude understanding that God uses specific materials to bring his grace to humans. Instead of a "thing" called grace, I receive the very presence of God the Father, whose divine attributes confront me with mercy, grace, and love directly; I receive the very presence of Jesus Christ, God the Son, whose loving sacrifice on my behalf is driven home to my heart directly; I receive the very presence of the Holy Spirit, whose ministry on my behalf causes me to become aware of the loving presence of the Triune God directly. Grace is *the manner* by which God's love operates toward human beings, not a substance infused within the human soul. Since I believe God confronts humans directly, even or especially beneath the material media or signs themselves, I do not see a need for some physical sign to be *the* channel of God's presence. What is it, then, that makes the participation with baptismal waters and bread and wine the "special" avenues of Christ's presence for us? Here I find myself in complete agreement with Barth. The New Testament discussion of baptism does not support the sacramental view. He states, "It is highly and even supremely probable that this Christian action is not to be understood as a divine work or word of grace which purifies man and renews him. It is not to be understood as a mystery or sacrament along the lines of the dominant theological tradition [*herrschend gewordenen theologischen Tradition*]" (*CD* IV/4:128; *KD* IV/4:140). As Barth explains, the New Testament traces a person's cleansing and renewal in "the history of Jesus Christ which culminates in his death, and they are mediated [*vermittelt*] through the work of the Holy Spirit" (*CD* IV/4:128; *KD* IV/4:140). There is no other mention of a "duplicate to this one divine act and word" as a "mediation of salvation [*Heilsvermittlung*]" (*CD* IV/4:128;

40. Dietrich Bonhoeffer, *Discipleship*, trans. Barbara Green and Reinhard Kraus, ed. Geffrey B. Kelly and John D. Godsey, Dietrich Bonhoeffer Works 4 (Minneapolis: Fortress, 2003), 43.

Pentecostals and Sacramentalism?

Among some Pentecostal scholars recently, there has been a turn toward taking up the concept of "sacrament" as something more than a Zwinglian memorial. Amos Yong has asked Pentecostals not to be "suspicious of sacramental language."[a] Along with this move, there has been an attempt to view the sacraments as divinely instituted means of grace that nourish Christians in their spiritual journey. Echoing Wesley, Kenneth Archer has described this well: "The sacramental ordinances, therefore, aid us in our salvific journey because they give the Holy Spirit necessary opportunities to keep the community on the right path—the way of salvation."[b] Here is a clear depiction of the channels through which the Holy Spirit operates in the community of faith. These are the means God ordained, through which we wait for the Spirit's movement, as Wesley said. Archer calls it "unfortunate" that some Pentecostals "deny any 'real grace' being mediated through the participatory ordinance to the community, thus reducing these mysteries to mere memorial rite, occasions solely for cognitive reflection devoid of the Spirit's presence and power."[c] Again, "real grace" seems to be conceived as a substance or thing. However, even if that is not Archer's meaning, why does the Christian faith *require* particular means through which the Holy Spirit then must work? Further, Archer seems to think that the only option besides seeing these sacraments as means of grace is to conceive of them as truncated to memorial rituals benefiting only cognition. It should be clear from what has transpired so far in this chapter that I do not support a "naked sign" or a "mere memorial" in the practice of the Supper. However, I also do not agree that these are means of grace as described by much of the tradition of the Christian church—even Wesley. Conceiving the sacraments in this way tends to allow them to become constitutive factors in one's ecclesiology.[d]

There is at least one other option besides these two presented by Archer—one that suggests that in these Christ-ordained practices, believers participate in some way in the history of Jesus Christ and are truly connected by means of the Spirit with the risen Christ, who is seated at the right hand of the Father. We *partici-*

KD IV/4:140). Baptism is "not a means of the divine work and revelation of salvation. It is neither a causative nor a cognitive *medium salutis* [means of salvation]" (CD IV/4:156).

Finally, one of the few "pauses" for me in this discussion has been the extent to which John Wesley viewed the sacraments as a means of grace. Working as a minister in the Church of England, Wesley held on to many of

pate in parallel action with our entire being, not merely some cognitive reflection. However, I find myself drawn to the discussion of Chris E. W. Green in relation to a Pentecostal theology of the Lord's Supper. While Green seems too beholden to the terms "sacrament" and even "means of grace," his ideas on the relation of mediated and unmediated presence in the Supper are quite in keeping with what I have been portraying. Once again I think the Anglican residue of Wesley's sacramental theology has cropped up here as well.[e]

For his own position, Daniel Tomberlin repeatedly notes that the sacraments are "charismatic, that is, they require the direct mediation (active presence) of Christ and the Spirit."[f] Even inanimate objects (like a prayer cloth anointed with oil) can become a means through which God offers healing to humans. Tomberlin continually refers to the sacraments as a means of grace through which the Spirit works. Indeed, he suggests that humans can become a "sacramental presence, mediators of the Spirit of grace,"[g] who participate in the "transference of divine grace" from God to humans. My own understanding of "means of grace" will be distinctly different from these current directions among Pentecostals. While I am no "mere memorialist," I am also no sacramentalist.

[a] Amos Yong, *The Spirit Poured Out on All Flesh: Pentecostalism and the Possibility of Global Theology* (Grand Rapids: Baker Academic, 2005), 156–57.

[b] Kenneth J. Archer, "Nourishment for Our Journey: The Pentecostal *via Salutis* and Sacramental Ordinances," in *Pentecostal Ecclesiology*, vol. 1, *A Reader*, ed. Chris E. W. Green (Leiden: Brill, 2016), 149.

[c] Archer, "Nourishment for Our Journey," 148.

[d] See Tom Greggs, *Dogmatic Ecclesiology*, vol. 1, *The Priestly Catholicity of the Church* (Grand Rapids: Baker Academic, 2019), 205, for an especially cogent argument against making Holy Communion a (or the) significant aspect of the church's life.

[e] See Chris E. W. Green, *Toward a Pentecostal Theology of the Lord's Supper: Foretasting the Kingdom* (Cleveland, TN: CPT, 2012), esp. 288–90. For the most extensive discussion on Pentecostals and the sacraments, see Daniel Tomberlin, *Pentecostal Sacraments: Encountering God at the Altar*, rev. ed. (Cleveland, TN: Cherohala, 2019).

[f] Tomberlin, *Pentecostal Sacraments*, 128.

[g] Tomberlin, *Pentecostal Sacraments*, 129.

the theological tenets of Anglicanism.[41] I believe that Wesley developed his idea on "means of grace" primarily from Anglican influences. How did Wesley define them? He saw more than the sacraments involved in these means of

41. Howard Snyder, *The Radical Wesley* (Downers Grove, IL: InterVarsity, 1980), offers the idea that Wesley remained faithful to Anglicanism in his sacramental and doctrinal ideas but also desired a renewal within the Church of England.

grace. Henry (Hal) Knight describes Wesley's means of grace as including a "wide range of activities associated with public worship, personal devotion, and Christian community and discipleship."[42]

At first glance Wesley's ideas do not seem to follow the traditional way this phrase was understood. The means of grace in Wesley provide us avenues for focusing on God's presence through our actions as well as "convey God's identity through remembrance and promise."[43] There certainly is nothing *ex opere operato* in Wesley's description of these "means," but there remains a residue of something almost medieval in the use of the phrase itself. For example, he begins his sermon "The Means of Grace" by asking whether there are in the Christian dispensation "any means ordained of God as the usual channels of his grace."[44] Since the days of the apostles, reasons Wesley, some began to mistake the means for the end, thereby making religion the goal instead of a means to the end of being renewed after the image of God.[45] Throughout this sermon, Wesley attempts to explain means of grace as "outward signs, words, or actions, ordained of God, and appointed for this end, to be the ordinary channels whereby he might convey to men, preventing, justifying, or sanctifying grace."[46] While humans have abused these means, they still remain God's avenues of blessing. Indeed, "all who desire the grace of God are to wait for it in the means he hath ordained."[47] To be sure, the work of the Holy Spirit within these means is necessary for them to be efficacious, yet God has ordained such physical, outward means of his grace. Wesley admits that he uses the expression "means of grace" "because I know none better."[48] Given the theological history of the phrase "means of grace," I think it should be abandoned in ways similar to abandoning the term "sacraments," so that no one will misunderstand the goal and intent of the language. While I agree that God *uses* media to encounter humans, I do not agree that God ordained a set of means by which God always channels grace (or his presence).

42. Henry H. Knight III, *The Presence of God in the Christian Life: John Wesley and the Means of Grace*, Pietist and Wesleyan Studies 3, ed. David Bundy and J. Steven O'Malley (Lanham, MD: Scarecrow, 1992), 2.

43. H. Knight, *The Presence of God in the Christian Life*, 199n11. This statement summarizes Knight's entire approach to Wesley's theology through the "means of grace" as the "context for Christian growth."

44. John Wesley, "The Means of Grace (Sermon 16)," in *The Works of John Wesley*, 3rd ed., Series of Sermons 1–39 (Grand Rapids: Baker Books, 2002), 5:185.

45. Wesley, "Means of Grace," in *Works*, 5:185.

46. Wesley, "Means of Grace," in *Works*, 5:187.

47. Wesley, "Means of Grace," in *Works*, 5:198.

48. Wesley, "Means of Grace," in *Works*, 5:187.

Participatory Christian Practices

Symbol and Participation

If these rituals are not means of grace, then what are they? John Calvin has provided us with a good start. He says that these actions are more than mere remembrances; they "may serve to establish and increase faith."[49] There is some benefit for believers in these practices because they reenact aspects of Christ's life, death, and resurrection that parallel aspects in every believer's life of faith. Participating in them helps to reinforce the truths they represent in the hearts (and bodies!) of all believers who engage in them.

Borrowing the idea of oath that arises from the Latin word *sacramentum*, Stanley Grenz has suggested that we call these practices "acts of commitment." In a rather ingenious theological move, he combines the idea of ritual or act with *sacramentum* (oath of fidelity) and suggests that believers need use not the terms "ordinance" or "sacrament" but rather "acts of commitment," since this more clearly describes the rite and its intention.[50] Since for Grenz these acts are primarily human actions in response to God's act in Christ, this phrase seems apt. We act out our commitment in these rituals. Grenz states,

> Through these acts, we confess our faith in a special manner. They are enacted pictures or symbols of God's grace given in Christ. . . . Acts of commitment become visual sermons, the Word of God symbolically proclaimed. Through our participation we not only declare the truth of the gospel, however, we also bear testimony to our reception of the grace symbolized. Hence, through these rites, we "act out" our faith. The acts of commitment become enactments of our appropriation of God's action in Christ. As we affirm our faith in this vivid symbolic manner, the Holy Spirit uses these rites to facilitate our participation in the reality of the acts symbolized.[51]

These acts are "performed by the church" with gestures and objects that "embody" our actions. The gospel story is made vivid by our participation in the reenactment of Christ's life, death, and resurrection (baptism and communion). If we had only the Word, then perhaps only part of our entire being would be addressed in the time of our gathering together. These rituals, however, add the *visual and kinetic dimensions* that embody our activity

49. Calvin, *Inst.* 4.14.9 (1284).
50. Grenz, *Theology for the Community of God*, 516.
51. Grenz, *Theology for the Community of God*, 516.

before God. As the community participates in these repeatable actions, they experience together some "muscle memory" in the faith.[52]

The symbolic nature of these practices is crucially important for the spiritual benefit of them. The symbolic gestures are enacted pictures of God's grace. These visual enactments of our faith require humans to do something—not for salvation, to be sure, but for obedience and spiritual growth. The church has always been harmed when it does not grasp the depth of symbols for human living; it has also been harmed when symbols have been elevated to the level of the transcendent in which God has been replaced with idols.[53] Symbols are a rich heritage in the Judeo-Christian religion by God's own design—just consider the Old Testament rituals and symbols in the tabernacle. Symbols need not be jettisoned because of misuse. In the biblical world, a symbol participated with the thing it signified (consider the importance of names in the OT).[54]

Richard R. Niebuhr has suggested Christian symbols "confederate us with our ultimate worths"; that is, they gather together in a simple sign those "deepest desires, the worths to which we entrust our own and our world's sustenation—and ultimate completion."[55] They are not mere signposts but signs that cause us to participate with the thing signified. These symbols create such participation "when we *enact* them and they *activate* us, when we incorporate them and they incorporate themselves into the tissue of our life and thought."[56] These acts are not merely signs of our obedience but are opportunities to participate in the life of God. Hence, the argument for performing communion only rarely in some Protestant churches reveals a lack of understanding of the meaningful repetition of these opportunities for participation in the life of God *through bodily action*. If we were meant to perform these rituals rarely, then the biblical language of participation (κοινωνία | *koinōnia*)—which implies repetition and continual sharing—does not make sense.

---

52. When I refer to "repeatable actions" here, I mean to imply not that baptism should be repeatable but merely that the community as a whole repeats this ritual together for those who are converted to Christ. As I will show, we all participate in someone's baptism by reflecting on our own baptism and conversion to Christ, thereby reaffirming our own commitment to be continuing disciples of Christ.

53. Clark Pinnock states, "We are impoverished when we have no place for festivals, drama, processions, banners, dance, color, movement, instruments, percussion, and incense. There are many notes on the Spirit's keyboard which we often neglect to sound, with the result that God's presence can be hard to access." See Clark Pinnock, *Flame of Love: A Theology of the Holy Spirit* (Downers Grove, IL: InterVarsity, 1996), 121.

54. Grenz, *Theology for the Community of God*, 516.

55. Richard R. Niebuhr, "Symbols in Reflection on God and Ourselves," *Princeton Seminary Bulletin* 20, no. 2 (1999): 142.

56. Niebuhr, "Symbols in Reflection on God and Ourselves," 147 (his emphasis).

While Grenz's substitution of "acts of commitment" for "sacraments" or "ordinances" is more in line with what I consider a helpful direction, it seems to focus the actions entirely on one's personal commitment, leaving out the corporate dimension of the church's action. The phrase is not communal enough and does not take into account all that is implied in the scriptural discussion of these practices. The crucial aspect for me is that these acts are opportunities for the corporate body of believers to *participate bodily* in the symbolic ritual and thereby reenact and remember the life, death, and resurrection of Christ. We participate in these symbolic gestures in a mystical, spiritual manner that cannot be rationally encompassed from this earthly dimension. Therefore, "ordinance" is a term that leaves this more fully orbed participatory reenactment somewhat pale and lifeless. It is a command—so obey! On the other hand, "sacrament" carries with it too much baggage from the history of Christian thought. Weber asks rightly if a term "freighted with problems" should be taken as "appropriate and helpful for interpretation."[57]

Donald Baillie has offered some useful reflection on what we are doing as a corporate body when we participate in the sacraments. He suggests this activity is not merely a "piece of symbolism" but rather a piece of *"dramatic symbolism."*[58] In order to explain his meaning, he describes the "sensible signs" of the sacrament of the Eucharist as consisting not only of the elements of bread and wine "but also of *the actions*, including the words spoken."[59] The meaning of the symbol is acted out—hence, it is *dramatic* symbolism. This is precisely what I am working toward by understanding these activities as participatory practices in the body of Christ. What does this mean? Allow me to sketch an outline of the meaning of dramatic symbolism or participatory practices with each of the three activities ordained by Christ for believers to continue performing.

In baptism, we reenact the life, death, and resurrection of Christ and our own participation with him. When we participate in this symbolic ritual of initiation, we "activate" this truth of God's action in our lives as well as "incorporate" it into the "tissue of our lives and thought" (to use Richard R. Niebuhr's phrases).[60] Through the repeated public witness of each baptism within our community of faith, we all remember our own baptism and renew our commitment of allegiance to our Lord.

In the Lord's Supper, we reenact the sacrificial death of Christ and our participation with him in that death; we also recall his resurrection and look

57. Weber, *Foundations of Dogmatics*, 2:592.
58. Baillie, *A Theology of the Sacraments*, 94 (his emphasis).
59. Baillie, *A Theology of the Sacraments*, 94 (his emphasis).
60. See Niebuhr, "Symbols in Reflection on God and Ourselves."

forward to the day when we will join together in the Marriage Supper of the Lamb. Hence, we look backward to remember his death for us and forward to anticipate his coming. We incorporate this truth into the tissue of our lives. Through the repeated performance of this ritual of Eucharist, we offer thanks to God the Father for the love demonstrated to us through his Son, Jesus Christ, and ask the Holy Spirit to shape our own embodied existence with the same sacrificial love for others.

In the act of footwashing, we reenact the servant life of Christ and his example of holiness and our participation with him in this. In this participatory Christian practice, we look neither to the past nor to the future but to the present. We stoop to serve others in this symbolic act, just as Christ did. Through the repeated performance of this ritual of footwashing, we find ourselves in need of continual cleansing and sanctifying as we wash others' feet and allow them to wash ours. We remind ourselves that we all are unclean without Christ. We remember that we all must serve as well as be served. Through the repeated performance of the practice of footwashing, we find ourselves so humbled by the simple act of washing another's feet and having our own washed that we sense the true nature of Christ's humbling in the incarnation as well as our own uncleanness by comparison. We trace Christ's movement to his knees and symbolically participate in taking up a towel to clean the feet of others, enacting in gathered assembly the servant nature of Christ.[61]

Through these three participatory Christian practices, the people of God bodily reenact and mystically participate in the life, death, and resurrection of Christ. The tracing of these actions of Christ within our own common lives today fosters a *Christoform* shape to our gathered group of believers. Speaking of baptism and the Lord's Supper, Gerhard Ebeling states, "Baptism is the appropriation of believers in Christ and the Lord's Supper is the appropriation of Christ in believers. We cannot speak of the form of these acts without immediately bumping into the gift, which is assigned through them."[62] Through these three participatory Christian practices, the people of God offer a public witness to their faith and allegiance to Christ before others in the believing community as well as before an unbelieving world. Through these three participatory Christian practices instituted by our Lord, the people of God may expect the presence of God to be manifest among us to help us be more like Christ in our everyday lives.

61. Obviously, footwashing has not been considered a sacrament or ordinance by most churches in the past, so I will need to make a case for that as a practice instituted by Christ just as much as baptism and communion.

62. Gerhard Ebeling, *Dogmatik des christlichen Glaubens*, vol. 3, *Der Glaube an Gott den Vollender der Welt*, 4th ed. (Tübingen: Mohr Siebeck, 2012), 315 (my translation).

If the Christ-ordained actions are not a means of grace by which God channels his gifts, then what are they? I propose that these human actions are *participatory Christian practices* in response to God's divine action in Christ, whereby the Spirit takes up our human actions and conforms them to the reality of Christ's own actions. The key point here is the *participatory* aspect of these rituals. In baptism, we physically participate in a symbolic reenactment of Christ's death and resurrection. In the Lord's Supper, we physically participate in a symbolic reenactment of the Passover night and the ensuing event of the crucifixion, remembering in the enactment that Christ gave himself up willingly for our sakes. In footwashing, we physically participate in a symbolic reenactment of Christ's own stooping down to wash the feet of others. There is also a bodily movement in line with the prior movement of Christ's own history. Thus, there is a *koinōnia*, a "sharing" or "participating" or a "fellowshipping" as we trace these aspects of Christ's life in our own lives. Through the Holy Spirit, believers experience the presence of Christ. These practices are not merely acts of commitment (as Grenz has suggested), although they are that as well.

Baptism

Some Preliminary Biblical Considerations

I have proposed that these special practices instituted by Christ are human actions within the corporate gathering of Christ's church that respond to God's gracious act in Jesus Christ. Water baptism is such an action. It is an initiatory ritual performed with water to symbolize cleansing from sins and engrafting of one into the body of Christ. This action of immersing under water, which is parallel with the death and burial of Christ, and the raising up from the water, which is attached to the resurrection of Christ, brings believers into a mystical union with their Savior. These are the simple New Testament approaches to this ritual. The waters of baptism do not cleanse us; they represent the cleansing blood of Jesus that saves us. However, the symbolic ritual allows us to participate with the thing it signifies, and therefore Peter points to an "antitype" (ἀντίτυπον | *antitypon*) of the ark of baptism, suggesting that it "saves" us by allowing us to have a good conscience toward God (1 Pet. 3:21). But it is Christ who cleanses the church, "cleansing her by the washing with water through the word" (Eph. 5:26). Christ has saved us, "not because of righteous things we had done, but because of his mercy. He saved us through the washing of rebirth [διὰ λουτροῦ παλιγγενεσίας | *dia loutrou palingenesias*]" (Titus 3:5). Does the water save us? Certainly not! Calvin says it correctly when he states, "For Paul did not mean to signify that our cleansing and salvation are accomplished by water, or that water contains in itself the power to cleanse, regenerate, and renew; nor that here is the cause of salvation, but only that in this sacrament are received the knowledge and certainty of such gifts."[63]

In addition to the symbolic cleansing that we see performed in baptism, there is the engrafting of believers as sons and daughters in the body of Christ represented by this act. "For we were all baptized by one Spirit [ἐν ἑνὶ πνεύματι | en heni pneumati] so as to form one body—whether Jews or Gentiles, slave or free—and we were all given the one Spirit to drink" (1 Cor. 12:13). The Spirit has merged us into the one body of Christ so that the symbolic ritual of baptism displays this truth. In this way we see that it is not only a "washing" but also a rite of welcoming into the family of God. Paul makes this relationship between baptism and adoption very clear: "So in Christ Jesus you are all children of God through faith, for all of you who were baptized into Christ have clothed yourselves with Christ" (Gal. 3:26–27). Baptism itself does not adopt us into the kingdom of God—only the Holy Spirit through the instrumentality of our faith in the work of Christ can do that. Indeed, only the grace of Christ offered to us in redemption and grasped by us through faith can accomplish this spiritual renewal by the Spirit. Yet Paul connects this joining of the family of God with the initiatory rite of baptism.

Finally, the act of baptism is something that we must choose to perform within the context of the gathered people of God. It is offered to us by the church. Therefore, it is something that is done to us. *We cannot baptize ourselves!* Indeed, we must do nothing in the process of baptism but relax in the arms of the one immersing us into the water (or pouring it over us). In this passive gesture, we participate with the death, burial, and resurrection of Christ. This is no mere empty sign to the world of our newfound experience of grace in Christ; this is a symbolic participatory practice in the very life and death of Christ. God has "anointed us, set his seal of ownership on us, and put his Spirit in our hearts as a deposit, guaranteeing what is to come" (2 Cor. 1:21–22). While the "seal" is not described here as baptism, it is distinct from the Spirit, who is elsewhere also called the seal of our redemption (Eph. 1:13). We are "marked" by the Spirit as belonging to God; baptism is a public display of that spiritual "marking." Therefore, we should not use the abundant grace of God as a license to sin. "We are those who have died to sin; how can we live in it any longer? Or don't you know that all of us who were baptized into Christ Jesus were baptized into his death? We were therefore buried with him through baptism into death in order that, just as Christ was raised from the dead through the glory of the Father, we too may

63. Calvin, *Inst.* 4.15.2 (1304).

live a new life" (Rom. 6:2b–4). In this way we can see baptism not as a "mere sign" but as a meaningful participatory practice whose symbolism draws us into the very life history of Christ's death and resurrection. "For if we have been united with him in a death like his, we will certainly also be united with him in a resurrection like his" (Rom. 6:5).

There is not only a spiritual reality toward which this sign points us but a mystical *participation* in that reality that somehow imitates and parallels the death and resurrection of Jesus Christ. When some Romans apparently challenged the expansive nature of God's grace by suggesting they could sin to their heart's delight, Paul points them first to their baptism—not a mere sign but a symbolic participation that engages believers in a different way of walking. What is also clear is that in the act of baptism, we participate in some real, spiritual, and significant sense with the death, burial, and resurrection of Jesus Christ when we perform the baptismal movement. It is this participation that reminds us of God's grace and allows us to walk in newness of life, as if the old self has been left in the grave, so to speak, and the new self has risen from the tomb of the baptismal pool. Again, this is no bare sign mutely pointing to a reality but is a genuine symbol in which we participate with the fullness of our spiritual and physical beings.

The Recipient of Baptism

Perhaps the most disagreements regarding baptism in the history of Christianity have revolved around the proper recipient of baptism. Who should be baptized? This seemingly benign question propels us into a consideration of soteriology and concomitant perspectives on faith, covenant, and grace. For example, I have described baptism as a human response to God's prior act of grace in Jesus Christ. Presupposed in such an understanding of baptism is that one has faith in Jesus Christ's work of atonement prior to witnessing publicly concerning that experience with Christ in baptism. Then the question becomes this: What is necessary for an individual to have faith? Since a person has to be able to respond to the story of the gospel and believe in his or her heart that God has raised Christ from the dead (Rom. 10:9), then the minimal requisite as described in the New Testament seems to be some cognitive ability to respond to the message of the gospel. In other words, can infants or very young children have such faith? It seems unlikely.[64]

64. Luther appeared to believe that infants held a faith (*fides infantium*) that was commensurate with their ability, and they therefore could be baptized on the basis of that faith. Martin Luther, *Defense and Explanation of All the Articles (1521)*, in *Luther's Works*, ed. Helmut T. Lehmann, vol. 32, *Career of the Reformer II*, ed. George W. Forrell, 14. In some way, faith is

Other issues of soteriology immediately rise to the surface as well. If an infant cannot be "saved" and therefore cannot be baptized, then what does this say about grace? Further, what does this say about humans who have intellectual hindrances—are they left out of salvation because they cannot meet a minimal level of intelligence to understand and respond to the gospel? Frankly, those who have supported believers' baptism (also called credobaptism) have left this question strangely unanswered.[65] Related to this concern is one that focuses on when a child is able to understand the gospel and the concept of baptism adequately so that faith and obedience can be judged genuine. How do pastors within this model of baptism discern when a four-year-old is grasped by the story of Christ and responds in faith versus an eight-year-old that appears insistent on being baptized because others in her Sunday school class have experienced the ritual? Or what is to be done in cases where intellectual challenges abound—or in cases where reasoning and language abilities are not present? Henry Mottu has asked this very thing concerning Barth's view that denies infant baptism. He sees this question of intellectual challenge as parallel with that of the question concerning infants in baptism. What he suggests Barth's view (and apparently mine as well) misses is that a human exists as part of a corporate group—there is no "I" apart from such grouping.[66]

Some Protestants who baptize infants and young children do so because of their view that God establishes a covenant with his people. This was clear in the Old Testament with Abraham, where the sign of that covenant was circumcision of male infants. When the new covenant was established with Christ, the sign of initiation into that covenant was transferred to baptism. Thus, baptism is simply a sign of that covenant in Christ. It includes entire families, just as it did in the old covenant. Is baptism a new sign of the new covenant that replaces circumcision in the old? There is a case for believing it may be. Following a number of the Reformers (Calvin, Zwingli, and Bullinger, in particular), the case for baptizing infants is not about individual faith but about belonging to God's covenanted people.[67] The sign of the new covenant

---

infused into infants at baptism. See Bernhard Lohse, *Martin Luther's Theology: Its Historical and Systematic Development*, trans. Roy A. Harrisville (Minneapolis: Fortress, 1999), 304.

65. Or they have created a theological security blanket called "the age of accountability."

66. Henry Mottu, "Les sacrements selon Karl Barth et Eberhard Jüngel," *Foi et Vie* 88, no. 2 (April 1989): 33–55, here 52. In Terry L. Cross, *The People of God's Presence: An Introduction to Ecclesiology* (Grand Rapids: Baker Academic, 2019), 6–7, 31–37, I have addressed this challenge about corporate faith and individual faith carefully and need only point to it here. However, I recognize that much more work needs to be done on this among those who support credobaptism.

67. For an exposition of Calvin's view of infant baptism, see Brian A. Gerrish, *Grace and Gratitude: The Eucharistic Theology of John Calvin* (Eugene, OR: Wipf & Stock, 2002), esp.

is open to all—male and female. It is also open to all humans—Jews and gentiles. In this way, infants and young children are gathered into the loving family of God through these covenantal signs and bonds.

The difficulty with this concept is that there is not a single New Testament passage that supports calling baptism a replacement for circumcision.[68] Yet the argument regarding the way circumcision as the old sign relates to baptism as the new sign of covenant remains especially strong in Reformed traditions. In response to the question "Should infants also be baptized?" the Heidelberg Catechism (1563) responds, "Infants as well as adults are included in God's covenant and people, and they, no less than adults, are promised deliverance from sin through Christ's blood and the Holy Spirit who produces faith. Therefore, by baptism, the sign of the covenant, they too should be incorporated into the Christian church and distinguished from the children of unbelievers. This was done in the Old Testament by circumcision, which was replaced in the New Testament by baptism."[69] While such baptism must not be seen as a rite of passage or initiation "into a particular culture or extended family" as some "remnants of a Germanic popular culture" that continues in some regions of Europe, the concept of covenant is certainly biblical.[70] "Just as circumcision was a sign of God's claim on those whom he accepted into

---

116–23. The value of Gerrish's explanation is that he sets the discussion of baptism within the context of both the Roman Catholic and the Anabaptist views.

68. Bruce A. Ware, "Believers' Baptism View," in *Baptism: Three Views*, ed. David F. Wright (Downers Grove, IL: IVP Academic, 2009), 46. Cf. also John Stevens, "Infant Baptism: Putting Old Wine into New Wineskins?," *Foundations: An International Journal of Evangelical Theology* 63 (September 2012): 18–42, here 24. The only possible exception to this claim is Col. 2:11–12: "In [Christ] you were also circumcised with a circumcision not performed by human hands. Your whole self ruled by the flesh was put off when you were circumcised by Christ, having been buried with him in baptism, in which you were also raised with him through your faith in the working of God, who raised him from the dead." While some read this circumcision by Christ as equivalent to being "buried with him in baptism," it appears to me that these are separate, even sequential, metaphors. First, this circumcision is clearly not referring to the literal old covenant sign; Paul uses it as a figure to speak of removal of the old self or "flesh." (In this way it is similar to Rom. 2:28–29, where circumcision in the new covenant is contrasted with that of the old by pointing to "circumcision of the heart, by the Spirit, not by the written code." In the Romans passage, there is no connection with baptism.) Second, the clause on baptism uses a different metaphor—namely, burial and resurrection with Christ. Paul speaks of "removal" of the old self and then burial with Christ in baptism—two different metaphors. He could have used crucifixion, burial, and resurrection instead, but his point was not simply death/burial but removal of the old flesh. Since I do not see Paul understanding baptism as removal of the old flesh in conversion, it is difficult to see circumcision here as equivalent to baptism. Third, the circumcision of the old self is done "by Christ," while baptism is participation with Christ in *his* burial and resurrection.

69. *Heidelberg Catechism*, 450th anniv. ed. (Grand Rapids: Faith Alive, 2013), 42, Q. 74.

70. This rather astute differentiation between a covenantal sign / rite of initiation and some festival of birth into a culture is a strong caution, especially given the history of infant baptism

the covenant, so baptism signifies the entrance into the eschatological community of Christ."[71] Hence, like circumcision, baptism is a sign and seal of the covenant of grace between God and his people.[72]

Nonetheless, there remains only indirect evidence that entire families were baptized in the New Testament. Regardless of the attempts of many theologians to support infant baptism in the New Testament, Weber's conclusion is undoubtedly the most appropriate: "As a *problem*, the issue of infant baptism is alien to the New Testament. It is not possible to come to an unequivocal position in regard to the probability that small children were actually baptized: the greater degree of probability is that this practice was not conducted."[73] The argument *for* infant baptism in the New Testament is essentially an argument of inference from the household baptisms mentioned there. Otherwise, there is silence. The salvation and baptism of the Philippian jailor in Acts 16 remains a consistent foundation for the baptism of infants and children.[74]

In the New Testament, baptism almost immediately follows repentance and acceptance of Christ as Lord and Savior. Nonetheless, it seems that the

connected to state churches in Europe from the time of the Reformation forward. This statement comes from van der Kooi and van den Brink, *Christian Dogmatics*, 607.

71. Van der Kooi and van den Brink, *Christian Dogmatics*, 607.

72. David Gibson, "'Fathers of Faith, My Fathers Now!': On Abraham and the Theology of Paedobaptism," *Themelios* 40, no. 1 (April 2015): 14–34, here 28.

73. Weber, *Foundations of Dogmatics*, 2:605 (his emphasis). In the last century, the early research of Joachim Jeremias seemed to support infant baptism in the NT, especially in the apostolic period. See Jeremias, *Die Kindertaufe in den ersten vier Jahrhunderten* (Göttingen: Vandenhoeck & Ruprecht, 1958); ET: *Infant Baptism in the First Four Centuries*, trans. David Cairns (London: SCM, 1960). However, Kurt Aland has leveled a profound critique of Jeremias's research that has yet to be countered. See Kurt Aland, *Die Säulingstaufe im Neuen Testament und in der Alten Kirche* (München: Kaiser, 1961); ET: *Did the Early Church Baptize Infants?*, trans. G. R. Beasley-Murray, The Library of History and Doctrine (1961; repr., Eugene, OR: Wipf & Stock, 2004). Aland came against Jeremias's argument concerning the NT evidence but in the end allowed for the practice on other grounds. In response, Jeremias wrote *Nochmals: Die Anfänge der Kindertaufe* (München: Kaiser, 1962); ET: *The Origins of Infant Baptism: A Further Study in Reply to Kurt Aland*, trans. Dorothea M. Barton (1962; repr., Eugene, OR: Wipf & Stock, 2004). Aland followed with two more books: *Die Stellung der Kinder in den frühen christlichen Gemeinden—und ihre Taufe* (München: Kaiser, 1967); and *Taufe und Kindertaufe* (Gütersloh: Gütersloher Verlagshaus, 1971). Also see Weber, *Foundations of Dogmatics*, 2:605n68. For a review of literature dealing with the historical question of infant baptism, see Everett Ferguson, *Baptism in the Early Church: History, Theology, and Liturgy in the First Five Centuries* (Grand Rapids: Eerdmans, 2009), 362n1.

74. I find it interesting that in defense of infant baptism, Sinclair Ferguson offers a *theological* reading of covenantal aspects in Scripture rather than a verse-by-verse explanation of how household baptisms can legitimately be inferred as infant baptism. See Sinclair B. Ferguson, "Infant Baptism View," in Wright, *Baptism: Three Views*, 77–111. For an insightful view opposing paedobaptism, see Ware, "Believers' Baptism View," 19–50, esp. 30–34.

expectation of baptismal candidates is that they possess faith in Jesus Christ. This also seems to be the implication in the Matthew 28:19–20 passage, where Jesus tells the disciples to "go and make disciples of all nations, baptizing them in the name of the Father and of the Son and of the Holy Spirit, and teaching them to obey everything I have commanded you." There seems to be an understanding in this command that making disciples and teaching them require people who have an ability to follow Christ and a capacity to understand what the disciples are teaching them. The main verb in this setting is "go and make disciples"—an imperatival force or command. Following this main verb of command are two participles, "baptizing" and "teaching," which grammatically are circumstantial, "describing the means of making disciples, with the 'teaching' accompanying the 'baptizing' ('make disciples by baptizing them and—at the same time—teaching them')."[75]

When engaging the Heidelberg Catechism on this question (Q. 74), Barth expresses a note of surprise. Since we have learned that baptism is confirmation of faith by the assurance of the blood of Christ and the Spirit (QQ. 69–70), we have assumed that such confirmation of faith and assurance applies to a believing person. "And now all of a sudden, in clear contradiction to what has been said before, the catechism speaks of the baptism of *infants*. Baptism is handled in this unexpected [*unvermuteten*] and unfounded way [*unbegründeten Weise*] in all classical Protestant theology, even in Calvin. All the previously discussed constitutive marks of baptism (especially the faith of the baptized) are suddenly ignored."[76] Barth has placed his finger on a very important problem: How can the Protestant principle of justification by faith support the doctrine and practice of infant baptism? In a rather wry and dry tone, Barth says, "One may not assume that babies believe. . . . Is faith mediated [*vermittelt*] to him by baptism? Or does the faith of others take his place . . . ? But how is all that related to what has previously been taught about baptism?"[77]

Barth's stunning questions—predictable in some sense in 1947 due to a previous teaching on baptism in 1943—led him to a most unlikely conclusion for a Reformed pastor and theologian. The "real reason [*eigentliche Grund*] for the persistent adherence to infant baptism is quite simply the fact that

75. Ferguson, *Baptism in the Early Church*, 137.
76. Karl Barth, *The Heidelberg Catechism for Today*, trans. Shirley C. Guthrie Jr. (Richmond, VA: John Knox, 1964), 102–3 (his emphasis). Cf. Barth, *Die christliche Lehre nach dem Heidelberger Katechismus: Vorlesung gehalten an der Universität Bonn im Sommersemester 1947* (München: Kaiser, 1949), 96.
77. Barth, *Heidelberg Catechism for Today*, 103; Barth, *Die christliche Lehre nach dem Heidelberger Katechismus*, 96.

without it the church would suddenly be in a remarkably embarrassing position [*plötzlich merkwürdig in die Luft gestellt wäre*]. Every individual would then have to decide whether he wanted to be a Christian. But how many Christians would there be in that case? The whole concept of a national church [or national religion; *Volkskirche*] would be shaken."[78] Barth's queries sound amazingly like the Anabaptists of the 1500s on some of these points.[79]

Along with Barth, I would not want to suggest that baptism offered in good faith in the past centuries has been invalid.[80] However, I do not see good biblical grounds for baptizing infants. While the practice of baptizing infants may be traced back to the late second century CE (around 180 to 200), this may be a tradition that needs reconsideration as we move into the future. It seems to me that New Testament baptism is connected with a change of life that demands repentance (*metanoia*) and therefore requires a direct encounter with God's Spirit whereby a person is addressed at the core of their being. Baptism follows this experience as obedience follows faith. Can such a level of commitment be possible for infants?

Water Baptism Today

What can we conclude about this practice called baptism? It is an ancient practice among Christians who desire to follow Christ in his own baptism. In itself, the performance of the action of immersion into water does nothing but get one wet. However, *as a response* to God's prior action toward us and our movement toward God, baptism is a human response to God's grace offered us in Christ. Baptism is a participatory sign in which the symbol of water points to the cleansing of our sin and the going down into the water points to our union with Christ in his life, death, burial, and resurrection. Participation in the sign does not "save" us; rather, it acknowledges that God has already acted in our lives and that we offer our own obedience in surrender to his will for baptism. As Tom Greggs says, "Baptism is a human act within and in response to the Spirit's act in the event of creating the church. Baptism is a willed act of human agency, for which the human is freed to will within and

---

78. Barth, *Heidelberg Catechism for Today*, 104; Barth, *Die christliche Lehre nach dem Heidelberger Katechismus*, 98.

79. Since Barth did not finish his *CD* IV/4, we have only a taste of his theology of baptism (which continues the sentiments found here in the 1940s yet with even greater rigor). Further, we have very little of how he understood this view of the sacrament to apply to the Lord's Supper. A proposal along these lines is offered by Paul D. Molnar, *Karl Barth and the Theology of the Lord's Supper: A Systematic Investigation*, Issues in Systematic Theology 1, ed. Paul D. Molnar (New York: Peter Lang, 1996).

80. He makes this clear in the last paragraph on Q. 74. Barth, *Heidelberg Catechism for Today*, 105; Barth, *Die christliche Lehre nach dem Heidelberger Katechismus*, 98.

along with the divine willing, within the movement of divine grace towards the creation in which the people of God are caught up and move."[81] Baptism makes room for God in our lives and demonstrates our intention to continue to make room for God as we walk together with fellow believers. "Baptism is a symbolic enactment, . . . which frees the believer to live not towards the individualized self (through the *cor incurvatum in se*) but towards God and the given neighbor in the life of the gathered community."[82]

The Lord's Supper

Just as baptism is a participatory practice that centers on initiation into the body of Christ, the Lord's Supper is a participatory practice that focuses on a "repeated reaffirmation of what we initially declared in baptism—namely, our new identity in Christ."[83] Both actions are human responses to God's grace in Christ and to Christ's command to perform them. As a people of God's presence, we participate in these rituals, expecting Christ to be present while we are gathered for this event. In *both* practices, we proclaim publicly through our actions our union with Christ.

The Lord's Supper makes room for God's presence to be among God's people while they remember Christ's sacrifice so that they are strengthened and nurtured by it. The sign in this practice is that of eating and drinking—nourishment. This is a spiritual eating, not a physical one, but an eating nonetheless. Just as baptism is not forgiveness of sins or regeneration in itself but a symbol of that prior event in one's life, so, too, the Lord's Supper is not renewal of life or grace from heaven in the form of food but a symbol of these things. By participating in them, we participate in the life of Christ, remembering and proclaiming his death until he returns.

As a people who live in the direct presence of God, we understand that when we gather corporately and enter into this practice of sharing wine (or juice) and bread, we participate in a symbolic reenactment that makes Christ's life, death, and resurrection truly present among us through the power of the Spirit. This is no small thing. The reality of what transpired on Golgotha in space and time, then and there, becomes *our* reality through which we experience the sacrificial love of Christ *for us*, here and now. Yet, more than assurance that it occurred in Jerusalem around 30 CE *outside of us* (*extra nos*), the Spirit assures us that it was done *for us* (*pro nobis*) so that the reality of salvation that has dawned with newness of life *in us* (*in nobis*) is a true and

81. Greggs, *Dogmatic Ecclesiology*, 1:166.
82. Greggs, *Dogmatic Ecclesiology*, 1:181.
83. Grenz, *Theology for the Community of God*, 531.

genuine experience with Christ that seals us with the Spirit as belonging to
the Triune God. Tracing the steps of Christ helps to shape our lives together
following Christ's own life of self-surrendering love.

Biblical Considerations

While there is not an explicit statement in the New Testament that speaks
of the *presence* of Christ at the Supper, there is an important implicit understanding of presence from Paul's exposition of the Supper in 1 Corinthians
10:16–22.[84] Let us consider it here:

> Is not the cup of thanksgiving for which we give thanks a participation in the
> blood of Christ? And is not the bread that we break a participation in the body
> of Christ? Because there is one loaf, we who are many, are one body, for we all
> share the one loaf.
>
> Consider the people of Israel: Do not those who eat the sacrifices participate
> in the altar? Do I mean then that food sacrificed to an idol is anything, or that
> an idol is anything? No, but the sacrifices of pagans are offered to demons, not
> to God, and I do not want you to be participants with demons. You cannot
> drink the cup of the Lord and the cup of demons too; you cannot have a part
> in both the Lord's table and the table of demons. Are we trying to arouse the
> Lord's jealousy? Are we stronger than he?

This passage deserves careful scrutiny. First, notice the multiple times that
"participation" is used in this text. It is either the noun *koinōnia* or a varia-
tion of it, such as the word "participants" (κοινωνοὺς | *koinōnous*) in verse
20. A synonym for *koinōnia* is used twice: once in verse 17, where "we all
share the one loaf" (μετέχομεν | *metechomen*), and once in verse 21b, where
"you cannot *have a part* in both the Lord's table and the table of demons"
(μετέχειν | *metechein*). If we combine all of the references in these verses, we
find the following:

1. The cup of thanksgiving is a *participation* in the blood of Christ.
2. The bread we break is a *participation* in the body of Christ.
3. The *one loaf* of bread that *we all share* is an analogy of the *one body*
   of the church.
4. Sacrificing and eating at the table of idols makes us *participants* with
   demons.

---

84. I do not have space to deal with the Gospels in their presentation of the Lord's Supper,
but the rehearsal of it by Paul in 1 Cor. 11 is helpful for our discussion.

5. One cannot *have a part* or *have a share* in both the table of demons and the Lord's Table.

What does this mean for my purposes with regard to the Lord's Supper? Paul's point seems to take us to his conclusion: the Corinthians who were eating sacrificial meals at pagan temples felt that they were not doing anything inappropriate, since the idols represented there were merely showpieces; Paul insists that such people need to know that they cannot *share* food and drink in pagan temples and at the same time participate in the Lord's Table. Reading this through the analogy of Israel's altar, Paul argues that eating of sacrificial food brings one into the position of participating in the altar—be it Israel's altar or another's (1 Cor. 10:18). Neither the food offered to idols nor the idols themselves are anything. The problem has nothing to do with the food, per se, but with the fact that *behind* the mute stone image lies the work of demons. So Paul admonishes, "I do not want you to be participants with demons" (1 Cor. 10:20b). Indeed, the Corinthians cannot eat and drink at the Table of the Lord and at the table of demons, because the participation with Christ and fellow believers at the Lord's Table precludes a similar type of participation with pagan worshipers and the table of idols. For surely one can see that the demonic work behind the ritual superstitions for idols should cause Christians *not* to participate in their sacrificial meals. "One is not merely eating with friends at the pagan temples; one is engaged in idolatry, idolatry that involves the worship of demons."[85] Due to the demonic nature behind the sacrificial meals and idolatrous rituals, a Christian who attended such meals would be participating with demons along with the idol's adherents. What sense does it make for a Christian, who participates with Christ's blood and body (in some sense), to move on to a nearby temple and participate with Apollo's sacrificial rituals?[86]

What, then, is Paul's point here about participation? At some spiritual level, I suggest that Paul found the idea of *koinōnia* with Christ during the

85. Gordon D. Fee, *The First Epistle to the Corinthians*, NICNT (Grand Rapids: Eerdmans, 1987), 473.

86. I have been assisted in my interpretation of this passage by Fee, *Corinthians*, 465–75. Fee carefully excises any sacramentalism from his interpretation. However, he seems to waffle on the question of what "participation" might mean in this pericope, especially in terms of the Christian meal. What does the word "participation" mean if (as Fee wishes) it refers only to horizontal table fellowship with other Christians (or Israelites, or pagans, as the case may be)? While the reference for "sharing" food that is eaten may clearly point to the horizontal relationships, is there not some manner in which the Christian meal is a *participation in* the body and blood of Christ? Paul freely engages a type of mystical union in various other areas of his writings, so why not also here at the point of communion? See Fee, *Corinthians*, 470–71.

Supper to be at a level comparable with the participatory action found in the practice of baptism in Romans 6:3–5. In some way, baptism participates symbolically in the very reality of Christ's death, burial, and resurrection so that through this participation we "were therefore buried with him through baptism into death in order that, just as Christ was raised from the dead through the glory of the Father, we too may live a new life" (Rom. 6:4). Paul then continues, "For if we have been united with him in a death like his, we will certainly also be united with him in a resurrection like his" (Rom. 6:5). Taken together, we have a picture of *koinōnia*—a sharing of something (burial) with someone (Christ)—in baptism. By participating in this practice of baptism, we retrace the steps of Christ's passion, being united or knit together with Christ in such a way as to join us with him in his death. The word "united" (σύμφυτοι | *symphytoi*) occurs only here in the New Testament (Rom. 6:5). It may be a horticultural term meaning "to make to grow together" or "plant along with."[87] It may also be a biological term meaning "to make the edges of a wound grow together" or "to fuse the ends of broken bones."[88] The idea seems to be that of "joined together."[89]

The upshot of this seems to be some type of participatory language in Paul's theological discussion of baptism. In the act of baptism, we are united (joined together) with Christ in death and burial, and are similarly united (joined together) with Christ in his resurrection, so that we may walk a new way through life with other believers.

Returning then to 1 Corinthians 10:16–22, Paul's language of "participation" seems to point at something deeper than mere attendance, especially since one who "attends" pagan rituals of sacrificial meals is actually doing more than sitting there; from Paul's perspective, he or she is participating in the worship of demonic forces. Therefore, we can infer that the Table of the Lord with its cup of blessing and its one loaf of bread cannot be less participatory than the table of demons. Indeed, Paul does not state that Christians are eating and drinking the Lord's body and blood but rather states that they are participating in a meal of mystical union with Christ's death similar to their baptism.

Historical Considerations from the Reformation

At this point I shall consider a few influential points on the Lord's Supper from the Reformation. Specifically, I will examine the views of Luther,

---

87. James D. G. Dunn, *Romans 1–8*, WBC 38A (Nashville: Thomas Nelson, 1988), 316.
88. Dunn, *Romans 1–8*, 316.
89. Douglas J. Moo, *The Epistle to the Romans*, NICNT (Grand Rapids: Eerdmans, 1996), 368n76.

Zwingli, and Calvin on the Eucharist as they relate to the idea of Christ's presence.

Luther on the Eucharist. In the Eucharist, Christ is really present in a literal physical sense as well as in a spiritual sense, but the bread and wine are not transformed into the body and blood of Christ. This was Luther's view—one that was difficult for other Reformers to distinguish from the Catholic view. Unlike medieval understandings of transubstantiation, Luther saw Christ as physically present in the Eucharist but not "magically" changed into the food of heaven, the partaking of which would bring one into the kingdom of heaven. For Luther, there was no change of the substance of bread and wine— the inner essence of the bread was still bread, and wine was still wine. Yet Luther held that what Jesus said in John 6—"Very truly I tell you, unless you eat the flesh of the Son of Man and drink his blood, you have no life in you. Whoever eats my flesh and drinks my blood has eternal life, and I will raise them up at the last day. For my flesh is real food and my blood is real drink" (John 6:53–55)—had to be understood literally, and therefore miraculously. Combining these words in John 6 with the words of institution of the Supper from the Synoptic Gospels, Luther believed he had clear scriptural evidence for his claim that we eat Christ's very flesh and drink his blood. "So we say, on our part, that according to the words, Christ's true body and blood are present when he says, 'Take, eat; this is my body.' If our belief and teaching go wrong here, tell us, what are we doing?"[90] Luther believed his opponents betrayed Christ by stating that these words were not to be understood literally. On this point, Luther declared, "There is no middle ground."[91]

The words of institution in Matthew and Mark make clear that "Christ gives his body to eat when he distributes the bread."[92] Therefore, we "eat and take to ourselves Christ's body truly and physically. But how this takes place or how he is in the bread, we do not know and are not meant to know. We should believe God's Word without setting bounds or measure to it. The bread we see with our eyes, but we hear with our ears that Christ's body is present."[93] Therefore, to say (as do Zwingli and Oecolampadius) that "This is my body" should really be "This signifies my body" is to speak in language that is the "arrogance and frivolous wickedness of the very devil."[94] For Luther,

90. Martin Luther, *That These Words of Christ, "This Is My Body," etc., Still Stand Firm against the Fanatics* (1527), trans. Robert Fischer and Amy Nelson Burnett, ed. Amy Nelson Burnett, in *The Annotated Luther*, ed. Hans J. Hillerbrand, Kirsi I. Stjerna, and Timothy J. Wengert, vol. 3, *Church and Sacraments*, ed. Paul W. Robinson (Minneapolis: Fortress, 2016), 180.
91. Luther, *That These Words of Christ*, 180.
92. Luther, *That These Words of Christ*, 183.
93. Luther, *That These Words of Christ*, 183.
94. Luther, *That These Words of Christ*, 186.

Luther's Christology and the Lord's Supper

Luther's Christology—especially his understanding of the way the two natures of Christ relate to each other—created another major influence concerning Christ's presence in the Lord's Supper. In the same 1527 treatise that I have been citing, Luther turns to the creed, where Christ is seated at the right hand of God the Father. The *Schwärmerei* (enthusiasts) say that it is impossible for the risen body of Jesus Christ to be both at the right hand of the Father *and* in the Supper where it is literally eaten. Luther responds first that the *Schwärmerei* misunderstand the phrase "right hand of God."[a] Scripture teaches us not that this right hand of God is a specific place where a body may be but "that it is the almighty power of God, which at one and the same time can be nowhere and yet must be everywhere."[b] One cannot circumscribe the immeasurable power of God! Therefore, the right hand of God is not at any one place. If these folks, "dumb as a clod,"[c] want to resist this understanding, then they must come to terms with the fact that God's power (his right hand) is not divisible into parts. Further, do they wish to deny the miracle that is needed for Christ's words to be true—namely, that "one body is in many places at the same time?"[d] This is Luther's doctrine of the ubiquity of Christ's risen body, which is everywhere present.[e] Following a line of thought

the figurative argument breaks down at these words of institution because they change the meaning and intent of Christ's own speech. As Luther states in a treatise from 1528, he believes that he has demonstrated sufficiently that "the body of Christ may be everywhere since God's right hand is everywhere."[95] Surely God is able to make Christ be both in heaven and on earth at the Lord's Table? Undoubtedly, God demonstrates his wisdom in reserving the precise nature of *how* he does this, because we humans "do not yet know the extent of his power."[96]

Zwingli on Communion. Huldreich Zwingli (1483–1531) wrote a treatise, *On the Lord's Supper* (1526), in which he attempted to prove that the phrase "This is my body" cannot be taken literally but must be understood as

95. Martin Luther, *Von Abendmahl Christi, Bekenntnis (1528)*, in WA 26:318, l.1 (my translation).
96. Luther, *Von Abendmahl Christi*, in WA 26:318, l.4–5. For what remains one of the most thorough treatments of Luther's doctrine of ubiquity, see Hans Grass, *Die Abendmahlslehre bei Luther und Calvin: Eine kritische Untersuchung*, Beiträge Förderung christlicher Theologie, ed. Paul Althaus, Hermann Dörries, and Joachim Jeremias, 2nd ser., vol. 47 (Gütersloh: Bertelsmann, 1954), 57–86.

from Cyril of Alexandria in the 430s CE, Luther sees the human and divine natures as united—almost mixed into a monophysite (one-nature) Christ. All of the attributes of divinity (including omnipresence) are *shared* with the risen body of Jesus Christ. (Theologically, this is called *communicatio idiomatum*: the sharing of attributes. Luther faulted Zwingli for separating the two natures of Christ, thereby charging him with the error of Nestorianism.) For Christ to be really present in the elements of the Lord's Supper, his risen body needs to be there as well. Luther asserts that this is precisely what has happened: the body of Christ is now everywhere present. He could not explain this miracle but felt it was necessary for the words of Christ to be taken literally.

[a] Martin Luther, *That These Words of Christ, "This Is My Body," Etc., Still Stand Firm against the Fanatics* (1527), trans. Robert Fischer and Amy Nelson Burnett, ed. Amy Nelson Burnett, in *The Annotated Luther*, ed. Hans J. Hillerbrand, Kirsi I. Stjerna, and Timothy J. Wengert, vol. 3, *Church and Sacraments*, ed. Paul W. Robinson (Minneapolis: Fortress, 2016), 202–3.

[b] Luther, *That These Words of Christ*, 204.

[c] Luther, *That These Words of Christ*, 204.

[d] Luther, *That These Words of Christ*, 210–11.

[e] Luther, *That These Words of Christ*, 213.

"figurative and symbolical."[97] Even Luther's railing about John 6 fails to see the key point there: "The Spirit gives life; the flesh counts for nothing" (John 6:63).[98] Therefore, when Christ refers to eating his flesh and drinking his blood, he means for us to understand that we should *believe in him*.[99] Thus, Jesus is not speaking about the sacrament of the Eucharist in John 6 but rather is teaching about believing on him. This bread is Christ's flesh, which he will give for the life of the world. Opponents "seize upon the first part" of his saying but ignore the latter part ("which I will give for the life of the world").[100]

In an early letter to Matthew Alber in 1524, Zwingli carefully describes his understanding of the Eucharist as opposed to the former Lutheran (now enthusiast) Andreas Bodenstein (also known as Karlstadt). Karlstadt had

97. Huldreich Zwingli, *On the Lord's Supper (1526)*, in *Zwingli and Bullinger*, ed. and trans. G. W. Bromiley, Library of Christian Classics, Ichthus ed. (Philadelphia: Westminster, 1953), 199.

98. Zwingli, *On the Lord's Supper*, 190.

99. Zwingli, *On the Lord's Supper*, 199. This same idea is expressed in Zwingli, *Subsidium sive coronis de Eucharistia (1525)*, in *Huldrici Zuinglii Opera: Completa Editio Prima* 3, Latinorum Scriptorum, ed. Melchiore Schulero and Johannis Schulthessio, pt. 1 (Turici: Schulthess und Höhr, 1832), 348–49.

100. Zwingli, *On the Lord's Supper*, 204.

suggested that when Jesus said, "This is my body," he was referring to his own body—his own self (*in se ipsum*).[101] Zwingli cautiously disagrees with Karlstadt, saying that "the opinions of Karlstadt are not approved by us."[102] For the first time, Zwingli discusses the proper way to understand "is" in the phrase "This *is* my body." It is to be read as "signifies" (*significare*), not "is" (*esse*).[103] Thus, "Take and eat! This *signifies* my body, which is given up for you" (*Accipite et comedite! Hoc* significat *corpus meum quod pro vobis traditur*).[104] Hence, the bread represents (*repraesentat*) his body.[105] For Jesus did not say that this bread is his body but that this represents his body. "In what way does the bread represent his body? Undoubtedly when it is eaten in this way, it calls back to our memory that Christ's own body was offered once for us."[106] This is how we "participate" in the Supper. "For Paul did not say: 'Participation is of bread and wine, but of blood and body.'"[107] The body of which Paul speaks in 1 Corinthians 10 is not the physical body of Christ—his flesh, nerves, and bones that we "eat"—but the people of God. "But who are the body of Christ? Of whom is that one the head and those ones are his members? The head (belongs) to whom? Those who follow Christ—who believe on him."[108] Communication or participation in the blood and body of Christ is not concerned with eating but with "sharing of the church" (*communicatione ecclesiae*).[109] Christ gives the bread to us to eat so that, eating him spiritually at the same time, we may coalesce into that very body, which is the body of Christ, the church (*hoc autem corpus ecclesia Christi est*).[110] By eating this bread together, we show our brothers and sisters that we are members of the body of Christ.

Later in his life after the Marburg Colloquy (1529), where he collided with Luther face-to-face on the issue of the presence of Christ in the Supper, Zwingli composes more positive expressions of the Supper, especially in terms of Christ's presence. Whereas he held in 1526 that the "communion" with the body and blood of Christ that is found in 1 Corinthians 10 is really to be

101. Huldreich Zwingli, *Ad Matthaeum Alberum Rutlingensium Ecclesiasten: de coena Dominica (1524)*, in *Zuinglii Opera*, 3:597.

102. Huldreich Zwingli, *De coena Dominica*, in *Zuinglii Opera*, 3:592 (my translation).

103. Zwingli, *De coena Dominica*, in *Zuinglii Opera*, 3:598 (my translation).

104. Zwingli, *De coena Dominica*, in *Zuinglii Opera*, 3:599 (his emphasis, my translation).

105. Zwingli, *De coena Dominica*, in *Zuinglii Opera*, 3:599.

106. Zwingli, *De coena Dominica*, in *Zuinglii Opera*, 3:599 (my translation). Latin: *Quomodo repraesentat panis corpus? Nimirum cum sic editur, revocatur in memoriam, Christum corpus suum pereutientibus praebuisse pro nobis.*

107. Zwingli, *De coena Dominica*, in *Zuinglii Opera*, 3:600 (my translation).

108. Zwingli, *De coena Dominica*, in *Zuinglii Opera*, 3:601 (my translation).

109. Zwingli, *De coena Dominica*, in *Zuinglii Opera*, 3:601 (my translation).

110. Zwingli, *De coena Dominica*, in *Zuinglii Opera*, 3:601.

understood as "community,"[111] by 1530 and 1531 Zwingli proposes clearly that Christ is present at the Supper in a spiritual sense and is therefore food for the nourishment of believers in a spiritual sense.[112] He could even state that we have a "spiritual participation" at the Lord's Supper, by which one's heart is "refreshed by this faith to which you bear witness by these symbols."[113] Christ is eaten in the Supper not literally but spiritually.[114] Therefore, Zwingli says that he holds to "the Lord's Supper distinguished by the presence of Christ."[115] This means that in the Eucharist,

> the true body of Christ is present by the contemplation of faith. This means that they who thank the Lord for the benefits bestowed on us in His Son acknowledge that He assumed true flesh, in it truly suffered, truly washed away our sins by His blood; and thus everything done by Christ becomes as it were present to them by the contemplation of faith. But that body of Christ in essence and really, i.e., the natural body itself, is either present in the supper or masticated with our mouth and teeth, as the Papists . . . assert, we not only deny, but constantly maintain to be an error, contrary to the Word of God.[116]

One notices in these later writings that the concept of memorial seems less prominent than that of spiritual contemplation and participation. It certainly is not an appropriate assessment of Zwingli's views on the Supper to claim that he was a bare memorialist or symbolist. Indeed, I find him pointing to spiritual participation in his less polemical moments more than to memorials themselves.[117]

Calvin on the spiritual nourishment of the Lord's Supper. When the Marburg Colloquy took place in 1529 between Luther and Zwingli on communion, John Calvin had not yet converted to Protestantism. By the time of his conversion

111. Zwingli, *On the Lord's Supper*, 236.

112. Huldreich Zwingli, *Exposition of the Christian Faith (1531)*, in *The Latin Works of Huldreich Zwingli*, trans. Samuel Macauley Jackson, ed. William J. Hinke (Philadelphia: Heidelberg, 1922), 2:252 (hereafter, *Exposition of the Christian Faith* [Macauley]).

113. Zwingli, *Exposition of the Christian Faith* (Macauley), 2:253–54.

114. Zwingli, *Exposition of the Christian Faith* (Macauley), 2:248.

115. Huldreich Zwingli, *Letter of Huldreich Zwingli to the Most Illustrious Princes of Germany (1530)*, in *The Latin Works of Hudreich Zwingli*, trans. Samuel Macauley Jackson, ed. William J. Hinke (Philadelphia: Heidelberg, 1922), 2:123.

116. Zwingli, *Account of the Faith*, 49.

117. I have left out an account of the well-known Marburg Colloquy of 1529, in part because Zwingli frequently gets labeled a pure symbolist by his rather warm responses to Luther's literalist view. I tend to see Zwingli as pressing Luther to agree to the point he is making by overstating his case. And such is the case with polemical theology. For an excellent discussion of Zwingli's more open view on presence in 1531, see W. P. Stephens, *The Theology of Huldrych Zwingli* (Oxford: Clarendon, 1986), 252–54.

Zwingli on Luther's Doctrine of the Ubiquity of Christ's Body

If Christ is seated at the right hand of God, how can he be eaten literally in the sacrament? Without naming Luther, Zwingli takes on the ubiquity of Christ's risen body: "You say: He is God. He can be everywhere. But note with what circumspection you say this. First you say: He is God. You give it to be understood that it is the property of God to be everywhere. But it is not the property of the body."[a] This is the crux of Zwingli's argument against Luther's doctrine of ubiquity: bodies are circumscribed by boundaries of time and space. By definition, bodies have limitations—even the risen body of our Lord. Indeed, "the flesh may fume, but the words of Christ stand firm: he sits at the right hand of the Father, he has left the world, he is no longer present with us. And if these words are true, it is impossible to maintain that his flesh and blood are present in the sacrament."[b] In other words, only the *divine* nature of Christ is ubiquitous, not the human.[c]

Luther misunderstands the clear literary devices used in the New Testament Greek language. Utilizing his thorough background in linguistics that came from his Swiss humanist training, Zwingli waxes eloquent on "figures and symbols, hyperbole and anaphora."[d] However, especially appropriate against Luther is the rhetorical device of metonymy. Luther had pressed the fanatics with the fact that Paul announces "that rock was Christ" (1 Cor. 10:4), not "that rock was *like* Christ" or "that rock signified Christ." Zwingli responds that Luther has missed the literary point of metonymy, whereby the name of one object is used for that of another, in this case "rock" and "Christ."[e] Therefore, Luther's argument that "This is my body" must be understood as a literal expression also misunderstands the figurative metonymy. Otherwise, figures of speech in Christ's words make

around 1534, "the debate over the Lord's Supper in the Protestant camp was in full swing."[118] However, within the next twenty years, Calvin would approach the question of Christ's presence in the Supper with a powerful answer that continues to offer rich resource for us today. Later in his life, Calvin did not agree with Luther—and in some ways, not even with Zwingli (as he understood him).[119]

---

118. Wilhelm Niesel, *Calvins Lehre vom Abendmahl*, 2nd ed., Forschungen zur Geschichte und Lehre das Protestantismus 3, ed. Paul Althaus, Karl Barth, and Karl Heim (Munich: Kaiser, 1935), 21 (my translation).

119. As Niesel describes it, Calvin did not appreciate Zwingli's earlier writings on the Lord's Supper, especially as they appeared in the 1525 *Commentary on True and False Religion*. It appears that Calvin did appreciate Luther's earlier writings on the Eucharist (e.g., *The Babylonian Captivity* [1520]) but was not acquainted until years later with Luther's doctrine of ubiquity. He

no sense. How are we to understand "I am the vine, you are the branches," if not with metonymy?[f]

Luther rightly says, "God's right hand, strength, majesty and power are everywhere," and Zwingli agrees. Even when Luther says, "Christ is at the right hand of God," he speaks correctly because the divine and human natures of Christ are indeed there. However, when Luther claims that the human body of the risen Christ is also at the right hand of God (by which he means "everywhere"), then Luther has confused the human with the divine and made the two into similar, uniform natures (*glychförmig*). Zwingli asserts that in his divinity Christ is everywhere that God is, because he is God himself. "But humanity is not the righteous God, for it is not the divine nature." With regard to Christ's humanity, it is not everywhere present in its "newly adopted nature," because the human nature is not synonymous with eternity—or then we would have two "infinite" natures.[g]

[a] Huldreich Zwingli, *On the Lord's Supper* (1526), in *Zwingli and Bullinger*, ed. and trans. G. W. Bromiley, Library of Christian Classics, Ichthus ed. (Philadelphia: Westminster, 1953), 214.

[b] Zwingli, *On the Lord's Supper*, 214–15.

[c] Zwingli, *On the Lord's Supper*, 219.

[d] Huldreich Zwingli, *Subsidium sive coronis de Eucharistia* (1525), in *Huldrici Zuinglii Opera: Completa Editio Prima* 3, Latinorum Scriptorum, ed. Melchiore Schulero Johannis Schulthessio, pt. 1 (Turici: Schulthess und Höhr, 1832), 335–36.

[e] Zwingli, *Subsidium sive coronis de Eucharistia*, in *Zuinglii Opera*, 3:336.

[f] Zwingli, *On the Lord's Supper*, 223.

[g] This discussion comes from Zwingli's treatise on Luther's book on the sacrament—namely, *Über Luthers Buch, das Sakrament betreffend* (1527). It is quoted in Hans Grass, *Die Abendmahlslehre bei Luther und Calvin: Eine kritische Untersuchung*, Beiträge Förderung christlicher Theologie, ed. Paul Althaus, Hermann Dörries, and Joachim Jeremias, 2nd ser., vol. 47 (Gütersloh: Bertelsmann, 1954), 61–62n1 (my translation).

Against Luther, he spoke strongly on the body of Christ not being everywhere present. The elements are true symbols, but not mere symbols, since Christ is made *spiritually present* in the elements.[120] There is true participation of the sign with the thing it symbolizes—and here Calvin parted ways with Zwingli's major philosophical point. When Jesus said, "This is my body," it was meant to be taken spiritually and analogically. To take Jesus's words literally makes no sense, especially when attempting to interpret the whole of Scripture.[121] Yet

will come to speak against Luther's understanding of the Eucharist, but mainly after Luther's death in 1546. See Niesel, *Calvins Lehre vom Abendmahl*, 33.

120. Calvin, *Inst.* 4.17.10 (1370).

121. R. Wallace, *Calvin's Doctrine of the Word and Sacrament*, 197.

this entire issue of the Supper points to a mystery of Christ and the church. By its very nature, it is therefore "incomprehensible."[122]

First, the sacrament of the Lord's Supper offers us the Word of God; only then does God offer us confirmation of our faith. Moreover, the light of the Spirit in our hearts illumines both the Word and the sacraments.[123] Calvin desired to find something of a middle ground between Luther and Zwingli; such an attempt garnered for him contempt from both camps. Luther understood Christ to be substantially and physically present in the Supper, and therefore Christ had to be there in his entirety. Zwingli believed Christ was not there substantially and physically, since the risen Christ's body is located at the right hand of God. In response to this, Calvin used the phrase "spiritually present" to speak of the reality of Christ at the Supper.[124] The *res* (matter) of the sacrament is Christ himself. The Supper, then, does not "feed our bodies with fading and corruptible food, but nourishes our souls on the best and most precious diet [*mais de nourrir noz ames de pasture meilleure et precieuse*]."[125] What we receive in the Eucharist is Jesus Christ himself—"the only food by which our souls are nourished [*la seule viande dont noz ames sont nourries*]."[126] Therefore, in Calvin's sacramental theology, the visible signs are offered on behalf of human weakness. The Eucharist is something like an "object lesson"—the Word of God in enacted form.[127] Yet contrary to his understanding of Zwingli's views, the sign is not "a bare figure [*une figure nue*] but is combined with the reality and substance [*mais conioincte avec sa verité et substance*]."[128] For Calvin, the Eucharist not only offers believers a reminder that Christ died for them in the past but also provides a vivid connection to Christ's body in the present.[129] The bread is called "body" because "it not only represents but also

122. Calvin, *Inst.* 4.17.1 (1361).

123. Calvin, *Inst.* 4.14.8 (1283–84).

124. Joseph McLelland, "Lutheran-Reformed Debate on the Eucharist and Christology," in *Reexamination of Luther and Reformed Traditions*, vol. 2, *Christology, the Lord's Supper and Its Observance in the Church* (New York: North American Area of the World Alliance of Reformed Churches and the USA National Committee of the Lutheran World Federation, 1964), 12.

125. John Calvin, *Short Treatise on the Supper of Our Lord in Which Is Shown Its True Institution, Benefit, and Utility (1541)*, in *John Calvin: Tracts and Letters*, vol. 2, *Tracts*, part 2, ed. and trans. Henry Beveridge (1849; repr., Carlisle, PA: Banner of Truth Trust, 2009), 166. For the French, see Calvin, *Petit Traicté de la Saincte Cene de Nostre Seigneur Jesus Christ*, in OS 1:504.

126. Calvin, *Short Treatise on the Supper*, 166; and Calvin, *Petit Traicté de la Saincte Cene*, in OS 1:505.

127. Gerrish, *Grace and Gratitude*, 127.

128. Calvin, *Short Treatise on the Supper*, 171; and Calvin, *Petit Traicté de la Saincte Cene*, in OS 1:509.

129. Gerrish, *Grace and Gratitude*, 127.

presents it to us [*puis que non seulement il le nous represente, mais aussi nous le presente*]."[130]

Therefore, for Calvin, it was enough to say simply that Christ was present—mysteriously and perhaps incomprehensibly present, but really present nonetheless. How do we know this? It is because the distinctive work of the Holy Spirit brings us into contact with Christ's very own substance.[131] It is the Spirit who causes the life of the body of Christ (located in heaven) to flow toward us as a root "transmits sap to the branches."[132] This is part of the mystery that Calvin's sacramental theology allows and part of the mystery that his understanding of Christology demands. However, to suggest (as Luther does) that this experience brings us into contact with the human, physical being of the historical Jesus at every table of the Supper throughout the world is unnecessary and highly speculative. "What, then, our mind does not comprehend, let faith conceive: that the Spirit truly unites things separated in space [namely, the body of Christ in heaven and his people on earth]."[133] When Christ ascended to heaven, he sent the Spirit on its descent into the world so that now we may be connected to Christ through the Spirit by spiritual means. When we eat and drink at the Supper, the Spirit makes Christ's presence real for us and makes effective the nourishment to our souls. "For we do not doubt that Christ's body is limited by the general characteristics common to all human bodies, and is contained in heaven (where it was once for all received) until Christ return in judgment [Acts 3:21]. So we deem it utterly unlawful to draw it back under these corruptible elements or to imagine it to be present everywhere."[134] From this attack against the ubiquity of Christ's body, Calvin then turns to explain the superfluous nature of such a doctrine. Who needs a universal, physical body of Christ when we have the Spirit? We are united to Christ through the Spirit. "The bond of this connection is therefore the Spirit of Christ, with whom we are joined in unity and is like a channel through which all that Christ himself is and has is conveyed to us."[135] And it is here that Calvin's emphasis shines clearest of all: the true gift in the sacraments is Jesus Christ himself.[136]

130. Calvin, *Short Treatise on the Supper*, 172; and Calvin, *Petit Traicté de la Saincte Cene*, in *OS* 1:509.

131. McLelland, "Lutheran-Reformed Debate," 13.

132. Gerrish, *Grace and Gratitude*, 129. Gerrish cites a letter from Calvin to a fellow Reformer, Peter Martyr Vermigli, from August 8, 1555. See John Calvin, *Ioannis Calvini opera quae supersunt omnia*, ed. Wilhelm Baum, Edward Cunitz, and Edward Reuss, 59 vols., Corpus Reformatorum 29–87 (Brunswick: Schwetschke and Son (Bruhn), 1863–1900), 15:722–23.

133. Calvin, *Inst.* 4.17.10 (1370). The bracketed explanatory remarks are mine.

134. Calvin, *Inst.* 4.17.12 (1373).

135. Calvin, *Inst.* 4.17.12 (1373).

136. See Niesel, *The Theology of Calvin*, trans. Harold Knight (Grand Rapids: Baker, 1980), 228.

If one were to ask Calvin *how* this mysterious union and communion occurs, he would confess ignorance without any shame.[137] Calvin admits that
it is a "secret too lofty for either my mind to comprehend or my words to
declare. And, to speak more plainly, I rather experience than understand it."[138]
Nonetheless, the Supper nourishes believers spiritually because "it is made
effectual by the secret and miraculous power of God [*par la vertu secrete et
miraculeuse de Dieu*], and that the Spirit of God is the bond of participation
[*et que l'Esprit de Dieu est le lien de ceste participation*], this being the reason
why it is called spiritual [*appellée spirituelle*]."[139]

The Lord's Supper Today

From the historical concerns about the Supper, we turn to the question
of how the church should conceive this practice today—especially in relation to Christ's presence. As I have described these participatory practices
instituted by Christ, it is clear that the Lord's Supper is a practice that has
both a backward recall and a forward leaning. When we partake of the bread
and wine (juice), we proclaim the Lord's death until he comes. This phrase,
"you [plural] proclaim" (καταγγέλλετε | *katangellete*) is not imperative, not a
command, but a declarative statement in the indicative mood (1 Cor. 11:26).
Through our actions, we are speaking about the death of Christ and the
immeasurable love required for such a selfless act of sacrifice. When we
break the bread and drink the cup, we are painting a picture of the Lord's
death for all to see, especially all the people of God who are assembled. The
Reformers are right in connecting the Word of God with this ritual, since
it is the gospel as illumined by the Spirit that gives life and meaning to the
symbolic reenactment in which we participate. The elements are meaning-
less unless we understand from the Word that Jesus died for our sins and we
have faith to receive that good news. This is the presuppositional ground for
the practice of the Lord's Supper. For those who do not know the Savior, the
Supper is just another perfunctory religious ritual, devoid of both meaning
and benefit. To the people of God's presence, however, the Supper represents
an occasion for the presence of Christ to be in our midst. "The Spirit makes
the crucified and risen Christ really present to us in the eucharistic meal."[140]

137. T. H. L. Parker, "John Calvin," in *A History of Christian Doctrine*, ed. Hubert Cunliffe-
Jones (Edinburgh: T&T Clark, 1978), 398.
138. Calvin, *Inst.* 4.17.32 (1403).
139. Calvin, *Short Treatise on the Supper*, 198; and *Petit Traicté de la Saincte Cene*, in *OS*
1:530.
140. *Baptism, Eucharist and Ministry*, Faith and Order Paper 111 (Geneva: World Council
of Churches, 1982), 13.

Nonetheless, this participatory action in the meal remains a human act, just as baptism does. There is no magical transformation of the bread and wine into the body and blood of Christ. We do not eat our way into eternal life. Yet there is participation with the very being of Christ through the Spirit that makes the Lord's Supper an occasion filled with expectation and extraordinary significance.

Weber grasps what John Calvin was aiming at when he states that we cannot speak of Christ's presence in the Supper in terms of subject/object or spiritual/physical. "If Jesus Christ is the Giver and the Gift of the Supper, then it must be dealt with pneumatically."[141] It is the Spirit of God who unites us to Christ in the first place, and this union is continued and enhanced through the mediation of Christ's presence in the Supper. We can *experience* Christ's presence. And this is what the people of God's presence do—they experience the presence of the crucified and risen One who lives forever. How is Christ present? By means of the Spirit, since this is the same way Christ is made present to us who believe in the first place.

Zwingli is also right in reminding us that the Supper is a sign—a symbol of what the people of God can never forget—namely, that Christ died for us. Therefore, in the Supper, we look backward in remembrance (ἀνάμνησιν | *anamnēsin*), recalling the love of Christ offered for us in the once-for-all sacrifice on the cross. Through our participation in tracing the events of Christ's passion, we remember him as he commanded us to do (1 Cor. 11:24). When we commune with the Savior during the Supper, we commune with the suffering, bleeding, crucified One, who took our punishment, bore our sorrows, and has been raised to life and is seated at the right hand of God, where he ever lives to make intercession for us.

The One who died is also the One who is alive and with whom we are presently communing through the Supper by means of the Spirit. Therefore, through participation in the Supper, the Spirit re-presents to us Jesus Christ in his death; yet, also through participation in the Supper, the Spirit re-presents to us Jesus Christ in his resurrection. Looking backward in remembrance, we find the reality of death that faced Christ and will face all of us one day. Looking forward in anticipation, we celebrate the victory that is Christ's over the grave. Hence, the Supper is not a gloomy, morose event but a joyous celebration of Christ's dying love and his living presence as well as his pending return. As Weber poetically states, "The Supper is the first gleaming of the Eschaton."[142] Or as *Baptism, Eucharist and Ministry* says it more prosaically,

141. Weber, *Foundations of Dogmatics*, 2:634.
142. Weber, *Foundations of Dogmatics*, 2:642.

"The eucharist is also the foretaste of his *Parousia* and of the final kingdom."[143]
One day we will eat and drink again with Jesus at the Marriage Supper of
the Lamb. While we await Christ's return, we participate in the practice of
the Lord's Supper to remember his dying love, to proclaim to all his death,
and to lift our heads in hope to the eastern skies.

What happens, then, in the Lord's Supper? While they eat the bread and
drink the wine, the people of God feast on the presence of Christ made real to
them by the Holy Spirit. This spiritual nourishment does not grant us eternal
life, but it strengthens our faith and solidifies the bond between Christ and us
through a continual reminder of his dying love as well as a perpetual pointer
toward his glorious return. Further, the people of God are brought together in
this Supper of recollection and anticipation in order to grow in unity with their
Master and each other. This is no mere empty sign but a robust celebratory
meal that is reminiscent of the banquet thrown by the father of the prodigal
son (Luke 15). There are moments of solemn reflection, to be sure, but these
never overcome the sheer joy of Christ's presence in our midst and the pure
anticipation of the day when we shall see Christ face-to-face, when God's
dwelling will be with humans for eternity. When the people of God feast at
the Supper, they retrace the events of the Lord's suffering and passion, helping to conform them into the image of Christ: "I want to know Christ—to
know the power [τὴν δύναμιν | *tēn dynamin*] of his resurrection and to know
the sharing/participation [τὴν κοινωνίαν | *tēn koinōnian*] in his sufferings,
being continually conformed [συμμορφιζόμενος | *symmorphizomenos*] to his
death" (Phil. 3:10, my translation).

With such a rich and meaningful meal at our disposal, why should we celebrate communion irregularly—or even just once a month? The traditional
response given by those who celebrate the Supper only occasionally is that
humans cheapen whatever ritual or practice they perform too often. Frankly,
this has never made sense to me. Something as deeply moving as the Lord's
Supper can become a vain repetition only to those who miss the point in the
first place! If we are enriched and strengthened by participating in this practice
of Christ's presence in the Supper—by retracing Christ's sacrificial steps of
love—then why should we limit our engagement of it? There may be many
reasons to perform certain actions or practices in moderation, but surely one
should not be simply that I might wear it out or come to lose interest while
I'm gathered in the presence of God and fellow believers. While that may
be true of a variety of activities, it cannot be true of an action that allows
me to participate by faith in the transcendent life of the God who loved us

143. *Baptism, Eucharist and Ministry*, 11.

enough to give his life for us. As Greggs notes, "Given the significance of the event and its importance within the community," there should be "no limits on the frequency of celebration."[144] Since the Supper is a communal activity that proclaims the Lord's death until he returns, why not perform the Supper whenever we gather for worship? If one comes to this Supper with the right disposition and faith, only spiritual nourishment from the presence of Christ can come from such repetition—and the shaping of our own character to the contours of Christ's life.

Footwashing

While I realize the radical nature of adding a "sacrament" or "ordinance" to the Protestant list of two sacraments, I cannot get away from the clear command of Christ to perform footwashing. For some churches, this ritual has been turned into a Maundy Thursday event where priests wash the feet of twelve individuals from the congregation. For other churches, it has been turned into a metaphor for service. While it has become common among Protestant congregations to interpret the John 13 passage on footwashing as a mere metaphor that encourages service among believers, I suggest it has a much greater depth of meaning than simply that of metaphor. Given the command of Christ regarding this practice, it seems clear that he intended his followers to perform footwashing as surely as the Supper or baptism.

I am not the first to think like this. Several churches after the Reformation established this practice (mainly those from the German Brethren movement), and several holiness and Pentecostal denominations continue to perform footwashing today (although rarely is it seen in practice).[145] In the early church, footwashing was considered a sacrament in Milan, Italy, for a number of years. Ambrose, bishop of Milan, clearly viewed it as a sacrament, although he recognized that the Church of Rome did not practice this ritual. He believed in it so fervently that he was willing to risk the consequences of continuing its practice.[146]

144. Greggs, *Dogmatic Ecclesiology*, 1:239.
145. Undoubtedly, the rarity of practice today is due to several factors: (1) the difficulty of coordinating and setting up such a ritual for a small or large number of people and (2) the potentially uncomfortable situation for some people (especially in the West) that allows others to touch or even view their feet (and vice versa). I would argue that these challenges can be overcome *if* the local congregation considers this practice to be one that is necessary today. Greggs notes that the "earthiness, practicality, and messiness of this action reduces its capacity to be a *regularized ritual* act and thereby its capacity to partake in the genus 'sacrament.'" Greggs, *Dogmatic Ecclesiology*, 1:158.
146. See John Christopher Thomas, *Footwashing in John 13 and the Johannine Community*, Journal for the Study of the New Testament Supplement Series 61 (Sheffield: Sheffield Academic, 1991), 178.

Let us consider the passage in John's Gospel that poses this practice.

Jesus knew that the Father had put all things under his power, and that he had come from God and was returning to God, so he got up from the meal, took off his outer clothing, and wrapped a towel around his waist. After that, he poured water into a basin and began to wash his disciples' feet, drying them with the towel that was wrapped around him.

He came to Simon Peter, who said to him, "Lord, are you going to wash my feet?"

Jesus replied, "You do not realize now what I am doing, but later you will understand."

"No," said Peter, "you shall never wash my feet."

Jesus answered, "Unless I wash you, you have no part with me."

"Then, Lord," Simon Peter replied, "not just my feet but my hands and my head as well!"

Jesus answered, "Those who have had a bath need only to wash their feet; their whole body is clean. And you are clean, though not every one of you." For he knew who was going to betray him, and that was why he said not every one was clean.

When he had finished washing their feet, he put on his clothes and returned to his place. "Do you understand what I have done for you?" he asked them. "You call me 'Teacher' and 'Lord,' and rightly so, for that is what I am. Now that I, your Lord and Teacher, have washed your feet, you also should wash one another's feet. I have set you an example that you should do as I have done for you. Very truly I tell you, no servant is greater than his master, nor is a messenger greater than the one who sent him. Now that you know these things, you will be blessed if you do them." (John 13:3–17)

Most Christians understand this as a simple lesson, a parable in action for the disciples to understand servanthood. Jesus used an ordinary Oriental custom of washing dusty feet in order to make a point, just as he used a farmer sowing in the fields to make a point. But there seems to be something going on here that is different from mere metaphor or parable.

Consider first of all the placement of this story in John's Gospel. While the Synoptic Gospels have a final supper with Jesus and the disciples, there is no institution of the Lord's Supper per se in John. There is a connection with eating Christ's body in the story of the miraculous feeding of the multitudes (John 6), but at the point where other Gospel writers place the institution of the Lord's Supper, John places the washing of the disciples' feet. It is entirely possible and perhaps even probable that the Johannine community (the one in which John lived and the one to which he left this Gospel as a legacy) viewed this chapter as the institution of another sacrament along with the Supper and baptism.[147]

Second, a natural reading of the narrative points one in the direction of reading this story as a literal command: as I have washed your feet, you "*should* [ὀφείλετε | *opheilete*] wash one another's feet" (John 13:14). This word implies "ought" or "necessity." He commanded his disciples to wash each other's feet; further, he emphasized that he had just performed this action as an *example* (ὑπόδειγμα | *hypodeigma*) for how it should be done (John 13:15).[148] One might come to the conclusion that there is a firmer basis for the institution of footwashing as a "sacrament" or "ordinance" than baptism or the Lord's Supper. As Chris Thomas says, "If the Johannine Jesus had intended to institute footwashing as a continuing religious rite, how else could he have said it to get his point across?"[149]

At least some in the first-century church took Jesus's commands literally. In a list of good works that widows should perform, the "washing of saints' feet" is one that Paul recognizes (1 Tim. 5:10). Other Christians in the early centuries of church history supported footwashing: Tertullian, Ambrose, John Chrysostom, Augustine, and John Cassian.[150]

Third, there is a blessing offered by Christ for those who perform this ritual: "You will be blessed [μακάριοί | *makarioi*] if you do them" (John 13:17). While a theology of baptism develops in Paul's writing that includes participation in the life, death, and resurrection of Jesus Christ and a theology of the Lord's Supper that also includes this participatory model of the mystery, neither of these rituals is assigned a "blessing" by Christ for those who do them. There is a promise and command in baptism and communion, but not a particularized blessing, as is found here for footwashing.

It seems that if one of the fundamental reasons for performing these participatory practices is the *dominical institution* of Christ, then footwashing is on firmer ground than the other two practices. Moreover, there is every reason to understand this text literally, as did a number of believers in the early centuries. Finally, there is a promised blessing attached to the performance of this ritual. It seems clear that footwashing is an act instituted by our Lord.

147. This is the basic thesis of Thomas's work. See Thomas, *Footwashing in John 13 and the Johannine Community*.

148. John Christopher Thomas, "Footwashing: Its Practice and Meaning," in *Ministry and Theology: Studies for the Church and Its Leaders* (Cleveland, TN: Pathway, 1996), 41.

149. John Christopher Thomas, "Footwashing within the Context of the Lord's Supper," in *The Lord's Supper: Believers Church Perspectives*, ed. Dale R. Stoffer (Scottdale, PA: Herald, 1997), 174.

150. Thomas, "Footwashing: Its Practice and Meaning," 43.

If footwashing is a sign, then what does the practice of it signify? The obvious meaning lies in the performance of this act of a servant, stooping to wash filth off someone's feet. In a manner analogous to baptism and the Supper, I believe that when we wash the feet of our fellow believers and receive that same act in return, we somehow participate in the humbling act and attitude of Christ. We put on the mind of Christ, who did not think it too far below him to come to earth and become a human being (Phil. 2:5–7). When we stoop to perform this participatory practice of service, surely the presence of Christ is shaping us into humbler servants.

However, the entire context of this passage forces us to consider other dimensions of the meaning of footwashing. What might the dialogue between Jesus and Peter actually mean in reference to this washing? John Christopher Thomas suggests a very provocative possibility here. The primary meaning of footwashing is made clear not only by the act of servitude but also by Jesus's statement: "Those who have bathed only need to wash their feet; their whole body is clean" (John 13:10). Thomas notes that the words "bathe" and "wash" are two completely different words and that for John's Gospel, the connotation of "bathe" is clearly connected with water baptism. What, then, might footwashing mean? Jesus connects it with the frequent cleansings of the feet necessary in daily life in the ancient world. Does one need to take an entire bath all over again when only one's feet are dirty from travel? Of course not! One needs only to wash the feet that have walked through the filth of the outside world during one's daily sojourns. The spiritual significance of this may be that the believer does not need to be "rebaptized" because he or she experiences the filthy effects of this life, but does need to undergo "footwashing which signifies the removal of sin that might accumulate as a result of life in this sinful world."[151] Thomas views footwashing as an "extension of baptism."[152] It might be said to deal with postbaptismal sins or even with the daily progress in sanctification.

Lisa P. Stephenson recognizes three themes within this ritual: cleansing, servitude, and love.[153] She also makes a profound point about intimacy involved in washing another's feet—the physical aspect of touch as related to such an embodied ritual.[154] "Footwashing necessitates embodied forgiveness. It

151. Thomas, "Footwashing: Its Practice and Meaning," 45.
152. Thomas, "Footwashing: Its Practice and Meaning," 45.
153. Lisa P. Stephenson, "Getting Our Feet Wet: The Politics of Footwashing," in *Pentecostal Ecclesiology: A Reader*, ed. Chris E. W. Green (Leiden: Brill, 2016), 161–77, here 170. Stephenson quotes the Mennonite Confession of Faith (Article 13), which addresses these three aspects of footwashing.
154. Stephenson, "Getting Our Feet Wet," 173.

requires a very intimate act of touching that makes the persistence of grudges and individual or social enmity difficult. Bodies are exposed in ways that enable honesty and equality. Footwashing provides a regular setting in which members of the community are forced to interact in a sentient and personal way with one another."[155] As a pastor who has led and shared in footwashing, I can witness to the experiential truth of this last statement. I have seen longtime grudges begin to melt away in tears when individuals wash each other's feet. Can this be done in other ways? Perhaps. Yet the church in the twenty-first century needs to be a bastion of genuine, authentic relationality. We must witness to the love that Christ has shown us by living out in public witness what has been done for us and in us. What better way to demonstrate equality and humility than the intimate act of footwashing? To be sure, it is not a beautiful ritual in the eyes of the world, but for those of us who have seen it in operation, it demonstrates the power and wisdom of God, which reverses the power and wisdom of the world. Many churches today (especially some Protestant evangelical churches) speak to the intellectual needs of people but do little to engage the entire body with the symbols of the faith. By engaging the participatory Christian practices, the entire array of senses are brought into the event of Christ's life and death, thereby helping to shape our own lives in the form of Christ. Footwashing seems especially effective in such engagement of the senses and bodily action, which points to the fact that our lives as Christians are not only internal and spiritual but external and physical.[156]

I see a dual meaning in Jesus's action: the humbling of oneself to wash and serve another and a reminder of the cleansing promised through the blood of Christ by participation in this practice. As with the previous two practices discussed, footwashing is a *human act* based on the prior action of Jesus's example (both in the incarnation and in this event of footwashing recorded in John 13). By performing this act, we participate in the humility of Christ and remind ourselves of the promise of cleansing from sins after baptism.

Whereas baptism and the Lord's Supper focus mainly on Christ's death and resurrection, footwashing causes us to focus on Christ's incarnation and humble life. The Spirit clearly allows us to see the life of Christ re-presented in

155. Stephenson, "Getting Our Feet Wet," 173–74.

156. As noted earlier, I fully recognize the logistical problems involved in preparing and engaging in footwashing for an entire congregation. Why not activate footwashing in small groups, house churches, and the like? While churches have prioritized equipment for indoor baptismal pools and communion sets that serve the people, they have not seen fit to incorporate basins and towels into their budgets or architectural considerations. Perhaps someday churches will have both the desire and the genius to figure out ways of bringing this most servant-like participatory practice into our corporate gatherings rather than merely leaving it as an ancient symbolic gesture of service.

the act of stooping, washing, and serving. In addition, baptism and the Lord's Supper require us to look both backward and forward, as we have seen. They are rituals of remembrance and yet also rituals of hope, involving us in the new eschatological age. The ritual of footwashing seems to focus neither on the past nor on the future, but *on the present*—namely, on how believers are to live their lives now on this earth in relation to other humans. By participating in this practice, the Spirit traces Christ's humility as a pattern on our own hearts and bodies, thereby making us more likely to participate in and reenact the servant-like attitude of Christ in our own present setting. Therefore, I see footwashing as a vital practice in the church—especially in today's world. While we do not wash our visitors' feet upon entry into our houses in modern life, we still can appreciate the humility required to stoop and wash another's feet. This participatory Christian practice helps to shape the character of Christ in our own lives together as well as to nurture the promise of Christ's forgiveness and cleansing for sins committed while we live and walk through this world.

Concluding Thoughts

The mission of Christ while he was on earth has been extended through his people. We bring the presence of Christ with us whenever we minister or serve those in need of the gospel message with whatever goods we may have to share. At the end of the book *The People of God's Presence*, I placed a discussion of the Word of God directly after the discussion of the mission of the church. I did so because the Word of God is fundamental to our existence as a church, but it is especially fundamental as an instrument through which the Spirit works in us to develop the character of God, which we encounter in his presence together. Similarly, I have placed a discussion on the participatory Christian practices at the end of this book because these practices that Christ ordained provide the entire body of Christ a way to embed and embody our faith deep within the "muscle memory" of our lives. Just as the Word of God deepens our understanding of who this God is who has met with us and commands us to go into all the world, so too the Christian practices of baptism, communion, and footwashing deepen our experience of this God as we act out key aspects of our Lord's life, death, burial, and resurrection in our gathered assemblies. Remembering the importance of the Word of God and Christian practices, the people of God's presence learn to hear God's voice together and to trace the character of Christ's life in our own lives. Gathered by the Spirit, we are built up by the Word and these corporate, bodily practices so that we may be sent out into the world of our everyday lives in the power of the Spirit and the presence of Christ.

Conclusion

The Jazz of Leading the Church

The ministry of Jesus Christ continues in the ministry of the people of God's presence through the paracletic empowerment of the Holy Spirit to service in the world, thereby ministering the presence of the crucified and risen Lord to a world broken by sin, for the purpose of glorifying God the Father.[1] This statement has been a guiding thesis for this book. As part of the universal priesthood of believers, Christians are called by God not to sit on a pew but to go forth into the world, continuing the ministry of Jesus Christ through the power of the Spirit, bringing God's holy presence into unholy situations, broken relationships, systemic sin and injustice, and individual suffering.

This is the mission of the people of God, who have experienced God's presence and are being transformed into the character of Christ through encounters together in the Spirit. Central to our transformation and mission together is worship—we gather together to experience God's direct presence and are transformed through these encounters and corporate practices. We experience life together in local congregations through upbuilding each other in the training ground of the church. As a priesthood of believers, we learn as a congregation how to do the work of ministry to which we are all called. Leaders are meant to guide us into discerning our own part to play in the mission of the church. The Spirit distributes gifts throughout the body of

---

1. This statement owes much to Ray S. Anderson, "A Theology of Ministry," in *Theological Foundations for Ministry: Selected Readings for a Theology of the Church in Ministry*, ed. Ray S. Anderson (Grand Rapids: Eerdmans, 1979); also Anderson, *The Shape of Practical Theology: Empowering Ministry with Theological Praxis* (Downers Grove, IL: InterVarsity, 2001).

Christ so that fellow believers and the world may be served well. It is in the sending out of the local congregation to do the work of their own ministry that the mission of God can be accomplished.

In all of this gathering, upbuilding, and sending, the vital dimension is learning to make room for God's presence among us so that we can thereby make room for God and others in our service. However, the structures we utilize to give form to the life together of our churches must reflect the other-regarding nature of the Triune God. Just as there is no hierarchy in the life of the Trinity, so there is no hierarchy in the life of God's people. There are leaders, to be sure, but Christian leaders are marked by the kenotic spirit of Christ, who came to serve and not be served. Just as the Son of God humbled himself to become human, so, too, the daughters and sons of God are to humble themselves in service of God and others. As Jesus said, "I am among you as one who serves" (Luke 22:27). It is time for the visible structures of our church to reflect more accurately the nature of our Lord's servant leadership.

Along with the structural scaffolding of the local congregation's life together, leaders form a critical aspect of service. They are not meant to be priests—the people of God are that together. They are not meant to be autocrats—the way of the world dominates others in such an over/under hierarchical model. Leaders are to model servanthood—the way Christ modeled service to his disciples. It is time for the leaders of congregations to reflect more genuinely the nature of our Lord's life and ministry.

The challenges facing the church of this century in Western societies are good for us. They demand more genuine vulnerability about how Christians really struggle in these difficult times. They demand more unpretentious responses to charges of irrelevancy. In the end, they demand that the church *be the church* and live up to the expectations of its Lord. If this drives Christian congregations back to the drawing board to reenvision better ways to live together as believers both among ourselves and with the world, then these challenges are good for us.

It has been my contention that this is too important a task awaiting us to attempt it without serious biblical engagement and theological dialogue. The radical nature of my proposals in this book has been crafted with precisely these challenges in mind. I have engaged both biblical and theological inquiries for the purpose of placing some of our long-held traditions under rather discomforting searchlights so that we may engage in self-examination and perhaps repent of ways that we have disguised rather than revealed the true nature of the church. A key to this investigation has been the biblically grounded concept of the universal priesthood of all believers—that we *all* are ministers/servants. The structures of leadership in our local congregations must encourage and equip the people of God to do the work of ministry. If this happens, then congregations will become active in their participation with God and others in the body of Christ. It is the leadership in any congregation, therefore, that holds the key to answering the challenges of this century concerning irrelevancy and inauthenticity by leading the way for God's people to understand their giftedness from the Spirit so they might fulfill their ministry functions as priests before God on behalf of others.

Leading the people of God's presence is not a simple task. There are so many factors present in any local congregation of believers that a one-size-fits-all approach is too simplistic. How, then, can we approach leading God's people? Clark Pinnock offers some insight into this delicate function of leadership: "Leaders are important to the community, yet community must not be too tightly controlled. Leaders should not be trying to control everything but foster life and discern gifts of those under their care. Ideally there should be a harmonious synergism of gift and office, a dialectic of charism and institution, for the Spirit is given not only to officeholders but to the whole congregation."[2] To weave such a tapestry of fostering life among the congregation while at the same time guiding the entire flock is challenging indeed. Such work should be left not to a single "professional" but to those leaders who are gifted and called to it. If the focus of the congregation is on the leaders rather than Christ or each other in the body, then the flaws of human leaders will shine unobscured. If the focus of the congregation is on the communal life shared with Christ and other members in the body, then leaders will be able to operate more in keeping with the Spirit's will. Leaders in this context understand that *they* are not the focal point, but rather Christ is. The gifts of the Spirit are given to operate *throughout* the body, not just among elders, deacons, or specially named leaders. In this regard, a community where God is present is one where leaders are honored but also one where everyone is prompted to fulfill their own calling to the glory of God.

Allow me to illustrate how leading in this manner might operate. William Carter, a pastor who is also a jazz musician, has described leading a church similar to the functioning of a jazz quartet. First, "a leader recognizes that a community has more gifts than an individual."[3] The unique feature of jazz ensembles is based precisely on this point: all three or four of the players

2. Clark Pinnock, *Flame of Love: A Theology of the Holy Spirit* (Downers Grove, IL: InterVarsity, 1996), 140.

3. William G. Carter, "Singing a New Song: The Gospel and Jazz," *Princeton Seminary Bulletin*, n.s., 19, no. 1 (1998): 48.

understand that their "community" produces something greater than one individual or simply its parts combined.

Second, "sometimes a leader must get out of the way and let other people do what they do best."[4] Leadership does not mean that the leader does everything! This is especially true if the leaders understand that their task has shifted from frenetic activity to careful, thoughtful discernment that nurtures ministries among the gifted individuals in the body of Christ. What happens with jazz as a result of this "making room" for others is a wonderful mixture of disciplined yet free music. The leader chooses the tune and tempo and then gets out of the way. As Carter comments, "This can only happen when the leader dares to trust everybody else. And if this should happen, work becomes like play."[5] What happens when church leaders foster, nurture, and release people into their ministries is a wonderful mixture of the free work of the Holy Spirit in the lives of people and the disciplined training to take the leader's cue and improvise within the established boundaries of the Word of God. A jazz musician must know how to play written notes but must equally know how the chords and notes connect to each other so that improvisation can occur, creating a new song. Composing and performing occur at the same time. It is risky, but if there is trust and discipline in the trio or quartet, it can become a thing of sheer delight.

In a jazz quartet (saxophone, piano, bass, and drums), the musicians collaborate in a collegial manner, always listening closely to the other players while at the same time knowing precisely what they themselves are playing. A jazz quartet is not about individual effort but is rather a team approach where one may take a lead part now and another may take lead later. While each "lead" is playing their "solo," the other three must follow along, filling in and backing it up. Without them playing along, the lead solo would sound hollow. This is a fine depiction of what the New Testament understands by leadership in the church. Carter makes this stunning challenge:

> Can you imagine music like this? Can you imagine a church that works like this? Only if God is God, and only if we relinquish all pretense and abandon all rigidity. Where did we ever get the idea that pews should be nailed to the floor? Why did we ever allow preachers (like myself!) to imply that worship should overdose on words? How did we ever develop forms of ministry that actually quench the Holy Spirit? Maybe the one thing most needful for us is to repent. To turn around. To come home. To fall in love with the One who

4. Carter, "Singing a New Song," 48.
5. Carter, "Singing a New Song," 49.

first loved us. God's new song can change us—provided we are willing to be changed.[6]

Like the Triune God who "makes room for" each of the persons of the Trinity, can the people of God's presence learn to "make room for" the gifts and callings of each other so that the mission of Christ may be fulfilled on earth? Given the challenges we face in this era, can we do less?

6. Carter, "Singing a New Song," 49–50.

Select Bibliography

Achtemeier, Paul J. *1 Peter: A Commentary on First Peter.* Hermeneia. Minneapolis: Fortress, 1996.

Adewuya, J. Ayodeji. *Holiness and Community in 2 Corinthians 6:14–7:1: Paul's View of Communal Holiness in the Corinthian Correspondence.* Studies in Biblical Literature. New York: Peter Lang, 2003.

Aland, Kurt. *Die Säulingstaufe im Neuen Testament und in der Alten Kirche.* Munich: Kaiser, 1961. Translated by G. R. Beasley-Murray as *Did the Early Church Baptize Infants?* The Library of History and Doctrine. Eugene, OR: Wipf & Stock, 2004.

———. *Die Stellung der Kinder in den frühen christlichen Gemeinden—und ihre Taufe.* Munich: Kaiser, 1967.

———. *The Shape of Practical Theology: Empowering Ministry with Theological Praxis.* Downers Grove, IL: InterVarsity, 2001.

———. *Taufe und Kindertaufe.* Gütersloh: Gütersloher Verlagshaus, 1971.

Anderson, Ray S. *Historical Transcendence and the Reality of God: A Christological Critique.* Grand Rapids: Eerdmans, 1975.

———, ed. *Theological Foundations for Ministry: Selected Readings for a Theology of the Church in Ministry.* Grand Rapids: Eerdmans, 1979.

Archer, Kenneth J. "Nourishment for Our Journey: The Pentecostal *Via salutis* and Sacramental Ordinances." In *Pentecostal Ecclesiology: A Reader*, edited by Chris E. W. Green, 144–60. Leiden: Brill, 2016.

Arrington, French L. *The Acts of the Apostles: Introduction, Translation, and Commentary.* Peabody, MA: Hendrickson, 1988.

Avis, Paul. *A Ministry Shaped by Mission.* Edinburgh: T&T Clark, 2005.

Baillie, Donald M., *A Theology of the Sacraments and Other Papers.* New York: Scribner's Sons, 1957.

241

Baptism, Eucharist and Ministry. Faith and Order Paper 111. Geneva: World Council of Churches, 1982.

Barth, Karl. *Church Dogmatics.* Edited by T. F. Torrance and G. W. Bromiley. Translated by G. W. Bromiley et al. 13 vols. Edinburgh: T&T Clark, 1936–68.

———. "The Church—the Living Congregation of the Living Lord Jesus Christ." In *God Here and Now*, translated by Paul M. van Buren, 75–104. New York: Harper & Row, 1964.

———. *Die christliche Lehre nach dem Heidelberger Katechismus: Vorlesung gehalten an der Universität Bonn im Sommersemester 1947.* Munich: Kaiser, 1949. Translated by Shirley C. Guthrie Jr. as *The Heidelberg Catechism for Today*. Richmond: John Knox, 1964.

Belleville, Linda L. "Women in Ministry: An Egalitarian Perspective." In Gundry, *Two Views on Women in Ministry*, 19–103.

Bender, Kimlyn J. *Karl Barth's Christological Ecclesiology.* Barth Studies Series, edited by John Webster, George Hunsinger, and Hans-Anton Drewes. Burlington, VT: Ashgate, 2005.

Blenkinsopp, Joseph. "On Clericalism." *Cross Currents* 17, no. 1 (Winter 1967): 15–23.

———. "Presbyter to Priest: Ministry in the Early Church." *Worship* 41, no. 7 (August-September 1967): 428–38.

Blomberg, Craig L. "Women in Ministry: A Complementarian Perspective." In Gundry, *Two Views on Women in Ministry*, 121–84.

Bonhoeffer, Dietrich. *Discipleship.* Edited by Geffrey B. Kelly and John D. Godsey. Translated by Barbara Green and Reinhard Kraus. Dietrich Bonhoeffer Works 4. Minneapolis: Fortress, 2003.

Bourdieu, Pierre. *The Logic of Practice.* Translated by Richard Nice. Stanford, CA: Stanford University Press, 1990.

Bradshaw, Paul F. *Rites of Ordination: Their History and Theology.* Collegeville, MN: Liturgical Press, 2013.

Branson, Mark Lau. "Forming Church, Forming Mission." *International Review of Mission* 92, no. 365 (April 2003): 153–68.

———. "Forming God's People." *Congregations* 29, no. 1 (Winter 2003): 23–27.

Brown, Raymond E. *Priest and Bishop: Biblical Reflections.* New York: Paulist Press, 1970.

Brunner, Emil. *Die Mißverständnis der Kirche.* Stuttgart: Evangelisches Verlagswerk, 1951. Translated by Harold Knight as *The Misunderstanding of the Church*. Philadelphia: Westminster, 1953.

Burgess, Stanley M. *The Holy Spirit: Ancient Christian Traditions.* Peabody, MA: Hendrickson, 1984.

Burke, Patrick. "The Monarchical Episcopate at the End of the First Century." *Journal of Ecumenical Studies* 7, no. 3 (Summer 1970): 499–518.

Calvin, John. *Institutes of the Christian Religion*. Edited by John T. McNeill. Translated by Ford Lewis Battles. 2 vols. Library of Christian Classics 21–22. Philadelphia: Westminster, 1975.

———. *Petit Traicté de la Saincte Cene de Nostre Seigneur Jesus Christ*. Vol. 1 of *Johannis Calvini Opera selecta*, edited by Peter Barth, Wilhelm Niesel, and Dora Scheuner. 5 vols. Munich: Kaiser, 1926–52.

———. *Short Treatise on the Supper of Our Lord in Which Is Shown Its True Institution, Benefit, and Utility*. Translated by Henry Beveridge. In *Tracts*, edited by Henry Beveridge. Vol. 2, pt. 2 of *John Calvin: Tracts and Letters*. Carlisle, PA: Banner of Truth Trust, 2009.

Campbell, Alister. *The Elders: Seniority within Earliest Christianity*. Studies of the New Testament and Its World, edited by John Riches. Edinburgh: T&T Clark, 1994.

Cervin, Richard S. "Does Κεφαλή Mean 'Source' or 'Authority Over' in Greek Literature? A Rebuttal." *Trinity Journal* 10 (1989): 85–112.

Chopp, Rebecca S. "Praxis." In *The New Dictionary of Catholic Spirituality*, edited by Michael Downey, 756–64. Collegeville, MN: Liturgical Press, 1993.

———. *The Praxis of Suffering: An Interpretation of Liberation and Political Theologies*. Eugene, OR: Wipf & Stock, 1986.

Collins, John N. *Are All Christians Ministers?* Collegeville, MN: Liturgical Press, 1992.

———. *Deacons and the Church: Making Connections between Old and New*. Harrisburg, PA: Morehouse, 2002.

———. *Diakonia: Re-interpreting the Ancient Sources*. New York: Oxford University Press, 1990.

———. "A Monocultural Usage: διακον—Words in Classical, Hellenistic, and Patristic Sources." *Vigiliae Christianae* 66 (2012): 287–309.

———. "Ordained and Other Ministries: Making a Difference." *Ecclesiology* 3, no. 1 (2006): 11–32.

———. "Re-interpreting *Diakonia* in Germany." *Ecclesiology* 5 (2009): 69–81.

Cross, Terry L. "Let the Church Be the Church: Barth and Pentecostals on Ecclesiology." In *Karl Barth and Pentecostal Theology: A Convergence of Word and Spirit*, edited by Frank Macchia, Andrew Gabriel, and Terry L. Cross. Systematic Pentecostal and Charismatic Theology Series, edited by Wolfgang Vondey and Daniela Augustine. New York: Bloomsbury, forthcoming.

———. *The People of God's Presence: An Introduction to Ecclesiology*. Grand Rapids: Baker Academic, 2019

"Danvers Statement, The, (1987): The Council on Biblical Manhood and Womanhood." In Piper and Grudem, *Recovering Biblical Manhood and Womanhood*, 469–72.

Dean, Kendra Creasy, and Ron Foster. *The Godbearing Life: The Art of Soul Tending for Youth Ministry*. Nashville: Upper Room Books, 1998.

Dean-Jones, Lesley. "The Cultural Construct of the Female Body in Classical Greek Science." In *Women's History and Ancient History*, edited by Sarah B. Pomeroy, 111–37. Chapel Hill: University of North Carolina Press, 1991.

Decree on the Ministry and Life of Priests (Presbyterorum Ordinis). In *Vatican Council II: The Conciliar and Post Conciliar Documents*, edited by Austin Flannery. Collegeville, MN: Liturgical Press, 1975.

Decretum de presbyterorum ministerio et vita (07 December 1965). In *Dogmatic Constitutions, Declarations, Decrees of the Second Vatican Council, 1962–1965 (Latin and English)*. Compiled by Kevin Simmons. Morrisville, NC: Lulu, 2012.

Dunn, James D. G. *Romans 1–8*. WBC 38A. Nashville: Thomas Nelson, 1988.

———. *Romans 9–16*. WBC 38B. Nashville: Thomas Nelson, 1988.

———. *A Theology of Paul the Apostle*. Grand Rapids: Eerdmans, 1998.

Dykstra, Craig. *Growing in the Life of Faith: Education and Christian Practices*. Louisville: Geneva, 1999.

Dykstra, Craig, and Dorothy C. Bass. "Times of Yearning. Practices of Faith." In *Practicing Our Faith: A Way of Life for a Searching People*, edited by Dorothy C. Bass, 1–12. San Francisco: Jossey-Bass, 1997.

Eastwood, Cyril. *The Priesthood of All Believers: An Examination of the Doctrine from the Reformation to the Present Day*. Eugene, OR: Wipf & Stock, 1960.

Faivre, Alexandre. "Clerc/laïc: Histoire d'une Frontière." *Revue des Sciences Religieuses* 57, no. 3 (1983): 195–220.

———. *The Emergence of the Laity in the Early Church*. Translated by David Smith. New York: Paulist Press, 1990.

———. "Préceptes laïcs (λαϊκὰ προστάγματα) et commandements humains (ἐμτάματα ἀνθρώπων): Les Fondements scripturaires de *1 Clement* 40:5." *Revue des Sciences Religieuses* 75, no. 3 (2001): 288–308.

———. "Quelques études sur la question des ministères." *Revue des Sciences Religieuses* 47, no. 1 (1973): 133–48.

Fee, Gordon D. *The First Epistle to the Corinthians*. NICNT. Grand Rapids: Eerdmans, 1987.

Ferguson, Everett. *Baptism in the Early Church: History, Theology, and Liturgy in the First Five Centuries*. Grand Rapids: Eerdmans, 2009.

———. "Laying On of Hands: Its Significance in Ordination." In *Ministry, Ordination, Covenant, and Canon*, 160–72. Vol. 1 of *The Early Church at Work and Worship*. Eugene, OR: Cascade Books, 2013.

———. "Ordination in the Ancient Church: IV; Ordination in the First Century." In *Ministry, Ordination, Covenant, and Canon*, 92–110. Vol. 1 of *The Early Church at Work and Worship*. Eugene, OR: Cascade Books, 2013.

Fox, Robin Lane. *Pagans and Christians*. New York: Knopf, 1987.

France, R. T. *The Gospel of Mark: A Commentary on the Greek Text*. NIGTC. Grand Rapids: Eerdmans, 2002.

Freire, Paulo. *Pedagogy of the Oppressed*. Translated by Myra Bergman Ramos. New York: Continuum, 2002.

Furnish, Victor P. *II Corinthians: Translated with Introduction, Notes and Commentary*. Anchor Bible 32A. Garden City: Doubleday, 1984.

Gibaut, John St. H. *The Cursus Honorum: A Study and Evolution of Sequential Ordination*. New York: Peter Lang, 2000.

Gibson, David. "Fathers of Faith, My Fathers Now! On Abraham and the Theology of Paedobaptism." *Themelios* 40, no. 1 (April 2015): 14–34.

Giles, Kevin. *Jesus and the Father: Modern Evangelicals Reinvent the Doctrine of the Trinity*. Grand Rapids: Zondervan, 2006.

———. *Patterns of Ministry among the First Christians*. 2nd ed. Eugene, OR: Cascade Books, 2017.

———. *The Rise and Fall of the Complementarian Doctrine of the Trinity*. Eugene, OR: Cascade Books, 2017.

———. *The Trinity and Subordinationism: The Doctrine of God and the Contemporary Gender Debate*. Downers Grove, IL: InterVarsity, 2002.

Gooder, Paula. "*Diakonia* in the New Testament: A Dialogue with John N. Collins." *Ecclesiology* 3, no. 1 (2006): 33–56.

Grass, Hans. *Die Abendmahlslehre bei Luther und Calvin: Eine kritische Untersuchung*. In Beiträge zur Förderung christlicher Theologie, edited by Paul Althaus, Hermann Dörries, and Joachim Jeremias, 2nd ser., vol. 47. Gütersloh: Bertelsmann, 1954.

Greggs, Tom. *Dogmatic Ecclesiology*. Vol. 1, *The Priestly Catholicity of the Church*. Grand Rapids: Baker Academic, 2019.

Green, Chris E. W. *Toward a Pentecostal Theology of the Lord's Supper: Foretasting the Kingdom*. Cleveland: CPT, 2012.

Grenz, Stanley J. "Biblical Priesthood and Women in Ministry." In Pierce and Groothuis, *Discovering Biblical Equality*, 272–86.

Groothuis, Rebecca Merrill. "Equal in Being, Unequal in Role: Exploring the Logic of Women's Subordination." In Pierce and Groothuis, *Discovering Biblical Equality*, 301–33.

Grudem, Wayne. "Appendix 1: The Meaning of *Kephalē* ('Head'): A Response to Recent Studies." In Piper and Grudem, *Recovering Biblical Manhood and Womanhood*, 425–68.

———. "Does *Kephalē* Mean 'Source' or 'Authority Over' in Greek Literature? A Survey of 2,336 Examples." *Trinity Journal* 6 (Spring 1985): 38–59.

———. "Prophecy—Yes, but Teaching—No: Paul's Consistent Advocacy of Women's Participation without Governing Authority." *Journal of the Evangelical Theological Society* 30, no. 1 (March 1987):11–23.

Gundry, Stanley, ed. *Two Views on Women in Ministry*. Counterpoints: Exploring Theology, edited by James Beck. Grand Rapids: Zondervan, 2005.

Gunton, Colin E. *Act and Being: Towards a Theology of the Divine Attributes*. Grand Rapids: Eerdmans, 2002.

Guthrie, Shirley C. *Christian Doctrine*. Atlanta: John Knox, 1968.

Haendler, Gerd. *Luther on Ministerial Office and Congregational Function*. Edited by Eric Gritsch. Translated by Ruth Gritsch. Philadelphia: Fortress, 1981.

Harper, Bradley, and Paul Louis Metzger. *Exploring Ecclesiology: An Evangelical and Ecumenical Introduction*. Grand Rapids: Baker Academic, 2009.

Harris, Murray. *The Second Epistle to the Corinthians: A Commentary on the Greek Text*. NIGTC. Grand Rapids: Eerdmans, 2005.

Harvey, A. E. "Elders." *Journal of Theological Studies*, n.s., 25 (1974): 318–32.

Hatch, Edwin. *The Organization of the Early Christian Churches: Eight Lectures, Delivered before the University of Oxford, in the Year 1880*. London: Longmans, Green, 1918.

Healy, Nicholas M. "The Logic of Karl Barth's Ecclesiology: Analysis, Assessment and Proposed Modifications." *Modern Theology* 10, no. 3 (July 1994): 253–70.

Hess, Richard S. "Equality with and without Innocence: Genesis 1–3." In Pierce and Groothuis, *Discovering Biblical Equality*, 79–95.

Hilbert, Gerhard. *Ecclesiola in Ecclesia: Luthers Anschauungen von Volkskirke und Freiwilligeitskirche in ihrer Bedeutung für die Gegenwart*. Leipzig: Deichert, 1920.

Hurley, James B. "Did Paul Require Veils or the Silence of Women? A Consideration of 1 Cor. 11:2–16 and 1 Cor. 14:33b–36." *Westminster Theological Journal* 35, no. 2 (Winter 1973): 190–220.

Jefford, Clayton N. "Understanding the Concept of Deacon in the *Didache*." In Koet, Murphy, and Ryökäs, *Deacons and Diakonia in Early Christianity*, 203–14.

Jeremias, Joachim. *Die Kindertaufe in den ersten vier Jahrhunderten*. Göttingen: Vandenhoeck & Ruprecht, 1958.

———. *Infant Baptism in the First Four Centuries*. Translated by David Cairns. London: SCM, 1960.

———. *Nochmals: Die Anfange der Kindertaufe*. Munich: Kaiser, 1962.

———. *The Origins of Infant Baptism: A Further Study in Reply to Kurt Aland*. Translated by Dorothea M. Barton. Eugene, OR: Wipf & Stock, 2004; orig. ed. 1962.

Jewett, Robert. *Romans: A Commentary*. Hermeneia. Minneapolis: Fortress, 2007.

Johnson, Mark. *The Meaning of the Body: Aesthetics of Human Understanding*. Chicago: University of Chicago Press, 2007.

Jones, Beth Felker. *Practicing Christian Doctrine: An Introduction to Thinking and Living Theologically*. Grand Rapids: Baker Academic, 2014.

Keener, Craig S. *Acts: An Exegetical Commentary*. 4 vols. Grand Rapids: Baker Academic, 2012–15.

———. *Paul, Women, and Wives: Marriage and Women's Ministry in the Letters of Paul.* 2nd ed. Grand Rapids: Baker Academic, 2013.

Knight, George W., III. "Husbands and Wives as Analogues of Christ and the Church: Ephesians 5:21–33 and Colossians 3:18–19." In Piper and Grudem, *Recovering Biblical Manhood and Womanhood,* 165–78.

Knight, Henry H., III. *The Presence of God in the Christian Life: John Wesley and the Means of Grace.* Pietist and Wesleyan Studies, edited by David Bundy and J. Steven O'Malley, no. 3. Lanham, MD: Scarecrow, 1992.

Koet, Bart J. "Dreaming about Deacons in the *Passio Perpetuae.*" In Koet, Murphy, and Ryökäs, *Deacons and Diakonia in Early Christianity,* 255–72.

———. "Isaiah 60:17 as a Key for Understanding the Two-Fold Ministry of Ἐπίσκόποι and Διάκονοι according to First Clement (*1 Clem.* 42:5)." In Koet, Murphy, and Ryökäs, *Deacons and Diakonia in Early Christianity,* 177–92.

Koet, Bart J., Edwina Murphy, and Esko Ryökäs, eds. *Deacons and Diakonia in Early Christianity.* WUNT, 2nd ser., 479. Tübingen: Mohr Siebeck, 2018.

Köstenberger, Andreas. "A Complex Sentence Structure in 1 Timothy 2:12." In *Women in the Church: A Fresh Analysis of 1 Timothy 2:9–15,* edited by Andreas Köstenberger, Thomas R. Schreiner, and H. Scott Baldwin, 117–62. 3rd ed. Wheaton: Crossway, 2016.

Laato, Anni Maria. "Tertullian and the Deacons." In Koet, Murphy, and Ryökäs, *Deacons and Diakonia in Early Christianity,* 245–54.

Lane, William L. *Hebrews 1–8.* Edited by Ralph P. Martin. WBC 47a. Dallas: Word Books, 1991.

———. *Hebrews 9–13.* Edited by Ralph P. Martin. WBC 47b. Dallas: Word Books, 1991.

Lieberg, Hellmut. *Amt und Ordination bei Luther und Melanchthon.* Göttingen: Vandenhoeck & Ruprecht, 1962.

Liefeld, Walter L. "Women, Submission and Ministry in 1 Corinthians." In *Women, Authority and the Bible,* edited by Alvera Mickelsen, 134–53. Downers Grove, IL: InterVarsity, 1986.

Lohse, Bernhard. *Martin Luther's Theology: Its Historical and Systematic Development.* Translated by Roy A. Harrisville. Minneapolis: Fortress, 1999.

Long, Thomas G. "Words, Words, Words: Baccalaureate Sermon, 1991." *Princeton Seminary Bulletin* 12, no. 3 (1991): 314–19.

Longenecker, Richard N. *The Epistle to the Romans.* NIGTC. Grand Rapids: Eerdmans, 1996.

Luther, Martin. *An den christlichen Adel Deutscher Nation: von des christlichen Standes Besserung (1520).* In *Reformatorische Schriften.* Vol. 1 of *Luthers Werke,* edited by Prof. Buchwald, Prof. Kawerau, Julius Köstlin, M. Räde, and Ew. Schneider. 3rd ed. Berlin: Schwetschke und Sohn, 1905.

————. *Answer to the Hyperchristian, Hyperspiritual, and Hyper-Learned Book by Goat Emser in Leipzig—Including Some Thoughts regarding His Companion, the Fool Murner (1521).* Translated by Eric W. Gritsch and Ruth C. Gritsch. In *Church and Ministry I*, edited by Eric W. Gritsch. Vol. 39 of *Luther's Works*, edited by Helmut T. Lehmann. Philadelphia: Fortress, 1970.

————. *The Babylonian Captivity of the Church (1520).* Translated by A. T. W. Steinhäuser, Frederick C. Ahrens, and Abdel Ross Wentz. In *Word and Sacrament II*, edited by Abdel Ross Wentz. Vol. 36 of *Luther's Works*, edited by Helmut T. Lehmann. Philadelphia: Fortress, 1959.

————. *Concerning the Ministry (1523).* Translated by Conrad Bergendoff. In *Church and Ministry II*, edited by Conrad Bergendoff. Vol. 40 of *Luther's Works*, edited by Helmut T. Lehmann. Philadelphia: Fortress, 1958.

————. *Daß eine christliche Versammlung oder Gemeinde Recht und Macht habe, alle Lehre zu Beurteilen und Lehre zu berufen, ein- und abzusetzen: Grund und Ursache aus der Schrift (1523).* In *Martin Luther: Kirche und Gemeinde.* Vol. 6 of *Luther Deutsch: Die Werke Martin Luthers in neuer Auswahl für die Gegenwart*, edited by Kurt Aland. Göttingen: Vandenhoeck & Ruprecht, 1983.

————. *De instituendis ministris ecclesiae ad clarissimum Senatum Pragensem Bohemiae (1523).* In *Varii Argumenti, Ad Reformationis Historiam (1521–1523)*, edited by Henricus Schmidt. Vol. 6 of *D. Martini Lutheri Opera Latina.* Frankfurt am Main: Heyderi et Zimmeri, 1872.

————. *The Sacrament of Penance (1519).* Translated by E. Theodore Bachmann. In *Word and Sacrament I*, edited by E. Theodore Bachmann, 3–22. Vol. 35 of *Luther's Works*, edited by Helmut T. Lehmann. Philadelphia: Muhlenberg, 1960.

————. *That These Words of Christ, "This Is My Body," Etc., Still Stand Firm against the Fanatics (1527).* Edited by Amy Nelson Burnett. Translated by Robert Fischer and Amy Nelson Burnett. In *Church and Sacraments*, edited by Paul W. Robinson. Vol. 3 of *The Annotated Luther*, edited by Hans J. Hillerbrand, Kirsi I. Stjerna, and Timothy J. Wengert. Minneapolis: Fortress, 2016.

————. *To the Christian Nobility of the German Nation concerning the Improvement of the Christian Estate (1520).* Translated by Charles M. Jacobs, James Atkinson, and James M. Estes. In *The Roots of Reform*, edited by Timothy J. Wengert. Vol. 1 of *The Annotated Luther*, edited by Hans J. Hillerbrand, Kirsi I. Stjerna, and Timothy J. Wengert. 5 vols. Minneapolis: Fortress, 2015.

Macchia, Frank D. *Baptized in the Spirit: A Global Pentecostal Theology.* Grand Rapids: Zondervan, 2006.

MacIntyre, Alasdair. *After Virtue: A Study in Moral Theory.* Notre Dame, IN: University of Notre Dame Press, 1981.

Mangina, Joseph L. *Karl Barth: Theologian of Christian Witness.* Louisville: Westminster John Knox, 2004.

Marcel, Gabriel. *Faith and Reality.* Vol. 2 of *The Mystery of Being*, translated by G. S. Fraser. The Gifford Lectures, 1949–50. South Bend, IN: St. Augustine's Press, 1950.

———. "On the Ontological Mystery." In *The Philosophy of Existentialism*, translated by Manya Harari, 9–46. New York: Citadel, 1956.

Marshall, I. Howard. *The Gospel of Luke: A Commentary on the Greek Text*. NIGTC. Grand Rapids: Eerdmans, 1978.

———. "Mutual Love and Submission in Marriage: Colossians 3:18–19 and Ephesians 5:21–33." In Pierce and Groothuis, *Discovering Biblical Equality*, 186–204.

Marshall, Jill E. *Women Praying and Prophesying in Corinth: Gender and Inspired Speech in First Corinthians*. WUNT, 2nd ser., 448. Tübingen: Mohr Siebeck, 2017.

Matthews, Alice. *Gender Roles and the People of God: Rethinking What We Were Taught about Men and Women in the Church*. Grand Rapids: Zondervan, 2017.

McLelland, Joseph. "Lutheran-Reformed Debate on the Eucharist and Christology." In *Christology, the Lord's Supper and Its Observance in the Church*. Vol. 2 of *Re-examination of Luther and Reformed Traditions*. New York: North American Area of the World Alliance of Reformed Churches and the USA National Committee of the Lutheran World Federation, 1964.

Merleau-Ponty, Maurice. *Phenomenology of Perception*. Translated by Donald A. Landes. New York: Routledge, 2014.

Migliore, Daniel L. *The Power of God and the gods of Power*. Louisville: Westminster John Knox, 2008.

Moltmann, Jürgen. *The Church in the Power of the Spirit: A Contribution to Messianic Ecclesiology*. Translated by Margaret Kohl. Minneapolis: Fortress, 1993.

Moo, Douglas J. *The Epistle to the Romans*. NICNT. Grand Rapids: Eerdmans, 1996.

———. "The Interpretation of 1 Timothy 2:11–15: A Rejoinder." *Trinity Journal*, n.s., 2 (1981): 198–222.

Moschos, Dimitrios. "Rezensionen: Alistair C. Stewart, *The Original Bishops*." *Zeitschrift für Antikes Christentum* 20, no. 3 (2016): 524–27.

Mottu, Henry. "Les sacrements selon Karl Barth et Eberhard Jüngel." *Foi et Vie* 88, no. 2 (April 1989): 33–55.

Mowezko, Margaret. "What Did Phoebe's Position and Ministry as Διάκονος of the Church at Cenchrea Involve?" In Koet, Murphy, and Ryökäs, *Deacons and Diakonia in Early Christianity*, 91–102.

Murphy-O'Connor, Jerome. "Corinthian Slogans in 1 Cor 6:12–20." *Catholic Biblical Quarterly* 40, no. 3 (1978): 391–96.

Muthiah, Robert A. *The Priesthood of All Believers in the Twenty-First Century: Living Faithfully as the Whole People of God in a Postmodern Context*. Eugene, OR: Pickwick, 2009.

Nature and Purpose of the Church: A Stage on the Way to a Common Statement. Faith and Order Paper 181. Geneva: World Council of Churches, 1998.

Nauck, Wolfgang. "Probleme des frühchristlichen Amtsverstandnisses (1 Ptr. 5:2f.)." *Zeitschrift für neutestamentliche Wissenschaft und die Kunde der älteren Kirche* 48, nos. 3–4 (1957): 200–220.

Niebuhr, Richard R. "Symbols in Reflection on God and Ourselves." *Princeton Seminary Bulletin* 20, no. 2 (1999): 127–49.

Niesel, Wilhelm. *Calvins Lehre vom Abendmahl.* 2nd ed. Forschungen zur Geschichte und Lehre das Protestantismus 3, edited by Paul Althaus, Karl Barth, and Karl Heim. Munich: Kaiser, 1935.

Odell-Scott, David W. "Let the Women Speak in Church: An Egalitarian Interpretation of 1 Cor 14:33b–36." *Biblical Theology Bulletin* 13 (1983): 90–93.

Ogden, Greg. *The New Reformation: Returning the Ministry to the People of God.* Grand Rapids: Zondervan, 1990.

On the Apostolic Tradition: Hippolytus; An English Version with Introduction and Commentary by Alistair C. Stewart. 2nd ed. Yonkers, NY: St. Vladimir's Seminary Press, 2015.

Ortlund, Raymond C., Jr. "Male-Female Equality and Male Headship: Genesis 1–3." In Piper and Grudem, *Recovering Biblical Manhood and Womanhood,* 95–112.

Osiek, Carolyn, and Margaret Y. MacDonald. *A Woman's Place: House Churches in Earliest Christianity.* Minneapolis: Fortress, 2006.

Packer, James I. "The Nature of the Church." In *Basic Christian Doctrines,* edited by Carl F. H. Henry. Grand Rapids: Baker, 1962.

Payne, Philip B. *Man and Woman, One in Christ: An Exegetical and Theological Study of Paul's Letters.* Grand Rapids: Zondervan, 2009.

Pierce, Ronald W., and Rebecca Merrill Groothuis, eds. *Discovering Biblical Equality: Complementarity without Hierarchy.* 2nd ed. Downers Grove, IL: InterVarsity, 2005.

Pinnock, Clark. *Flame of Love: A Theology of the Holy Spirit.* Downers Grove, IL: InterVarsity, 1996.

Piper, John, and Wayne Grudem. "An Overview of Central Concerns: Questions and Answers." In Piper and Grudem, *Recovering Biblical Manhood and Womanhood,* 60–94.

———, eds. *Recovering Biblical Manhood and Womanhood: A Response to Evangelical Feminism.* Wheaton: Crossway, 1991.

Poythress, Vern S. "The Church as Family: Why Male Leadership in the Family Requires Male Leadership in the Church." In Piper and Grudem, *Recovering Biblical Manhood and Womanhood,* 233–47.

Saliers, Don E. *Worship as Theology: Foretaste of Glory Divine.* Nashville: Abingdon, 1994.

Schoedel, William R. *Ignatius of Antioch: A Commentary on the Letters of Ignatius of Antioch.* Hermeneia. Philadelphia: Fortress, 1985.

Scholer, David M. "1 Timothy 2:9–15 and the Place of Women in the Church's Ministry." In *Women, Authority and the Bible*, edited by Alvera Mickelsen, 193–224. Downers Grove, IL: InterVarsity, 1986.

Schreiner, Thomas R. "Women in Ministry: Another Complementarian Perspective." In Gundry, *Two Views on Women in Ministry*, 263–322.

Schweizer, Eduard. *Church Order in the New Testament*. Translated by Frank Clarke. Eugene, OR: Wipf & Stock, 2006.

Smith, James K. A. *Imagining the Kingdom: How Worship Works*. Cultural Liturgies 2. Grand Rapids: Baker Academic, 2013.

Snyder, Howard. *The Radical Wesley*. Downers Grove, IL: InterVarsity, 1980.

Stephenson, Lisa P. "A Feminist Pentecostal Theological Anthropology: North America and Beyond." *PNEUMA: A Journal of the Society for Pentecostal Studies* 35 (2013): 35–47.

———. "Getting Our Feet Wet: The Politics of Footwashing." In *Pentecostal Ecclesiology: A Reader*, edited by Chris E. W. Green, 161–77. Leiden: Brill, 2016.

———. "Made in the Image of God: A Theological Apologetic for Women Preachers." In *Toward a Pentecostal Theology of Preaching*, edited by Lee Roy Martin, 141–53. Cleveland: CPT, 2015.

Stevens, John. "Infant Baptism: Putting Old Wine in New Wineskins?" *Foundations: An International Journal of Evangelical Theology* 63 (Sep 2013): 18–42.

Stewart, Alistair C. *The Original Bishops: Office and Order in the First Christian Communities*. Grand Rapids: Baker Academic, 2014.

Tertullian. *De baptismo / Traité du baptême*. Edited by François Refoulé. Translated by Maurice Droozy. Sources chrétiennes 35. Paris: Cerf, 2011; orig. ed. 1952.

———. *De exhortation castitatis / Exhortation à la chasteté*. Edited by Jean-Claude Fredouille. Translated by Claudio Moreschini. Sources chrétiennes 319. Paris: Cerf, 1985.

———. *Ee praescriptione haereticorum*. Edited by François Refoulé. Translated by Pierre de Labriolle. Sources chrétiennes 46. Paris: Cerf, 1957.

———. *Tertullian's Homily on Baptism*. Edited and translated by Ernest Evans. London: SPCK, 1964.

Thiselton, Anthony C. *The First Epistle to the Corinthians: A Commentary on the Greek Text*. NIGTC. Grand Rapids: Eerdmans, 2000.

Thomas, John Christopher. *Footwashing in John 13 and the Johannine Community*. Journal for the Study of the New Testament Supplement Series 61. Sheffield: Sheffield Academic, 1991.

———. "Footwashing: Its Practice and Meaning." In *Ministry and Theology: Studies for the Church and Its Leaders*, 39–48. Cleveland: Pathway, 1996.

———. "Footwashing within the Context of the Lord's Supper." In *The Lord's Supper: Believers Church Perspectives*, edited by Dale R. Stoffer, 169–86. Scottdale, PA: Herald, 1997.

Torjesen, Karen Jo. *When Women Were Priests: Women's Leadership in the Early Church and the Scandal of Their Subordination in the Rise of Christianity.* San Francisco: HarperSanFrancisco, 1993.

Torrance, Thomas F. "The Ordering and Equipping of the Church for Ministry." In Anderson, *Theological Foundations for Ministry*, 390–429.

———. *Royal Priesthood: A Theology of Ordained Ministry.* 2nd ed. Edinburgh: T&T Clark, 1993.

———. "Service in Jesus Christ." In Anderson, *Theological Foundations for Ministry*, 714–33.

van der Kooi, Cornelius, and Gilbert van den Brink. *Christian Dogmatics: An Introduction.* Translated by Reinder Bruinsma with James D. Bratt. Grand Rapids: Eerdmans, 2017.

Villafañe, Eldin. *Beyond Cheap Grace: A Call to Radical Discipleship, Incarnation, and Justice.* Grand Rapids: Eerdmans, 2006.

Volf, Miroslav. *After Our Likeness: The Church as the Image of the Trinity.* Grand Rapids: Eerdmans, 1998.

von Campenhausen, Hans Freiherr. *Ecclesiastical Authority and Spiritual Power in the Church of the First Three Centuries.* Translated by J. A. Baker. Peabody, MA: Hendrickson, 1997.

———. *Kirchliches Amt und geistliche Vollmacht in den ersten drei Jahrhunderten.* Beiträge zur Historischen Theologie 14, edited by Gerhard Ebeling. Tübingen: Mohr, 1953.

Wallace, Daniel B., and Michael H. Burer. "Was Junia Really an Apostle?" *Journal for Biblical Manhood and Womanhood* 6, no. 2 (2001): 4–11.

Wallace, Ronald S. *Calvin's Doctrine of the Word and Sacrament.* Grand Rapids: Eerdmans, 1957.

Weber, Otto. *Foundations of Dogmatics.* Translated by Darrell L. Guder. 2 vols. Grand Rapids: Eerdmans, 1983.

Wesley, John. "The Means of Grace (Sermon 16)." In *The Works of John Wesley*, 5:185–201. 3rd ed. Series of Sermons. 14 vols. Grand Rapids: Baker Books, 2002.

Westfall, Cynthia Long. *Paul and Gender: Reclaiming the Apostle's Vision for Men and Women in Christ.* Grand Rapids: Baker Academic, 2016.

Whitehouse, W. A. "Christological Understanding." In Anderson, *Theological Foundations for Ministry*, 216–29.

Willimon, William H. *Pastor: The Theology and Practice of Ordained Ministry.* Nashville: Abingdon, 2002.

Wink, Walter. *Engaging the Powers: Discernment and Resistance in a World of Domination.* Minneapolis: Fortress, 1992.

Wolters, Al. "The Meaning of Αὐθεντέω." In *Women in the Church: An Interpretation and Application of 1 Timothy 2:9–15*, edited by Andreas J. Köstenberger and Thomas R. Schreiner, 65–116. 3rd. ed. Wheaton: Crossway, 2016.

Zwingli, Huldreich. *An Account of the Faith of Huldreich Zwingli (1530)*. Vol. 1 of *The Latin Works of Huldreich Zwingli*, edited by William J. Hinke, translated by Samuel Macauley Jackson. Philadelphia: Heidelberg, 1922.

———. *Ad Matthaeum Alberum Rutlingensium Ecclesiasten: De coena Dominica (1524)*. In *Huldrici Zuinglii Opera: Completa Editio Prima* 3. Latinorum Scriptorum, edited by Melchiore Schulero and Johannis Schulthessio, pt. 1. Turici: Schulthess und Höhr, 1832.

———. *Exposition of the Christian Faith (1531)*. Vol. 2 of *The Latin Works of Huldreich Zwingli*, edited by William J. Hinke, translated by Samuel Macauley Jackson. Philadelphia: Heidelberg, 1922.

———. *On the Lord's Supper (1526)*. In *Zwingli and Bullinger*, edited and translated by G. W. Bromiley. Library of Christian Classics. Ichthus ed. Philadelphia: Westminster, 1979.

———. *Subsidium sive coronis de Eucharistia (1525)*. In *Huldrici Zuinglii Opera: Completa Editio Prima* 3. Latinorum Scriptorum, edited by Melchiore Schulero and Johannis Schulthessio, pt. 1. Turici: Schulthess und Höhr, 1832.

Author Index

Scripture and Ancient Sources Index

Subject Index